MW00352939

Effective Mathematics Teaching
from Teachers' Perspectives

Effective Mathematics Teaching from Teachers' Perspectives

National and Cross-National Studies

Jinfa Cai
University of Delaware, USA

Gabriele Kaiser
University of Hamburg, Germany

Bob Perry
Charles Sturt University, Australia

Ngai-Ying Wong
The Chinese University of Hong Kong, Hong Kong-SAR-China

SENSE PUBLISHERS
ROTTERDAM/BOSTON/TAIPEI

A C.I.P. record for this book is available from the Library of Congress.

ISBN: 978-90-8790-820-1 (paperback)
ISBN: 978-90-8790-821-8 (hardback)
ISBN: 978-90-8790-822-5 (e-book)

Published by: Sense Publishers,
P.O. Box 21858, 3001 AW
Rotterdam, The Netherlands
http://www.sensepublishers.com

Printed on acid-free paper

© Frontcover picture by Thomas Raupach. The photo was made at a mathematical modelling week at the University of Hamburg.

All Rights Reserved © 2009 Sense Publishers

No part of this work may be reproduced, stored in a retrieval system, or transmitted in any form or by any means, electronic, mechanical, photocopying, microfilming, recording or otherwise, without written permission from the Publisher, with the exception of any material supplied specifically for the purpose of being entered and executed on a computer system, for exclusive use by the purchaser of the work.

TABLE OF CONTENTS

Preface   vii

1. What is Effective Teaching? A Study of Experienced Mathematics Teachers from Australia, the Mainland China, Hong Kong-China, and the United States   1
   Jinfa Cai, Bob Perry, Ngai-Ying Wong, and Tao Wang

2. What is Effective Mathematics Teaching? International Educators' Judgments of Mathematics Lessons from the TIMSS 1999 Video Study   37
   Karen Bogard Givvin, Jennifer Jacobs, Hilary Hollingsworth, and James Hiebert

3. What is "Good" Mathematics Instruction? Mathematics Teachers' Individual Criteria for Instructional Quality and Attributions for Instructional Success   71
   Sebastian Kuntze and Franziska Rudolph-Albert

4. Good Mathematics Teaching and the Role of Students' Mathematical Thinking: High School Teachers' Perspectives   93
   Patricia S. Wilson and Kanita K. Ducloux

5. In Search of Effective Mathematics Teaching Practice: The Malaysian Mathematics Teachers' Dilemma   123
   Chap Sam Lim

6. What are Teacher's Beliefs about Effective Mathematics Teaching? A Qualitative Study of Secondary School Teachers in Germany   141
   Katja Maass

7. Examining the Nature of Effective Teaching through Master Teachers' Lesson Evaluation in China   163
   Rongjin Huang and Yeping Li

8. Teachers' Beliefs, Instructional Practices, and Culture: Understanding Effective Mathematics Teaching in the Philippines   183
   Catherine P. Vistro-Yu and Rosemarievic Villena-Diaz

9. Effective Mathematics Teaching in Finland Through the Eyes of Elementary Student Teachers   203
   Raimo Kaasila and Erkki Pehkonen

10. On the Quality of Mathematics Lesson: Do Elementary Mathematics
    Teachers Have Similar Views as Students and Their School?   217
    Yeping Li, Gerald Kulm, Rongjin Huang, and Meixia Ding

11. Beliefs about Mathematics and Effective Teaching among Elementary
    Mathematics Teachers in Hong Kong   235
    *Qian-Ting Wong, Ngai-Ying Wong, Chi-Chung Lam,
    and Qiao-Ping Zhang*

12. "Effective Teaching of Mathematics" by Teachers, for Teachers: An
    Australian Case Study   259
    Will Morony

13. The Presidential Award for Excellence in Mathematics Teaching:
    Setting the Standard   281
    Iris R. Weiss, P. Sean Smith, and Sharon K. O'Kelley

14. Studying Effective Teaching from Teachers' Perspectives: The Journey
    has Just Begun   305
    Jinfa Cai, Tao Wang, Ning Wang, and Tiffany Garber

Editors and Contributors   319

PREFACE

INTRODUCTION

Classroom instruction is accepted as a central component for understanding the dynamic processes and the organization of students' mathematical thinking and learning (Cai, 2004; Gardner, 1991; Rogoff & Chavajay, 1995). Because classroom instruction plays such a central role in students' learning, researchers have long tried to characterize the nature of the classroom instruction that maximizes students' learning opportunities (Brophy & Good, 1996; Floden, 2001). Teachers are central to classroom instruction in mathematics and have a major impact on students' learning. Consequently, if our aim is to improve students' learning of mathematics, one fruitful line of endeavor is to investigate the characteristics of effective mathematics teaching.

Much of the early research on the effectiveness of mathematics teaching focused on teacher knowledge of mathematics (Thompson, 2004). Teachers' beliefs about mathematics, mathematics learning and mathematics instruction can also impact on teachers' instructional practices (Beswick, 2007; Leder, Pehkonen, & Törner, 2002; Wilkins, 2008), although the contextual nature of beliefs means that it is unwise to expect consistent links between beliefs and practice. While teachers' beliefs have been described by Pajares (1992, p. 307) as "a messy construct", their influence on instruction is sufficiently accepted to warrant further investigation.

This book focuses particularly on how teachers view effective teaching of mathematics. One of the unique features of the book is this reliance on the views of teachers as the primary sources of data for each chapter. Hence, teachers' voices are heard and celebrated throughout the chapters. Another feature of the book is the geographical and cultural spread of the teachers (and authors) involved in the development of the chapters. While this is a reflection of the spheres of contact in which the editors have worked over many years, it also reflects a particular strategy through which the editors aimed deliberately to include the views of teachers from different cultural backgrounds, taking into account that beliefs on effective mathematics teaching and its features are highly culturally dependent.

ORIGIN OF THE BOOK

The initial impetus for this book comes from the work of its editors over the last 15 years in the areas of effective mathematics teaching; teacher beliefs about mathematics, mathematics learning and mathematics teaching; and cross-cultural comparisons of mathematics teaching and learning. Both alone and in conjunction with each other, we have compiled an extensive collection of publications in these areas.

In October, 2002, all of us were invited participants in the 13th ICMI Study Conference held at the University of Hong Kong. This study, *Mathematics Education in Different Cultural Traditions: A Comparative Study of East Asia and the West* (Leung, Graf, & Lopez-Real, 2006), brought together many mathematics education researchers to consider how cultural traditions might impact on mathematics teaching and learning. All of the editors of this book were invited to present papers at the Study Conference (Cai, 2006; Kaiser, Hino, & Knipping, 2006; Perry, Wong, & Howard, 2006; Wong, 2006) and during discussions the seeds for this book were sown.

Work continued on the impact of cultural traditions on mathematics teaching with three of the editors (Cai, Perry, and Wong) conducting a study during 2004/ 2005 which gathered data from outstanding elementary/middle school teachers in Australia, Mainland China, Hong Kong SAR-China and the United States of America on what these teachers perceived an effective teacher of mathematics to be and to do. This study was presented at the 2006 conference of the International Group for the Psychology of Mathematics Education (PME) in a working group entitled *What is effective mathematics teaching? East meets West.*

The international study of what teachers perceived as effective mathematics teaching was published as an issue of *ZDM – The International Journal on Mathematics Education* (Volume 39(4), 2007) entitled *What is Effective Mathematics Teaching? A Dialogue between East and West.* All the editors of this book contributed to this special issue.

Growing from both the PME Working Group and the *ZDM* issue, invitations were extended to colleagues working in the area of teachers' views of effective mathematics teaching and this book is the result. It is a collection of chapters themed to teachers providing their views about what they see as effective mathematics teaching. There have been many fine studies of cultural differences among mathematics teachers and teaching, most of them based on the observation and detailed analysis of classrooms and lessons (for example, Clarke, Keitel, & Shimizu, 2006; Stigler & Hiebert, 1999). This book, however, represents the first purposeful cross-cultural collection of studies concerning teachers' views of effective mathematics teaching.

Research is presented from many parts of the world representing both Eastern and Western cultural traditions. Included are Australia, China – both Mainland and Hong Kong SAR, Czech Republic, Finland, Germany, Japan, Switzerland, Malaysia, Netherlands, Philippines, and United States of America. National or cross-national studies are presented in 12 chapters and are compared in a final chapter that discusses the methodologies and findings from each of these studies. Always, the emphasis is on what practicing teachers see effective mathematics teaching to be.

Another chapter which does not report a research study is also included in the book. This chapter reports on an initiative taken by the Australian Association of Mathematics Teachers to develop standards by which effective mathematics teaching might be identified and celebrated. In many ways, this chapter provides a culmination for the research studies reported in the book, showing just how teachers' views of effective mathematics teaching can be used not only to improve teaching and learning but also to improve the image of teaching within societies.

ACKNOWLEDGEMENTS

The editors would like to express their thanks to many people for assisting them in bringing this book to fruition. First and foremost, thanks are due the many chapter authors who have diligently worked at preparing, revising and finalizing their chapters within timelines that were, probably, unreasonable. Secondly, thanks to the professionals at Sense Publishers, particularly Peter de Liefde, for their patience and expertise in leading us through the production of the book. Thirdly, thanks to our families who have had to endure our absences while we undertook the task of putting this book together. Finally, we should thank each other. It is not easy to bring a book together when the four authors are on four different continents in the world. However, it is very gratifying to have worked in a team so dedicated to the task, in spite of the local distractions that are always present in busy lives. We hope that the book will provide future readers and scholars with the stimulus to take the ideas presented and expand on them in ways that help improve mathematics education for children, teachers and researchers in both the East and the West.

REFERENCES

Beswick, K. (2007). Teachers' beliefs that matter in secondary mathematics classrooms. *Educational Studies in Mathematics, 65*(1), 95–120.

Brophy, J. E., & Good, T. L. (1996). Teacher behavior and student achievement. In M. C. Wittrock (Ed.), *Handbook of research on teaching* (3rd ed., pp. 328–375). New York: Macmillan.

Cai, J. (2004). Why do U.S. and Chinese students think differently in mathematical problem solving? Exploring the impact of early algebra learning and teachers' beliefs. *Journal of Mathematical Behavior, 23*, 135–167.

Cai, J. (2006). U.S. and Chinese teachers' cultural values of representations in mathematics education. In F. K. S. Leung, K.-D. Graf, & F. J. Lopez-Real (Eds.), *Mathematics education in different cultural traditions: A comparative study of East Asia and the West* (pp. 465–481). New York: Springer.

Clarke, D., Keitel, C., & Shimizu, Y. (2006). *Mathematics classrooms in twelve countries.* Rotterdam, The Netherlands: Sense.

Floden, R. E. (2001). Research on effects of teaching: A continuing model for research on teaching. In V. Richardson (Ed.), *Handbook of research on teaching* (4th ed., pp. 3–16). Washington, DC: American Educational Research Association.

Gardner, H. (1991). *The unschooled mind: How children think and how schools should teach.* New York: Basic Books.

Kaiser, G., Hino, K., & Knipping, C. (2006). Proposal for a framework to analyse mathematics education in eastern and western traditions. In F. K. S. Leung, K.-D. Graf, & F. J. Lopez-Real (Eds.), *Mathematics education in different cultural traditions: A comparative study of East Asia and the West* (pp. 319–351). New York: Springer.

Leder, G. C., Pehkonen, E., & Törner, G. (Eds.). (2002). *Beliefs: A hidden variable in mathematics education?* Dordrecht: Kluwer.

Leung, F. K. S., Graf, K.-D., & Lopez-Real, F. J. (Eds.). *Mathematics education in different cultural traditions: A comparative study of East Asia and the West.* New York: Springer.

Pajares, M. F. (1992). Teachers' beliefs and educational research: Cleaning up a messy construct. *Review of Educational Research, 62*, 307–332.

Perry, B., Wong, N. Y., & Howard, P. (2006). Comparing primary and secondary mathematics teachers' beliefs about mathematics, mathematics learning and mathematics teaching in Hong Kong and

Australia. In F. K. S. Leung, K.-D. Graf, & F. J. Lopez-Real (Eds.), *Mathematics education in different cultural traditions: A comparative study of East Asia and the West* (pp. 435–448). New York: Springer.

Rogoff, B., & Chavajay, P. (1995). What's become of research on the cultural basis of cognitive development? *American Psychologist, 50,* 859–877.

Stigler, J., & Hiebert, J. (1999). *The teaching gap: Best ideas from the world's teachers for improving education in the classroom.* New York: Free Press.

Thompson, A. G. (2004). The relationship of teachers' conceptions of mathematics and mathematics teaching to instructional practice. In B. Allen & S. J. Wilder (Eds.), *Mathematics education: Exploring the culture of learning* (pp. 175–194). London: Routledge Falmer.

Wilkins, J. L. M. (2008). The relationship among elementary teachers' content knowledge, attitudes, beliefs, and practices. *Journal of Mathematics Teacher Education, 11,* 139–164.

Wong, N. Y. (2006). From "Entering the Way" to "Exiting the Way": In search of a bridge to span "Basic Skills" and "Process Abilities". In F. K. S. Leung, K.-D. Graf, & F. J. Lopez-Real (Eds.), *Mathematics education in different cultural traditions: A comparative study of East Asia and the West* (pp. 111–128). New York: Springer.

JINFA CAI, BOB PERRY, NGAI-YING WONG, AND TAO WANG

WHAT IS EFFECTIVE TEACHING?

A Study of Experienced Mathematics Teachers from Australia,
the Mainland China, Hong Kong-China, and the United States

INTRODUCTION

While family and students' out-of-school experiences play important roles in their learning (Cai, 2003; Lave, 1988), students acquire much of their knowledge and develop their thinking skills from classroom instruction. Thus, researchers have long tried to understand the nature of classroom instruction to maximize students' learning opportunities. Because classroom instruction is a complex enterprise (Leinhardt, 1993), researchers have attempted to identify its important aspects in order to investigate the kinds of classroom instruction that are effective in fostering students' learning (Brophy & Good, 1996; Carpenter, Franke, Jacobs, Fennema, & Empson, 1998; Good, Grouws, & Ebmeier, 1983; Hiebert & Wearne, 1993; Perry, VanderStoep, & Yu, 1993). One of the important aspects of classroom instruction that has been considered for such investigation is on the beliefs[1] of teachers about mathematics, mathematics learning and mathematics teaching (Battista, 1994; Beswick, 2007; Leder, Pehkonen, & Törner, 2002; Pehkonen & Törner, 1998; Perry, Howard, & Tracey, 1999; Thompson, 2004; Wong, Marton, Wong, & Lam, 2002).

However, beliefs about mathematics and its learning and teaching are not the only teacher beliefs that need to be considered when we are looking for influences on the effectiveness of teaching (Gates, 2006; Sztajn, 2003). Mathematics educators recently have begun to examine other sets of beliefs that influence mathematics teaching practices. Skott (2001) showed how beliefs not directly related to mathematics teaching also help one understand mathematics teachers' practices. In his study, he considered micro-aspects of the social contexts of mathematics classrooms. He presented the teacher's overarching concern about students' self-esteem as justification for mathematics teaching episodes.

It seems that teachers' beliefs about their students and how the students are situated in social contexts that may not be well understood by the teachers are closely related to the students' motivation to learn, and their performance in mathematics (Philippou & Christou, 2002; Zevenbergen, 2003). This, in turn, seems to be related to the effectiveness of the mathematical instruction provided (McLeod, 1992; Pehkonen & Törner, 1998).

J. Cai, G. Kaiser, B. Perry and N.-Y. Wong (eds.), Effective Mathematics Teaching from Teachers'
Perspectives: National and Cross-National Studies, 1–36.
© *2009 Sense Publishers. All rights reserved.*

The idea that teachers' instructional practices are influenced by both their cultural beliefs and their conceptions of effective teaching is not new (Cai, 2005; Perry, Wong, & Howard, 2006; Stigler & Hiebert, 1999). In fact, teachers do draw upon their cultural beliefs as a normative framework of values and goals to guide their teaching (Rogoff, 2003). A teacher's manner of presenting mathematics is an indication of what he/she believes to be most essential, thereby influencing the ways that students understand and learn mathematics (Cai, 2004; Cooney, Shealy, & Arvold, 1998; Greeno, 1987; Thompson, 1992). Some researchers are even calling for changes in teachers' cultural beliefs concerning who should learn mathematics, what mathematics should be learned, and how mathematics should be taught, in order to change mathematics teaching practice in classrooms (Tirosh & Graeber, 2003).

Over the last two decades, researchers have developed theories about teachers' beliefs and the way these beliefs impact teachers' classroom practice (see, for example, Leder et al., 2002; Thompson, 1992). However, these theories were mainly developed from studying Western mathematics teachers in Western mathematics classrooms (Biggs, 1994; Graf, Leung, & Lopez-Real, 2006; Wong, 2004). Only in recent years have researchers started to cross-culturally explore teachers' beliefs and look at how teachers' culturally constructed beliefs impact their teaching and the learning of their students (Cai, 2004, 2005; Gao & Watkins, 2001; Stigler & Hiebert, 1999). However, in all of these works, there are few studies examining teachers' beliefs about effective teaching (an exception to this is the recent special issue, Volume 39, Number 4 in 2007, of ZDM – *The International Journal on Mathematics Education*) containing papers by the authors of this chapter.

The study reported in this chapter examines teachers' beliefs about effective teaching in mathematics from a cross-cultural perspective. It is designed to address the following fundamental question: What is effective teaching for teachers in Eastern and Western cultures? From a cross-national perspective, this study aims to develop a deeper understanding of teachers' cultural beliefs concerning effective mathematics instruction.

Theoretically, the findings from this study will make a significant contribution to our understanding of teaching and teachers' belief systems from a cross-cultural perspective. Practically, such an investigation should provide insightful information about what can be learned from instructional practices in different countries in order to improve students' learning of mathematics. This study not only helps us understand the relationship between teachers' conceptions and instructional practices from an international perspective, but it also helps us interpret the differences in the teaching and learning of mathematics found in previous cross-national studies (e.g., Cai, 2000).

Systems of Beliefs about Effective Mathematics Teaching

Ernest (1989) identified three main components of teachers' mathematical belief systems: teachers' views of the (1) nature of mathematics, (2) features of mathematics teaching, and (3) process of learning mathematics. According to Ernest, the teachers' view of the nature of mathematics is the most fundamental because it impacts two other closely related beliefs about mathematics teaching and learning, although it has also been suggested that the components are inter-related in many ways (Perry et al., 1999; Speer, 2005; Thompson, 1992). While there are many ways in which teachers' beliefs about mathematics and its teaching and learning have been characterized (Kuhs & Ball, 1986; Leder et al., 2002; Lerman, 1990), in this study, we have used Ernest's ideas of teachers' belief systems as our primary organizer for designing the study and conducting the data analysis.

View of the nature of mathematics. A teacher's conception of the nature of mathematics can be viewed as that teacher's conscious or subconscious beliefs, concepts, meanings, rules, mental images, and preferences concerning the discipline of mathematics. Those beliefs, concepts, views, and preferences constitute the beginnings of a philosophy of mathematics, although, for some teachers, they may not be developed and articulated into a coherent philosophy. For many people, mathematics is a discipline characterized by abstract knowledge, accurate results, and strong logical procedures. However, people's views vary greatly about the origin of this abstract knowledge system and how people can partake of it.

According to Ernest (1989), teachers view mathematics from at least two perspectives: functional and structural. From a functional perspective, mathematics is seen as "a bag of tools ... made up of an accumulation of facts, rules and skills" (p. 250). Ernest characterized this view as "instrumentalist." Teachers who view mathematics from a structural perspective see it as a "unified body of knowledge, a crystalline realm of interconnecting structures and truths, bound together by filaments of logic and meaning" (p. 250). Ernest called the second view the Platonist view. While the instrumentalists pay more attention to the functions of mathematics knowledge on the external world, Platonists put their emphasis on the complicated internal structure of the knowledge itself.

In practice, an individual teacher's beliefs about the nature of mathematics often include changeable combinations of instrumentalist and Platonist views. The effects of these beliefs on teacher' actions in relation to teaching mathematics are impacted by the contexts in which the teachers are working. Using Green's (1971) concept of the relative centrality of a belief within a teacher's belief system, Beswick (2007) has claimed that

> The relative centrality of an individual's beliefs will vary from context to context. Failure to enact a particular belief evident (via words and/or actions) in one context or another, can thus be seen as the result of different beliefs taking precedence in the different situations (p. 97).

View of the mathematics teaching and learning. Teachers' beliefs about teaching mathematics, according to Thompson (1992), can be revealed in following aspects: desirable goals of the mathematics program, a teacher's role in teaching, appropriate classroom actions and activities, desirable instructional approaches and emphases, and legitimate mathematical procedures. Similarly, teachers' beliefs about the learning of mathematics cover the processes of learning mathematics, what behaviors and mental activities are involved on the part of the learner, and what constitute appropriate and prototypical learning activities (Thompson, 1992).

Kuhs and Ball (1986) identified four views concerning teachers' beliefs about mathematics teaching and learning. These have been summarized by Speer (2005) in the following way.

> The "learner-focused" view centers on the learner's personal construction of mathematical knowledge through active involvement in doing mathematics. The teacher's role is as a facilitator of student learning. The second view, "content-focused with an emphasis on conceptual understanding," focuses on the logical relations among mathematical ideas. "Content-focused with an emphasis on performance" is similar to the previous one in its focus on mathematical content, but emphasizes rules and procedural mastery. The fourth view, "classroom-focused," emphasizes classroom activity that is structured, efficiently organized, where teachers present material clearly and students practice individually (p. 366).

Ernest (1989) has proposed three teaching models to reflect the various roles a teacher might play in a classroom: instructor model, explainer model, and facilitator model. The intended outcome for an instructor often focuses on student skill mastery and correct performance; for an explainer, conceptual understanding with unified knowledge; and for a facilitator teacher, student confidence in problem posing and solving. There are clear links among the three characterizations of beliefs about mathematics teaching and learning the two views held about mathematics itself. These commonalities will be used in the analysis of data from the current study.

Cross-cultural comparisons of teachers' beliefs. The formative work around the development of understandings of teachers' belief systems about mathematics, mathematics teaching and mathematics learning has been conducted in Western countries by Western researchers. Recently, there have been some attempts to understand teachers' beliefs from cross-cultural perspectives. A few studies have demonstrated the value and feasibility of cross-national studies in investigating teachers' beliefs about effective teaching (Cai, 2004, 2005; Marton, Tse, & dall'Alba, 1996; Stigler & Hiebert, 1999; Perry et al., 2006; Perry, Vistro-Yu, Howard, Wong, & Fong, 2002). For example, Marton et al. (1996) examined teachers' views of memorization and understanding and suggested that in Western countries memorization and rote learning are generally considered the same. Western educators also believe that memorization does not lead to understanding. However, through extensive interviews with 20 Chinese teacher educators, Marton et al. (1996) provided a new way of seeing the relationship between memorization and understanding. For Chinese educators, memorization does not necessarily lead to rote learning; instead, it can be used to deepen understanding.

Recent studies (Cai, 2004, 2005; Cai & Wang, 2006) examined Chinese and U.S. teachers' cultural values of representations in instruction. They found that Chinese and U.S. teachers hold different curricular expectations. Chinese teachers expect 6th graders to be able to use equations to solve problems, but U.S. teachers have that expectation only for 7th or 8th grade students. The fact that U.S. and Chinese teachers have differing curricular expectations is not surprising since the curricula of the two countries are very different. However, on a deeper level, the differences in expectations may reflect the differences in cultural beliefs about mathematics. Although both the Chinese and U.S. teachers agreed that mathematics has wide applications in the real world, the true beauty of mathematics for Chinese teachers was its purity, generality, and logic. Thus, a solution strategy that lacks generality (e.g., a visual approach) should be discouraged. In contrast, U.S. teachers heavily emphasized the pragmatic nature of mathematics, leading, at least for some of the U.S. teachers, to a belief that as long as it works, students can choose whatever representations and strategies they like.

Stigler and Hiebert (1999) found that, to a large extent, the different beliefs held by Eastern and Western teachers explain the different mathematics instructional patterns they observed in East Asian and U.S. classrooms. For example, they found that Asian teachers teach mathematics in a coherent way because they believe that mathematics is a set of relationships between concepts, facts, and procedures. In contrast, Stigler and Hiebert describe U.S. teachers' understanding of school mathematics as "a set of procedures" and "skills." Based on classroom observation, Stigler and Perry (1988) found that U.S. teachers tend to believe that young children need concrete experiences in order to understand mathematics. Chinese teachers, however, believe that even young children can understand abstraction and that concrete experience only serves as a mediator for understanding (Stigler & Perry, 1988).

These studies have indicated the value and feasibility of investigating teachers' beliefs about teaching mathematics from an international perspective. However, there is more to be done, particularly in terms of how teachers from the East and West view and practice effective mathematics teaching. The aim of the current study is to contribute substantially to this work.

METHODS

When teachers' views about effective teaching are studied, the first problem is to determine the criteria to be used for judging teaching effectiveness (Cai, 2005). In this study, we take the position that the quality of mathematics instruction can be judged by two criteria: desirable outcomes in students' learning and the processes that yield those desirable learning outcomes. This position has strong support from the extant literature on mathematics learning and research on teaching and teacher development (e.g., Bransford, Brown, & Cocking, 2000; Cobb, 1994; Floden, 2001; Hatano, 1993; Schoenfeld, 2000).

In this study, we are particularly interested in teachers' views about the characteristics of effective teachers, characteristics of effective lessons, memorization and understanding, and the role of practice in students' learning. The study adopts a descriptive approach in order to understand teachers' belief systems in different cultures and does not judge or evaluate these beliefs. The study builds on previous work by the authors which has tried to understand cultural differences in teachers' beliefs on the nature of mathematics, the teaching and learning of mathematics in general, and effective mathematics teaching in particular (e.g., Cai, 2005; Cai & Wang, 2006; Perry et al., 2006).

It is clear that there is no single educational region that can represent the East (or the West), and we cannot draw a line on the globe to divide the East from the West. However, the purpose of this study was to make cultural contrasts about the beliefs of effective teachers of mathematics. Australia, the Mainland China, Hong Kong SAR[2], and the United States were selected for the study because they represent a spectrum of Eastern and Western cultures. The U.S. can be considered Western and the Mainland China the Eastern. Hong Kong is clearly influenced by Chinese culture, but it is also influenced by the more than a century of Western (British) colonization. Australia is also strongly influenced by British colonization but, over the last 60 years, has grown into one of the world's most multicultural nations and represents a highly diverse cultural melting pot. To some extent, Hong Kong and Australia can be considered to be some where between the Eastern and Western extremes exemplified by the Mainland China and the U.S., respectively, with Hong Kong SAR "closer" to China than Australia and Australia "closer" to the U.S. than Hong Kong SAR.

Effective teachers of mathematics were identified in each jurisdiction using local definitions of effectiveness. Each of the selected teachers was interviewed using semi-structured questions in order to understand each teacher's views about mathematics, teaching mathematics, and learning mathematics. Through semi-structured interviews, we can understand not only what teachers believe, but also why they hold these beliefs.

Selection of Teachers

Thirteen Australian teachers, 9 from China, 12 from Hong Kong, and 11 from the U.S. were selected for the study. The U.S. teachers were selected from Delaware, Milwaukee (WI), and Philadelphia (PA). Chinese teachers were selected from Guiyang, Guizhou, a developing province in the southeast of China, and from the Hong Kong SAR. The Australian teachers were selected from three states – Tasmania, New South Wales and Victoria – and the Australian Capital Territory. There is no suggestion that the sample of teachers in this study is representative of the effective teachers of mathematics in their regions[3]. Rather, in each case, effective teachers were identified through processes appropriate to the local context.

All the selected teachers were distinguished mathematics teachers in their regions. Local criteria were used to select the teachers. In the U.S. for example, teachers who had received recognition for their teaching excellence, such as the presidential award in teaching or the teacher of the year award were chosen. For teachers from Guizhou, Chuna, those who had been recognized as special class or first class teachers (the highest ranks for the teaching profession in China), were selected.

As for Hong Kong SAR, though such a special class/first class system is not established, all teachers except one possessed over 10 years of teaching experience, and most of them were actively involved in professional bodies; as well, three had earned Masters of Education degrees. At the time of selection of the teachers, Australia did not have a process for recognizing excellence in mathematics teaching except through the state and national mathematics teaching professional associations. The Australian teachers for this study were selected after a request was made to the Australian Association of Mathematics Teachers (the national professional association) and the Mathematics Association of New South Wales for them to nominate, from their membership, elementary school teachers who were excellent teachers of mathematics. The association made the nominations and checked with the nominees to be sure that they were willing to be involved in the study. Tables 1-4 (in Appendix) show more detailed background information about the selected teachers in the study.

It goes without saying that teachers are recognized as distinguished teachers of mathematics in their regions because they represent the culturally accepted values of effective mathematics instruction. Therefore, the inclusion of distinguished mathematics teachers may facilitate the process of identifying cultural values and criteria of effective mathematics teaching.

Interview Questions and Data Analysis

Semi-structured interviews were conducted and three sets of interview questions were used in this study.

About Mathematics:

In your view, what is mathematics? What is the substance of it?

Some people believe: A lot of things in mathematics must simply be accepted as true and remembered and there really aren't any explanations for them. What do you think?

Some people believe: Mathematics is abstract; therefore, we need to help students think abstractly. What do you think?

About Learning:

Many people believe: Learning mathematics with understanding is essential. What do you think? What is "understanding" anyway? What do you think a teacher should do to help students learn mathematics with understanding?

Many people believe: In order to help students learn mathematics with understanding, concrete experiences are necessary. What do you think? What concrete experiences do they refer to?

What role does memorization play in students' learning of mathematics?

What role does practice play in students' learning of mathematics?

About Teaching:

We all know some teachers are more effective than others in teaching. In your view, what characteristics does an effective teacher have?

We also know some lessons are better than others. What is an ideal, excellent lesson? What characteristics should an ideal, excellent lesson have?

How should teachers use manipulatives and/or concrete representations in their teaching?

Interviews were either videotaped or audiotaped and transcribed. In data analysis, we adopted three phases to code and analyze transcribed data. Firstly, researchers began with open coding of all transcribed interview data. The purpose of this open coding phase was to find unanticipated salient examples of cultural beliefs from the teachers. Second, we re-examined all the data using a start list of codes that were developed to specifically address the research questions about teachers' beliefs on the nature of mathematics as well as the teaching and learning of mathematics. We looked for commonly expressed themes in teachers' responses. Finally, we compared the similarities and differences among teachers' beliefs from the four regions. This process helps us develop a grounded theory (Miles & Huberman, 1994; Strauss & Corbin, 1990) to understand the cultural differences about the teachers' beliefs.

Translation Equivalence

In a cross-national study involving interviews in two languages, it is absolutely essential to ensure the equivalence of the two language versions of the instruments. To address this, a process of English-back translation was used. In this process, two people, each literate in both Chinese and English, contributed to the translation of the instruments. The interview questions were originally in English. The first person translated them from English into Chinese. The second person then translated the Chinese back into English. This final translation was then compared to the original to ensure equivalence and consistency, except for intentional changes involving culturally appropriate words like personal names, object names, contexts, and terminology. Any inconsistencies were resolved through discussion. This was used with the Chinese teachers in Guizhou only. All other teachers in the study were asked and answered the questions in English.

RESULTS

In this chapter, the results are discussed through techniques of comparison and contrast. In this way, the similarities and differences among teachers from Australia, the Mainland China, Hong Kong SAR, and the United States can be seen. Detailed findings about the beliefs of effective teachers of mathematics in each region can be found in Perry (2007), Wang and Cai (2007a, 2007b), and Wong (2007).

Teachers' Views about Mathematics

What is the nature of mathematics? Of the three fundamental questions investigated in this study, this one received the most varied responses among teachers from the four regions. Overall, teachers from Australia and U.S. both hold more to the functional view of mathematics, which focuses on its usage in the physical world. Teachers from the Chinese mainland and Hong Kong are of the Platonist view, meaning that they focus more on the internal structure of mathematical knowledge (Ernest, 1989). A discussion of some of the major similarities and differences across the four regions follows.

Mathematics is practical. Of all the common themes among the four regions, the utilitarian aspect of mathematics was dominant. There is agreement among teachers from Australia, the Chinese mainland, Hong Kong SAR, and the U.S. that mathematics is applicable to real life problems and that it is a necessary skill for living. All of the teachers interviewed from four regions felt that mathematics has many utilitarian aspects, including being applicable to other disciplines.

For Australian teachers, mathematics is *one of those essential subjects that allow us to function in the world.* (AU1)

For teachers from the Chinese mainland, mathematics is practical in daily life and can help people solve real life problems in an efficient way. It is *a science as well as a necessary tool for life.* (CH8)

For teachers from Hong Kong SAR, the practical significance of mathematics constituted a salient theme in the teachers' responses.

> In daily life, [a] child may face problems in books. When they grow older, they use it in buying [a] house. I think that we learned some skills and methods of calculation, then apply them in life to solve problems continually. (HK11)

For U.S. teachers, mathematics could provide a new perspective for looking at the world:

> I see it as a tool in order to solve problems. ... But it's a tool that enables people to do things or to reach goals that they have. The substance of mathematics would be things like a set of rules, a set of methods that allow me to achieve goals or achieve things I'm trying to do or other people are trying to do. (US5)

Mathematics is a language. Mathematics as a language was the second-most common theme relating to the nature of mathematics across the four groups of teachers. Though this belief was held more prevalently in some regions than others, what is meant by mathematics having the nature of a language is the same: it is a system of knowledge that provides the means of description and explanation of natural phenomenon. Yet, it is very different from commonly used languages like Chinese or English. The formal language of mathematics is a logical framework of rules and terms that can be used effectively to solve problems of many kinds and

9

communicate the problem-solving procedures to others in a somewhat universal dialect.

The emphasis on mathematics being a language decreased as the analysis moved through data from the Mainland China, Hong Kong SAR, the U.S., and Australia, respectively. It is possible that the description of mathematics as a language is held more strongly in the Mainland China and Hong Kong SAR because of the language's relation to the Platonist view of mathematics (i.e., language, being a structure itself, is related to the *structural view*). On the other hand, this view is held less by Australian and U.S. teachers because of their emphasis on the *functionality* of mathematics.

Mathematics is derived from real life. Only the teachers from the Mainland China explicitly argue that mathematics is derived from real life, though it is implicit in some of responses of Hong Kong SAR teachers. All of the nine teachers from the Mainland China believe that mathematics is an abstract and generalized knowledge system refined from real life problems.

> Mathematics stems from real life ... but it is the knowledge refined [tilian] from real life. Once our ancestors help us get the knowledge, we can directly apply the general knowledge without considering some unnecessary features of each specific real life problem. (CH3)

This view extends the orientation of mathematics as practical that is held by the majority of teachers from all four regions.

Mathematical knowledge is abstract. This particular characteristic of mathematics drew out a sharp distinction among the four groups of teachers: specifically between the Eastern and Western regions. Teachers from the Mainland China and Hong Kong SAR had considerably more to say (both quantitatively and qualitatively) about the abstract nature of mathematics than did teachers from Australia and the U.S. There was a decreasing emphasis on the abstract nature of mathematics, in the following order: the Mainland China, Hong Kong SAR, Australia, and the U.S.

All nine of the teachers from the Mainland China differentiate mathematics knowledge from real life problems in that mathematics is an abstract and generalized knowledge system refined from real life problems. The real life problems provide the raw materials that can be purified and abstracted as mathematics knowledge.

The majority of the interviewed teachers from Hong Kong SAR said that developing abstract thinking in students is one of the objectives of teaching mathematics. Unlike teachers from the Mainland China, they did not give deep descriptions of what they thought abstraction is. However, they spoke mainly of the process of developing abstract, logical thinking in the classroom and, while they did not use the term, expressed this abstraction as a facet of mathematization (De Lange, 1996; Gravemeijer, Cobb, Bowers, & Whitenack, 2000).

In Australia and the U.S., few teachers explicitly report that mathematics is abstract. The reluctance to teach and encourage students to learn abstract principles is evident, especially in the U.S. For the most part, that which is concrete is the focus in the classroom and lessons of Australia and the U.S.

This distinction between the Eastern and Western cultures in regards to the abstract nature of mathematics and how it affects mathematics education is predicttable in light of the previously discussed views of the usefulness of mathematics. It follows from the Mainland China and Hong Kong SAR's structural or Platonic view that the teachers place greater importance on the abstraction of mathematics than the countries that hold more to a functional view.

Teachers' Views about Mathematics Learning

To discuss teachers' views about mathematics learning, we focus on the three main themes derived from Cai (2007):
- The nature of understanding – This includes the teacher's belief of what understanding is and how the teacher should help the students gain understanding of mathematical ideas.
- Memorization and understanding – What role, if any, does memorization play in a student's development of understanding? Should memorization come before or after understanding?
- The role of practice – What role does practice play and how much is necessary? What kind of practice develops understanding?

The Nature of understanding. In terms of the importance of understanding, teachers from the four regions all agree that understanding is the ultimate goal of learning mathematics and that using real-life problems and concrete experiences can facilitate mathematical understanding.

Understanding means being able to apply knowledge flexibly.

Teachers from the four regions agree that an indicator of mathematical understanding is the flexible application of what has been learned to problem situations that require the students to use what they have learned in different ways.

> For understanding, I think the first step is they can accept the rule as a fact ...
> Second, when the rule appears in another format, s/he can still think in the
> reverse manner. I think this is understanding. (HK2)

> [Understanding] is being able to use what you are able to apply in many
> different situations rather than just applying a skill or a piece of knowledge in
> one situation repeatedly. (AU12)

Another common theme in terms of the nature of understanding is that students are able to communicate what they have learned. When students are able to communicate with others using mathematical language, they display their understanding of the ideas being communicated. Teacher AU11 exemplifies this theme:

> Understanding is achieved when they are able to explain the "why," the "how,"
> and the "do" in a situation using mathematical language to support their
> explanation.

Understanding at concrete and abstract levels. Teachers from the four regions agree that mathematics understanding should start from students' concrete experiences. However, different regional groups of teachers have different views on how concrete examples should be used in mathematical learning. While the U.S. teachers put their emphasis on helping students realize the relatedness between mathematics and real life problems, teachers from the Mainland China tend to encourage students to derive abstract concepts and thinking from concrete examples. All of the teachers from the Mainland China argue that the ultimate goal of introducing concrete examples is to help students derive abstract mathematics concepts. Once the students' understanding reaches this abstract level, they can be freed from the constraints of concrete representations. After the students have established some abstract mathematical concepts, the teachers should emphasize the importance of connecting different concepts and integrating them into a systematic knowledge system. While most teachers from the Mainland China emphasize the importance of helping students master abstract and connected mathematics concepts, only one U.S. teacher (US7) explicitly mentions that helping students connect abstract concepts is important. Instead, most U.S. teachers express their reluctance to encourage students to learn mathematics on an abstract level (e.g., deriving formulas) especially in 6th or 7th grade classrooms. It seems that most of the U.S. teachers think their students at this stage are cognitively incapable of thinking abstractly. Teachers from the Mainland China thought differently.

While teachers from the Mainland China and the U.S. seem to hold quite different views about understanding at the concrete and abstract levels, teachers from Australia and Hong Kong SAR hold views between these extremes. For Australia and Hong Kong SAR teachers, while concrete experiences offer great opportunities for fostering mathematical understanding, the individual characteristics of the learner need to be taken into account before offering particular materials.

Some of the interviewed teachers from Australia and Hong Kong SAR explicitly point out that concrete materials are particularly relevant for certain groups of children (such as slow learners or students have missed out on learning a particular topic) and not for others (such as the more able or gifted learners). The level of abstraction teachers can expect students to reach depends on the characteristics of students and nature of the mathematics to be learned.

Memorization and Understanding. Though they all agree that memorization plays an important role in mathematical understanding, teachers from the four regions do not fully agree on what that role is or to what degree memorization is important. There was also an over-riding concern as to whether memorization should come before or after understanding. For teachers from the Mainland China and Hong Kong SAR, memorization can come before or after understanding. However, for Australia and U.S. teachers, memorization can only come after understanding. Nevertheless, memorization after understanding is held in higher regard than memorization before understanding (or rote memorization), though some of the teachers from teachers in the Mainland China say that perhaps the latter could be an intermediate or transitional step towards understanding the mathematics.

While students start with rote memorization (without understanding), they should be able to gradually come to understanding by practicing. (CH8)

While teachers in the Mainland China express the value of memorization, they also make a distinction between what they call live knowledge and dead knowledge. Live knowledge is easy to transfer when solving new problems. In particular, CH1 uses the Chinese idiom juyifansan (knowing one concept and applying it into three situations[4]) to describe live knowledge. In contrast, dead knowledge cannot last long and is difficult to apply and transfer into a new situation. It seems that the teachers in the Mainland China believe that even that knowledge which is memorized before understanding must eventually be converted to live knowledge.

In general, teachers from Hong Kong SAR do not believe that memorization has a central role in mathematics learning.

Memorization may have some effect on mathematics learning, but it is not an important component. (HK4)

However, when asked what kind of memorization (if and when used) is best, a higher regard for memorization after understanding than for rote memorization was expressed. The majority of teachers in the Hong Kong SAR group view rote memorization as a final alternative for the student when she does not have understanding of that knowledge:

If there is something we really cannot understand, we should memorize it first as to tackle the examination. (HK9)

Though there is a general inclination among the teachers from Hong Kong not to make memorization (whether before or after understanding) an imperative, the teachers value the type of memorization that follows understanding and therefore makes the knowledge mentally available for application:

After the students understand, then memorization is important. It would be useful if s/he has a good memory. In fact, if s/he understands, memory would be useful to future application. (HK8)

Many of the Hong Kong SAR teachers were able to distinguish between memorization after understanding or even memorization and understanding enhanced in parallel. These teachers seemed to have a preference for the former type of memorization.

Many of the Australian teachers give high regard to memorization as the recall of pertinent information. They support the process of memorization as a key factor in learning almost as strongly as teachers from the Mainland China.

Memory is very important. They have to start off with a core amount of information. (AU2)

> I think there's a place for memorization. I'm glad to see that the new syllabus puts some emphasis back on learning times tables. I think that is very important. Along with that comes understanding. (AU1)

However, Australian teachers do not necessarily believe that rote memorization can serve as a transitional step to understanding. The majority sees rote memorization – retaining facts without understanding – as something to be avoided. When the Australian teachers speak of memorization, they tend to add words such as "reinforce," "connections," and "understanding." In general, the Australian teachers believe memorization should follow understanding.

The U.S. teachers are all in agreement that memorization after understanding is the type of memorization that is valuable. They believe it is necessary for retaining knowledge, applying the knowledge to solve problems, and learning new knowledge. However, when it comes to rote memorization, the interviewed teachers from the U.S. display a variety of views. Some believe it has little to no use, while others see it has something that is necessary.

> I think that if they encounter something enough times, they're just going to remember it anyway. That rote memory is not something they are going to remember. (US8)

In contrast, US9 suggests:

> I think some people that follow the NCTM standards[5] very closely would disagree with me, but I still think there's a place for memorization and rote memorization of basic facts.

In summary, the idea of understanding before memorization seems to be the most prominent trend. The teachers interviewed from the Mainland China, Hong Kong SAR and Australia explicitly affirm that rote memorization can be useful in making knowledge quickly accessible and as a last resort for examination when understanding is not fully developed. Only teachers from the Mainland China expressed the view that rote memorization could also be useful as a transition to understanding.

Role of practice. All teachers from the four regions view practice as important, but to varying degrees. Teachers from the Mainland China place as much value on it as they did on memorization. Teachers from Hong Kong SAR, much like teachers from the Mainland China, view practice as a means to facilitate understanding, but some also present a minimalist view:

> They don't need a lot of exercises, [just] one in each type. If you understand, you just have to have a quick glance [to understand] and don't need to do a lot. (HK7)

This minimalist view is also observed in U.S. responses such as:

> I don't do a lot of practice ... students in my classroom don't necessarily get a lot of practice repeatedly on [a] particular concept. They may only be

exposed one or two times to a particular concept, and then we move on. (US11)

One significant difference among teachers from the four regions is that teachers from the Mainland China were the only group who did not mention the risk of over-burdening the students with 'drill and kill' practice. Teachers from Hong Kong SAR, Australia, and the U.S. all shared concern that practice can be overdone and student's interest in the subject can be dulled.

> Yes they [exercises] are important, but I do not agree on letting students do the same kind of exercises too much unless there are variations. The worst case is that students do not think over the question after doing massive exercises. I do not agree with mechanical training. (HK5)

Teachers from Australia and the U.S. seemed to share similar concerns related to practice:

> I think that you only need to go so far as realizing that most people are confident with the idea and not flogging it to death. (AU13)

> I find that if you give too much, it's like they'll just turn off from it ... especially with word problems. You know, you don't want to turn them off either. (US10)

Teachers' Views about the Teacher and Teaching

While understanding teachers' views about mathematics and learning of mathematics can provide an important context, the major focus of this study is to understand the teachers' views about effective mathematics teaching. How a teacher decides to run a classroom is, to a great extent, a reflection of her/his goals for maximizing students' learning and her/his beliefs and values in relation to the subject being taught. Hence, questions in this study about teachers' views about mathematics teachers and mathematics teaching have elicited much core information.

Characteristics of an effective teacher of mathematics. The question of what characterizes an effective teacher of mathematics has accentuated the differences in the beliefs of teachers from the Eastern and Western regions. For example, teachers from Australia and the U.S. had much more to say about the teacher's enthusiasm and rapport with the students than teachers from the Mainland China and Hong Kong SAR. On the other hand, teachers from the Mainland China and Hong Kong SAR focused on how well the teacher prepares and presents a lesson and the ability to provide clear explanations of the points to be covered in the lesson.

– *Strong background in mathematics*

Nearly all the teachers from Australia, the Mainland China, and Hong Kong SAR make a strong point of this characteristic of effective teachers of mathematics.

According to their statements, well-grounded knowledge and understanding of the subject is a crucial element in being able to effectively teach mathematics. In addition, teachers from the Mainland China place a very strong emphasis on understanding of the curriculum and the texts being used. According to teachers in the Mainland China, it is clear that an effective mathematics teacher should explore and study textbooks intensively and carefully and should try to predict the possibly difficult concepts for their students so that they can devise instructional strategies to overcome the difficulties. Teachers from Australia and Hong Kong SAR also emphasize deep understanding of the curriculum content and structure.

> They have to have an understanding of the syllabus to start with and what they should be teaching. (AU5)

– Adept in instructional skills

All of the interviewed teachers agreed that an effective teacher should possess the skills needed to instruct properly. For teachers from Australia, this point was made implicitly through their discussion about making the lessons relevant to current society and balancing humor and authority. The following three specific instructional skills were mentioned consistently by teachers from the four regions:

> *Clear communication and explanation of the topic and goals (which requires their own knowledge of mathematics and of the curriculum).*
> *Being able to use a variety of methods of instruction (manipulatives, thought-provoking lecture, etc.) according to the students' needs.*
> *Building interest and maintaining it by varying methods and/or by making the topic, when possible, relevant to the students' experiences.*

Although the teachers from all four regions agree that personal magnetism and solid mathematical understanding are both important traits of an effective math teacher, there is again a general difference between the teachers from the Mainland China and Hong Kong SAR, and teachers from Australia and the U.S. While teachers from the Mainland China and Hong Kong SAR highlight the need for the teacher's ability to provide insightful explanation and stimulate thinking, teachers from Australia and the U.S. focus more on how well the teacher can listen to their students and get them to interact with their teachers and one another.

– Knowing and caring for the students

The teachers from Australia, the Mainland China, and the U.S. all explicitly agree on the necessity of knowing and caring for their students. Hong Kong SAR teachers did not mention this point as a characteristic of an effective mathematics teacher. This does not suggest that these teachers do not believe that they should care for their students. However, it is clear that this point is not at the forefront of their thinking. The general theme among the teachers from Australia, the Mainland China, and the U.S. is that a teacher should understand the needs of the students and have the desire to understand their needs. For example, CH1 argues that a good teacher is always passionate in caring about students both in and out of the classroom. CH2 further argues that this kind of passion not only builds a positive rapport between the teacher and students but also could directly impact on students' learning.

Overall, however, the teachers from Australia and the U.S. had more to say about building this positive rapport with the students than teachers from the Mainland China did.

> Once there is a level of empathy with the student so that you know this person reasonably well, at least in terms of their interests, you can start to get somewhere. (AU9)

> The [effective teachers] are caring. They relate to the students. ... I show them respect and they show me respect . . . (US10)

– *Classroom management*

Classroom management seemed to be much more important to the teachers interviewed from the U.S. than for any of the other three regions. One teacher asserted:

> Well, first of all, I think the classroom management is truly important. If that's not there, we're not going to. . . nothing will be accomplished. (US2)

US5 also heavily emphasized this need:

> In the public school, the number one thing that you have to have is you have to control the classroom. From my experience of teachers that appeared not to be as effective, it's more of a discipline issue and a control issue.

The teachers interviewed from the Mainland China did not mention anything about classroom management being a concern. This may reflect that, in most educational environments in the Mainland China, classroom management is simply not an issue. Neither does it appear to be an important issue with teachers from Hong Kong SAR or Australia, as nothing was said by the teachers from these two regions in regards to classroom management. It must be remembered that the interviewed teachers in all four regions were chosen for the study because they were effective mathematics teachers. Consequently, they would be expected to have solved issues around classroom management in their own teaching.

According to Ernest (1989), there are three basic teaching models related to the responsibilities that a teacher has in the classroom: facilitator model, explainer model, and instructor model. The first model, the facilitator, has the goal of having students develop confidence in establishing and solving problems. The explainer's aim is that the students gaining conceptual understanding with cohesive knowledge. Finally, the instructor's intention is that the student masters the skills necessary for proper performance. There are some teachers in the sample accessed in this study that fit more into one model than another. The description of an effective teacher according to teachers from the Mainland China and Hong Kong SAR seems to fit more into the instructor model. For teachers from Australia, it would seem that their description of an effective teacher is somewhat between the explainer and facilitator: one who helps the students connect the knowledge mentally, yet encourages them to confront and solve mathematical problems themselves. The U.S. teachers' descriptions of an effective teacher generally seem to fit the facilitator model. This analysis is reinforced by the common belief among Eastern teachers that it is simply infeasible to facilitate individualized guidance with the large numbers of students present in their classrooms. These teachers believe that the role of classroom teaching is the transmission of knowledge: Ernest's explainer. It is often believed by these teachers that other facets of teaching/learning should be left to out-of-class hours.

Characteristics of an effective mathematics lesson: As might be expected, some of the aspects that were mentioned in regards to what makes a teacher effective were reiterated in the responses to the characteristics of an effective lesson, albeit from a different angle. There is a tendency for the teachers from the Eastern regions (the Mainland China and Hong Kong SAR) to emphasize the teacher-led aspects of the mathematics education in the classroom, while the Western region teachers (Australia and U.S.) emphasize the student-centered aspects (Leung, 2004). The possibilities of having a teacher-led yet student centered' classroom among Eastern regions should be noted (for details, please refer to Wong, 2004). It is noteworthy that Watkins (2008) even put forth the notion of learning center-ness and not just learner centerness.

– *Active engagement of students*

All eleven U.S. teachers agree that active student engagement in the classroom is necessary to keep the students interested. Therefore, concrete examples are often implemented into the lesson:

> I usually start off talking about why we're going to learn this topic, why we need this topic. Let's say with percent. And I have the kids say, well we need it for sales tax, to leave a tip at a restaurant ... so we talk about why we're dealing with this topic. Then I try to go into what does it really mean. (US7)

For the majority of the U.S. teachers, active student engagement also involves hands-on manipulative activities for the purpose of student exploration:

> I think that investigation by students and allowing them to find rules, allowing them to find the way things behave is very effective compared to just always lecturing and giving formulas and telling them how things behave. (US5)

The teachers from Australia emphasize the students' verbal involvement more than the physical involvement as a characteristic of an effective lesson. There was little said specifically about the use of hands-on manipulatives. To them, active student engagement can arise by tapping the students' curiosity:

> I think curiosity is a big thing with kids. . .and active student involvement. (AU2)

[An effective mathematics lesson is] one where all the conversation is about the maths, the students are engaged and there is not too much teacher talk. (AU13)

Such verbal engagement is also expressed as a respectful exchange between the student and teacher on what is being taught:

You try to make sure that children have the opportunity to question, to discuss, to answer and that there's an atmosphere where the children and teacher respect each other's views and that those are listened to. (AU1)

For teachers from Hong Kong SAR, student participation and involvement are the keys for understanding as well as achieving the learning objectives. Student participation is also the source of satisfaction in learning. For teachers from Hong Kong SAR, participation mainly refers to the vocalized interactions in classrooms.

Teachers from the Mainland China acknowledged that there was a necessity for a lively and comfortable learning environment. CH1 asserts that:

A terrible lesson is the teacher lecturing the whole lesson without student participation because you would have no idea whether your students understand the material.

In following this point made by CH1, all the teachers from the Mainland China seem to agree that concrete types of examples serve a purpose in helping the students understand mathematical concepts. However, there are varying opinions about how this should be practiced. For some teachers from the Mainland China, in order to understand a concept clearly, students should physically operate the concrete examples and tools. However, due to constraints of time and class size, other teachers argue that, in real teaching, a teacher often just demonstrates the process without having students manipulate tools.

It was also expressed by teachers from the Mainland China that the hands-on manipulatives should be used only for the objective of bringing about under-standing, and, therefore, the teachers need to have the students contribute mentally and verbally to what they have just done physically.

– *Group activities/in-class student collaboration*

Significantly more was said about group activities and in-class student colla-boration by the U.S. teachers than by those from Australia, the Mainland China, and Hong Kong SAR. Teachers from the Mainland China and Hong Kong SAR made no mention of this being a characteristic of an effective lesson. The teachers from Australia held a more middle-road view: small group activity was neither a necessity nor an impediment to an effective lesson, though the majority of Australian teachers interviewed utilize this pedagogical approach in their classrooms.

At times you need to have groupings. So you might have a core lesson and some work that the children who have obtained or [understood] that knowl-edge can go on with. Then you can spend some intense time with the ones that don't. (AU7)

For U.S. teachers, in-class peer interaction is essential to a lesson being effective.

And to have a problem like that where the kids are, you know, four of them together, are communicating mathematically, trying to solve a problem. Maybe not one of them individually could solve it, but all of them could solve it. (US3)

In general, it seems that the U.S. teachers are more comfortable with having group activities and discussion during the class time than are the teachers from the other three groups.

– *Coherence*

Of the four groups of teachers interviewed in this study, only teachers from the Mainland China and Hong Kong SAR explicitly addressed the issue of having a well-structured, coherent lesson for the class. All nine teachers from the Mainland China maintain that an effective lesson should coherently develop a well-planned content. The following statement is typical for teachers from the Mainland China:

An effective lesson should have all the steps [of instruction] closely serve the essential points…so that students can actively participate in each step. (CH3)

About half of the Hong Kong SAR teachers interviewed made mention that an effective math lesson is one which is well structured. For example:

One should think about what one is going to teach before a lesson, but should not pack too many objectives into a single lesson . . .another important point is the flow of the lesson [well-designed]. (HK5)

The teachers from Australia did not give as many specific responses that emphasized the need for coherence of a lesson as the teachers from the Mainland China and Hong Kong SAR. However, there was mention that lesson objectives should be made clear and that there needs to be a structured routine in the classroom:

I have clear goals to be reached, they know where the journey is going, it's very clear and they have to be focused. (AU4)

There were no comments about the coherence of lessons from the U.S. teachers interviewed.

– *Flexibility of teaching fits individual students' needs*

Teachers from Australia and the U.S. addressed the issue of flexibility with significantly more emphasis than did teachers from the Mainland China and Hong Kong SAR.

For the U.S. teachers, flexibility is a prominent characteristic of an effective mathematics lesson. However, it is primarily addressed through the characteristics of an effective mathematics teacher.

Being able to observe, and judge, and evaluate each student and meeting their individual needs probably is the most difficult and probably one of the most crucial parts [for an effective teacher]. (US4)

In regards to the math lesson itself, there is acknowledgment that the lesson needs to be appropriate to the students' stages of development.

[I]f you can gear a lesson so that it's just at the right spot for where the students are developmentally, where it stretches them just enough so they're not frustrated but it challenges them at the same time. (US9)

Australia's teachers were specific about how the lessons themselves should be both planned and yet flexible.

Most of my lessons are planned ... For example, you would have to have the resources you needed there, and if there is a child who needs concrete material, then you have to have it available. There has to be an ability to change. (AU7)

When new ideas have been discovered, when perhaps what I had planned is not what we've done at all, which is what happened to us this week because somebody came up with something and we've gone off on a tangent and discovered something totally new, then that is an excellent lesson. (AU3)

Some of the teachers from the Mainland China acknowledged the need for teaching flexibly in order to address students' needs. They agreed about the necessity of flexibility in the lesson, though that the flexibility is constrained both by the large number of students in the class and the amount of content that is required to be taught in a lesson. One teacher argues:

In terms of how to unfold a planned lesson, the teacher should always flexibly adjust his path according to student status. After a student answered a question, [I can find] what is still not understood by him. Then I will continue [to] explain it carefully. Therefore, I cannot just rigorously follow the plan. (CH2)

Only one teacher from Hong Kong SAR explicitly commented on the need for flexibility in order to be sensitive to the developmental pace of the students:

The teaching pace should be adjusted with the response of the students in the lesson. The teacher should not just blindly follow the lesson plan and let the lesson go on without considering students' response. (HK2)

– *Cultivating students' interests*

All four groups of teachers highlighted this characteristic of an effective mathematics lesson. For example, six teachers from Hong Kong SAR commented on the cultivation of student interest, giving various ideas on how this might be achieved.

> Teaching aids, games, real-life examples, introducing various activities and outside readers to them [can help cultivate students' interests]. (HK8)

Other ways in which students' interest could be stimulated include drawing connections between different mathematical ideas in the syllabus.

> They would feel surprised and this would initiate their thinking [too]. (HK7)

The importance of a teacher using a good question and answer technique in order to stimulate interest was canvassed by teachers from both Hong Kong SAR and the Mainland China.

> [One has to] ask questions, from which can inspire students to further imagine ... [One should ask] how can we make use of questions to guide students to think something new, deeper, and those things they have never thought before. (HK1)

> In order to broaden student participation, the teacher should design questions with different levels of difficulty to take care of good students, average students, and slow students. Therefore, in my class, I never invite one student to answer a question more than three times so that more students can have chances to answer questions. (CH2)

Many of the Australian teachers believe that cultivating interest in students is important. Some of these teachers point out that if one is able to begin the lesson in an interest-capturing way, then the student's interest is more likely to be maintained for the rest of the lesson.

> When it is time for math groups it should be "Yes! Off we go to maths" and they should be coming into the classroom excited. For all sort of reasons, the mathematics classroom should be a place where they feel really good about themselves, where they're feeling really enthused to be there ... Not every-body feels like that all the time but there are times when the recess bell has gone and I am shooing them out the door and they're still not going. (AU3)

> I like to start the lesson off with something that makes the children think. It doesn't have to be anything to do with the particular topic that you're learning but it just means that you are trying to get the answer to something. (AU13)

There is no specific comment made by teachers from the U.S. on the cultivation of student interest being a characteristic of an effective lesson. However, other comments reported above from U.S. teachers suggest that they see such cultivation as important. The majority of teachers from the Mainland China seem to agree. For example, cultivation of student interest can lead to ongoing motivation to learn mathematics.

> At the beginning, they can learn some mathematics, and then they are willing to learn more mathematics. Finally, they enjoy mathematics. (CH8)

REFLECTION AND DISCUSSION

Mathematics impacts the way we understand our environment, control our finances, construct enterprises, and conduct business. Effective mathematics teaching is clearly of the utmost importance in developing the mathematical skills, knowledge and understanding required to enable this impact to be realized. Effective mathematics teaching requires effective mathematics teachers. The beliefs of such teachers about mathematics, mathematics teaching and mathematics learning are critical to ensure that there is sufficient mathematical capital being developed (Leder et al., 2002; McLeod, 1992). Hence, hearing the perspectives of teachers from a variety of regions about the effective teaching is invaluable.

The study reported in this chapter provides a cross-cultural (East compared with West) perspective on teachers' beliefs about effective mathematics teaching. Australia, the Mainland China, Hong Kong SAR, and the U.S. were selected for the study because they represent a spectrum of Eastern and Western cultures.

Though one may argue that beliefs constitute only one aspect of teachers' professional expertise, the link with teachers' teaching practices has been acknowledged (Furinghetti, 1998; Leder et al., 2002; McLeod, 1992; Pehkonen & Törner, 1998). The words of the 18th century Chinese scholar, Yuan Mei, that "*Knowledge is like the bow, ability like an arrow; but it is wisdom which directs the arrow to bull's eye*" (Siu, Siu, & Wong, 1993, p. 223) is pertinent to our thinking that teachers' beliefs about mathematics and about how mathematics should be learned and taught will influence their teaching practice.

Nature of Mathematics

Some of the beliefs of teachers from Australia, the Mainland China, Hong Kong SAR, and the U.S. about the nature of mathematics, and the learning and teaching of mathematics showed an East/West cultural dichotomy while others resulted in much more of an East/West cultural continuum. For example, the teachers from the Mainland China and Hong Kong SAR view the nature of mathematics from a Platonic view: their focus is on the internal, logical structure of mathematics, which reflects mathematics as an abstract body of knowledge. In contrast, the teachers from Australia and the U.S. place much emphasis on the functional view of mathematics: mathematics is a useful tool that is utilised everyday to solve real-life problems. For example, teachers from Australia and the U.S. placed more emphasis on mathematics being a language by which physical phenomenon can be described and explained than did those from the Mainland China and Hong Kong SAR. This does not mean that there is no acknowledgment by teachers from the Mainland China and Hong Kong SAR of the usefulness of mathematics in helping to solve real life problems. Rather, there is not as much emphasis placed on its functionality by teachers from the Mainland China and Hong Kong SAR as there is by teachers from Australia and the U.S.

Understanding, Memorization, and Practice

In regards to the nature of understanding, there was not a great deal of variance among the four groups of teachers. Teachers from the four regions by and large agreed that the goal of mathematics education is that the students gain under-standing of the mathematics being taught. They also agreed that both the student's ability to apply the mathematics to various problems and her/his ability to communicate the learned mathematics to the teacher or other students indicate the presence of understanding. However, there is significant difference among the four groups of teachers in terms of their descriptions of the relationship between understanding and memorization.

Two types of memorization were identified: memorization *before* understanding (sometimes designated rote memorization) and memorization *after* understanding. For teachers from the Mainland China and Hong Kong SAR, memorization can come before or after understanding. However, for Australian and U.S. teachers, memorization can only come after understanding. For teachers from the Mainland China, memorization before understanding could serve as an intermediate step towards understanding; in other words, as long as this type of memorization leads to understanding, then the memorized knowledge is not simply dead knowledge. In general, however, teachers from all four regions agreed that understanding after memorization is ideal, though it is also acknowledged by those teachers that this is not always the case in the classroom. It seems that memorization is regarded as a means and understanding as the goal, though automation (memorizing by heart) is also regarded as important, especially when one needs to solve mathematics problems fluently (Kerkman & Siegel, 1997; Wong, 2006). Other research supports the hypothesis that the excellent academic performance of Asian learners on international mathematical comparison programs may be due to a synthesis of memorizing and understanding which is not commonly found in Western students (Marton et al., 1996; Marton et al., 1997; Watkins, 1996).

In terms of the role of practice, it seems that the teachers from the Mainland China are the most comfortable ones with having students practice since there was no concern expressed about over doing it; there were only indications of its value. Hong Kong SAR teachers place nearly as high a value on practice as teachers from the Mainland China do, but only if that practice is constituted as exercises with variations. Australian and U.S. teachers, in general, are not as committed as the Mainland China and Hong Kong SAR teachers are to the value of practice. Teachers from Australia and the U.S. shared a common concern that practice can be overdone and, therefore, dull student interest. None of the teachers from the Mainland China, however, expressed this concern.

Characteristics of an Effective Teacher

Teachers from the Mainland China, Hong Kong SAR, and Australia agree that competence in mathematics is a necessary characteristic of an effective teacher. It was also stated (especially by teachers from the Mainland China) that a teacher's in-depth understanding of the curriculum and textbooks is key for an effective teacher. The U.S. teachers did not note this as an important point in their responses.

Teachers from all regions concurred that a teacher should both understand the needs of her/his students and have an interest in catering to these needs. Teachers from the U.S. believed that effective teachers need to have appropriate classroom management skills, particularly in terms of discipline and control. Teachers from the other three regions did not address this issue, possibly because classroom discipline does not seem to be as major an issue with them, particularly for teachers from the Mainland China and Hong Kong SAR. The general difference here was that the teachers from the Mainland China and Hong Kong SAR emphasize the ability of a teacher to provide the information with clarity and to stimulate thinking, while the teachers from Australia and the U.S. emphasize the ability of the teachers to listen to the students and to get them to respond with interest.

Characteristics of an Effective Lesson

Based on the responses of the teachers from the four regions, it appears that the teachers from Australia and the U.S. are more comfortable with frequent use of hands-on manipulatives than teachers from the Mainland China and Hong Kong SAR are. Hong Kong SAR teachers, in particular, suggested that if physical manipulatives are used, they are commonly used by the teacher for purposes of demonstration and not by the students, mainly because of time restraints. The teachers from the Mainland China tend to stress verbal engagement over physical engagement on the part of the students. The teachers from the Mainland China and Hong Kong SAR did not mention in-class group activities, yet this is stated as a characteristic of an effective lesson by many of the U.S. teachers. In fact, group activities are usually included in U.S. teachers' lesson plans, but not in those from Mainland Chinese teachers (Cai, 2005; Cai & Wang, 2006). Teachers from Australia saw group activity neither as a necessity nor an impediment to mathematical understanding. U.S. teachers tended to focus on students' engagement and interaction during mathematics lessons while teachers from the Mainland China and Hong Kong SAR emphasized the importance of coherence of a lesson. In summary, what do teachers consider characterizes an effective lesson? Teachers from the East tend to have more of a teacher-led view of classroom instruction than do teachers from the West, who hold more of a student-centered view.

It is impractical to look for a national/regional script of mathematics teaching. Yet classroom practices are often shaped by cultural, environmental, and societal assumptions. Watkins and Biggs (2001) have warned that teaching and learning traditions that appear to work well in a certain culture may not necessarily work in another. For instance, when a high-stake examination is the ticket to the future, fast and accurate solutions to mathematics problems are needed. The ramifications of such high-stake examinations are often manifested through parental expectations and their impacts on classroom practices. When there are larger class sizes, such as is the case in both the Mainland China and Hong Kong SAR, hands-on explorations can become difficult and individual care is often left to after-class hours (Gao & Watkins, 2001; Wong, 2004).

In this study, we see a broad-stroke linkage between teachers' beliefs in mathematics, their image of an effective mathematics lesson, and that of the effective teacher. For instance, for the two Eastern regions (the Mainland China and Hong Kong SAR), since the mathematics teachers generally hold a Platonic view, mathematics knowledge and structure are stressed in the teachers' responses about effective mathematics teaching. It is important to let the student understand the generalization (Cai, 2004). Consequently, practice plays a central role. Though these teachers fully understand the importance of individual guidance, cultural norms such as class size and current practices seem to have determined that this can only be done after class (Gao & Watkins, 2001; Wong, 2004). For these teachers, the major task of classroom teaching lies in the transmission of knowledge. The teacher must be well prepared and have the lesson well structured, so as to run a teacher-led, yet student-centered mathematics lesson. As Watkins (2008) pointed out, the focus should be put on learning, or more precisely, the tripartite interactions among teacher, student and learning. Two things are prerequisites: thorough understanding by the teacher of the curriculum and textbook and the establishment of a classroom routine by the students and teacher. This may explain partially why classroom management is not a major concern among Eastern mathematics teachers. Students are accustomed to the various routines in the flow of classroom teaching—when to talk, when to do seat work, when to open one's book, when to look at the chalk-board (or computer projection), and so on early at an early age (Wong, 2004)—students know the routines and implement them. In the two Western regions, there is a much stronger emphasis both on student-centered approaches to mathematics teaching and learning and on the need for the mathematics being learned to be practical and relevant to the learners. While teachers' understanding of the mathematics being taught is seen as important, reliance on planning, knowledge of the syllabus and textbooks is not as strongly emphasized as is the case with the teachers from the Mainland China and Hong Kong SAR. Both U.S. and Australian teachers see that part of their being effective teachers relies on their knowledge of the students and their understanding of the students' needs. Consequently, the functional understanding of mathematics leads to less structured lessons that are more able to reflect flexibly the needs of the students.

In this study, we have confined our investigations to teachers' perspectives on the effectiveness of mathematics teaching. Many similarities and some differences have been discerned across the four regions considered. The qualitative methodology used in our research and the small numbers in our regional samples could be seen as a limitation in our study. Further investigation is needed to see if these similarities and differences are sustainable across the populations concerned.

There are many other international studies that take different starting points than those of the current study, and they have found results that both contrast and comparison with those presented in this chapter (Clarke & Keitel, 2006; Fan et al., 2004; Leung et al., 2006; Stigler & Hiebert, 1999). It is possible that asking different questions of different people in different ways might result in different conclusions. What is notable are the similarities that have resulted from these different approaches.

On the other hand, long term research on the CHC (Confucian Heritage Culture) learning phenomena has shifted its attention from looking for cultural attributes for the success of Asian learners to identifying good practices in both Eastern and Western cultures (Wong, 2004). More needs to be done to uncover what is happening every day in the mathematics classrooms of different regions. Detailed investigations in mathematics classrooms need to be continued. Classroom observations, interviews, telling of teachers' and students' life-stories, among many other methodologies could be used (Clarke & Keitel, 2006). The perspectives of pre-service and novice teachers and school students need to be canvassed further in a consistent, valid cross-cultural methodology. We need to strive for as full a picture as possible of effectiveness in mathematics teaching and learning so that future generations of students in all regions can benefit. The current study is but one approach that seems to have proved fruitful results.

ACKNOWLEDGEMENTS

The research involving teachers from the Mainland China and U.S. was supported, in part, by grants from the Spencer Foundation. Any opinions expressed herein are those of the authors and do not necessarily represent the views of the Spencer Foundation.

The assistance of the Australian Association of Mathematics Teachers and the Mathematics Association of New South Wales in the recruitment of teachers for this study is gratefully acknowledged.

NOTES

[1] Though there had been extensive discussions on the distinctions among terminologies like "conception," "belief," "view," "image," ... (see, e.g., Pehkonen, 1998; Philipp, 2007), in this chapter, we used them quite interchangeably.

[2] Special Administrative Region

[3] Since Hong Kong SAR is not a country, we use "region" throughout this chapter to designate the four jurisdictions in which the study was conducted.

[4] Words of Confucius quoted in Chapter 1 of the Analects.

[5] The mathematics curriculum and evaluation standards published by the National Council of Teachers of Mathematics of the U.S. in 1989 and 2000.

REFERENCES

Battista, M. T. (1994). Teacher beliefs and the reform movement in mathematics education. *Phi Delta Kappan, 75*, 462–463 & 466–468.

Beswick, K. (2007). Teachers' beliefs that matter in secondary mathematics classrooms. *Educational Studies in Mathematics, 65*(1), 95–120.

Biggs, J. B. (1994). What are effective schools? Lessons from East and West [The Radford Memorial Lecture]. *Australian Educational Researcher, 21*, 19–39.

Bransford, J. D., Brown, A. L., & Cocking, R. R. (2000). *How people learn: Brain, mind, experience, and school.* Washington, DC: National Research Council.

Brophy, J. E., & Good, T. L. (1996). Teacher behavior and student achievement. In M. C. Wittrock (Ed.), *Handbook of research on teaching* (3rd ed., pp. 328–375). New York: Macmillan.

Cai, J. (2000). Mathematical thinking involved in U.S. and Chinese students' solving process-constrained and process-open problems. *Mathematical Thinking and Learning, 2*, 309–340.

Cai, J. (2003). Investigating parental roles in students' learning of mathematics from a cross-national perspective. *Mathematics Education Research Journal, 15*, 87–106.

Cai, J. (2004). Why do U.S. and Chinese students think differently in mathematical problem solving? Exploring the impact of early algebra learning and teachers' beliefs. *Journal of Mathematical Behavior, 23*, 135–167.

Cai, J. (2005). U.S. and Chinese teachers' knowing, evaluating, and constructing representations in mathematics instruction. *Mathematical Thinking and Learning: An International Journal, 7*, 135–169.

Cai, J. (2007). What is effective mathematics teaching? A study of teachers from Australia, Mainland China, Hong Kong SAR, and the United States. *ZDM - The International Journal on Mathematics Education, 39*(4), 265–270.

Cai, J., & Wang, T. (2006). U.S. and Chinese teachers' conceptions and constructions of representations: A case of teaching ratio concept. *International Journal of Mathematics and Science Education, 4*, 145–186.

Carpenter, T. P., Franke, M. L., Jacobs, V. R., Fennema, E., & Empson, S. B. (1998). A longitudinal study of invention and understanding in children's multidigit addition and subtraction. *Journal for Research in Mathematics Education, 29*, 3–20.

Clarke, D., & Keitel, C. (Eds.). (2006). *Mathematics classrooms in twelve countries*. Rotterdam: Sense Publishers.

Cobb, P. (1994). Where is the mind? Constructivist and sociocultural perspectives on mathematical development. *Educational Researcher, 23*, 13–20.

Cooney, T. J., Shealy, B. E., & Arvold, B. (1998). Conceptualizing belief structures of preservice secondary mathematics teachers. *Journal for Research in Mathematics Education, 29*(3), 306–333.

Dahlin, B., & Watkins, D. A. (2000). The role of repetition in the processes of memorising and understanding: A comparison of the views of Western and Chinese school students in Hong Kong. *British Journal of Educational Psychology, 70*, 65–84.

De Lange, J. (1996). Using and applying mathematics in education. In A. J. Bishop, K. Clements, C. Keitel, J. Kilpatrick, & C. Laborde (Eds.), *International handbook of mathematics education* (pp. 49–98). Dordrecht: Kluwer.

Ernest, P. (Ed.). (1989). *Mathematics teaching: The state of the art*. Basingstoke: Falmer Press.

Fan, F., Wong, N. Y., Cai, J., & Li, S. (Eds.). (2004). *How Chinese learn mathematics: Perspectives from insiders*. Singapore: World Scientific.

Floden, R. E. (2001). Research on effects of teaching: A continuing model for research on teaching. In V. Richardson (Ed.), *Handbook of research on teaching* (4th ed., pp. 3–16). Washington, DC: American Educational Research Association.

Furinghetti, F. (1998). Beliefs, conceptions and knowledge in mathematics teaching. In. E. Pehkonen & G. Törner (Eds.), *The state-of-art in mathematics-related belief research: Results of the MAVI activities* (Research Report 195) (pp. 37–72). Helsinki, Finland: Department of Teacher Education, University of Helsinki.

Gao, L., & Watkins, D. A. (2001). Towards a model of teaching conceptions of Chinese secondary school teachers of physics. In D. A. Watkins & J. B. Biggs (Eds.), *Teaching the Chinese learner: Psychological and pedagogical perspectives* (pp. 27–45). Hong Kong: Comparative Education Research Centre, The University of Hong Kong.

Gates, P. (2006). Going beyond belief systems: Exploring a model for the social influence on mathematics teacher beliefs. *Educational Studies in Mathematics, 63*(3), 347–369.

Good, T., Grouws, D., & Ebmeier, M. (1983). *Active mathematics teaching*. New York: Longman.

Graf, K.-D., Leung, F. K. S., & Lopez-Real, F. J. (Eds.). *Mathematics education in different cultural traditions: A comparative study of East Asia and the West*. New York: Springer.

Gravemeijer, K., Cobb, P., Bowers, J., & Whitenack, J. (2000). Symbolizing, modelling, and instructional design. In P. Cobb, E. Yackel, & K. McClain (Eds.), *Symbolizing and communicating in mathematics classrooms* (pp. 225–273). Mahwah, NJ: Lawrence Erlbaum.

Green, T. F. (1971). *The activities of teaching.* New York: McGraw-Hill.

Greeno, J. G. (1987). Instructional representations based on research about understanding. In A. H. Schoenfeld (Ed.), *Cognitive science and mathematics education* (pp. 61–88). New York: Academic Press.

Hatano, G. (1993). Time to merge Vygotskian and constructivist conceptions of knowledge acquisition. In E. A. Forman, N. Minick, & C. A. Stone (Eds.), *Contexts for learning: Sociocultural dynamics in children's development* (pp. 153–166). New York: Oxford University Press.

Hiebert, J., & Wearne, D. (1993). Instructional tasks, classroom discourse, and students' learning in second-grade arithmetic. *American Educational Research Journal, 30*(2), 393–425.

Kerkman, D. D., & Siegel, R. S. (1997). Measuring individual differences in children's addition strategy choices. *Learning and Individual Differences, 9*(1), 1–18.

Kuhs, T. M., & Ball, D. (1986). *Approaches to teaching mathematics: Mapping the domains of knowledge, skills, and dispositions.* East Lansing, MI: Center on Teacher Education, Michigan State University.

Lave, J. (1988). *Cognition in practice: Mind, mathematics and culture in everyday life.* Cambridge: Cambridge University Press.

Leder, G. C., Pehkonen, E., & Törner, G. (Eds.). (2002). *Beliefs: A hidden variable in mathematics education?* Dordrecht: Kluwer.

Leinhardt, G. (1993). On teaching. In R. Glaser (Ed.), *Advances in instructional psychology* (Vol. 4, pp. 1–54). Hillsdale, NJ: Erlbaum.

Lerman, S. (1990). Alternative perspectives of the nature of mathematics and their influence on the teaching of mathematics. *British Educational Research Journal, 16*(1), 53–61.

Leung, F. K. S. (2004). The implications of the Third International Mathematics and Science Study for mathematics curriculum reforms in Chinese communities. In D. Pei (Ed.), *Proceedings of the conference on the curriculum and educational reform in the primary and secondary mathematics in the four regions across the strait* (pp. 122–138). Macau: Direcção dos Serviços de Educação e Juventude.

Marton, F., Tse, L. K., & dall'Alba, G. (1996). Memorizing and understanding: The keys to the paradox? In D. A. Watkins & J. B. Biggs (Eds.), *The Chinese learner: Cultural, psychological and contextual influences* (pp. 69–83). Hong Kong: Comparative Education Research Centre, The University of Hong Kong and Melbourne: The Australian Council for Educational Research.

Marton, F., Watkins, D. A., & Tang, C. (1997). Discontinuities and continuities in the experience of learning: An interview study of high-school students in Hong Kong. *Learning and Instruction, 7,* 21–48.

McLeod, D. B. (1992). Research on affect in mathematics education: A reconceptualization. In D. A. Grouws (Ed.), *Handbook of research on mathematics teaching and learning* (pp. 575–596). New York: Macmillan.

Miles, M. B., & Huberman, A. M. (1994). *Qualitative data analysis: An expanded sourcebook* (2nd ed.). Thousand Oaks, CA: Sage.

Pehkonen, E. (1998). On the concept "mathematical belief." In E. Pohkonen & G. Törner (Eds.), *The state-of-art in mathematics-related belief research: Results of the MAVI activities* (Research Report 195) (pp. 11–36). Helsinki: Department of Teacher Education, University of Helsinki.

Pehkonen, E., & Törner, G. (Eds.). (1998). *The state-of-art in mathematics-related belief research: Results of the MAVI activities* (Research Report 195). Helsinki: Department of Teacher Education, University of Helsinki.

Perry, B. (2007). Australian teachers' views of effective mathematics teaching and learning. *ZDM - The International Journal on Mathematics Education, 39*(4), 271–286.

Perry, B., Howard, P., & Tracey, D. (1999). Head mathematics teachers' beliefs about the learning and teaching of mathematics. *Mathematics Education Research Journal, 11*(1), 39–53.

Perry, B., Vistro-Yu, C., Howard, P., Wong, N.-Y., & Fong, H. K. (2002). Beliefs of primary teachers about mathematics and its teaching and learning: Views from Singapore, Philippines, Mainland China, Hong Kong, Taiwan and Australia. In B. Barton, K. C. Irwin, M. Pfannkuch, & M. O. J. Thomas (Eds.), *Mathematics education in the South Pacific: Proceedings of the twenty-fifth annual conference of the mathematics education research group of Australasia* (pp. 551–558). Auckland: MERGA.

Perry, B., Wong, N. Y., & Howard, P. (2006). Comparing primary and secondary mathematics teachers' beliefs about mathematics, mathematics learning and mathematics teaching in Hong Kong and Australia. In K. D. Graf, F. K. S. Leung, & F. Lopez-Real (Eds.), *Mathematics education in different cultural traditions: A comparative study of East Asia and the West* (pp. 435–448). New York: Springer.

Perry, M., VanderStoep, S. W., & Yu, S. L. (1993). Asking questions in first-grade mathematics classes: Potential influences on mathematical thought. *Journal of Educational Psychology, 85*(1), 31–40.

Philipp, R. A. (2007). Mathematics teachers' beliefs and affect. In F. K. Lester, Jr. (Ed.), *Second handbook on research on mathematics teaching and learning: A project of the National Council of Teachers of Mathematics* (pp. 257–315). Charlotte, NC: Information Age Publishing.

Philippou, G., & Christou, C. (2002). A study of mathematics teaching efficacy beliefs of primary teachers. In G. C. Leder, E. Pehkonen, & G. Törner (Eds.), *Beliefs: A hidden variable in mathematics education?* (pp. 211–231). Dordrecht: Kluwer.

Rogoff, B. (2003). *The cultural nature of human development.* Oxford: Oxford University Press.

Schoenfeld, A. H. (2000). Models for the teaching process. *Journal of Mathematical Behavior, 18*, 243–261.

Siu, F. K., Siu, M. K., & Wong, N. Y. (1993). Changing times in mathematics education: The need for a scholar-teacher. In C. C. Lam, H. W. Wong, & Y. W. Fung (Eds.), *Proceedings of the international symposium on curriculum changes for Chinese communities in Southeast Asia: Challenges of the 21st century* (pp. 223–226). Hong Kong: Department of Curriculum and Instruction, The Chinese University of Hong Kong.

Speer, N. M. (2005). Issues of method and theory in the study of mathematics teachers' professed and attributed beliefs. *Educational Studies in Mathematics, 58*(3), 361–391.

Stigler, J. W., & Hiebert, J. (1999). *The teaching gap.* New York: Free Press.

Stigler, J. W., & Perry, M. (1988). Cross cultural studies of mathematics teaching and learning: Recent findings and new directions. In D. A. Grouws, T. J. Cooney, & D. Jones (Eds.), *Effective mathematics teaching* (pp. 104–123). Reston, VA: National Council of Teachers of Mathematics.

Strauss, A., & Corbin, J. (1990). *Basics of qualitative research: Grounded theory procedures and techniques.* Newbury Park, CA: Sage.

Sztajn, P. (2003). Adapting reform ideas in different mathematics classrooms: Beliefs beyond mathematics. *Journal of Mathematics Teacher Education, 6*, 53–75.

Thompson, A. G. (1992). Teachers' beliefs and conceptions: A synthesis of the research. In D. A. Grouws (Ed.), *Handbook of research on mathematics teaching and learning* (pp. 127–146). New York: Macmillan.

Thompson, A. G. (2004). The relationship of teachers' conceptions of mathematics and mathematics teaching to instructional practice. In B. Allen & S. J. Wilder (Eds.), *Mathematics education: Exploring the culture of learning* (pp. 175–194). London: Routledge Falmer.

Tirosh, D., & Graeber, A. O. (2003). Challenging and changing mathematics teaching classroom practices. In A. J. Bishop, M. A. Clements, C. Keitel, J. Kilpatrick, & F. K. S. Leung (Eds.), *Second international handbook of mathematics education* (pp. 643–687). Dordrecht: Kluwer.

Wang, T., & Cai, J. (2007a). Mainland Chinese teachers' views of effective mathematics teaching and learning. *ZDM - The International Journal on Mathematics Education, 39*(4), 287–300.

Wang, T., & Cai, J. (2007b). U.S. teachers' views of effective mathematics teaching and learning. *ZDM - The International Journal on Mathematics Education, 39*(4), 315–327.

Watkins, D. (1996). Hong Kong secondary school learners: A developmental perspective. In D. A. Watkins & J. B. Biggs (Eds.), *The Chinese learner: Cultural, psychological and contextual influences* (pp. 107–119). Hong Kong: Comparative Education Research Centre, The University of Hong Kong and Melbourne: The Australian Council for Educational Research.

Watkins, D. A. (2008, February). Learning-centered teaching: An Asian perspective. Keynote address at the 2nd international conference on learner-centered education. Manila, the Philippines.

Watkins, D. A., & Biggs, J. B. (Eds.). (2001). *Teaching the Chinese learner: Psychological and pedagogical perspectives.* Hong Kong: Comparative Education Research Centre, The University of Hong Kong and Melbourne: The Australian Council for Educational Research.

Wong, N. Y. (2004). The CHC learner's phenomenon: Its implications on mathematics education. In L. Fan, N. Y. Wong, J. Cai, & S. Li (Eds.), *How Chinese learn mathematics: Perspectives from insiders* (pp. 503–534). Singapore: World Scientific.

Wong, N. Y. (2006). From "entering the way" to "exiting the way": In search of a bridge to span "basic skills" and "process abilities." In K. D. Graf, F. K. S. Leung, & F. Lopez-Real (Eds.), *Mathematics education in different cultural traditions: A comparative study of East Asia and the West* (pp. 111–128). New York: Springer.

Wong, N. Y. (2007). Hong Kong teachers' views of effective mathematics teaching and learning. *ZDM - The International Journal on Mathematics Education, 39*(4), 301–314.

Wong, N. Y., Marton, F., Wong, K. M., & Lam, C. C. (2002). The lived space of mathematics learning. *Journal of Mathematical Behavior, 21,* 25–47.

Zevenbergen, R. (2003). Teachers' beliefs about teaching mathematics to students from socially disadvantaged backgrounds: Implications for social justice. In L. Burton (Ed.), *Which way social justice in mathematics education?* (pp. 133–151). Westport, CT: Praeger.

Jinfa Cai
University of Delaware

Bob Perry
Charles Sturt University

Ngai-Ying Wong
Chinese University of Hong Kong

Tao Wang
The University of Tulsa

APPENDIX: DETAILS OF PARTICIPANTS

Table 1. Details of Australia participants

Code	Gender	Qualifications	Years of teaching	Other relevant data
AU1	M	DipTeach	30+	Fellow of College of Teachers, London; Fellow of Royal Geographic Society; Excellence in Teaching award from Australian College of Education; Former Head of Mathematics/Deputy Headmaster of prestigious independent school
AU2	F	BTeach	11	School art coordinator; Count Me In Too[1] training
AU3	F	DipTeach	20	Professional development in gifted and talented education and systemic mathematics program
AU4	F	B.Ed; GradCert (Productive Pedagogy)	20	Extensive Count Me In Too training; Former mathematics consultant; Taught in England and Ecuador
AU5	F	B.Ed	25	Training and experience in special education; Former mathematics consultant
AU6	F	B.Ed	32	Conference presenter
AU7	M	B.Ed	30	Extensive Count Me In Too training; Assistant Principal
AU8	F	DipTeach	20+	National Literacy and Numeracy Award; Former mathematics consultant; Extensive Count Me In Too training
AU9	M	B.Ed	25+	Council Member, Mathematical Association of Victoria; School Numeracy Coordinator
AU10	F	B.Ed	28+	Conference presenter; School Numeracy Coordinator
AU11	F	B.Ed, GradCert (Teaching)	18	School Numeracy Coordinator
AU12	M	B.Ed, M.Ed	19	Taught in Canada for 8 years
AU13	F	B.A, GradDip (Primary)	20	Taught Spanish in primary schools for 13 years

[1] Count Me In Too is a systemic numeracy program introduced into the majority of New South Wales government schools.

Table 2. Details of participants from the Mainland China

Code	Gender	Qualifications	Years of teaching	Other relevant data
CH1	F	Graduate from a Normal School	19	Active participant of an instructional improvement project
CH2	F	Graduate from a Normal School, Received a bachelor's degree through advanced training	25	Frequent contributor to books or teaching journals for teachers Gave model lessons
CH3	F	Graduate from a Normal School, Advanced training in mathematics and mathematics education	22	Active participant of an instructional improvement project Gave many model lessons for other teachers
CH4	F	Graduate from a Normal School, Advanced training in mathematics and mathematics education	30	Gave model lessons for other teachers Wrote articles for a local teaching journal
CH5	F	Graduate from a Normal University, took additional mathematics courses in another Normal University	19	Became a teacher researcher two years ago, she does not teach in class, but helps other teachers to teach
CH6	M	Graduate from a Normal School, took additional mathematics courses from a University	23	Active participant of an instructional improvement project
CH7	M	Graduate from a Normal School, took courses from another University and received a bachelor's degree	34	Has been a teacher researcher for 11 years, he does not teach in class, but helps other teachers to teach Gave many model lessons for other teachers
CH8	F	Graduate from a Normal School, was taking classes from a University	21	Has been a teacher researcher for three years Received a prize for a teaching competition
CH9	F	Graduate from a Normal School, was taking additional courses in math and math education courses from a Normal University	20	Gave model lessons for other teachers Wrote articles for a local teaching journal

Table 3. Details of Hong Kong participants

Code	Gender	Qualifications	Years of teaching	Other relevant data
HK1	M	Teacher Cert., B.Ed.	17	Member of the editorial board of a local mathematics education periodical
HK2	F	Teacher Cert., B.Ed.	6	Council member of a local mathematics education professional body served at the government Education Department as seconded teacher for a year
HK3	F	Teacher Cert., B.Ed.	10+	Council member of a local mathematics education professional body
HK4	F	Teacher Cert., B.Ed., M.Ed.	10	Council member of a local mathematics education professional body
HK5	F	Teacher Cert.	25	Teaching practice supervisor of a university
HK6	M	B.S., PGDE	5	Head mathematics teacher in school
HK7	F	Teacher Cert.	22	Curriculum leader in school Team member of a university project on students' motivation of learning
HK8	M	Teacher Cert., B.Ed.	15	Principal member of the government's Curriculum Development Council (mathematics)
HK9	F	Teacher Cert., B.Ed.	15	Head mathematics teacher in school team member of a university project on students' motivation of learning
HK10	F	Teacher Cert., B.Ed., M.Ed.	17	Member of the government's Curriculum Development Council (mathematics)
HK11	M	B.S., PGDE	10+	Senior teacher in school
HK12	F	B.Ed., M.Ed.	12	Member of the editorial board of a local mathematics education periodical teaching practice supervisor of a university

Table 4. Details of U.S. participants

Code	Gender	Qualifications	Years of teaching	Other relevant data
US1	F	B.A.; M.Ed.; Received National Board Certification	12	Led workshops for other mathematics teachers; Attended mathematics education conferences or workshops regularly
US2	F	B.S., Completed 18-credit in-service training	5	Received the Outstanding First Year Teacher award; Member of teacher leadership team for two years; Attended mathematics education conferences or workshops regularly
US3	F	B.S.; Completed 25-credit in-service training	9	Received the Outstanding First Year Teacher award; Member of teacher leadership team for four years; Led workshops; Attended mathematics education conferences or workshops regularly
US4	F	B.A.; Received National Board Certification	14	Led workshops for other mathematics teachers; Lead teacher at summer enrichment academy; Attended national and regional mathematics education conferences or workshops regularly
US5	M	B.A.; Six credits away from receiving a M.Ed.	11	Participated in a math education project; Led workshops for other mathematics teachers; Attended national and regional mathematics education conferences regularly
US6	F	B.A.	11	Received Presidential Award for Excellence in Science and Mathematics Teaching Led workshops; Participated in several math education projects; Attended national and regional mathematics education conferences or workshops regularly

US7	M	B.S.; M.Ed.; and Ed.D.	32	Participated in several math education projects; Led workshops; Attended mathematics education conferences or workshops regularly
US8	F	B.A.; Enrolled in a M.Ed. program	14	Led workshops; Participated in several math education projects; Attended mathematics education conferences or workshops regularly
US9	M	B.A.; M.Ed.	10	Led workshops; Participated in several math education projects; Attended mathematics education conferences or workshops regularly
US10	F	B.A.	23	Led workshops; Mathematics Department Chair; Attended national and regional mathematics education conferences or workshops regularly
US11	F	B.S.	7	Led workshops; Participated in several math education projects; Attended mathematics education conferences or workshops regularly

KAREN BOGARD GIVVIN, JENNIFER JACOBS, HILARY
HOLLINGSWORTH, AND JAMES HIEBERT

WHAT IS EFFECTIVE MATHEMATICS TEACHING? INTERNATIONAL EDUCATORS' JUDGMENTS OF MATHEMATICS LESSONS FROM THE TIMSS 1999 VIDEO STUDY

It has been well documented that classroom mathematics teaching differs across countries (Clarke et al., 2006a; Givvin et al., 2005; Hiebert et al., 2003a, 2003b; LeTendre et al., 2001; Leung, 1995; Stigler & Hiebert, 1999). Much less is known about whether leading educators in different countries differ in their views about what kinds of teaching *should be* occurring. Do the differences in classroom practices across countries mirror differences in experts' views or do the differences exist in spite of shared views among experts? The goal of this chapter is to address this question. Specifically, we address whether there is variability in the vision of mathematics educators in five different countries[1] with respect to what constitutes effective practice.

There is, of course, a growing literature on what constitutes effective mathematics teaching. Recent summaries of the research (e.g., Hiebert & Grouws, 2007; National Research Council, 2001; Reynolds & Muijs, 1999) note that what counts as "effective" depends on a variety of factors, including the particular learning goals of interest. For example, one set of instructional practices has been shown to be effective for helping students develop quick execution of skills whereas another set of practices has been shown to be effective for helping students develop conceptual understanding. Other factors influencing one's view of "effective" include what role one plays in the educational system. Teachers' views can differ, at least in emphasis, from those of researchers and policy makers (Wilson, Cooney, & Stinson, 2005). We raise these issues simply to make it clear that the aim of this chapter is *not* to contribute directly to this literature on what should count as effective teaching but rather to describe differences and similarities in views that currently exist among mathematics educators. That is, we do not aim to promote a particular perspective on effective teaching or to advocate for a particular form of instruction but rather to enrich our understanding of how mathematics educators in different countries evaluate teaching with respect to its effectiveness.

Our central question is whether mathematics educators in different countries judge the effectiveness of teaching differently and, if so, in what ways. There are reasons to believe that mathematics educators across countries could make similar judgments with regard to effectiveness. That is, mathematics educators in different

J. Cai, G. Kaiser, B. Perry and N.-Y. Wong (eds.), Effective Mathematics Teaching from Teachers'
Perspectives: National and Cross-National Studies, 37–69.
© *2009 Sense Publishers. All rights reserved.*

countries might share visions of effective classroom practice. The increasing communication among international educators with international audiences through journals, international handbooks and other publications, and international associations and meetings, provide opportunities for collaboration and discussion around issues of mathematics teaching and learning. Common ideas and recommendations might be developed and adopted across countries. In addition, international comparisons (of the kind represented in this chapter) could themselves lead to increasingly shared views among mathematics educators (Clarke et al., 2006b). Even the process of constructing and using a shared achievement instrument for international comparisons imposes some level of homogeneity across countries (Keitel & Kilpatrick, 1999). These activities are more likely, of course, to influence the views of mathematics educators involved in these joint activities than of classroom teachers more removed from international communications.

It is also possible to formulate plausible hypotheses for why mathematics educators across countries might differ in their views of effective teaching. Variations in visions could emerge from the same kinds of differences in cultural traditions that have been proposed as explanations for differences in teaching itself (Stigler & Hiebert, 1999). Leung (1995, 2001), Cai, Perry, and Wong (2007), and Tweed and Lehman (2002) noted differences between Eastern and Western cultures that might affect educators' views of effective teaching. In particular, Leung (1995, 2001) suggests that Eastern values could lead to greater emphases on mathematical content and teacher-directed practices whereas Western values could promote greater emphases on the processes of learning and student-centered practices. We interpret Leung's argument to open the possibility that deep cultural differences, of varying kinds, might lead to differing views across countries in what counts as effective mathematics teaching.

No single study can answer definitively the question of whether, and to what degree, mathematics educators across countries share views of effective teaching. But we believe the study we report begins to address the question with a unique set of empirical results. The study was enabled by the Third International Mathematics and Science Study (TIMSS) 1999 Video Study. The Video Study provided a common set of videotaped eighth-grade mathematics lessons that mathematics educators could evaluate. A shared set of concrete referents reduces the implicit differences that often exist in verbal descriptions of teaching in the abstract. By asking the mathematics educators to watch a common set of lessons, we had a common basis on which to compare educators' views of mathematics teaching.

This chapter describes the judgments of mathematics education groups drawn from most of the participating countries in the TIMSS 1999 Video Study and provides comparative information about their views of teaching. Do they focus on similar or different features when evaluating mathematics teaching? Do they identify similar or different features when they compare what they see with what they believe to be effective mathematics teaching?

METHOD

Sample

The countries that participated in the mathematics portion of the TIMSS 1999 Video Study were Australia, the Czech Republic, Hong Kong SAR, Japan,[2] the Netherlands, Switzerland, and the United States. Random, nationally-representative samples of eighth-grade mathematics lessons were videotaped in each of these countries. All of these countries, except the United States, are considered to be high achieving in eighth-grade mathematics, based on their scores on the TIMSS 1995 mathematics achievement test (Beaton et al., 1996; Gonzales et al., 2000), which was used to select countries for inclusion in the TIMSS 1999 Video Study. For more information about the sample of lessons collected for the TIMSS 1999 Video Study, see Hiebert et al. (2003a).

Groups of mathematics educators from five of the seven countries that participated in the TIMSS 1999 Video Study participated in this study: Australia, the Czech Republic, Hong Kong SAR, Switzerland, and the United States.[3] The educators were selected by the country's National Research Coordinator, who served as the country liaison for the TIMSS 1999 Video Study.[4] The educators were experienced mathematics teacher educators and/or researchers, and typically were on the faculty of prominent universities in their country or researchers at national research institutes.[5] Aside from the North American educators (who were all members of the TIMSS 1999 Video Study steering committee), and the National Research Coordinators, the educators in the other countries did not have a particular connection to the Video Study. In each country, three to nine mathematics educators participated in the meetings. The National Research Coordinator joined the discussion at times to offer opinions of the lessons or otherwise guide the nature of the discussions. It should be noted that no group of that size can adequately represent the perspectives shared across an entire nation. Small numbers of educators may, even within one culture, come to different judgments. Therefore, the size of the educator groups should be kept in mind when interpreting results.

Procedures

Selecting the lessons. The data for this study were the educators' judgments of lessons drawn from six of the seven countries. New lessons from Japan were not collected for the 1999 Video Study, so educators from Japan were not part of the international research team and Japanese lessons were not viewed during this study.

Because our goal was to compare judgments of the lessons (rather than the lessons themselves), it was critical that all groups of educators viewed the same set of lessons. We asked each country's team of coders[6] to select from the full set of lessons up to five lessons that captured the common features of teaching in each country. The code developers and the director of the mathematics portion of the TIMSS 1999 Video Study reviewed the lessons and chose two from each country for the educators to view.[7] The exception to this was Switzerland, from which three lessons were chosen (i.e., one from each language area: French, German, and Italian).

Selecting two (or three) lessons that capture the common features of teaching in each of the six countries is, of course, nearly impossible. No single lesson, or pair of lessons, represents teaching in a country. But it is possible to select lessons that reveal some practices commonly seen across the full data set within a country and to avoid lessons that are clear outliers. Taken together, the selected lessons displayed some of the variation apparent in the teaching practices across the six countries and served as a common referent for the educators' comments about effective teaching.

Analyzing the videotaped lessons. Meetings of each group of educators were held in each country. During these meetings the educators watched and discussed the selected lessons from each country. Switzerland hosted three mathematics educator groups, one in each language region. Each of the Swiss groups is treated separately in this report.

The mathematics educator groups were told to watch the set of lessons from each country in whatever order they preferred. They were asked to focus on the *methods* used to teach mathematics—in particular, the kinds of learning opportunities provided for the students and the nature of the mathematical reasoning that was evident by the teacher or the students. The task was quite open-ended, and comments on other dimensions of similarity and difference deemed especially striking were invited. The written task given to all participants is included as Table A1.

The groups were asked to devote approximately two hours to each of the six countries, watching and discussing the designated lessons. A written report based on these discussions was requested, and thus the groups were asked to keep notes during their meetings. It was suggested that the written report indicate the dimensions that the group members used to compare the lessons, along with comments about each country's lessons along those dimensions. In addition, the groups were asked to summarize their conclusions regarding major similarities and differences among the lessons.

The mathematics educator meetings were conducted in 2001 or 2002, for two or three day periods. In each country, the meetings were hosted by the National Research Coordinator of the TIMSS 1999 Video Study from that country. At least one member of the TIMSS 1999 Video Study mathematics code development team was also present to assist in organizational and technical details. The math educators viewed the 13 lessons over the computer, using specially designed software that allowed them to hear the lesson in its native language, and see a running English transcript.

RESULTS

Each group of mathematics educators wrote a report summarizing their judgments about the videotaped lessons they viewed.[8] The specific organization and nature of those reports was not heavily dictated beforehand, and they varied substantially. Some groups wrote comments on each lesson whereas other groups combined their comments for the set of lessons from a country. Some groups had more to say about certain lessons or countries than others. By request, the submitted reports represented the consensus views of all members of the group.

Summarizing the comments from each mathematics educator group took place in several stages. First, at least two of the authors of this chapter reviewed the comments made by each educator group. They examined comments from each country in turn, keeping a written record of those that applied to all lessons in a country. When comments within an educator group differed across the lessons within a given country, the authors noted that as well. Next, the authors discussed the results of their review, considering issues of inclusion as well as language. In particular, the authors considered whether all common notions were captured and adequately supported by the data, and whether the language they used to summarize the content of the educators' comments was as close as possible to the original language (or its English translation). Discussion continued until consensus was reached. Finally, the comments were loosely classified as addressing the role of the teacher, the role of the students, the mathematics content, or the climate of the lessons. These four classifications emerged from the data and served as a means of organizing the data without theoretical bias. There is considerable overlap between these categories and they are not intended as reliable distinctions. Rather they serve to help organize the array of data and are intended to be a useful device for the reader. The result of this process appears in the Appendix as Tables A2 through A7.

It is important to keep in mind that the original data (i.e., individual educators' comments on the lessons) have undergone multiple phases of aggregation. Individual educators' comments formed the basis for discussion among the members of the educator groups, the result of which was recorded by one of the group members, in some cases translated into English, and then interpreted and further aggregated by our research team. It is certainly possible that successive aggregation made subtle intercultural differences less visible, which may lead to the incorrect assumption that each country has a unified voice. To help accurately convey the perspectives of each educator group, we maintain their language as much as possible and frequently provide direct quotations from their reports.

In the sections that follow, we present a summary of the judgments offered by the educators about each country's lessons, in turn. We then look across the comments of the different lessons offered by each country's group and attempt to characterize the primary concerns voiced by each country. These two ways of aggregating and juxtaposing educators' comments begin to address the question of whether mathematics educators from different countries hold similar or different views of effective mathematics teaching.

Comments on the Australian Lessons

As seen in Table A2, most of the mathematics educator groups had a good deal to say about the two Australian lessons. There was a high level of agreement among the groups, with the exception of the Australian educators' comments about the role of students.

Teacher's role. All of the mathematics educator groups felt that the Australian teachers played a strong, guiding role. They characterized the lessons as teacher-"directed," "led," or "guided."

Students' role. With the exception of the Australian educators, all of the mathematics educator groups described the Australian students as having a rather small and undemanding role. For example, the Czech educators stated that the students "show little activity." The Swiss-Italians maintained that "the students participate in a guided activity that does not present any meaning to their learning." And, the Swiss-French educators wrote that "not much is asked of [students]... [The] teacher seems resigned to ask a minimum of intellectual effort from his students." Similarly, the North Americans noted that the teachers made things easy for the students. They wrote that the "teacher seems to protect students from thinking." By contrast, the Australian educators felt that the videotaped teachers attempted to involve their students through classroom activities.

Content. There was widespread agreement that the mathematics content in the Australian lessons was at a low level and too heavily focused on procedures or rules, with not enough attention to mathematical concepts and reasoning. Specifically, the group from Hong Kong SAR referred to the lessons as having "superficial mathematics content" and as being "rule-oriented." The Swiss-German educators claimed that "the development takes place on a purely procedural level, without an in-depth understanding of the mathematical concepts that stand behind those procedures." The Swiss-French educators referred to the lessons as being "very algorithmic." Even the Australian educators agreed that the two lessons were "sometimes unfocused, so significant features may be unclear at the end."

A number of the mathematics educator groups (including the Australian, Czech, Swiss-French, and Swiss-German groups) felt strongly that the teachers did not place a strong enough emphasis on the correct use of mathematical language. The Czech educators noted that "the covered material is focused on practical application, which sometimes leads to inaccuracy in terminology." The Swiss-German group noted that there was a "low level of accuracy in defining mathematical terminology." Their Swiss-French colleagues provided a more elaborated comment, stating that "we have the feeling that the level of expectation has been lowered to negotiate the students' participation. This translated into the teacher's tendency to use 'easy' terms for the students. He ends up speaking without rigor and with limited correctness." The Australians offered another explanation, stating that there was a "deliberate de-formalizing of maths as though teachers acknowledged that it was unpalatable to students."

Three of the educator groups pointed out that the mathematics content was contextualized. Specifically, the Australians described "definite attempts to involve students and show relevance." The Czechs described the content as "based on application" and the North Americans used the word "situated."

Climate. Most of the groups commented on the climate in the Australian lessons and agreed that it was informal. However the Hong Kong SAR educators felt the "laissez-faire" atmosphere led to a lack of discipline, while the Swiss-Germans felt that the classes were "relaxed" and "well-disciplined."

Comments on the Czech Lessons

The Czech Republic lessons provoked a relatively large number of comments by most of the educator groups. There was general consistency among their impressions, particularly with respect to the content (see Table A3). The educators tended to speak positively about the content, although they had more mixed impressions regarding the role of the students.

Teacher's role. The mathematics educator groups agreed that the Czech teachers played a dominant role in their classrooms. They used words such as "authority" "dominated," "directed," and "controls" in their descriptions of the Czech teachers and their behavior. However, the North Americans added that the teachers did not "shoulder the entire workload."

Students' role. There was some discrepancy among the educator groups regarding the extent of the students' participation in the Czech lessons. Most of the groups noted that the students demonstrated their knowledge, especially when they were publicly examined. On the other hand, several described the Czech students as having few opportunities for choice and rarely asking questions. The educators from Hong Kong SAR wrote that among the participating countries, students in the Czech Republic had the lowest degree of choice in the mathematics they were to learn. The Swiss-German educators commented that "Czech students learn by reproducing the cognitive structure that has been presented by the teacher ... There is hardly any leeway for alternative solution methods." Interestingly, the Czech educators described the students as "passive." On the other hand, a number of educator groups pointed out that high expectations or demands were placed on the Czech students. The Swiss-French described this mixture of roles as "responsibility without autonomy."

Content. The educator groups largely shared positive impressions regarding the mathematics content in the Czech lessons. Words used to describe the content included "demanding," "difficult," "dense," and "rich." Several groups mentioned that there was an emphasis on rules and procedures as well as concepts and processes. For instance, the Swiss-German group wrote that "next to the 'how' of the procedures also the 'why' of the procedures has central meaning." Both the

North American and Swiss-German educators discussed their positive impression that the content was developed in a logical, linear fashion, with the Swiss-Germans stating that "the content is taught in small steps and meaningful units that build on each other." The Australians, North Americans, and Swiss-Germans noted the use of correct mathematical language.

Climate. Comments on the climate in the Czech lessons were largely related to formality. The educators described the atmosphere as "formal," "serious," "respectful," and "very intense, focused, and disciplined." Two of the groups (Australian and Czech) mentioned that there was a conspicuous distance between the teacher and students.

Comments on the Hong Kong SAR Lessons

Many of the comments regarding the Hong Kong SAR lessons were similar in nature to those made about the Czech Republic lessons. However, there was somewhat less agreement among the educator groups regarding the nature of the mathematics content in the Hong Kong SAR lessons, as seen in Table A4. Specifically, the groups varied with respect to how much emphasis they felt was placed on reasoning as opposed to computation.

Teacher's role. The mathematics educator groups all agreed that the Hong Kong SAR lessons were dominated or highly directed by the teacher. Several groups noted that the teachers provided much of the information to their students. For example, the Czechs referred to the lesson as being "conducted as a lecture" and the Swiss-Germans felt that the "teacher walks through [the material] step by step in a clear and direct way." The group from Hong Kong SAR expressed the opinion that "knowledge was given by the teacher."

Students' role. There was a shared sense that the Hong Kong SAR students did what they were told but were not active participants in the lessons. For example, some groups noted that although the Hong Kong SAR students answered the teachers' questions or worked at the board, their involvement still appeared to be minimal. The Australian group wrote that students were "absolutely quiet and submissive" and the Swiss-Germans wrote that student participation was limited to very short, predictable comments or statements. Similarly, the Swiss-Italians wrote that "one does not see a willingness to invent the occasions for the students to discover the learning process themselves." Even the Hong Kong SAR educators agreed and declared that the "students seem to be treated as calculation and computation machines." The Hong Kong SAR and North American educator groups both described the demand placed on the students as moderate. Specifically, the North American group wrote that "students were not expected to struggle ... but they were expected to think. To engage."

Content. Opinions about the nature of the content varied. Some groups felt that the difficulty level was high (the Swiss-French) and that reasoning or deep understanding of concepts was encouraged (the Australians and Swiss-Germans). However, the Hong Kong SAR and Swiss-Italian educators were more critical and saw the lessons as too focused on teaching technical abilities and rules, with not enough emphasis on mathematical concepts.

The Australians and Swiss-Germans noted the use of correct mathematical language in Hong Kong SAR lessons. In addition, the Australian and North American groups discussed the important role played by the textbook in guiding the structure of the lessons and providing examples. Specifically, the North American educators wrote that "both of the lessons were based on examples worked out in the students' book."

Climate. The climate in the Hong Kong SAR mathematics lessons was perceived as "disciplined," and "formal." The Australians commented that there was a "sense that the work was serious and important." Most groups felt that the students worked hard, and the Swiss-German and Swiss-Italian groups described the students as learning to be "competitive." Three of the educator groups (the Australians, Czechs, and Swiss-Italians) mentioned that there was a noticeable distance between the teacher and students.

Comments on the Dutch Lessons

The mathematics educator groups had mixed impressions of the Dutch lessons with respect to all four areas considered – teacher's role, students' roles, content, and climate (see Table A5). Most of the groups described both positive and negative qualities of the lessons, but the Swiss-Italians were especially critical.

Teacher's role. Most of the mathematics educator groups felt that the teacher's role in the Dutch lessons was largely as a guide or partner, rather than directing or dominating the lesson. For example, the Swiss-Germans said that "teachers in the Netherlands play the role of facilitators, whereas in all the other countries teachers try at least for part of the time to transmit or demonstrate knowledge." And, although the Czech educators called the lessons "frontal" and teacher directed, they also described a "partner-like attitude of the teacher toward the student."

Students' role. Comments on the role of the students in the Dutch lessons were varied. Two of the educator groups (the Czechs and Swiss-Germans) noted that the Dutch students were afforded a large degree of responsibility and control over their own learning and pointed out that the students worked with their peers. For example, the Swiss-German educators commented that "during seatwork phases the students have a high degree of control. The students solve the problems independently, sometimes without any prior introduction or knowledge." At the same time, three of the educator groups (the Australian, Hong Kong SAR, and Swiss-Italian educators) felt that the Dutch students were not involved enough in the public portions of the lessons. The Australian educators felt that there was "little evidence of student understanding or involvement."

Content. Most of the educator groups agreed that the content in the Dutch lessons was not particularly demanding, and saw little emphasis placed on reasoning and higher order thinking. For example, the Hong Kong SAR educators felt that although the lessons covered many mathematical problems, mathematical concepts were not explored. The Australians referred to the lessons as "procedure-bound."

Although some groups were largely critical of the content in the Dutch lessons (the Swiss-Italians felt that the lessons were "without any real occasions to learn"), other educators had more positive judgments. Specifically, the North Americans commented that the "ideas are sophisticated for eighth graders" and that the topics appeared to be mathematically challenging. The Swiss-German educators noted that the Dutch lesson style teaches students how to solve problems by exploring on their own, stating that "the Dutch students are self-proficient learners who explore procedures and who are supposed to construct their own mathematical understanding."

Several groups discussed the dominant roles played by homework (the Czechs and Swiss-Germans) and the textbook (the Australians and North Americans) during Dutch lessons. These groups described the textbook as setting boundaries on the content presented and helping to determine the learning structure. The North American group, for instance, stated that "the book has the role of giving a set of problems for students to work and in the working the mathematics will be developed."

Climate. Mathematics educators described the climate in the Dutch lessons as "casual," "informal," "laissez-faire," and "permissive." Some groups (Hong Kong SAR, Swiss-Germans, and Swiss-Italians) believed that these qualities were problematic, and further described the lessons as lacking discipline and rapport between the teachers and students. Specifically, the Hong Kong SAR group called the lesson "out of control" and the Swiss-Italians claimed that "the teacher finds it difficult to relate to the students. Therefore there is not a real educational rapport." The educators from the Czech Republic theorized that "Dutch liberalism is recognizable in the schools. The informal and even partner-like relationship between the teacher and a student during instruction reflects this liberal attitude."

Comments on the Swiss Lessons

The number of comments included in Table A6 regarding the Swiss lessons is somewhat fewer than that of the other countries. This is largely due to the fact that the mathematics educator groups had varying impressions of the three Swiss lessons they watched. Some of the groups, particularly the North American and Swiss-French, made only a few comments that extended to all three lessons.

However, there was a good deal of consistency across the educator groups with respect to their comments that did apply to all of the Swiss lessons.

Teacher's role. Most of the mathematics educator groups felt that the Swiss teachers played a strong role, and two described the lessons as "teacher-led." For example, the Swiss-German educators noted that "knowledge is often developed in a teacher-led instructional conversation. The teachers show significant effort to provide opportunities for discovery and individual problem solving." On the other hand, the Swiss-French educators perceived the teachers as providing "indirect or subtle guidance." The lessons were also praised as "well prepared," "well planned," or "highly structured" by the Czech, Hong Kong SAR, and Swiss-German educator groups, respectively.

Students' role. There was general approval among the mathematics educator groups in terms of the roles played by the Swiss students. For example, the Czech and Swiss-German educators noted that students actively participated in "problem solving." The Swiss-German and Swiss-Italian groups saw some opportunities for the students to discover and "construct cognitive steps independently." The Hong Kong SAR educators felt that there was "quite high demand on students' work" and "a lot of student involvement" whereas the North American educators felt that the degree of thinking students were asked to do ranged across the three lessons from low to moderate.

Content. Mixed opinions were expressed regarding the difficulty of the mathematics content in the Swiss lessons. Some of the educator groups (Australian, Hong Kong SAR, Swiss-German educators) felt that there was evidence of mathematical thinking and reasoning, and opportunities for students to gain a deeper understanding of the material. For instance, the Australians commented that "in different ways all three lessons encouraged mathematical thinking." The Swiss-German educators wrote that "teachers often address with their comments and questions the 'why' of mathematical steps" and that there is "an attempt on the side of the teachers to trigger constructive thinking processes rather than receptive ones." However, the Swiss-Italian educators felt that "the educational objectives are different" across the three lessons, and the Czech educators described the content as "little, but well connected."

Climate. Comments on the climate in the Swiss lessons were quite positive. The educator groups described the lessons as "enjoyable," "respectful," and "serene," and consisting of "motivated" students. The Czech educators found that a "friendly relationship between the teacher and students is prominent."

Comments on the U.S. Lessons

Most of the mathematics educator groups had a considerable amount to say regarding the U.S. lessons, especially regarding the students' role and the nature of the mathematics content (see Table A7). Their impressions, particularly with respect to these two dimensions, were generally consistent and largely negative.

Teacher's role. The mathematics educator groups agreed that the U.S. teachers played a strong role, and guided the students step-by-step through the lessons. As the Swiss-Germans explained, "the teachers demonstrate the content to be learned in front of the whole class." The Czechs wrote that the "teacher has control over the lesson."

The North American educators observed that a main role of the teachers in the videotapes appeared to be helping their students prepare for tests. Specifically, they said of one lesson that "the entire period was devoted to the upcoming quiz ... [The teacher] was comprehensive in his coverage of all that would be on the quiz." The Czech and Swiss-German groups commented that the assessments served as a motivating factor for the students. The former group wrote that "students use [the teacher's] presence to learn material they do not know, so that they can succeed in taking a test."

Students' role. Almost all of the groups mentioned that students' involvement in these lessons was relatively infrequent and/or of limited depth. Specifically, the Swiss-German group wrote that "verbal participation of students is infrequent and limited. Often these are answers to 'fill-in-the-blank' type questions, which focus on the immediately following step." The Hong Kong SAR educators noted that the "students [were] not expected to think deeply" and were given "low-level tasks only." The Swiss-French educators noted that "to participate, students don't need a great intellectual implication." Similar concerns raised by the North American and Swiss-Italian educators were that students did not engage in processes that involved discovery or reasoning. The Swiss-Italians wrote that "the lessons are based on knowledge already known to the students. One does not see a willingness to invent the occasions for students to discover the learning process themselves." The North Americans commented that "no reasoning was asked of the kids."

Content. The content in the U.S. lessons was deemed to be lacking and was widely criticized. The educator group from Hong Kong SAR described "computation and factual recall. Superficial math content (content is 'slim')." Other educator groups described the lessons as being too focused on procedures and rote learning. Missing was any justification of techniques involved, attention to relational under-standing, and learning about higher order mathematical principles. Educators from the Czech Republic and North America used the words "content: little" and "not very demanding," respectively. The Swiss-German educators wrote that "there is a great redundancy of content."

The North American educators noted that the content in the lessons seemed constrained by what was in the textbook or other published materials. They said that "the text plays the dominant role. The teacher uses problems and review sheets that are provided by the text" and "the teacher added no value to the problems provided by the text ... The teacher just blindly follows the text without clueing the kids into how this fits with what they have been doing or where they are going." The role of the textbook was not brought up by any of the other groups.

Climate. The educators described the climate in the U.S. lessons in mostly positive terms such as a mixture of an "easy," "respectful" relationship between the teacher and the students. The group from Hong Kong SAR noted that "order was kept."

Characteristics of Educators' Comments

To get a more direct sense of the similarities and differences among the views of the educator groups with regard to effective mathematics teaching, we looked at the recurring themes within the comments of each mathematics educator group. What features of teaching did the educators in, say, Australia focus on and how do these features compare to those most frequently voiced by the mathematics educators in the other countries? By looking across Tables A2-A7, we abstracted those features of lessons that were frequently identified by each group. Table 1 contains our interpretation of these themes. Readers are encouraged to review Tables A2-A7 and check our interpretation against their own. Because classroom climate is such a culturally-bound and difficult construct to interpret and summarize, we included only the teacher's role, the students' role, and the mathematics content in Table 1.

It is apparent to us that all of the mathematics educator groups shared concern about two issues: who is doing the mathematical work during the lesson (teacher and/or students) and how demanding or challenging is the content. Concern with who does the mathematical work is evident by the nearly unanimous focus on the level of dominance or guidance with respect to the teacher's role and an almost equally frequent focus on the involvement of students. The demand of the content was sometimes voiced with respect to the mathematical nature of the content (e.g., that it requires deep, conceptual understanding) and sometimes with respect to the expectations for students (e.g., that students be actively engaged in reasoning and in presenting their thinking).

At a general level, there was some indication that most educator groups agreed not only on the importance of these two features of teaching, but on the way in which these features define effective teaching. With regard to who does the mathematical work, the groups indicated that students must participate in doing some of the work and that teachers frequently do too much of the work. Teachers do too much by demonstrating a procedure step-by-step and leaving students to practice, by controlling the discussion too tightly, by not providing students opportunities to reason about and make sense of the material, and so on. With regard to content, most groups expressed concern that the content in at least some lessons was not challenging enough, and that there was little mathematically to learn.

Table 1. Major Themes of Educator Groups' Comments

Educator Group	Teacher's role	Students' role	Content
Australia	– Level of dominance or guidance	– Degree of involvement (what are students doing, in what activities are they engaging)	– Nature and amount of reasoning required – Degree of structure and coherent sequencing (including use of textbook toward this end) – Use of technical language
Czech Republic	– Level of dominance or guidance	– Degree of involvement (are students active or passive)	– Level of demand – Degree, nature of structure in activities
Hong Kong SAR	– Level of dominance or guidance – Degree of apparent planning	– Degree of involvement (do students present their ideas) – Level of demand/expectations – Student choice in mathematics/activities – Degree of collaborative work	– Richness vs. shallowness – Degree of conceptual thinking vs. rules/computation
North America	– Level of dominance or guidance – Degree to which textbook is followed	– Level of demand/expectations	– Degree of focus on rules – Degree of structure determined by text
Swiss-French	– Level of dominance or guidance	– Degree of involvement (are students asked to do mathematical work and to do problems at the board) – Degree of responsibility and autonomy	– Level of demand – Nature and amount of reasoning required – Use of technical language
Swiss-German	– Level of dominance or guidance (control)	– Degree of involvement (are students asked to provide independent constructions) – Extent of student choice – Degree of cooperative work	– Extent of conceptual development – Use of technical language
Swiss-Italian	*Varied, no prominent theme*	– Degree of involvement (are students asked to provide independent constructions)	– Extent of learning opportunities (how does content allow students to learn) – Degree of focus on technical competence – Clarity of lesson objectives

Behind this general agreement, there were some interesting differences in how these constructs were defined or at least what aspects of these constructs were emphasized. Student involvement, for example, meant somewhat different things to different groups of educators. Some mathematics educators (e.g., Australia) focused on involvement through participation in lesson activity, often in solving real-life problems. Other mathematics educators (e.g., Swiss-German, Swiss-Italian) spoke about involvement as opportunities to construct ideas independently. The extent to which students can choose how they participate was also mentioned by some groups (e.g., Hong Kong SAR, Swiss-German), as was the degree of responsibility and autonomy held by students (Swiss-Italian).

A second example of differences in nuance behind more general agreement can be found in the groups' commentaries about the mathematics content and its level of demand. The educators in Hong Kong SAR, for example, expressed a clear separation in the richness of content from whether it is mostly about rules versus concepts. That is, some lessons were judged to be rich mathematically *and* mostly about rules or procedures. In these cases, the Hong Kong SAR group looked for the ways in which the rules were developed. This same disaggregation between richness versus shallowness from rules versus concepts was not apparent in all groups.

All of the educator groups indicated that many of the lessons did not meet their standard of effective teaching. In fact, several groups commented that none of the videotapes depicted the type of teaching they would like to see in eighth-grade mathematics classes. Although these comments do not mean that all groups held exactly the same vision of effective teaching, it does suggest that they set a similar level of standard for what counts as effective.

CONCLUSIONS

Shared Images of Effective Teaching

At a general level, the mathematics educators from all countries—Australia, Czech Republic, Hong Kong SAR, North America, and Switzerland—tended to agree on the features they were looking for in effective mathematics teaching. First, all groups indicated that students should play a significant role in the classroom rather than having it dominated by the teacher. They agreed that the teacher should allow students to actively participate in making sense of the mathematics. Second, all of the groups commented on the degree of challenge posed by the mathematics content in the lessons. Those lessons deemed mathematically demanding were held in greater esteem than those whose content was considered slim or minimal. Also noted by the educators was the extent to which the content was developed. They reacted negatively to lessons that simply demonstrated rules and procedures and asked students to practice.

It is interesting that mathematics content was identified and described so often by the groups, given that the task description encouraged the participants to focus on instructional methods rather than content (see Table A1). Clearly, all mathematics educator groups viewed content as an essential aspect of methods—as a main ingredient in defining effective mathematics teaching.

Differences Among the Educator Groups

Differences among the educator groups appeared to revolve around the ways they defined some of the general constructs, such as student involvement, as well as the degree to which they judged a desired attribute, was present in the videotaped lessons. In the case of student involvement, the Swiss-German and Swiss-Italian educator groups looked for evidence that students provided independent constructions. The Hong Kong SAR and Swiss-French educators looked for students to present their ideas and work. The Swiss-French were interested also in whether students were asked to *do* mathematical work. The Australian educators took a broader view, examining the activities in which students were engaged, and the Czechs were more general still, noting whether students were active or passive.

In many cases the educators agreed on the qualities they wanted to see, but differed in their interpretations of how prominently those qualities were displayed in the particular lessons they viewed. For instance, with regard to the mathematical content in the Hong Kong SAR lessons, all of the educators wanted to see evidence of reasoning and conceptual thinking. However, some of the groups more than others were confident that these features were present in the lessons.

On a few occasions the educator groups agreed on the presence (or absence) of lesson features, but disagreed about whether these features were positive or negative. This was particularly true with respect to their comments about lesson climate. For example, all of the educator groups who commented on the climate in the Dutch lessons agreed that it was casual and informal, yet two of the groups saw the relaxed atmosphere in a positive light, whereas three of the groups felt that it led to discipline problems.

Occasionally, the mathematics educators viewed the lessons from their own country differently from their international colleagues. For example, most of the educator groups described the two videotaped Australian teachers as playing a strong, guiding role, while leaving the students relatively uninvolved in demanding mathematics. By contrast, the Australian educators felt these two teachers did not assume a dominant role and did attempt to involve their students, although they acknowledged that some of their attempts might have failed. Each educator group's frame of reference is likely shaped by their experiences working with many teachers within their country. The Australian educators' comments might have been made in relation to other Australian teachers they have worked with and observed. Indeed, these different frames of reference for the various educator groups underscore the significance of the fact that, on the whole, the educators' impressions of lessons from their home country were in agreement with the impressions of the educators from (at least some of) the other countries.

What Does This Tell Us?

Before returning to the question of whether educators across countries share a vision of effective mathematics teaching, we need to insert an important caveat. We have been implying, by naming the mathematics educator groups with the countries in which they work, that a group represents the views of an entire country. This cannot be true because surely there is greater variation among mathematics educators within a country than represented by the small number of group members who participated in this study and, further, we have no way of knowing how representative of the country are the views of the group members. Having said this, we do believe that the National Research Coordinators in each country invited participants who were credible mathematics educators in each country. In addition, there was no apparent connection among the participants across countries. Consequently, the results can be interpreted as judgments of respected mathematics educators in each country arrived at independently of the judgments of those in other countries.

Given this context, we believe it is fair to conclude that the mathematics educators across the five countries in this study share some significant components of a vision of effective teaching. To address the opening question of the chapter, the data we have presented suggest that the differences in classroom teaching across countries (as analyzed and reported elsewhere; see Hiebert et al., 2003a, 2003b) do not result from translating into practice different visions of effective teaching promoted by mathematics educators in the respective countries. In general, the visions of effective teaching expressed by mathematics educators across countries show much more similarity than do the country's classroom practices. In other words, many of the differences in classroom practices across countries appear to exist in spite of experts' views rather than because of them. As noted in the introduction, this might be due to the much greater level of communication and collaboration across country boundaries by mathematics educators than by classroom teachers.

Reinforcing this conclusion is the fact that all the mathematics educators participating in this study expressed some disappointment in the quality of classroom practices revealed on the videotapes, including lessons in their own country. In their judgment, their visions of effective teaching were not being realized in the classroom. All of these countries share the problem of translating visions into practice. Recall that the countries selected for inclusion in the TIMSS 1999 Video Study, with the exception of the United States, had high mathematics achievement as measured by the TIMSS 1995 assessment. Therefore, it is particularly interesting that the examples of teaching from these countries did not meet the standard set by this group of international educators.

There is a sense in which the findings on educators' judgments parallel our earlier work on classroom practices. At a general level of description, classroom practices look quite similar; at a more specific level, there are interesting and educationally significant differences (Givvin et al., 2005; Hiebert et al., 2003b). It might be fair to say the same thing about educators' judgments. Mathematics educators in different countries identified common, key features of effective instruction, but defined some of the general constructs in different ways. We believe these differences could be the basis for productive international discussions among mathematics educators. We see the forums for international communications and collaborations not only as possible explanations for the current similarities of views but also as forums for continued discussions about differences. We conjecture that the learning opportunities of such discussions will increase if they are centered on concrete referents of teaching. Imagine, for example, the learning opportunities for the mathematics educators who participated in this study if we could have arranged a joint conference of all participants to share and discuss their judgments of the videotaped lessons. Visions of effective teaching in each country clearly could be enriched through such collective examinations.

NOTES

[1] For convenience, in this chapter Hong Kong SAR is referred to as a country. Hong Kong is a Special Administrative Region (SAR) of the People's Republic of China. We held separate meetings with educators in each of the language regions of Switzerland, but here count Switzerland as a single country.

[2] The Japanese lessons collected for the TIMSS 1995 Video Study were reanalyzed for the TIMSS 1999 Video Study.

[3] A meeting of Dutch mathematics educators was planned but did not take place due to logistical difficulties. Because Japanese mathematics educators did not participate in the 1999 data collection, they were not part of this study. We will refer to the group that met in the United States as North American; 4 of the members were from the United States and 1 was from Canada.

[4] The National Research Coordinators for the TIMSS 1999 Video Study were: Australia – Jan Lokan (1998-2001) and Barry McCrae (2002-2003), Australian Council for Educational Research; Czech Republic – Jana Strakova, formerly at the Institute for Information on Education; Hong Kong SAR – Frederick Leung, The University of Hong Kong; Switzerland – Kurt Reusser, University of Zurich; and United States – Patrick Gonzales, National Center for Education Statistics.

[5] In the case of the Czech Republic, the National Research Coordinator selected experienced mathematics teachers to participate.

[6] An international group of specially trained coders analyzed the TIMSS 1999 Video Study data. They were fluently bilingual and could therefore watch the lessons in their original language. In most cases, they were born and raised in the country whose lessons they coded (Jacobs et al., 2003).

[7] With the exception of one Hong Kong SAR classroom, the lessons viewed by the mathematics educators are not the same as those released publicly for the mathematics component of the TIMSS 1999 Video Study. Most of the lessons viewed by the mathematics educators are considered "restricted use," meaning that permissions were not obtained for these lessons to be shown publicly. However, copies of the lessons for public release, either in their entirety or as a series of clips, are available from http://www.pearsonachievementsolutions.com/bkstore/index.cfm?action=dsr.

[8] Reports written in a language other than English were translated into English.

REFERENCES

Beaton, A., Mullis, I. V. S., Martin, M. O., Gonzalez, E. J., Kelly, D. L., & Smith, T. A. (1996). *Mathematics achievement in the middle school years: IEA's third international mathematics and science study.* Chestnut Hill, MA: Boston College.

Cai, J., Perry, R., & Wong, N.-Y. (2007). What is effective mathematics teaching? A dialogue between East and West. *Zentralblatt fuer Didaktik der Mathematik (International Journal of Mathematics Education)*, *39*(4).

Clarke, D. J., Emanuelsson, J., Jablonka, E., & Mok, I. A. C. (Eds.). (2006a). *Making connections: Comparing mathematics classrooms around the world.* Rotterdam: Sense Publishers.

Clarke, D. J., Emanuelsson, J., Jablonka, E., & Mok, I. A. C. (2006b). The learner's perspective study and international comparisons of classroom practice. In D. J. Clarke, J. Emanuelsson, E. Jablonka, & I. A.

C. Mok (Eds.), *Making connections: Comparing mathematics classrooms around the world* (pp. 1–22). Rotterdam: Sense Publishers.

Givvin, K. B., Hiebert, J., Jacobs, J. K., Hollingsworth, H., & Gallimore, R. (2005). Are there national patterns of teaching? Evidence from the TIMSS 1999 Video Study. *Comparative Education Review*, *49*(3), 311–343.

Gonzales, P., Calsyn, C., Jocelyn, L., Mak, K., Kastberg, D., Arafeh, S., et al. (2000). *Pursuing excellence: Comparisons of international eighth-grade mathematics and science achievement from a U.S. perspective, 1995 and 1999* (NCES 2001-028). Washington, DC: U.S. Department of Education, National Center for Education Statistics.

Hiebert, J., Gallimore, R., Garnier, H., Givvin, K. B., Hollingsworth, H., Jacobs, J., et al. (2003a). *Teaching mathematics in seven countries: Results from the TIMSS 1999 video study*. NCES (2003-013). U.S. Department of Education. Washington DC: National Center for Education Statistics.

Hiebert, J., Gallimore, R., Garnier, H., Givvin, K. B., Hollingsworth, H., Jacobs, J., et al. (2003b). Understanding and improving mathematics teaching: Highlights from the TIMSS 1999 video study. *Phi Delta Kappan, 84*(10), 768–775.

Hiebert, J., & Grouws, D. A. (2007). The effects of classroom mathematics teaching on students' learning. In F. K. Lester (Ed.), *Second handbook of research on mathematics teaching and learning* (pp. 371–404). Charlotte, NC: Information Age Publishing.

Jacobs, J., Garnier, H., Gallimore, R., Hollingsworth, H., Givvin, K. B., Rust, K., et al. (2003). *TIMSS 1999 video study technical report: Volume 1: Mathematics study* (NCES 2003-012). U.S. Department of Education. Washington, DC: National Center for Education Statistics.

Keitel, C., & Kilpatrick, J. (1999). The rationality and irrationality of international comparative studies. In G. Kaiser, L. Eduardo, & I. Huntley (Eds.), *International comparisons in mathematics education* (pp. 241–256). London: Falmer Press.

LeTendre, G. K., Baker, D., Akiba, M., Goesling, B., & Wiseman, A. (2001). Teachers' work: Institutional isomorphism and cultural variation in the U.S., Germany, and Japan. *Educational Researcher, 30*, 3–15.

Leung, F. K. S. (1995). The mathematics classroom in Beijing, Hong Kong, and London. *Educational Studies in Mathematics, 29*, 297–325.

Leung, F. K. S. (2001). In search of an East Asian identity in mathematics education. *Educational Studies in Mathematics, 47*, 35–51.

National Research Council. (2001). Adding it up: Helping children learn mathematics. In J. Kilpatrick, J. Swafford, & B. Findell (Eds.), *Mathematics learning study committee, center for education, division of behavioral and social sciences and education*. Washington, DC: National Academy Press.

Reynolds, D., & Muijs, D. (1999). The effective teaching of mathematics: A review of research. *Journal of Leadership & Management, 19*(3), 273–288.

Stigler, J. W., & Hiebert, J. (1999). *The teaching gap: Best ideas from the world's teachers for improving education in the classroom.* New York: Free Press.

Tweed, R. G., & Lehman, D. R. (2002). Learning considered within a cultural context: Confucian and Socratic approaches. *American Psychologist, 57*, 89–99.

Wilson, P. S., Cooney, T. J., & Stinson, D. W. (2005). What constitutes good mathematics teaching and how it develops: Nine high school teachers' perspectives. *Journal of Mathematics Teacher Education, 8*, 83–111.

Karen Bogard Givvin
LessonLab Research Institute

Jennifer Jacobs
University of Colorado, Boulder

Hilary Hollingsworth
Education Consultant

James Hiebert
University of Delaware

AUTHOR NOTE

The TIMSS 1999 Video Study was funded by the National Center for Education Statistics and the Office of Educational Research and Improvement of the U.S. Department of Education, as well as the National Science Foundation. It was conducted under the auspices of the International Association for the Evaluation of Educational Achievement (IEA). Support was also provided by each participating country through the services of a research coordinator who guided the sampling and recruiting of participating teachers. In addition, Australia and Switzerland contributed direct financial support for data collection and processing of their respective samples of lessons. The views expressed in this chapter are the authors and do not necessarily reflect those of the IEA or the funding agencies.

Special thanks are extended to each of the mathematics educators who participated in this task. Their significant contribution towards encouraging and extending international discussions of mathematics education is greatly appreciated. Thanks also go to the National Research Coordinators (listed in endnote 4) for organizing the educator meetings in each country and providing guidance throughout the project.

Correspondence concerning this chapter should be addressed to Karen Bogard Givvin, Karen.givvin@gmail.com

APPENDIX

Table A1. The Task Given to Each Educator Group

Task Goal

The goal of the task is to provide an overall assessment of some key similarities and differences in eighth-grade mathematics teaching among the six participating countries based on viewing two "typical" lessons from each country. We would like you to focus on the methods used to teach mathematics rather than other features, such as the level of the content. In particular, we are interested in the kinds of learning opportunities provided for the students and the nature of the mathematical reasoning that is evident. However, we also welcome your comments on other dimensions of similarity and difference that you find especially striking.

Task Description

We would like you to spend about two hours per country--watching the lessons and discussing the nature of teaching that you see. We have edited the lessons so that you can view both lessons in about an hour; however, you are free to view the entire lesson if you would like. Please prepare a consensus written report (indicating any areas where there is disagreement among yourselves) that addresses the goal of the task described above. Don't worry about the written form of the report. Unpolished statements that capture your main impressions are fine. Examples are helpful.

Suggested format for your report. To increase the likelihood that meaningful comparisons can be made among the reports from each country, we suggest that you organize your comments in the following way.
1. Identify the dimensions you used to compare the lessons and provide all of the comments you made about each country's lessons along these dimensions (some dimensions might be relevant only for some countries). This requires keeping notes of your discussions while reviewing the lessons.
2. Summarize your conclusions about major similarities and differences among the lessons.
3. Suggest the major "stories" that you think can be told from these lessons (assuming the remaining lessons in the sample are similar to these).
4. Provide whatever comments you would like about the lessons from this set that you think are high quality or exemplary and identify the key elements that distinguish high quality lessons from the rest.

Table A2. Educator Groups' Impressions of the Australian Lessons

Educator Group	Teacher's role	Students' role	Content	Climate
Australia	– Guide students to understanding	– Attempts to involve students through activities – Little emphasis on public performance of students	– Deformalizing the math and showing its relevance – Sometimes unfocused, so significant features may be unclear at the end – Sequence and structure of the math not emphasized – Reasoning not directly encouraged – Technical language underused	– Casual and informal – Many social interactions
Czech Republic	– Teacher directed ("frontal") – No clear lesson structure	– Little activity or involvement	– Not very demanding – Inaccurate terminology sometimes used – Based on practical applications	– Teacher is "natural authority" – Informal attitude of students toward teacher
Hong Kong SAR	– Teacher-led – Not well planned	– Few hands-on activities – No collaborative work – No student presentation – Relatively low expectations of students	– Low-level computation – Superficial (shallow) math content – Rule-oriented	– Laissez-faire atmosphere – Lack of discipline
North America	– Teacher helps students figure out the rules, makes things easy for them, is ally of the students, prepares them for tests – Follows the spirit of the textbook, but not totally bound to it	– Students are protected from thinking very hard – Low math demand on students	– Focus is on rules and procedures rather than concepts and conceptual understanding – The math is situated	*Opinions across the lessons were mixed*

Educator Group	Teacher's role	Students' role	Content	Climate
Swiss-French	– Teacher provides strong guidance, intervenes when there are errors – "Transmissive" – little autonomy given to students – Authoritarian, directed by the teacher	– Little is asked of students, low expectations of students	– Fragmented, low-level – Little emphasis on mathematically correct language	– Amicable
Swiss-German	– Teacher takes control of the cognitive process and leaves little leeway in making independent steps – Teacher shows the correct solution or solution method in response to mistakes	– Students expected to repeat and automate procedures demonstrated by the teacher in small steps – No opportunity to discover or construct math structures – Opportunities for cooperation between students not observed	– Purely procedural, without an in-depth understanding of the math concepts that are behind the procedures – Lower emphasis on correct mathematical terminology – Terms are defined, developed, and then applied – a deductive instructional pattern	– Relaxed but well disciplined – Sympathetic and respectful teacher-student relationship – Motivation is extrinsic – to produce correct solutions on the test
Swiss-Italian	– Completely teacher guided	– Students learn by repetition, not by math reasoning – Don't create their own spontaneous knowledge	– Very minimal content – Great attention to application of rules – No real learning opportunities	*No comments made*

GIVVIN, JACOBS, HOLLINGSWORTH, HIEBERT

Table A3. Educator Groups' Impressions of the Czech Lessons

Educator Group	Teacher's role	Students' role	Content	Climate
Australia	– Teacher is dominant	– Lesson is for teaching – Learning through student activity or practice is separate or elsewhere – Student's publicly assessed in beginning	– Appropriate technical language	– Little social interaction between teacher-students and students-students
Czech Republic	– Teacher directed ("frontal") and dominated – Lesson highly structured/ ordered/routinized	– Passive – Some use of groups	– Demanding – Formal material covered	– Formal and authoritative – Teacher keeps a distance from students
Hong Kong SAR	– Teacher-led – Continuous formative assessment – Teacher has authoritative role	– A lot of student presentation – Little student choice of the mathematics to learn – High expectations of students	– Math content dense and rich – Emphasis on computation and factual recall – Both process and the correct solution are stressed	– Clear classroom routines – Serious atmosphere
North America	– Lessons carefully planned – Teacher explores ideas beyond what happened in the book – Teacher does not shoulder the entire workload	– Held accountable for learning – Expected to do some learning on their own – High math demand on students – Students examined at the beginning	– Focus is on rules, technical aspects of math language, and symbol manipulation – Linear organization to the math development, learning one idea or skill in preparation for the next	*No comments made*
Swiss-French	– Teacher is authority – Activity guided by the teacher	– Students are involved – Their work is important – Students used as "technical assistants" and take part in the teaching workload	– High level of difficulty	– Students pay attention, have respect for the teacher

Educator Group	Teacher's role	Students' role	Content	Climate
		– Given responsibility without autonomy (i.e. rarely ask questions) – Students are responsible for doing a problem on the board; they get judged by their peers and graded by the teacher		
Swiss-German	– Teacher organizes the lesson linearly and controls every detail of the instruction, even during private time – Through direct teaching, teacher makes the deep structure of the math procedures transparent – Lessons carefully planned and organized efficiently	– Students reproduce the cognitive structure demonstrated by the teacher, with little leeway for alternative solution methods – Students' mistakes are exhibited publicly and recognized as learning opportunities – Phases of seatwork, but cooperation is prohibited – Students are given public feedback on their performance in the form of grades	– Content is composed of small steps and meaningful units that build on each other – Knowing the "how" and "why" of procedures is important – Correct mathematical language is valued	– Intense, focused, and disciplined atmosphere – High degree of pressure put on students – Emphasis on social comparison
Swiss-Italian	– Teacher concerned about the students' learning process	– The math is carried through dialogue – Students don't ask questions but have an active role doing "research" and inductive thinking	– Goal is to reach technical ability, but at the same time allow students to understand why a certain mathematical process is followed – Heavy emphasis on the technical aspects – Problems aren't very practical	– Good environment – Teacher has control of the classroom – Teacher and students share the same values and respect the same rules

Table A4. Educator Groups' Impressions of the Hong Kong SAR Lessons

Educator Group	Teacher's role	Students' role	Content	Climate
Australia	– Teacher is dominant	– Student involvement not highly valued	– Well structured – Sequencing is important – Textbook provides much of the learning structure – Encourages mathematical thinking and reasoning – Stress on relational understanding as opposed to rote understanding – Appropriate technical language	– Students quiet and submissive – The work is serious and important – Little social interaction between teacher-students and students-students
Czech Republic	– Teacher directed ("frontal") – Lecture-like	– Minimal activity	– Formally structured – Variety	– Formal and authoritative – Great distance between students and teacher – Based on "Asian discipline"
Hong Kong SAR	– Teacher-led – Knowledge is given by the teacher – Well planned	– Students seem to be treated as calculation and computation machines – A lot of student presentation – No collaborative work – Moderate mathematics demand placed on students	– Rich content – Computation/calculation emphasized – Rule-oriented – Low emphasis on concepts – Teacher mathematically competent	– Clear classroom routines
North America	– Teacher dominated	– Moderate math demand on students	– Very textbook driven, based on examples worked out in the students' book	*Opinions across the lessons were mixed*
Swiss-French	– Teacher is authority – Activities guided by the teacher	– Students given responsibility without autonomy (i.e. rarely ask questions, must do what	– High level of difficulty	– Students highly disciplined – Students put forth a high degree of concentration and

Educator Group	Teacher's role	Students' role	Content	Climate
		is proposed) – Often work out problems at the board that are judged by the teacher and peers		effort, and have respect for the teacher
Swiss-German	– Teacher walks through step by step in a clear and direct way – Teacher shows the correct solution or solution method in response to mistakes – Teacher often answers their own questions	– No independent cognitive constructing of the math structural knowledge – Students often answer teachers' questions together in sync ("choir style") – Participation limited to short, predictable statements	– Opportunities for students to acquire a deeper understanding of math structures and principles – Training of procedural skills, with logical math explanations for the prescribed method – Incorrect student comments are eliminated through strong teacher guidance – Emphasis on correct use of math terminology – Following a review, new content is introduced and then practiced	– Disciplined and work-intensive atmosphere – A high degree of pressure to succeed and a competitive character – Extrinsic incentives are emphasized
Swiss-Italian	– Repetition-imitative method – Seems to be a clear contract between the teacher and students	– Very few instances when the students can actively participate – Students don't discover the learning process themselves – Goal is for students to gain instrumental competence and be competitive	– Focused on competence in technical abilities – Lessons based on knowledge already known to students – No real "learning experiences" – Lesson objectives not clearly explained	– Competitive – Use of microphone affects rapport between students and teacher

GIVVIN, JACOBS, HOLLINGSWORTH, HIEBERT

Table A5. Educator Groups' Impressions of the Dutch Lessons

Educator Group	Teacher's role	Students' role	Content	Climate
Australia	– Not teacher dominated	– Little emphasis on public performance of students	– Sequence and structure of the math not emphasized – Textbook provides much of the learning structure	– Casual relationships between teacher and students – Many social interactions
Czech Republic	– Teacher directed ("frontal")	– Much student responsibility – Active – Some use of groups	– Not very demanding – Structured scheme: homework, new material, practice, then test	– Equality and partner-like relationship between teacher and students – Mutual tolerance – Liberal – Informal
Hong Kong SAR	– Low requirement on the teacher – Teacher plays a "friendly" role	– No student presentation – No collaborative work – Students willing to ask questions – Low expectations of students	– Superficial (shallow) math content – Lesson covers a lot of questions (math problems), but there are no mathematics concepts involved	– Laissez-faire atmosphere – Lack of discipline – Class out of the teacher's control
North America	– Teacher does not go farther than the textbook: "If the book does not ask, the teacher does not ask"	– Student's task is to work on assigned textbook problems independently – High math demand on students	– Challenging topics and problems	*Opinions across the lessons were mixed*
Swiss-French	– Teacher guides and simplifies the work for students	*Opinions across the lessons were mixed*	– Focus is on rules and results – Opportunities for math reasoning are not well exploited	*Opinions across the lessons were mixed*

Educator Group	Teacher's role	Students' role	Content	Climate
Swiss-German	– Teacher is coach, providing individual learning support – Teacher plays the role of facilitator – Lessons are guided only to a small degree by the teacher	– Students have a high degree of control to explore procedures and construct their own math understanding – Mistakes are recognized as learning opportunities – Can get help from their classmates and tutoring from the teacher	– Learning to solve problems by exploring, without instruction on standard solution procedures – Opportunities for students to acquire a deeper understanding of math structures and principles – Development of higher order thinking not observed – Relevant to real-life, and not very abstract – Little observable emphasis on correct mathematical language – Math terminology is casual and undemanding – Extensive discussion of prior homework, then new problems assigned and worked on independently for much of the lesson	– Noise level is high, and discipline of students is a frequent issue – Chaotic – Very permissive and relaxed environment – No extrinsic motivators present
Swiss-Italian	*Opinions across the lessons were mixed*	– Students not involved, either due to teacher's lack of attempts or difficulty in finding the appropriate strategies	– A division exists between theory and practice – No real occasions to learn	– Teacher seems to be detached or has difficulty relating, and students seem distracted and uninterested – Efforts between the teacher and students to interact fail – Teacher and students lack rapport

GIVVIN, JACOBS, HOLLINGSWORTH, HIEBERT

Table A6. Educator Groups' Impressions of the Swiss Lessons

Educator Group	Teacher's role	Students' role	Content	Climate
Australia	– Teacher is dominant	– Student activity and involvement valued	– Sequence and structure of the math emphasized – Math thinking and reasoning encouraged – Appropriate technical language	*Opinions across the lessons were mixed*
Czech Republic	– Teacher works together with students – Well prepared	– Active in problem solving – Focused, disciplined, motivated	– Structure focuses on problem solving – Not very demanding, but well connected	– Good working morale and discipline – Friendly relationship between teacher and students
Hong Kong SAR	– Teacher-led – Well planned	– High student engagement and involvement – A lot of oral student presentation – Individual student care, but no collaborative work – A lot of student choice of mathematics/activities – Quite high demand on students' work	– Rich math content – Thinking process emphasized – Calculation not emphasized	– Enjoyable atmosphere for students, self-motivation is quite high
North America	*Opinions across the lessons were mixed*	– Degree of thinking students asked to do varies – Math demand on students varies from low to moderate	*Opinions across the lessons were mixed*	*No comments made*
Swiss-French	– Teacher may provide indirect or subtle guidance	– Students are involved and participate in doing the work	*Opinions across the lessons were mixed*	*No comments made*

Educator Group	Teacher's role	Students' role	Content	Climate
Swiss-German	– Teacher prepares and highly structures the lessons based on didactics – Knowledge is often developed in a teacher-led instructional conversation – During individual work, teacher tries to diagnose mistakes and provide hints	– Students participate actively – Some student directed learning situations, where they construct cognitive steps independently – Discovery and individual (or group) problem-solving – Mistakes are recognized as learning opportunities	– Focus is on understanding and meaning, rather than procedures – Students have opportunities to acquire a deeper understanding of math structures and principles	– Respectful climate – Lack of focus on extrinsic motivators
Swiss-Italian	*Opinions across the lessons were mixed*	– Student's role varies from repeating procedures established by the teacher to time for "thought-reflection" and discovery	– The degree to which the lessons involve "learning situations" varies – The educational objective of the lesson is not always clearly defined	– Quiet, serene, responsible environment

Table A7. Educator Groups' Impressions of the U.S. Lessons

Educator Group	Teacher's role	Students' role	Content	Climate
Australia	– Teacher is dominant	– Student involvement not highly valued – Little emphasis on public performance of students	– Reasoning not directly encouraged – Stress on rote understanding as opposed to relational understanding – Technical language overused	– Easy relationship between teacher and students – Teachers accept a low level of student attention
Czech Republic	– Teacher-controlled	– Independent work under teacher's guidance – Goal is to pass test	– Material presented schematically without emphasis on fundamentals	– Teacher is "natural authority" – Firm discipline

GIVVIN, JACOBS, HOLLINGSWORTH, HIEBERT

Educator Group	Teacher's role	Students' role	Content	Climate
Hong Kong SAR	– Teacher-led	– Students not expected to think deeply and given low-level tasks – A lot of student choice of activities	– Some structure – Not very demanding – Superficial ("slim") and simple math content – Emphasis on computation and factual recall	– Order kept
North America	– Teacher helps students prepare for tests and doesn't explore ideas beyond what happened in the book	– Students not asked to reason – Students not asked to make personal records of their work and the work of the class – Low math demand on students	– Lessons tightly linked to materials in the text or provided by the publisher	*No comments made*
Swiss-French	– Step by step guidance	– Students don't hesitate to ask questions, but exchanges are only at an elementary level	– Focus is on knowing "how" – Little or no justification of techniques and reasoning – Prior homework is discussed, but they don't get into what the difficulties were	– Good ambiance and relative freedom of students
Swiss-German	– Teacher demonstrates and students practice – Teacher demonstrates the content quickly but also with redundancy – Teacher shows the correct solution or solution method in response to mistakes	– Verbal participation is infrequent and often limited to fill-in-the-blank questions – Even during seatwork, students guided step-by-step by the teacher – No opportunity for group work observed	– Emphasis on procedural skills, not meaning – Procedures are not connected and integrated into a coherent knowledge structure – Higher order mathematical principles are not taught – Problems solved in small steps according to prescribed	– Respectful climate – Motivation is extrinsic – to do well on the test

Educator Group	Teacher's role	Students' role	Content	Climate
			– procedures and rules – General, "open" problems not posed – Correct math terminology valued highly	
Swiss-Italian	*Opinions across the lessons were mixed*	– Very few instances when students can actively participate – Students don't discover the learning process themselves	– Learning opportunities vary from none to learning only technical aspects – Lessons based on knowledge already known to students – Lesson objectives not clearly explained	– The living experience of the students appears to be positive

SEBASTIAN KUNTZE AND FRANZISKA RUDOLPH-ALBERT

WHAT IS "GOOD" MATHEMATICS INSTRUCTION?

Mathematics Teachers' Individual Criteria for Instructional Quality and Attributions for Instructional Success [1]

INTRODUCTION

In TIMSS and PISA, the mathematics achievement results for students from Germany and Switzerland differed considerably. Although the cultural environments in Germany and the German-speaking part of Switzerland are relatively close, there might be different cultural characteristics framing mathematics instruction. As teachers' beliefs about what can be considered as "good" mathematics instruction probably reflect components of their professional knowledge and their instruction-related beliefs in a cumulative way, we focus on teachers' views about criteria for instructional quality and their attributions of personal instructtional success. In the following, we give an outline of the theoretical background of our study.

THEORETICAL BACKGROUND

Mathematics instruction in the classroom is a complex interactional interplay orchestrated by teachers. Typical roles and interactional patterns of students and teachers, as well as the mutual social expectancies between them, are influenced by cultural factors. Stigler and Hiebert (1999, pp. 87–88) describe these interdependencies in the following way:

> Cultural activities, such as teaching, are not invented full-blown but rather evolve over long periods of time in ways that are consistent with the stable web of beliefs and assumptions that are part of the culture. The scripts for teaching in each country appear to rest on a relatively small and tacit set of core beliefs about the nature of the subject, about how students learn, and about the role that a teacher should play in the classroom. These beliefs, often implicit, serve to maintain the stability of cultural systems over time.

As indicated by Stigler and Hiebert (1999), different teaching scripts for mathematics instruction in different countries have been identified in international research projects focusing on classroom practice like the TIMSS Video Studies of 1995 and 1999 (cf. Stigler et al., 1999; Neubrand, 2006; Baumert et al., 1997). These different instructional patterns have to be considered as influenced by

J. Cai, G. Kaiser, B. Perry and N.-Y. Wong (eds.), Effective Mathematics Teaching from Teachers' Perspectives: National and Cross-National Studies, 71–92.
© *2009 Sense Publishers. All rights reserved.*

culture-specific expectations of students, teachers, parents, school administration and other social environments. For instance, there are probably more or less shared notions of what should happen in a good mathematics lesson, how teachers and students should interact, and how learning opportunities should be framed in the classroom. Even though there is a considerable variance within countries, such shared expectations may contribute to culture-typical patterns in instructional practice (Neubrand, 2006; Kaiser, Hino & Knipping, 2006). Moreover, individual perceptions of experiences of teachers and students with classroom situations are likely to play a role in the stability of culture-specific teaching scripts, because they might follow socially shared criteria. For example, teaching traditions and corresponding reference criteria are often transmitted to the next generation of teachers within the community of teachers of a country (Hiebert, Stigler & Manaster, 1999).

As the teacher plays an important role when orchestrating interactional processes and learning opportunities in the classroom, we would like to concentrate on the teachers' belief structure regarding such possibly culture-specific expectations and perceptions related to instructional practice. We expect that there is a "backing" for culture-specific teaching scripts in professional knowledge and instruction-related beliefs of the teachers (c.f. e.g. Perry et al., 2006; An et al., 2006). As theoretical background for professional knowledge and instruction-related beliefs, we refer to the model by Shulman (1986a, 1986b, 1987), distinguishing between pedagogical knowledge, subject matter knowledge, and pedagogical content knowledge. As it is difficult to make a clear distinction between knowledge and instructtion-related beliefs, we consider such beliefs as part of the professional knowledge of a teacher.

Several studies have found connections and interdependencies between instructtional practice and professional knowledge (e.g. Staub & Stern, 2002; Stipek et al., 2001; Fennema, Carpenter, & Peterson, 1989; Schoenfeld, 1983; Wholhuter, 1996). Taking a look at the teacher variables included in these studies, we observe that especially in the domain of pedagogical content beliefs, the constructs considered are mostly linked to different aspects or orientations of what good mathematics instruction according to different underlying criteria should look like. For example, the "cognitive constructivist or direct-transmission views of teaching and learning" of Staub and Stern (2002) refer to different aspects of how learning opportunities should be organized in order to be effective. Most likely, convictions regarding characteristics for instructional quality play an important role for the process of decision-making in the classroom (Malara, 2003, Escudero & Sanchez, 1999; Sullivan & Mousley, 2001), or even for building up interactional patterns and routines for classroom situations, to which the attribution of individual success in classroom situations can also contribute. In some of the studies cited above, the investigated components of professional knowledge are related to particular theoretical frameworks in a top-down manner. If teachers' convictions about instructional quality are examined in a bottom-up way, it could be possible to obtain a more cumulative picture of this area of professional knowledge. This is why we focused on mathematics teachers' individual criteria for instructional quality and the perception of reasons for own instructional success.

In order to get a rough orientation, we would like to refer to criteria for the quality of mathematics instruction from the perspective of empirical research. Based on the German sample of the TIMSS 1995 Video Study and the Swiss sample of the TIMSS 1995 Video Study, Clausen, Reusser and Klieme (2003) identified four basic dimensions of instructional quality using high-inference ratings, namely *instructional efficiency, student orientation, cognitive activation, and clarity/structure. Instructional efficiency* is associated with positive ratings of classroom management as well as time-on-task and low values for wasting time, disciplinary problems, and aggressions. *Student orientation* is linked to characteristics such as a positive way of learning from mistakes, diagnostic competency of the teacher in the social domain, individual learning supported by the teacher, and multiple authentic contexts. *Cognitive activation* encompasses mathematical productivity, the mediator role of the teacher, pacing, and the teacher's ability to motivate the students. Finally, the basic dimension of *clarity/structure* is characterized by structuring help from the teacher, clarity of instruction, and diagnostic competency focusing on achievement (Clausen, Reusser, & Klieme, 2003, p.129). We assert that these criteria are valid at least for Germany and the German-speaking part of Switzerland. For this reason, we consider the results of this study as a base of reference for our study.

Parts of the scales used by Clausen, Reusser, and Klieme (2003) were presented by Gruehn (2000), who mainly adopted a perspective of the learners for different criteria concerning the quality of instructional practice. According to Clausen (2002), the perspective of the teachers can differ considerably from the students' perceptions of instructional quality and from ratings of external observers. For this reason, it is interesting to compare individual criteria for instructional practice of the teachers to criteria linked to the perspective of learners or external observers like they are reflected in the basic dimensions of instructional quality by Clausen, Reusser and Klieme (2003).

According to Leinhardt and Greeno (1986) and Bromme (1992, 1997), professional knowledge is often organized episodically. For this reason, criteria for instructional quality might be primarily context-specific, i.e. specific for a particular content or for particular instructional situations (cf. Kuntze & Reiss, 2005). Even though there are general aspects of the quality of mathematics instruction like classroom management or cognitive activation, the individual criteria of teachers for "good" mathematics lessons might be activated by them according to particular situations. For example, the situation of having to judge on instructional quality observing the lesson of a colleague might differ from the situation in which factors for the success of an own lesson that has turned out well are analyzed. Apparently, the question of the stability of convictions concerning more general individual criteria for instructional quality under varying contexts should not be omitted when investigating this component of professional knowledge.

A second critical point partly linked to the previous is how close to instruction-related decision-making (Sullivan & Mousley, 2001) these criteria for instructional quality really are. For instance, criteria for instructional quality which are seen as rather theoretical and not very relevant for practice by the teachers are not very likely to have an important impact on the teaching practice. These are two reasons why research identifying individual criteria for instructional quality should integrate different formats of questions, using different degrees of situatedness in order to gain additional information about the potential relevance of the individual criteria.

Summing up, it seems very probable that there is a backing in professional teacher knowledge for culture-specific teaching scripts. As the convictions about instructional quality and beliefs concerning factors of successful teaching might be of particular importance for instructional practice and decision-making in the classroom, we focus on that component of professional knowledge. As a reference for criteria of instructional quality, we refer to the basic dimensions identified by Clausen, Reusser and Klieme (2003). It should be taken into consideration whether individual criteria for instructional quality are stable given different formats of questions, e.g. under varying degrees of relatedness to particular classroom situations. Perceptions of individual experiences and attributions linked to instructional success might give additional information.

Between Germany and the German-speaking part of Switzerland, differences in mathematical competence have been found in TIMSS and the PISA studies of 2000 and 2003 (TIMSS: Germany: M=509, SD=90; Switzerland: M=545, SD=88; German-speaking part of Switzerland: M=590; cf. Baumert et al., 1997, p. 90; PISA 2000: Germany: M=490, SD=103; Switzerland: M=529, SD=100; cf. Deutsches PISA-Konsortium, 2001, p. 173; PISA 2003: Germany: M=503, SD=103; Switzerland: M=527, SD=98: cf. Deutsches PISA-Konsortium, 2004). These differences suggest that there are differences in mathematics instruction between the two countries.

The study of Clausen, Reusser, and Klieme (2003) compared Swiss and German mathematics lessons. The cross-cultural differences found in this study indicated that in the domain of *instructional efficiency*, the lessons from the German-speaking part of Switzerland showed an emphasis on classroom management without disciplinary problems, whereas in one quarter of the German lessons, disciplinary problems, a certain struggle for ordered working processes and signs of wasted time were observed. Moreover, Clausen, Reusser, and Klieme (2003) found a higher *student orientation* in the Swiss lessons than in the German lessons: The Swiss classrooms showed more individualization in the working processes and better ways to provide learning opportunities when reacting to mistakes of the students. Clausen et al. see this as a consequence of a certain reform orientation in the German-speaking part of Switzerland, including the introduction of student-centered learning environments (cf. Stebler & Reusser, 2000). For *cognitive activation* and for *clarity/structure*, the cultural differences found by Clausen et al. (2003) were rather small.

These findings can be seen as in line with the description of the typical teaching script for German mathematics lessons in the TIMSS 1995 Video Study (Stigler et al., 1999; Neubrand, 2006), comparing them to lessons in Japan and in the U.S. According to this script, the teacher plays a dominant role in an interaction characterized by rather small-step questions of the teacher. Moreover, algorithmical abilities are emphasized. This teaching script offers limited possibilities for individualized working forms. The differences in student orientation are likely to be influenced also by the social framing of mathematics instruction. According to the results of the bi-national cross-cultural study of Lipowsky et al. (2003) on professional knowledge and the perceived professional environment, the Swiss teachers report a more positive perception of their school environment (cf. also Fend, 1998), higher interest of the parents and a higher self- efficacy than the German teachers, who saw their instructional practice as more difficult and demanding. This means that Swiss teachers might see more possibilities of influencing the success of instructional situations.

As already discussed above, individual instructional experiences might play an important role for judgements on instructional quality and for the development of professional knowledge in general. Seen from this point of view, the attribution of reasons for lessons to have turned out successful or less successful is not only a question of self-efficacy (for attributional styles and self-efficacy cf. e.g. Dweck, 1986, Bandura, 1977), but it could also influence the teachers' perception, where they see possibilities to improve the quality of lessons. Such pedagogical content beliefs could influence their views on criteria of instructional quality. For this reason, finding out about personal experiences of successful or unsuccessful lessons as well as the attribution of success can provide additional insight.

The sample of the study of Lipowsky et al. (2003) was statistically representative for Germany and Switzerland. The variables concerning professional knowledge included in the study of Lipowsky et al. showed only small differences between Swiss and German teachers compared to the professional knowledge discrepancies between school types within the two countries. One of the differences consists in a higher favoring of the direct-transmission view of teaching and learning (cf. Staub & Stern, 2002) by the Swiss teachers compared to their German colleagues. It is one of the aims of this study to contribute also to answering the question whether such convictions and dispositions might be explained by individual criteria of instructional quality and attributions of factors favoring the success of the own teaching practice.

RESEARCH QUESTIONS

Against this theoretical background, we focus on the following research questions:
– What are the individual criteria for instructional quality that mathematics teachers refer to when asked to judge on classroom practice?
– To which causes do teachers attribute instructional success of their own instruction when asked about personal experiences of "good" lessons or about experiences of lessons not having turned out well? How do they judge their possibilities of influencing the success of these instructional situations they experienced?

DESIGN, METHOD AND SAMPLE

The sample of this study consisted of 42 German and 10 Swiss upper secondary in-service mathematics teachers coming from 11 German and 4 Swiss schools. These schools were located in south-German and Swiss small-town environments. Some characteristics of the sample are displayed in Table 1.

Table 1. Characteristics of the sample

	age (years)				professional practice in years (SD)	female	male
	35 or less	36–45	46–55	more than 55			
German teachers	19	8	13	2	11.3 (9.8)	14	28
Swiss teachers	4	3	1	2	13.6 (10.9)	3	7

The teachers were participants of an in-service teacher training project. However, the study we report on here only focused on data from questionnaires the teachers were asked to complete prior to the teacher training, so that we can assume that their responses were not influenced by any of the interventions of the training. As participation in the teacher training was voluntary, a possible process of self-selection of the sample might have taken place, even though the recruitment of the participants was rather top-down, i.e. via the school directors.

The data for this study were collected in two paper-and-pencil-questionnaires the teachers were asked to fill out. The first one of these questionnaires contained a unit on individual criteria of instructional quality and a unit on individual views on instructional success, i.e. on their own lessons having turned out well or unsatisfactory according to the teachers' view.

In the unit on individual criteria of instructional practice, in an open item, the participants were asked to name characteristics of good mathematics instruction, which are accessible by an external observation. They were told to imagine that they were assisting a lesson of a colleague and that, independently from the feedback they would give her or him, they would have to make an honest judgement on the quality of instruction for themselves, for which they should name the underlying criteria. On a three-point Likert scale, the importance given to each of these criteria could be marked on the questionnaire. In order to limit the answers to rather non-artificial criteria, which are likely to be present in the every-day life of the teachers, the teachers were asked not to spend more than ten minutes on this part of the questionnaire. The questionnaire unit contained a default space for six criteria. This questionnaire unit is presented in the appendix.

The unit on individual views concerning the perception of instructional success, i.e. their own lessons that the teachers qualified as having turned out well or unsatisfactory, was an instrument developed by A. Buff and E. Klieme (this instrument is presented in Rakoczy, Buff & Lipowsky, 2005, p. 220). The teachers were asked to imagine situations in which they were very satisfied or not satisfied at all from lessons they had taught before. For successful and unsatisfactory lessons, they were asked separately to name reasons for the success of the satisfactory lessons or the failure of for the unsatisfactory lessons. There was space for three reasons respectively, and these reasons had to be given in the order of their importance. For additional items on the attribution of these reasons, the teachers were asked whether for the corresponding reason, it was an external influence or a factor they attributed to themselves, and therefore, in the case of the unsatisfactory lessons, saw the possibility of doing better.

The second questionnaire was also administered prior to the interventions of the teacher training. It referred to two particular videotaped classroom situations the teachers had been shown before answering the questions in the questionnaire. Again, the teachers were asked about their individual criteria of instructional quality in a part of this questionnaire, this time when really making judgements on the classroom situations. In this way, the teachers focused on a situation-specific context while answering this unit, whereas the unit on individual criteria for instructional quality in the first questionnaire was more hypothetical in character.

In the two videotaped classroom situations, two classrooms were shown in lessons on introducing geometrical proof, respectively. One of the situations contained a teacher-centered interaction comparable to the small-step-question teaching script dominant in Germany, and the other situation showed a teacher-centered interaction which was marked by elements of discourse and short argumentations by the students. In both situations, a first example of a geometrical proof was elaborated.

The questionnaire unit for judgements on the classroom situations is presented in the appendix as well.

The answers of the teachers to the questions presented above were coded following a bottom-up-approach. This bottom-up-analysis was based on an inter-pretative paradigm similar to grounded theory (Straub, Kempf, & Werbik, 1997). The coding was done by two raters who analyzed the teachers' responses by consensus against the background of possible context information in the question-naires in order to establish primary codes very close to the teachers' individual responses. In a second step of this interpretative work of the raters, the codes were grouped according to their semantic proximity or contiguousness. This process was continued unless the remaining codes/responses could no longer be grouped into a greater common semantic domain. The grouping of primary codes was controlled by reviewing the original responses of the teachers during the consensus process.

RESULTS

Individual Criteria for Instructional Quality

As described in the third section, a bottom-up-analysis was used to code the responses of the teachers concerning their individual criteria for instructional quality. In the first questionnaire, the 299 criteria provided by the teachers could be labelled with 105 codes. These 105 codes could be grouped (following the bottom-up-approach) into 12 semantic domains, which encompassed 90.3% of all teachers' responses on the primary code level. In the bottom-up-analysis of the responses in the second questionnaire related to judging instructional quality of the two videotaped classroom situations, these semantic domains could be replicated together with an additional semantic domain "communication/interaction in the classroom." In order to obtain a better comparability, this thirteenth semantic domain was included in the analysis of the first questionnaire and a few corresponding primary codes formerly classified in the category "other" were assigned to this semantic domain.

We would like to illustrate the process of the bottom-up-analysis using an example. One of the teachers provided the following criteria for instructional quality: "The students are given the opportunity to reflect and discuss among themselves." This response was coded by the primary codes "discussion of students on problems" and "student-centered work and reflection." Later in the analysis, both of these primary codes were grouped in the semantic domain of "use of preferred teaching methods (in the sense of forms of organization of working processes in the classroom,, e.g. group work, seatwork etc.),," together with other primary codes like "integrate phases of student-centered work," "use of adequate working forms according to content," or "students solve problems in small groups." As can be seen from this example, the semantic domains often encompassed a range of detailed aspects that are related to a common area of criteria formed by semantic proximity or contiguousness. For more information about the semantic domains created in the bottom-up-analysis, an overview of the semantic domains and examples of codes they were based on is given in the appendix.

The percentages of teachers providing responses in the semantic domains are displayed in Figure 1 and 2. Generally, in the second questionnaire referring to the videotaped instructional situations, there were less or less-varied criteria named by the teachers (cf. Figures 1 and 2). The twelve semantic domains produced for the first questionnaire were reproduced for the second. In addition, a thirteenth domain emerged. The number of "other" primary codes not related to the semantic domains receded in the second questionnaire.

Comparing the percentage values for the two questionnaires, certain shifts can be seen: For example, the semantic domains "activation of the students" and "communication/interaction in the classroom" got more attention in the second questionnaire than in the first, whereas the domains "discipline" and "use of preferred teaching methods" occurred less frequently. These results reflected the content of the videotaped classroom situations. For example, disciplinary problems were not shown in the classroom situations.

Even though comparisons between the cultural groups of the teachers should be handled with special care given the rather low number of Swiss teachers, some careful observations can be made: There was a relatively stronger emphasis by the Swiss teachers on content-related criteria and less attention on criteria like discipline or the focus on students especially in the first questionnaire compared to their German counterparts.

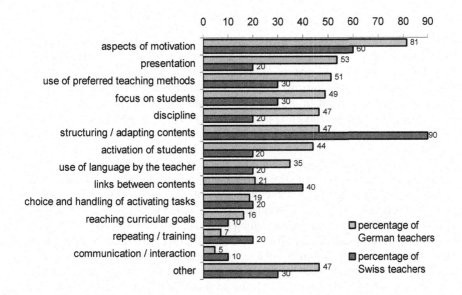

*Figure 1. First questionnaire: Criteria for instructional quality
(percentages of teachers making comments classified in the semantic domains)*

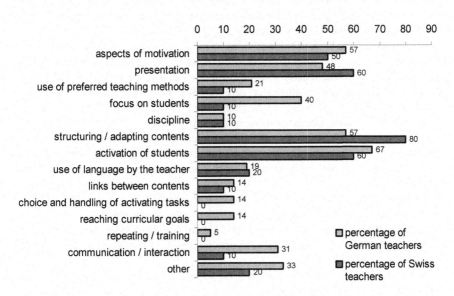

*Figure 2. Second questionnaire: Criteria for instructional quality of videotaped classroom
situations (percentages of teachers making comments classified in the semantic domains)*

Attributions Linked to Experiences of Successful or Unsuccessful Lessons

The analyses of the responses to the questions on reasons for a satisfactory or unsatisfactory results of own lessons were done in the same way as for the findings presented in section 4.1, that is, deriving semantic domains for the teachers' responses in a bottom-up process. Nine semantic domains were found (cf. Fig. 3), which were not congruent to the semantic domains presented in section 4.1. The number of reasons to be classified was lower in Figure 3 than in Figures 1 and 2, because a maximum of three reasons could be given in the questionnaire by the teachers.

For example, two-thirds of the German teachers and less than one-third of the Swiss teachers attributed their own instructional success to aspects of motivation or interest of the students or sometimes also of the teachers. Close to aspects of motivation, there was an additional second, separate domain of "classroom ambiance," which was seen as contributing to the success of mathematics lessons.

Lessons were unsatisfactory for more than 40% of the German teachers when they were not able to reach their learning goals and more than 60% saw their own planning and preparation as responsible for the lack of own instructional success. Sixty percent of the Swiss teachers attributed the unsatisfactory results of lessons to the domain of non-optimal didactical structuring of contents, and half of the Swiss teachers identified disciplinary problems as a hindering factor in the success of their own lessons. However, as the number of participating Swiss teachers was rather low, these findings indicating differences between the two nationality groups should again be interpreted very carefully.

For the role of teachers in their attempt to raise the quality of their instruction, the domains in Figure 3 probably played different roles, as the perceived possibilities of influence for the teachers may vary. For example, the mood of students as an aspect of the classroom ambiance or external conditions (e.g., the timetable) may be seen as hard to influence by teachers, whereas the planning and preparation of a lesson or the didactical structuring of contents could be perceived as rather in the teachers' hands. This is why the teachers were asked additionally to evaluate their influence on the reasons for instructional success they gave. The results of this part of the study on attributions of instructional success are described in the following.

An overall result was that reasons for instructional success were attributed to internal causes for 66% of the reasons provided by German teachers and 84% of the reasons given by the Swiss participants. Unsatisfactory lessons were attributed to internal causes for 71% of the reasons provided by German teachers and 57% of those given by Swiss teachers.

These results may have had to do with the different nature of reasons mentioned by the teachers. There are domains which were almost exclusively attributed to internal influence like "planning/preparation of lesson" and other domains were seen rather dependent on external factors like "external conditions for instruction." The domains "motivation/interest," "reaching learning goals/curricular goals," and "activity and involvement of students" showed varied attributions. Some teachers

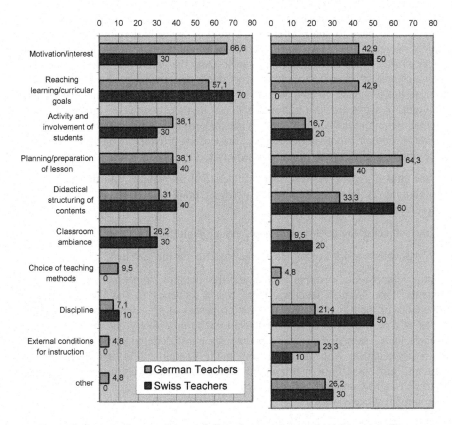

Figure 3. Reasons for satisfactory (left) and unsatisfactory (right) results of lessons (percentages of teachers making comments classified in the semantic domains)

saw possibilities of influence on instructional success. However, for other responses, less personal influence was perceived.

In order to give more evidence about the perceptions of the own influence on instructional success, we would like to discuss some examples of responses. For instance, typical responses of German teachers referring to the domain "motivation/ interest" were the following:

"There was interest and enjoyment of the subject matter of the lesson."

"The students are concentrating, collaborate enthusiastically, and at the culmination [of the lesson], a 'whispering' runs across the class."

"The students were interested, and liking to get to know something."

"Questions by the students showed their interest, i.e. interest was sparked."

An observation here seems to be a subliminal understanding that the role of the students was seen mostly as rather passive, and that the teacher was regarded as the person to have to spark interest and motivation. Additionally, sometimes the subject matter of the lesson itself (perceived as an external factor for teacher and students) was expected to generate interest. Only the activity of asking "questions showing interest" seemed to add a more active component of the student role in these responses. Such understandings of roles might also have influenced whether individual reasons for instructional success in this area were attributed to the internal domain of influence of the teachers or seen as external conditions.

For the domain "motivation/interest," the reasons provided by the Swiss teachers were similar to those of the German teachers, e.g.

"the students show that they have understood the subject and that they are ambitious at learning new things (which manifests itself by continuing questions)"

"the subject or the question [of their lesson] is interesting"

"I was able to spark the interest of the students for the problem."

Another interesting example concerned the domain "didactical structuring of contents." For German teachers, there was a tendency to see the influence on the quality of their own lessons in stable properties of the content, as if the subject matter of a lesson given by the curriculum would completely determine the attractiveness of a lesson and hence its potential for instructional success. Conversely, the Swiss teachers who saw a reason in the domain "didactical structuring of contents" attributed their instructional success to their own influence. Examples of responses of German teachers which referred to this domain as inhibiting own instructional success were

"The subject is not so interesting for students and possibly also for teachers"

"boring subject"

"uninteresting subject matter"

"boring concept [of the lesson], e.g. a pure exercise lesson without 'highlights'"

"instruction oriented too strongly by exterior conditions (e.g. curriculum, test ...)."

Typical responses of the Swiss participants were

"instructional sequencing with too little structuring or logic"

"problem was too difficult"

"subject/complexity/pre-knowledge misjudged"

"the students were overstrained by me as far as the subject matter was concerned"

"the subject matter was inscrutable, too complicated for students."

An interesting detail was that most of the cited German responses showed a link to motivational aspects, even though the idea of the subject matter seemed predominant. Very probably, these teachers saw the content of lessons as rather statically given by units of subject matter as, for instance, defined in the curriculum. In this perspective, even having to give a "pure exercise lesson" might have been perceived as an external task hardly allowing own ideas for attractive structuring. The Swiss teachers emphasized rather the complexity of tasks or contents as well as their structuring.

The domain "classroom ambiance" as a negative influence was seen as dependent on external factors by the Swiss teachers, whereas there was a considerable portion of the German teachers admitting to have been able to do something against this negative influence on instructional quality. "Discipline" as a negative factor on own instructional success was seen as a rather external influence by Swiss teachers; the views of the German teachers concerning this domain were varied. An example of a response referring both to "classroom ambiance" and "discipline" named by a German teacher was the following reason for an unsatisfactory lesson: "no ambiance was emerging, i.e. during the information phase [i.e. introduction of new content], the students were distracted." This response could be seen in line with convictions that one of the teacher's tasks consists of creating an ambiance at the beginning of each lesson which allows one to pursue the teaching script that this teacher judges to be successful.

According to the data in Figure 3, the domain "reaching learning goals/curricular goals" played an important role in attributing instructional success or failure, especially for German teachers. Responses related to this domain can offer additional insight in instruction-related convictions which might be linked to the dominant teaching script in German classrooms:

"All of the learning contents that were planned (after deliberate considerations and with good reasons) could be communicated."

"All learning goals were met (one has forged ahead well)."

"A task given at the beginning [of the lesson] could be solved stepwise by the students by means of the [teacher's] instructional guidance."

Examples of responses concerning unsatisfactory results from lessons linked to the domain "reaching learning goals/curricular goals" were the following:

"No self-contained lesson, in the middle of important thoughts the bell rings."

"A completely different progression of the lesson than planned (e.g. problems where I had not suspected any)."

"Some students don't understand certain coherences, although they have been explained a hundred times and the rest of the class moan already and laugh."

In these responses, convictions about what the participating German teachers judged to be characteristics of instructional quality in their own mathematics lessons seem to be reflected. Meeting learning goals in the sense of "forging ahead," solving problems stepwise in a teacher-guided classroom interaction, and explanation as an important part of a teacher-centered classroom interaction were some aspects of instruction-related convictions that can be seen well in-line with the dominant teaching script in Germany (cf. Baumert et al. 1997).

DISCUSSION

Individual Criteria for Instructional Quality

In the first place, it is interesting to compare the results concerning the individual criteria for instructional quality to the basic dimensions of instructional quality identified in the study of Clausen, Reusser and Klieme (2003) and described in the theoretical background section. Given the small sample of Swiss teachers, we focus on the responses of the 42 German teachers for these considerations. Looking at the non-situation-specific data in Figure 1, some results appear to be in line with the basic dimensions of Clausen, Reusser, and Klieme (2003): For example, the existence of the component "discipline" in the semantic domain of "instructional efficiency" or the semantic domain of "focus on students" indicate that links can be seen with the basic dimensions—which also cover these aspects. However, the semantic domains of "reaching curricular goals," "language/expression of the teacher," or "use of preferred teaching methods" cannot be classified among the characteristics of the basic dimensions of instructional quality. Moreover, the domain "aspects of motivation" encompasses a much wider semantic area than the sub-characteristic "teacher's ability to motivate the students" of the basic dimension "cognitive activation." Generally speaking, for the teachers, rather global criteria on an intuitive level of perception seem to play an important role.

Conversely, some characteristics of the basic dimensions of instructional quality by Clausen, Reusser, and Klieme (2003) appear very rarely or even not at all in the responses of the teachers. Among these, there are characteristics that are considered meaningful in research, as for example, "time on task," "pacing," "learning from mistakes," or "argumentational exchange in classroom interaction." Criteria in the domain "choice and handling of activating tasks" were provided only by a relatively small number of teachers. This may be seen as an astonishing result, because the role of activating tasks was at the center of recent reform movements in Germany about which the teachers could have been informed.remarked. A possible conclusion from these results can be seen in the possibility to focus on these criteria in in-service teacher trainings, in order to draw the attention of teachers to such characteristics of their instruction, which, seen from the perspective of empirical research, can be very relevant for fostering mathematical competencies of the students.

A second domain of the discussion of the results refers to potential inter-cultural differences. Given the low number of Swiss teachers in the sample, the interpretation of the results must be handled with extreme care. Considering the descriptive results in Figure 1, the Swiss teachers showed more emphasis on content-related semantic domains like structuring and adapting contents, links between contents, and repeating and training, whereas the German teachers focused, on average, more on criteria in the areas of discipline, modes of presentation, aspects of motivation, use of preferred teaching methods, or focus on students. These possible differences can be seen as consistent with results of Clausen, Reusser, and Klieme (2003). If, for example, the struggle for discipline is a current feature in German classrooms, as stated by Clausen, Reusser, and Klieme, it is plausible that discipline and an ordered presentation, as well as a good classroom ambiance (as part of "aspects of motivation"), are considered to be important criteria for instructional quality by the German teachers. In Switzerland, where a higher valuing of classroom management was observed and discipline concerns might have played a minor inhibiting role for instruction, teachers might have more opportunity to focus on mathematical content as a characteristic for "good" mathematics instruction.

Moreover, the results appear to be plausible compared to the results of the representative study of Lipowsky et al. (2003). In that study, Swiss teachers showed higher values of a direct-transmission view on teaching and learning than did German teachers. The results, that there are lower values for "focus on students" or "use of preferred teaching methods" (which were mostly student-centered) for the Swiss teachers, and their stronger focus on the content area, may be seen as consistent with the findings of Lipowsky et al., even though there is an inverse observation concerning the domain of "presentation."

As a third aspect, the comparison of Figure 1 and 2 can give evidence for how stable individual criteria of instructional quality might be. As the semantic domains were reproduced with the exception of "communication/interaction," the results indicate, on the one hand, a certain stability of the perceived criteria. On the other hand, we can observe shifts of attention between the responses on criteria of the global unit and the unit in the second questionnaire related to the judgements on the videotaped instructional situations. A part of these shifts of attention can be explained by the fact that, confronted with a videotaped instructional situation, some aspects are hardly observable or judgeable. For example, whether the curricular goals of the teacher are met or whether there is enough subsequent repeating/ training of the contents introduced in the videotaped classroom situations. Another aspect is that the attention of the teachers might concentrate on criteria which *made a difference between* the two classroom situations presented, as they were asked to *judge* the instructional quality according to the criteria they chose. Under this perspective, the results are plausible again, because "activation of students" and "communication/interaction" indeed belonged to the characteristics that allowed making a difference between the two videotaped situations from the point of view of our research on the videotaped classroom situations (see Kuntze, 2008, for examples of transcripts of the classroom situations; cf. also Kuntze & Reiss, 2004). Summing up, individual criteria for the quality of mathematics instruction appear to be relatively stable from a macroscopic point of view, but the attention of the teachers seems to vary according to the situation, in which they apply this component of professional knowledge. According to the results displayed in Figures 1 and 2, this is likely to have been the case for teachers of both nationalities.

Attributions Linked to Experiences of Successful or Unsuccessful Lessons

The results concerning attributions of reasons for a "good" or an unsatisfactory result of lessons can be seen as an additional control for the results presented in section 4.1. As we can observe by a comparison of the results, the reasons provided by the teachers often concern aspects which are also covered by the criteria of instructional quality in Figures 1 and 2. Additional aspects like "planning/ preparation of lessons" can be explained by the particular format of the question. Again, tendencies of possible differences between the Swiss and German teachers can be seen as plausible with the results of Clausen, Reusser, and Klieme (2003) and Lipowsky et al. (2003). For example, the Swiss teachers seem to see their influence somewhat stronger in the didactical structuring of contents and attribute reasons for unsuccessful lessons more often externally. The German teachers more often perceive reasons beyond their influence as factors favoring their instructional success, and give rather intuitive criteria—like motivation and interest. Frequently, an unsatisfactory lesson seems to be attributed to internal factors.

CONCLUSIONS

In this study, we reported findings on teachers' perceptions of "good" mathematics instruction on three levels of observation. The rather general question on observable criteria of instructional quality probably gives insight on the level of non-situated preferences and instruction-related beliefs. The comparison with the answers in the situated format (judging on videotaped classroom situations) shows stability, but also shifts of awareness linked to the classroom situations shown. The third level of observation on attributions the teachers made concerning their own experiences of "good" or unsuccessful lessons may give an insight into the teachers' own evolution, as the subjective evaluation of own experiences is likely to influence their subsequent instruction-related decision-making. On all three levels of observation, some central characteristics of "good" mathematics lessons could be observed in the teachers' responses, which were most frequently related to the domain of motivation, interest, and classroom ambiance – often showing little specificity and a rather intuitive character. Moreover, some basic characteristics of instructional quality emerged in the different analyses, as, for instance, presentation, structuring of content, activation of students, and reaching curricular goals. For the most part, the criteria do not seem inconsistent with the teacher-centered, small-step classroom interaction dominant in Germany, as it was observed by Baumert et al. (1997). Unfortunately, criteria corresponding to an improved classroom culture, such as the awareness for a productive learning from mistakes or for the quality of tasks, were rare or even absent.

The question in the title "what is 'good' mathematics instruction" is not answered in a simple way by the mathematics teachers. One of the outcomes of this study can be seen in the finding, that multiple and differing criteria are used by the teachers to judge effective teaching. If conflicting goals for meeting requirements of "good" mathematics instruction are seen as the reason for this observation, the existence of such conflicts may represent a real difficulty for mathematics teachers when making instruction-related decisions. Under this perspective, developing priorities for such conflicting criteria together with mathematics teachers could be a way of supporting the quality of their instruction.

On all three levels of observation, some tendencies of differences between the German and Swiss teachers may be seen, which seem in line with findings in existing studies on other domains of professional knowledge or classroom practice. For the German teachers, the results show an outline of their instruction-related beliefs on instructional quality, suggesting that often, rather intuitive criteria are used for describing the quality of instructional practice. Since criteria for instructional quality are a base of reference for improving classroom practice, this may be interpreted as a need for further development of professional expertise in this domain, e.g. by in-service teacher trainings.

NOTES

[1]   This study has been supported by the Robert Bosch Stiftung (Bew.-Nr. 32.5.8050.0037.0).

REFERENCES

An, S., Kulm, G., Wu, Z., & Wang, L. (2006). The impact of cultural differences on middle school mathematics teachers' beliefs in the U.S. and China. In F. Leung, K.-D. Graf, & F. Lopez-Real (Eds.), *Mathematics education in different cultural traditions* (pp. 449–464). New York: Springer.

Bandura, A. (1977). Self-efficacy: Toward a unifying theory of behavioural change. *Psychological Review, 84,* 191–215.

Baumert, J., Lehmann, R., et al. (1997). *TIMSS - Mathematisch-naturwissenschaftlicher Unterricht im internationalen Vergleich.* Opladen: Leske + Budrich.

Bromme, R. (1992). *Der Lehrer als Experte. Zur Psychologie des professionellen Wissens* [The teacher as an expert. On the psychology of professional knowledge]. Bern: Hans Huber.

Bromme, R. (1997). Kompetenzen, Funktionen und unterrichtliches Handeln des Lehrers [Competencies, functions and instructional actions of teachers]. In F. Weinert (Ed.), *Enzyklopädie der Psychologie: Psychologie des Unterrichts und der Schule* (pp. 177–212). Göttingen: Hogrefe.

Cai, J. (2006). U.S. and Chinese teachers' cultural values of representations in mathematics education. In F. Leung, K.-D. Graf, & F. Lopez-Real (Eds.), *Mathematics education in different cultural traditions* (pp. 465–481). New York: Springer.

Clausen, M. (2002). *Unterrichtsqualität: Eine Frage der Perspektive?* [Instructional quality: A question of perspective?]. Münster: Waxmann.

Clausen, M., Reusser, K., & Klieme, E. (2003). Unterrichtsqualität auf der Basis hoch-inferenter Unterrichtsbeurteilungen: Ein Vergleich zwischen Deutschland und der deutschsprachigen Schweiz. [Using high-inference ratings to assess quality of instruction: A comparison between Germany and the German-speaking part of Switzerland]. *Unterrichtswissenschaft, 31*(2), 122–141.

Deutsches PISA-Konsortium. (Ed.). (2001). *PISA 2000.* Opladen: Leske + Budrich.

Deutsches PISA-Konsortium. (Ed.). (2004). *PISA 2003.* Münster: Waxmann.

Dweck, C. (1986). Motivational processes affecting learning. *American Psychologist, 41,* 1040–1048.

Escudero, I., & Sanchez, V. (1999). The relationship between professional knowledge and teaching practice: The case of similarity. In O. Zaslavsky (Ed.), *Proceedings of the 23th conference of the international group for the psychology of mathematics education* (Vol. 2, pp. 305–312). Haifa: PME.

Fend, H. (1998). *Qualität im Bildungswesen.* Weinheim: Juventa.

Fennema, E., Carpenter, T., & Peterson, P. (1989). Learning mathematics with understanding: Cognitively guided instruction. In J. Brophy (Ed.), *Advances in research on teaching* (Vol. 1, pp. 195–221). Greenwich, CT: JAI Press.

Gruehn, S. (2000). *Unterricht und schulisches Lernen: Schüler als Quellen der Unterrichtsbeschreibung* [Instruction and learning at school: Students as sources for the description of instruction]. Münster: Waxmann.

Hiebert, J., Stigler, J., & Manaster, A. (1999). Mathematical features of lessons in the TIMSS video study. *Zentralblatt für Didaktik der Mathematik, 31*(6), 196–201.

Kaiser, G., Hino, K., & Knipping, C. (2006). Proposal for a framework to analyse mathematics education in eastern and western traditions. In F. Leung, K.-D. Graf, & F. Lopez-Real (Eds.), *Mathematics education in different cultural traditions* (pp. 319–351). New York: Springer.

Kuntze, S. (2008). Zusammenhänge zwischen allgemeinen und situiert erhobenen unterrichtsbezogenen Kognitionen und Überzeugungen von Mathematiklehrerinnen und -lehrern. *Unterrichtswissenschaft, 36*(2), 167–192.

Kuntze, S., & Reiss, K. (2004). Unterschiede zwischen Klassen hinsichtlich inhaltlicher Elemente und Anforderungsniveaus im Unterrichtsgespräch beim Erarbeiten von Beweisen - Ergebnisse einer Videoanalyse. *Unterrichtswissenschaft, 32*(4), 357–379.

Kuntze, S., & Reiss, K. (2005). Situation-specific and generalized components of professional knowledge of mathematics teachers – Research on a video-based in-service teacher learning program. In H. L. Chick & J. L. Vincent (Eds.), *Proceedings of the 29th conference of the international group for the psychology of mathematics education (PME)* (Vol. 3, pp. 225–232). Melbourne: University.

Leinhardt, G., & Greeno, J. (1986). The cognitive skill of teaching. *Journal of Educational Psychology, 78,* 75–95.

Leung, F., Graf, K.-D., & Lopez-Real, F. (Eds.). *Mathematics education in different cultural traditions* [The 13th ICMI Study]. New York: Springer.

Lipowsky, F., Thußbas, C., Klieme, E., Reusser, K., & Pauli, C. (2003). Professionelles Lehrerwissen, selbstbezogene Kognitionen und wahrgenommene Schulumwelt - Ergebnisse einer kulturvergleichenden Studie deutscher und Schweizer Mathematiklehrkräfte [Professional teacher knowledge, self-related cognitions and perceived school environment - Results of a cross-culture study of German and Swiss mathematics teachers]. *Unterrichtswissenschaft, 31*(3), 206–237.

Malara, N. (2003). Dialectics between theory and practice: Theoretical issues and aspects of practice from an early algebra project. In N. Pateman et al. (Eds.), *Proceedings of the 27th conference of the international group for the psychology of mathematics education* (pp. 33–48). Honolulu: PME.

Neubrand, J. (2006). The TIMSS 1995 and 1999 video studies. In F. Leung, K.-D. Graf, & F. Lopez-Real (Eds.), *Mathematics education in different cultural traditions* [The 13th ICMI Study] (pp. 291–318). New York: Springer.

Perry, B., Wong, N.-Y., & Howard, P. (2006). Comparing primary and secondary mathematics teachers' beliefs about mathematics, mathematics learning and mathematics teaching in Hong Kong and Australia. In F. Leung, K.-D. Graf, & F. Lopez-Real (Eds.), *Mathematics education in different cultural traditions* (pp. 435–464). New York: Springer.

Rakoczy, K., Buff, A., & Lipowsky, F. (2005). Befragungsinstrumente. In E. Klieme, C. Pauli, & K. Reusser (Eds.), *Dokumentation der Erhebungs- und Auswertungsinstrumente zur schweizerisch-deutschen Videostudie "Unterrichtsqualität, Lernverhalten und mathematisches Verständnis"* (Vol. 1). Frankfurt a. M.: DIPF.

Schoenfeld, A. (1983). Beyond the purely cognitive: Belief systems, social cognitions, and metacognitions as driving forces in intellectual performance. *Cognitive Science, 7,* 329–363.

Shulman, L. (1986a). Paradigms and research programs in the study of teaching: A contemporary perspective. In M. Wittrock (Ed.), *Handbook of research on teaching* (pp. 3–36). New York: Macmillan.

Shulman, L. (1986b). Those who understand: Knowledge growth in teaching. *Educational Researcher*, *15*(2), 4–14.

Shulman, L. (1987). Knowledge and teaching: Foundations of the new reform. *Harvard Educational Review*, *57*(1), 1–22.

Staub, F., & Stern, E. (2002). The nature of teacher's pedagogical content beliefs matters for students' achievement gains. *Journal of Educational Psychology*, *94*(2), 344–355.

Stebler, R., & Reusser, K. (2000). Progressive, classical, or balanced – A look at mathematical learning environments in Swiss-German lower-secondary schools. *Zentralblatt für Didaktik der Mathematik (ZDM)*, *32*(1), 1–10.

Stigler, J., & Hiebert, J. (1999). *The teaching gap: Best ideas from the world's teachers for improving education in the classroom.* New York: The Free Press.

Stigler, J., Gonzales, P., Kawanaka, T., Knoll, S., & Serrano, A. (1999). *The TIMSS videotape classroom study: Methods and findings from an exploratory research project on eighth grade mathematics instruction in Germany, Japan, and the United States.* Washington, DC: National Center of Educational Statistics. Retrieved from www.ed.gov/nces

Stipek, D., Givvin, K., Salmon, J., & MacGyvers, V. (2001). Teachers' beliefs and practices related to mathematics instruction. *Teaching and Teacher Education*, *17*, 213–226.

Straub, J., Kempf, W., & Werbik, H. (Eds.). (1997). *Psychologie. Eine Einführung Grundlagen, Methoden, Forschungsfelder.* München: Deutscher Taschenbuch Verlag.

Sullivan, P., & Mousley, J. (2001). Thinking teaching: Seeing mathematics teachers as active decision makers. In F.-L. Lin & T. J. Cooney (Eds.), *Making sense of mathematics teacher education* (pp. 33–52). Dordrecht: Kluwer.

Wahl, D. (1991). *Handeln unter Druck* [Acting under pressure]. Weinheim: Deutscher Studienverlag.

Wholhuter, K. A. (1997). The geometry classroom: The influence of teachers' beliefs. *Proceedings of PME-NA 19*, *2*, 459–463.

Sebastian Kuntze
University of Education Ludwigsburg

Franziska Rudolph-Albert
University of Munich

APPENDIX

FIRST QUESTIONNAIRE: QUESTION ON CRITERIA OF INSTRUCTIONAL QUALITY

How would you judge on the quality of mathematics instruction?
Imagine that a mathematics teacher colleague asks you to attend and watch one of her/his lessons and to judge on the quality of instruction.
Independently from the feedback you give to your colleague, you have to make an honest judgement on the instructional quality of the observed mathematics lesson for yourself.
In order to judge on the quality of mathematics instruction, you probably have a couple of criteria. Please note in the space below such criteria which are important to you and which you can observe in the lesson. […] For the criteria you note, please indicate how important they are for you respectively.
Please limit the time you spend for this page of the questionnaire to about 10 minutes at most.

Criteria for the quality of mathematics instruction *(for additional remarks you may use the space on the following page)*	*Importance*
	☐ very important ☐ important ☐ less important

The questionnaire provided five more boxes like the one given above in the form of lines of a table.

SECOND QUESTIONNAIRE: JUDGEMENTS ON CLASSROOM SITUATIONS ACCORDING TO INDIVIDUAL CRITERIA OF INSTRUCTIONAL QUALITY

In order to judge on the quality of the mathematics instruction observed in the videos, you probably have a couple of criteria which are important to you. Please list criteria that are the most important for you and mark on the right hand side how well this criteria was fulfilled/how successful it was met in the videotaped instructional situation.

(example: well ful-filled, suc-cessfully met   ✕————————✕   not fulfilled, deficits) for this criterion

Please indicate for the criteria you noted how important they are for you.

Criteria for the quality of mathematics instruction *(for additional remarks you may use the space on the following page)*	*Importance*	*...in video A:*
Criterion:	criterion ☐ very important ☐ important ☐ less important	well fulfilled, success-fully met ●————————● not fulfilled, deficits for this criterion

The questionnaire provided five more lines like the one above and one more row for evaluating the second videotaped classroom situation in video B. Moreover, space for additional remarks was offered.

SEMANTIC DOMAINS AND EXAMPLES OF PRIMARY CODES

Criteria for instructional quality (first questionnaire): Semantic domains:

Aspects of motivation – examples of codes:
- Good classroom ambiance/good ambiance for learning
- Praise
- (Sparking) motivation/interest
- Appreciation of individual students/emotional link to students
- Sparking curiosity/interest
- Humor
- Emphasis on the interesting

Presentation (quality of presentation) – examples of codes:
- Good, well-structured blackboard and transparencies
- Good use of media (choice and way of presentation)
- Presentation/instruction without the aid of notes
- Change of media

Use of preferred teaching methods – examples of codes:
- Integrate phases of student-centered work
- Use of adequate working forms according to content
- Students solve problems in small groups
- Student-centered work and reflection
- Discussion of students on problems

Focus on students – examples of codes:
- Taking students, their questions, and their problems seriously
- Following the ideas and suggestions of students
- Activation of less active and lower-achieving students
- Encouragement of the students to ask questions
- When the students cannot follow anymore, the teacher remarks it
- Patience with students responding hesitantly
- Opportunities to ask the teacher
- Help provided when students ask questions

Discipline – examples of codes:
- Discipline
- Discipline in communication/discussion

Structuring/adapting contents – examples of codes:
- Logical and plausible structure
- Clear structure of lesson/lesson structured
- Chain of thought and emphasis transparent in lesson
- Content goals given clearly
- Justification of the lesson's content
- Difference between important and unimportant contents clearly laid out
- Explanations understandable
- Easy contents first, then more complex problems
- Basic knowledge provided
- Mathematical competence of the teacher

Activation of students – examples of codes:
- Many students take part in the instructional conversation
- Degree of activation of students
- Concentration and activity of students

Use of language by the teacher – examples of codes:
- Use of a language close to the student's language
- Precise use of language/emphasis on correct mathematical language
- Well-weighted use of mathematical language
- Good choice of linguistic "images" (metaphors)

Links between contents – examples of codes:
- Providing links to other contents
- Relationships to applications visible
- Embedding of contents in a larger context
- Showing relationships to everyday contexts
- Significance against the background of the history of science
- Fostering insight into the value of mathematical thinking
- Link to practice

Choice and handling of activating tasks – examples of codes:
- Well-chosen tasks/examples/rich tasks
- Discussion on tasks/ search for alternative ways of solving tasks
- Complexity of the chosen tasks
- Additional tasks for higher-achieving students
- Homework
- Different levels of complexity of tasks

Reaching curricular goals – examples of codes:
- Reaching a curricular goal/the goals of the curriculum
- Work for reaching exam results

Repeating/training – examples of codes:
- Repetition of contents
- Learning contents with practicing/training
- Training phases

Communication/interaction – examples of codes:
- Fostering precise, reciprocal explanation
- Exchange/communication between all students/teacher in the classroom

PATRICIA S. WILSON AND KANITA K. DUCLOUX

GOOD MATHEMATICS TEACHING AND THE ROLE OF STUDENTS' MATHEMATICAL THINKING

High School Teachers' Perspectives

INTRODUCTION

The notion of good mathematics teaching is an elusive concept that, nevertheless, has permeated the literature for decades. Often the construct is ill-defined and subject to interpretation. Constructs such as student-centered instruction, students' mathematical thinking, and constructed knowledge are used by researchers, teacher educators and often by teachers, but it is not clear that they agree upon the meaning. Although there is a considerable body of research emerging on the notion of becoming a good teacher (e.g., see Mathematics Teachers in Transition edited by Fennema & Nelson, 1997), what is often missing in that literature is what teachers think constitutes good teaching, and what teachers think about the role of students' mathematical thinking in good teaching. Our purpose is to add research reporting teachers' perspectives.

In this chapter we present data and interpretations from two studies on teachers' views about good teaching. The original study, in 2000, was based on interviews with practicing teachers about good teaching and was reported in the Journal of Mathematics Teacher Education (JMTE). In that article, Wilson, Cooney, and Stinson (2005) presented various scholars' views about good teaching and the views of nine experienced and professionally active teachers. The authors identified significant overlap in scholars' views and teachers' views, but they also recognized differences. In particular, they noted that teachers advocated characteristics of teacher-centered instruction in contrast to researchers' call for student-centered instruction. In particular, teachers did not describe good teaching in terms of students' thinking, or discuss the role that students' thinking played in their planning and instruction. However researchers argued for a constructivist orientation to learning and emphasized the role of students' thinking as a basis for designing instruction. A second study, conducted five years later within the same teacher education program, investigated teachers' perspectives about the role that high school students' thinking played in planning and implementing mathematical instruction.

We begin this chapter with an abridged version of the article from the Journal of Mathematics Teacher Education (Wilson, Cooney, and Stinson, 2005) followed by a report on the second study investigating teachers' perceptions about the role of

J. Cai, G. Kaiser, B. Perry and N.-Y. Wong (eds.), Effective Mathematics Teaching from Teachers' Perspectives: National and Cross-National Studies, 93–121.
© *2009 Sense Publishers. All rights reserved.*

students' mathematical thinking in good teaching. We conclude with a discussion of possible implications for mathematics teacher education. We urge readers to read the complete JMTE article for a more detailed analysis of relevant literature and teachers' perceptions about good teaching. The JMTE article contains an additional analysis of teachers' descriptions of how they learned to teach mathematics well.

PERSPECTIVES ON GOOD TEACHING

Educational scholars often emphasize the broader, more process-oriented goals of education when they address issues about teaching. For example, Dewey (1916) defined education as "the reconstruction or reorganization of experiences which add to the meaning of experience, and which increases ability to direct the course of subsequent experiences" (p. 76). Dewey is adamant that education is not just about the learning of the three traditional basic subjects of reading, writing, and arithmetic, but should be conceived from a much broader perspective, one in which citizens become literate and capable of directing their own lives through informed and reasoned choices. Such a broad perspective strongly suggests that Dewey would define good teaching as that which enables students to realize these broader educational goals.

Polya (1965) argued that the primary aim of mathematics teaching is to teach people to think. He wrote, "'Teaching to think' means that the mathematics teacher should not merely impart information, but should try also to develop the ability of the students to use the information imparted" (p. 100). Polya listed ten commandments for teachers, including: be interested in the subject; know your subject; know about ways of learning; give students "know how", attitudes of mind, and habit of methodical work; and suggest it – do not force it down their throats (p. 116). Polya's commandments emphasize a process-oriented teaching style consistent with Dewey's notion of education.

Davis and Hersh (1981) emphasized acertain pluralism in the teaching of mathematics in which students see mathematics as more than a formalistic science. They spoke explicitly against authoritarian presentations. To them, the ideal teacher is one who invites students to "Come, let us reason together" rather than one who uses "proof by coercion" (p. 282). It seems clear that through the decades, scholars envisioned teaching as an activity that promotes thinking and problem solving rather than the accumulation of information. This perspective is consistent with standards developed by the National Council of Teachers of Mathematics (NCTM). In the original set of Standards, it is stated, "Finally, our vision sees teachers encouraging students, probing for ideas, and carefully judging the maturity of a student's thoughts and expressions" (NCTM, 1989, p. 10). In the more recent set of standards (NCTM, 2000) the Teaching Principle is stated as follows: "Effective mathematics teaching requires understanding what students know and need to learn and then challenging and supporting them to learn it well" (p. 16). The Teaching Principle has a decidedly constructivist orientation in that effective teaching is defined in terms of the teacher basing instruction on students' thinking. A condition for effective teaching is that "teachers must know and understand deeply the mathematics they are teaching and be able to draw on that knowledge with flexibility in their teaching tasks" (NCTM, 2000, p. 17).

The various statements about teaching in the NCTM documents[1] clearly embrace the importance of teachers emphasizing the processes of doing mathematics and of connecting with students' understanding of mathematics. From this perspective, we can see considerable convergence between the NCTM's definition of effective or good teaching and those "definitions" emanating from scholars such as Dewey, Polya, and Davis and Hersh who consistently emphasized teaching as a process that promotes analysis, thinking, and problem solving. It is largely this convergence that defines the authors' notion of good teaching and that provides the foundation for developing teacher education programs.

Good Teaching as Reflected in Research

Although research seldom addresses the issue of good teaching directly, the notion of effective teaching is implicit, particularly when the dominant research methodology is deterministic. Because the notion of what characteristics best capture or exemplify good teaching seems to vary according to the philosophical underpinnings of the research, we divide this section into two subsections that distinguish findings between deterministic studies and interpretivist studies.

Deterministic Studies

Most of the deterministic studies in education and in mathematics education in the United States occurred during the 1960s and 1970s under the guise of either process-product or experimental studies. Rosenshine and Furst's (1971) review of educational research revealed 11 variables from process-product studies that were associated with effective teaching: clarity, variability, enthusiasm, task-oriented or business like behaviors, opportunity to learn, the use of student ideas and general indirectness, criticism, the use of structuring comments, types of questions, probing, and the level of difficulty of instruction.

Good, Grouws, and Ebmeier's (1983) extensive study of mathematics teaching led to the development of a model that they felt represented effective mathematics teaching. Their model was based on time allocation for a single class period: review and practice on mental computation (8 minutes), developmental portion of the lesson (20 minutes), seatwork (15 minutes), and assignment of homework (2 minutes). The model was offered as a heuristic for teachers to guide their teaching.

McKinney's (1986) review of research on expert-novice teachers examined behaviors of these two kinds of teachers. In general, expert teachers were more efficient in organizing and conducting lessons, had a better knowledge of the content than did novice teachers, had clearer lessons, and were more adept at explaining why, how, and when mathematical concepts are used. McKinney quantified differences between expert and novice teachers. Similarly, Leinhardt (1988) studied expert and novice teachers and found that expert teachers could weave what the author called segments and routines of lessons together in a more coherent and flexible way than could novices, and could draw upon richer representations of concepts than could novice teachers. Again, the focus of the research was on highly quantifiable aspects of teaching as a means of characterizing effective mathematics teaching.

Research based on deterministic methodologies was often criticized in terms of the kind of limited mathematics that defined student achievement and thus teacher effectiveness. Further, it was generally the case that the research was grounded in a more teacher-centered orientation to teaching and thus focused on ways of making direct instruction more effective. Effective teaching was defined primarily in terms of what teachers could do as an activity in itself rather than as an activity based on students' thinking. In this sense, there is a certain disparity between what this kind of research defined as effective or good teaching and how the NCTM documents defined good teaching.

Interpretative Studies

As one might expect, interpretative studies, especially those involving case studies, emphasize teachers' beliefs and actions in classrooms. Here, good teaching must be inferred from what the researcher is studying because it is usually not focused on specific behaviors. We will examine several studies that fit this type of methodology as we consider how these researchers defined, implicitly, the notion of good teaching.

Wilson and Goldenberg's (1998) study of Mr. Burt, a middle school mathematics teacher who was interested in reforming his teaching, represents a case in point. The researchers worked with Mr. Burt in an effort to help him reform his teaching and make it more conceptually oriented and aligned with students' thinking. They concluded that, "Mr. Burt's approach generally portrayed mathematics as a rigid subject to be mastered and correctly applied, rather than as a way of thinking or as a subject to be explored" (p. 287). Although Wilson and Goldenberg did not address the notion of good teaching directly, it seems reasonable to assume from their comments that, to them, good teaching involves a student-centered instructional style in which mathematics is treated conceptually. Even though Mr. Burt's teaching became more conceptually oriented, his primary mode of instruction remained teacher-centered thus suggesting that Mr. Burt's notion of good teaching differed from that of Wilson and Goldenberg.

The notion of good teaching as that in which teachers reflect on their own understanding as well as on their students' understanding is illustrated in the work of Schifter (1998) who concluded that "teachers must come not only to expect, but to seek, situations in their own teaching in which they can view the mathematics in new ways, especially through the perspectives that their students bring to the work" (p. 84). Schifter's approach provided a context in which teachers could experience mathematics, not as a formalized subject, but as a subject that resulted from human invention. In some sense, Schifter was defining, implicitly, good mathematics teaching as that kind of teaching in which teachers reflect on what students know and consequently see mathematics in terms of the students' constructions of mathematical ideas. From this perspective, Schifter's study is consistent with the implicit notion of good teaching that permeates what the previously cited scholars said about teaching.

METHODOLOGY IN THE ORIGINAL STUDY

Participants in Original Study

Nine secondary mathematics teachers who participated in a three-year federally funded project (1997–2000) at the University of Georgia entitled PRIME: Partnerships and Reform in Mathematics Education served as informants for this study. The purpose of PRIME was to provide the best possible field-experiences for student teachers and their mentors by enhancing professional relationships between university teachers (UT), mentor teachers (MT), and student teachers (ST); by providing mentor teachers with opportunities to dialogue with one another and university faculty and staff; and by supplying a knowledge base to encourage an open discussion regarding reform mathematics and a consistent experience for pre-service teachers between campus and field.

Procedure in Original Study

Each teacher participated in three audio-recorded interviews. The two overarching questions that governed the study and the interviews were:
    What constitutes good mathematics teaching? How do the skills necessary for good mathematics teaching develop?
    The first two interviews were semi-structured and consisted of seven questions framed by a discussion of what constitutes successful mathematics lessons and how a teacher develops the skills necessary for teaching such lessons. Because research (e.g., Raymond, 1997; Skott, 2001) has illustrated the possibility of inconsistency between teachers' beliefs and actual classroom practices, the questions were intended to motivate discussions about what the teachers considered to be the practices of good mathematics teaching, rather than discussions about their beliefs about good mathematics teaching and its development per se, allowing for the fact that beliefs and practice are intertwined. Therefore, the questions What do you believe constitutes good mathematics teaching? and How did you develop the skills of good mathematics teaching? were never asked of the participants. The questions from the first interview focused on the teachers' practices in a good mathematics lesson (e.g., Describe what you consider to be one of your most successful lessons. Why was it such a good lesson? Where would you expect a student teacher to develop the knowledge and skills necessary to teach the lesson as well as you taught it?). The second interview centered on the teachers' views of their student teachers' planning and implementing of a good mathematics lesson (e.g., What was the best lesson that you have observed by your student teacher? Why was it such a good lesson? What likely contributed to the student teacher's knowledge and skills that led to such a good lesson?). The questions were based on

Schön's (1983) theory about how practitioners reflect in and on their own practice. Before the third interview, participants were provided transcripts of the first two interviews and were asked to highlight those points that they deemed important. This third interview focused on what the teachers highlighted and asked them to elaborate on those points. The third interview was also transcribed.

In addition to the collection of interview data, the researchers met with a group of seven PRIME teachers to discuss the data analysis and initial findings of the study, and to receive input from these teachers as to what they thought constituted good mathematics teaching; only one of the teachers in this summer work session was a participant in the study. Both the summer work session and the third interview offered face validity to the research study, as "analytical categories and emerging conclusions were continually recycled back through the respondents" (Lather, 1986, p. 74), the respondents being PRIME teachers.

TEACHERS' PERSPECTIVES ON GOOD TEACHING

As teachers discussed their best lesson in the first interview, the attributes of their student teachers in the second interview, and summary points in the third "review" interview, they painted a picture of what good teaching meant to them. Although the brush strokes varied from teacher to teacher, the composition of the individual paintings was the same. All nine teachers emphasized the importance of pre-requisite teacher knowledge, promoting mathematical understanding, engaging students, and effectively managing the classroom environment.

In the following sections, we examine the nature of these four characteristics of good teaching. Using quotes and summaries from interview transcripts, we have tried to capture the wisdom of the group and at the same time delineate the similarities and the differences in teachers' perspectives.

Good Teaching Requires Prerequisite Knowledge

Our interviewees reported that mathematics teachers needed to have an extensive knowledge of both mathematics and their students in order to teach well. They needed knowledge of mathematics in order to teach for understanding, sequence lessons, make transitions between topics, understand student questions, provide good examples, and maintain the necessary confidence in front of a class of students. Seven of the nine teachers explained how mathematical knowledge supported good teaching. Yvonne (1)[2] focused on the importance of a comprehensive knowledge of mathematics:

> I think that a lot of mathematics comes from knowing the upper level math. I can tell my class and I can exude a love of mathematics, even when I am talking about the reflexive property, because I know how it fits into the bigger whole.

Some teachers alluded to not only knowing more mathematics, but also knowing it in a way that supported the teaching strategies that they wanted to use. Anna (1) thought it was important to know enough mathematics to make connections between mathematical ideas and create useful transitions between topics. The mathematical knowledge that the teachers valued consisted of more than being able to work all the assigned problems. They were calling for knowledge of the structure of mathematics. They reasoned that mathematical knowledge provided confidence and a freedom to move away from a textbook and a rigid curriculum.

Teachers also emphasized the need to know their students. They tended to emphasize personal knowledge of the student or knowledge of the students' skill levels in contrast to knowing how a student was learning or constructing mathematical ideas. Nick (1) warned, "... a student teacher just needs to keep in mind that these are ninth grade students taking it [Algebra I] for the first time and stop and think what they know, don't take it for granted." At another point in the interview, he explained that one of the most important assets of a student teacher is the ability to "maintain a professional relationship with your kids and at the same time understand the difficulties and the problems they are having as a ninth grader." Melanie (3) and Holly (2) emphasized the importance of prerequisite knowledge explicitly advising student teachers to pay attention to what topics appeared earlier in the textbook to help them understand what students knew.

Good Teaching Promotes Mathematical Understanding

Teachers frequently explained that their goal was to teach so that their students understood the mathematics. They wanted their students to be able to use their mathematics outside of the classroom as well as in the study of other mathematics. As teachers described good lessons, we inferred different types of mathematical understanding that we coded as procedural, conceptual, or related to the nature of mathematics. Two teachers explained that they wanted their students to understand the versatility of mathematics. Only a few comments referred to the importance of procedural learning: Nick (2) praised a student teacher for going "step-by-step, so the kids had a system they could use to get the correct answer"; and Melanie (2) was pleased that the student teacher was "making it more concise for the students so that they can understand it better." Although some of the teachers' statements were ambiguous and could have been interpreted as wanting students to understand either a procedure or a concept, more than half of the coded statements related to understanding referred explicitly to conceptual understanding. Upon a reflection of her learning experiences, one of the mentors provided a description that gave us a working definition of teaching for conceptual understanding:

> I really didn't start enjoying math until I really started understanding it, because just to memorize things and do things because the teachers tells you, to me is, you know, that's not good enough.... I am very big on kids exploring a topic or thinking about it before I just start throwing definitions at them. (Elizabeth, 1)

All nine teachers were interested in student understanding that moved beyond the instrumental understanding involved with using a formula or explaining a mathematical procedure. The teaching strategies that they recommended, their described uses of technology, and the reported mathematical activities were accompanied by claims that these practices would help students understand mathematics.

As teachers talked about teaching for understanding, a few pedagogical strategies were repeated and emphasized. In referring to their own teaching or discussing strategies that student teachers needed to develop, our interviewees highlighted: connecting mathematics, visualizing mathematics, and assessing students' understanding. They emphasized the need to refrain from just telling students what you want them to know because it was not an effective way to help students understand.

Connecting Mathematics

Seven of the nine teachers made explicit references to connecting mathematics. In general, the reason to make connections was to enhance student understanding but the kind of connections advocated varied. Some said it was important to make mathematical connections and smooth transitions between mathematical topics. Peggy (1) explained, "You can do it graphically, you can model it algebraically, there are just so many different things that you can do with it to kind of help the kids understand why and where it is going." Brian (2) argued the importance of stressing "where the idea comes from, and why we do use it, and what areas we would want to use it in." Other teachers valued connecting mathematics to the world of the students and making applications of the mathematics specific. The responsibility for making the connections belonged to the teacher; the student's responsibility was to understand.

Visualizing Mathematics

Four of the nine teachers made specific references to helping students visualize mathematics by using computers or calculators, drawings, or concrete materials. Elizabeth (1) argued for the power of using visual representations to increase understanding about the unit circle and trigonometric functions after a successful experience with her students.

Teachers who advocated a visual approach emphasized it throughout the interviews. Some teachers did not specifically talk about a visual approach but discussed using hands-on materials and laboratory activities that suggested a visual and tactile approach. Occasionally, the strategy appeared to be motivated by a need to keep the students' attention, but usually the teachers advocated a visual presentation as an effective means of helping students "see" the mathematics.

Assessing Students' Understanding

Six of the nine teachers mentioned the need to assess student understanding. The need was made explicit, but the nature of the assessment was focused on quick procedures. For example, Anna (1) suggested, "looking into the eyes of the students, and see what they need."

Teachers reported a need for frequent, quick evaluation that would inform the instructor whether or not to proceed. Quick assessment was important to inform the instruction, but substantial assessment was not part of their descriptions of good lessons. For example, the interviews did not uncover examples of probing students for the limits of their understanding or challenging students to explain where they were having difficulties.

Refrain from Telling

Eight of the nine teachers discussed good lessons as moving away from the teacher providing information that the students had to memorize or mimic. Yvonne (1) explained why mathematics required a non-telling approach:

> ...mathematics is different because it is just not giving content, ... not just giving a lecture ... it is developing something, modeling something, and showing something. ... Mathematics involves a lot of thinking, so it is not just listening, writing down notes.

Teachers realized the inadequacy of telling students and realized that it did not lead to their goal of students understanding mathematics. They believed that just knowing what the teacher tells students does not prepare them to solve real problems or use mathematics outside the classroom.

Teachers wanted students to discover properties and ideas, and they were dedicated to using activities, employing technologies, and designing lessons that led to a specific conclusion. They expected students to discover a piece of mathematics that the teacher thought was important, and worked hard to guide students and, on occasion, advocated directly leading students to the desired conclusion. Teachers tried to balance what needed to be told and what could be discovered, but the goal was clearly for the students to learn what the teacher had planned:

> ... not telling [students] ahead of time what the relationship would be ... get them to tie it together, not telling them necessarily how it all fits together, but making sure before they leave the room they've seen how it ties together. (Anna, 2)

Teachers felt a pressure to be sure that the students understood "the concept" before they left the class period. If the "discovery" did not work, it was necessary to do more guiding and telling.

Good Teaching Engages and Motivates Students

The importance of engaging students was discussed by eight of the nine teachers. The idea of engaging students is very compatible with the teachers' emphasis on understanding and with their belief that "just telling" was not an adequate way to promote understanding. One of the most frequently discussed strategies for engaging students was to use various approaches. Teachers mentioned using technology, having students write, doing group work, and using hands-on activities such as measuring distances, applying mathematics, and laboratory activities. Alice (2) explained:

I know that every day you can't come in here and be an entertainer, I don't mean that. But come with new activities or new ways to do things so that kids don't just, OK, open the book. ... I've had really good experiences with that.

One of the popular ways to vary instruction was to use groups of students. Teachers argued for group work as a way for students (a) to help each other, (b) to share ideas, (c) to do problem solving, and (d) to compile and validate data. Although teachers reasoned that "teacher telling" was not useful, some of the value of group work was reported as an opportunity for students to tell other students how to work problems.

Four teachers specifically referred to students physically moving around the room in order to engage them. Sometimes the physical movement was as mundane as going to the board to explain a problem or moving to work with a partner, but physical movement was a substantial part of engaging students.

Teachers also recommended engaging students by meeting them at their mathematical level. Although teachers wanted to reach high school students at the level where they were, two teachers cautioned that we needed to continue to challenge students even when it is uncomfortable. Peggy (3) lamented,

Nobody wants to make anybody else uncomfortable and a lot of people don't want to get out of their comfort zone so we don't push them in the directions as much as we should.

Anna (2) argued, "... if they struggle with this [the mathematics], they [students] tend to make it their own and they are going to be proud of it in the end." Although these two comments were not typical, they do exemplify the challenge teachers face when trying to (a) engage students at their existing knowledge level, and (b) inspire them to move to a less comfortable, but more advanced zone.

Good Teaching Requires Effective Management

As teachers described good teaching, they usually mentioned the necessity of good management to achieve their goals. For most of the teachers, "management" covered a host of skills and ideas to keep the lesson moving and the students under control. Another aspect of having effective management skills was the notion of flexibility, which was repeatedly mentioned by the teachers. Alice (1) argued that teachers need to be prepared with "as many ways as they can to describe whatever it is they are trying to do." The theme of flexibility permeated teachers' descriptions of their lessons and their comments about lessons of student teachers. It was a management technique, and the purpose was to keep students engaged and motivated. They wanted to find a hook that would meet students where they were.

Rather than trying to assess how each student was thinking, teachers recommended taking a variety of approaches with the assumption that there would be at least one approach that would reach each learner.

Reflecting on Good Teaching

Teachers' perspectives about good teaching illustrate how teachers assume most of the responsibility for what is accomplished in a classroom. Teachers felt responsible for making lessons go smoothly. Although teachers were emphatic that good teaching was not telling, they believed that they should guide the students and even tell in instances where guiding was unsuccessful. Teachers believed that good teaching involved teaching for understanding, and they reported reading students' facial expressions to assess that understanding. It is certainly reasonable that teachers' descriptions of good teaching would focus on their responsibilities for making lessons go smoothly, but there was little evidence in their remarks to suggest that students should feel responsible for making lessons go smoothly. The lessons were organized to help students understand the teachers' mathematics, and the teacher assumed the responsibility for guiding students toward that mathematics.

HEARING THE ECHOES

Although teachers seldom use the words of researchers or scholars, to what extent did these nine teachers' ideas align with ideas of researchers and scholars? Without question, the teachers emphasized the need to know mathematics, the foundation on which their teaching rested. This disposition is in keeping with Polya's (1965) commandment "Know your subject," and with the very premise of the various NCTM documents, but may not be as extensive as Ma's (1999) idea of deep and profound understanding.

Repeatedly, the teachers emphasized the need to know their students as emerging adults. But also they emphasized the need to know if students were keeping up with the taught mathematics. Despite the teachers' emphasis on attention to students' understanding, there remains the question of whether they are assessing students' understanding as a means of shaping their instruction or whether assessment consists primarily of determining the extent to which students are "with the teacher" as the class follows a predetermined curriculum. The interviews suggest that the teachers considered it important to assess in order to appropriately pace instruction rather than shape instruction. This perspective differs from Schifter's (1998) constructivist-based notion that the mathematics to which teachers should be attending is not that of a predetermined curriculum but rather the mathematics in the students' mind. There is considerable variance between how our teachers defined good teaching in terms of assessing students' understanding as they move through a predetermined curriculum and the constructivist notion that assessment is what determines what gets taught next. Schifter's constructivist perspective does not seem to capture what our teachers had in mind. Furthermore, the teachers' reference to "understanding students" did not reflect the NCTM documents' emphasis on basing instruction on how students are constructing mathematics.

It seems fair to say that the teachers' comments reflected an essentially teacher-centered classroom although not one necessarily dominated by lecture. They felt comfortable with a teacher-centered approach so long as their instruction included a variety of instructional styles and they could exercise different ways of reaching out to students. The mathematics was predetermined by textbooks or county or state objectives. Although the teachers embraced part of the NCTM reform-based notions about teaching and learning, that acceptance was limited to those aspects of reform that could be realized in a teacher-centered classroom.

CONCLUDING THOUGHTS OF ORIGINAL STUDY

Dewey (1916) thought of education as a reconstructive process that is grounded in thinking and that allows the individual being educated to make informed choices. These are lofty goals, indeed. Did the teachers of this study convey the essence of Dewey's philosophy? Yes, in the sense that the teachers wanted their students to understand mathematics as it related to other aspects of their lives. But we did not uncover much of an emphasis on reflective thinking or on students learning how to monitor their own learning. Teachers reflected those notions of good teaching that were grounded in a teacher-centered classroom in which the teacher had the primary if not the sole responsibility for directing learning.

It should be kept in mind that these were experienced teachers who took considerable pride in their profession. Based on their participation in Project PRIME, it would be reasonable to conclude that they were well established and well respected by both students and administrators. At the very least, they were initiators and leaders in their own school districts. So perhaps it should not be surprising that their notions of good teaching echoed that of many scholars and researchers who have written about the teaching and learning of mathematics. Although the teachers may not hold to Dewey's (1916) notion of good teaching in its broadest sense, their notions are grounded in a substantial body of literature.

The teachers' perspectives also reflected much in the NCTM documents. The notion of solid mathematics, connecting and visualizing mathematics, and engage-ing students in doing mathematics are all precepts that pervade the Standards. Furthermore, the teachers' use of technology, specifically connected to visualizing mathematics, is another indication that the teachers are "living" the Standards, but they did not fully embrace the Standards' constructivist leanings. Whereas the NCTM documents present effective teaching in terms of the teacher basing instruction on students' thinking, this orientation is not consistent with how the teachers discussed good teaching.

We can take some comfort, however, in the fact that one can find considerable overlap between the teachers' espoused beliefs and the writings of those who have devoted their time thinking and reflecting about the act of teaching. Although there may exist a fundamental inconsistency between the views of the two groups (i.e., teachers are viewing good teaching in the paradigm of a teacher-centered classroom whereas scholars of decades past and the NCTM documents are viewing good teaching in the paradigm of a student-centered classroom), this potential conflict poses a significant challenge for teacher educators or reformers who advocate a more student-centered approach to teaching. There is a risk that when good teaching is the focal point of the discussion, teachers and teacher educators are picturing the phenomena in fundamentally different ways. In order to improve the conversation and to facilitate the development of good teaching, teacher educators would be wise to listen to how teachers are thinking about good teaching.

FURTHER INVESTIGATIONS INTO TEACHERS' PERSPECTIVES ON STUDENTS' MATHEMATICAL THINKING

Although the original study found considerable overlap between the teachers' espoused beliefs and the writings of scholars and researchers, there seemed to be a fundamental difference with respect to the influence of students' mathematical thinking on instruction. Researchers argued for student-centered instruction and teachers described teacher-centered instruction. Researchers argued that students' mathematical thinking was not only a goal of effective instruction, but also a component that should inform instructional decisions. In the original study, we did not find evidence that teachers used students' mathematical thinking to inform their instruction. Teachers emphasized the importance of knowing your students, but they did not include understanding students' mathematical thinking as an essential part of knowing their students. In describing good teaching, they emphasized knowing students at a personal level, and knowing what students could do procedurally so they could remediate or move to the next topic. Neither one of these ways of knowing students is synonymous with understanding and using the mathematical thinking of students.

Although scholars and policy makers were urging practitioners to utilize students' mathematical thinking in planning and implementing instruction, our group of teachers failed to mention the role students' mathematical thinking played in planning or implementing effective instruction. We were curious about this missing component in teachers' descriptions of good teaching, and sought to better understand how teachers viewed the role of their students' mathematical thinking.

According to the Principles and Standards for School Mathematics (NCTM, 2000), teachers are responsible "for creating an intellectual environment where serious mathematical thinking is the norm" (p.18). It further stated, "effective teaching involves observing students, listening carefully to their ideas and explanations, having mathematical goals, and using the information to make instructional decisions" (p. 19). This emphasis on students' mathematical thinking could influence instruction in two important ways. First, it suggests that teachers need to access students' thinking and adjust their lessons to take advantage of their new insights. It also implies that teachers should shift their attention from trying to implement a set lesson plan to continuously listening to students and probing their thinking. In their work with elementary teachers using Cognitively Guided Instruction (CGI), Franke and Kazemi (2001) reported that the mathematics teachers' expectations of their students' understanding increased dramatically and they began listening more and telling less when they started focusing on what their students were thinking.

Teachers also realized that they needed to listen to their students' mathematical explanations to create strategies and questions to elicit more and better explanations (Franke & Kamezi, 2001). Furthermore, when teachers focused on students and listened to their thinking, the teachers often experienced a transformation into a new role, that of a learner (Franke & Kazemi, 2001; Sharp & Hoiberg, 2001).

Second, a focus on students' mathematical thinking requires lessons and tasks that promote students' thinking. Teachers can not gain access to students' thinking if the lessons and tasks do not provide opportunities for students to demonstrate or share their thinking. The selection of the tasks plays a crucial role in potentially fostering higher levels of thinking among students (Doyle, 1988; Sharp & Hoiberg, 2001). NTCM (1991) is a strong advocate for choosing worthwhile mathematical tasks and it is addressed in one of the six standards for the teaching of mathematics. It is not only important to select good tasks, but it is critical to maintain a high level of cognitive demand that encourages student thinking (Stein, Smith, Henningsen, & Silver, 2000). Cuoco, Goldenberg & Mark (1997) argue that the goal of mathematics teaching is to develop habits of mind that are useful across a variety of mathematics problems. They urge teachers to focus less on a specific topic and to emphasize the processes of doing mathematics. They point out that we should not describe mathematics as studying triangles or equations but rather as ways to solve problems. They propose teaching students to see patterns, play with the mathematics, experiment, visualize, and invent approaches. In short they promote the idea that students should learn to think mathematically and develop habits of mind.

> A curriculum organized around habits of mind tries to close the gap between what the users and makers of mathematics *do* and what they *say*. Such a curriculum lets students in on the process of creating, inventing, conjecturing, and experimenting; it lets them experience what goes on behind the study door before new results are polished and presented. It is a curriculum that encourages false starts, calculations, experiments, and special cases (p. 376).

Influenced by the first study, we revised our preparation of mathematics teachers to include more attention to students' mathematical thinking. Pre-service teachers created mathematical tasks and discussed how to help learners maintain a high level of thinking as they worked on a task (Stein et al., 2000). They watched experienced teachers and were able to talk with teachers about what they saw. They interviewed secondary students about learning mathematics. The PRIME project hosted a meeting for mentor teachers, university teachers and student teachers where we shared our goals for student teaching and explained our emphasis on accessing students' mathematical thinking and using it to inform instruction. Although the PRIME participants talked about "students' thinking," most classes remained teacher-centered. We analyzed the post student teaching surveys to help us understand how teachers (i.e., mentor teachers, university teachers, and student teachers) were thinking about the role of students' mathematical thinking in good teaching. We gained insights into how students' thinking was accessed by teachers and what barriers may have interfered with implementing the visions of researchers and policy makers who advocate using students' thinking to drive instruction in mathematics.

METHODOLOGY IN THE SECOND STUDY

Participants in Second Study

In contrast to the first study where all participants were mentor teachers, we wanted to understand how all of the teachers involved with the PRIME project viewed students' thinking. Forty-six pre-service secondary mathematics student teachers (ST), 44 secondary in-service teachers serving as mentor teachers (MT), and eleven doctoral students serving as university teachers (UT) participated in this study. The new structure of PRIME required mentor teachers to commit to a non-traditional student teaching field-experience in the spring. We tried to shift the focus from an apprentice experience to a more collaborative experience where the mentor teacher, student teacher, and university teacher worked together to improve the mathematical learning of the high school students. An important difference was the requirement that mentors, student and university teachers meet once a week as a group to discuss mathematics, students' thinking and/or instructional issues. The fall field-experience, preceding spring student teaching, included a total of four weeks, spread throughout the semester, when pre-service teachers visited at least two schools. During the fall field-experience the pre-service teachers observed mathematics classes, tutored small groups of students, and taught a unit lesson that lasted three to five days. Mentor teachers allowed groups of pre-service teachers to observe and discuss their instructional practices during the fall semester. Additionally, PRIME mentor and university teachers were invited to attend an evening work session that focused on reforming the teaching of mathematics by building on students' thinking. During the work session, both university and mentor teachers received and discussed information regarding the semester schedule, student teaching goals and suggested activities. Student teachers also received and discussed this information in their teaching methods course. Each student teacher was given a bound notebook so that they could record information about their students, observed instruction, and reflections. Student teachers could share their notebooks with their mentor teachers or university teachers at their own discretion.

Procedure in the Second Study

All university and student teachers were required to complete a post-student teaching survey, and mentor teachers were strongly encouraged to complete the survey. The survey asked the university and mentor teachers to evaluate each student teacher that they supervised with respect to specified student teaching goals. Student teachers provided a self-evaluation. University teachers were also asked to evaluate the mentors, with whom they worked, in terms of the type of assistance needed and whether or not the mentors attended to the goals of student teaching. Student teachers reported on the effectiveness of their mentor and university teachers. Data analyzed for this study included all university and student teacher reports and reports from the thirty mentor teachers who completed reports. (Fourteen mentor teachers did not complete the report.) In an effort to understand the participants' views on the role of students' mathematical thinking in good teaching, we analyzed the participants comments related to the first goal of the field experience. All teachers were asked to provide comments that evaluated the student teachers with respect to the following goal: *Student teachers will learn to teach mathematics based on the mathematical thinking of their secondary students.* Although using the post student teaching survey required a high level of inference about teachers' perspectives, we were able to avoid asking teachers to report directly on instances of using students thinking. We did not want to pressure teachers to search for instances that appeared to focus on students' thinking. We were more interested in understanding how students' mathematical thinking influenced their ideas about good teaching.

Using qualitative methods of coding the survey data as "a progressive process of sorting and defining and defining and sorting" (Glesne, 1999, p. 135), the initial analysis revealed five categories related to the first student teaching goal. Tally charts were developed to display the frequency of comments about students' thinking by teacher group (i.e., MT, ST, UT). We chose to collapse the groups rather than make distinctions among the groups, because the groups were continually interacting and working together. Further analysis of the charts produced three robust categories related to teaching based on students' mathematical thinking: (1) students' misconceptions and competencies, (2) students' questions, and (3) thinking or teaching differently based on students' thinking. The first two categories explained how teachers accessed students' thinking and the third category provided insights into the role that students' thinking played in teachers' instruction. We noted various approaches used to identify students' thinking and to make instructional adjustments. Although highly inferential, teachers' perspectives on students' thinking helped us to understand some of the reasons why teachers' descriptions of good teaching were based on teacher-centered classrooms rather than student-centered classrooms that are advocated by many researchers.

TEACHERS' PERSPECTIVES ON STUDENTS' MATHEMATICAL THINKING

Teachers talked about their students' mathematical thinking in two major contexts. They discussed how they accessed students' thinking and they reported ways in which their students' mathematical thinking altered their thinking or the way that they taught. It is important to remember that there were no direct observations of teaching, or any interviews inquiring about the role of students' mathematical thinking. We analyzed the reports of mentor teachers, university teachers, and student teachers that explained how they *thought* about their instruction. Their reports offered a window into how they conceived of the nature of their students' mathematical thinking and the role it played in their instruction.

Accessing Students' Thinking

Learning how to teach by focusing on or trying to understand students' mathematical thinking is not an easy feat especially for pre-service and beginning mathematics teachers, but it was posed as an important goal for the student teaching experience. As one student teacher commented:

> One of the hardest and most enjoyable things I had to learn while student teaching was how to get inside of my students' heads. It became obvious from the beginning that my students would not be able to learn everything they needed to just by writing down everything I put on the board (ST)[3].

The most popular way mentioned to access students' mathematical thinking was to analyze student work or artifacts. Student artifacts included homework, tests and quizzes, and various alternative assessments.

The three groups of teachers each made specific references to how student teachers used student artifacts to learn about students' thinking. Grading and analyzing artifacts afforded teachers the opportunity to learn where their students experienced difficulty with the mathematical content. Teachers were drawn to student misconceptions and errors when grading student work and frequently reported that this helped them to learn about students' thinking.

> Throughout my student teaching, through assessment and lots of communication with my students, I was able to better understand the various ways of thinking within my classroom. I not only learned common mistakes, reasons for those, and ways to circumvent them, but I learned how to make understanding student thinking a continuous process throughout my teaching. (ST)

> [ST] spent a good bit of time reflecting on the errors that students were making on homework and assessments to help shape his lesson plans (MT).

> They [the group of student teachers] learned to spend some time investigating the mathematical thinking of these students to ferret out misconceptions and gaps, correct those conditions, and then present new material (UT).

Questioning students and listening to students' questions offered insights into students' thinking. Student teachers claimed that they improved in their ability to access students' thinking through questioning, and they learned that questions had to be constructed carefully in order to provide useful information. The teachers' comments about questioning suggested that teachers gained more access to students' thinking through questioning than through assessments of student artifacts, but much of the questioning focused on exposing misconceptions. Very few teachers talked about students' understanding exposed through questioning.

> Her greatest challenge in this regard was that her students often seemed to understand the concepts and could "do the work," but actually, they often missed connections and the purpose of what they were doing. She became more adept at asking questions that exposed these problems (UT).

He would also use the warm-up activity to help determine what misconceptions were there. He allowed the students to work the problems on the board for the class and explain what they did and why they chose that method. Seeing their work on the board gave him an insight as to what they were thinking when approaching a problem (MT).

I also became better at asking students to explain their thinking when solving problems and better at understanding their thinking and determining when the thinking was correct or incorrect (ST).

A third source of information about students' thinking came from assumptions based on tracked placements (i.e., low-level algebra, advanced algebra) or interpretations of student work by colleagues. This source was cited less frequently, but seemed to be influential. Student teachers reported learning by observing and talking with their more experienced mentor teachers especially about students and their common mathematical mistakes and misconceptions. It appeared that teachers frequently consulted with each other to determine the causes of student misconceptions, but they rarely reported providing students opportunities to discuss errors or explain their thinking.

When I graded papers, I tried to examine problems that students answered incorrectly to see if I could tell what they were thinking. This helped me fix misconceptions that students may have. There were several occasions when I wasn't sure why the students made the mistakes and (MT) helped me understand what they were thinking. I guess that over the years she has seen almost everything (ST).

(MT) would [alert] (ST) to things she thought the students would find hard and how to sequence tasks in a meaningful way for the students (UT).

Although the teachers mostly emphasized the students' deficiencies in mathematical knowledge when trying to focus on students' thinking, there was some mention of their capabilities in mathematics.

(ST) made a conscious effort to be aware of her students' mathematical thinking. The notes in (ST's) PRIME notebook allude to the fact that she is focusing on her students' knowledge. She writes questions, asking herself what they know already, whether they understood a concept she taught and how to assess it the next day (UT).

By using alternative assessments we are able to assess the different levels of mathematical thinking. While some students excel in computation, others excel in design and visual representations of the content. I believe through my alternative assessment, I was able to determine the level at which my students were thinking mathematically (ST).

Teachers used a variety of ways to access students' thinking, but most were based on assessment of products. Although they focused on misconceptions, it seemed that they were trying to establish a level of proficiency. Teachers tended to assess knowledge or level of understanding rather than the thinking process used by a student.

Adjusting Instruction Based on Students' thinking

In reporting on progress toward the goal of learning "to teach mathematics based on the mathematical thinking of their secondary students" about two-thirds of the teachers who responded (i.e., 52% MT, 65% ST, 90% UT) explained that instruction had been adjusted based on students' thinking. We used their comments about adjusting instruction to infer teachers' views about the nature of students' thinking and role it could play in adjusting instruction. In their respective reports, the mentor teachers and university teachers commented on how student teachers had adjusted their lessons, and student teachers gave self-reports on adjusted lessons. The participants wrote about what led to adjusting instruction and how it was adjusted, but none of the participants discussed how the adjustment in instruction impacted student learning or students' thinking.

There were a total of 90 comments that referred to adjusting instruction based on students' thinking. Table 1 shows the frequency of various reasons that teachers provided.

Table 1. Comments Related to Adjusting Instruction Based on Students' thinking.

Reasons for adjusting instruction	Number of comments	%
Total	90	
Student	32	36%
Deficiencies		
Misconceptions	17	
Low level of understanding	4	
Lack of knowledge	5	
Lack connections	1	
Not on task or motivated	5	
Vague reference to understanding	15	17%
Generic understanding	6	
Generic "students' thinking"	9	
Student competencies	7	8%
High level of understanding	2	
Probed understanding	5	
Student Questions/Comments	12	13%
Student Teacher's lesson	13	14%
Poorly taught lesson	3	
Insights from previous lesson	10	
Feedback	8	9%
From MT or UT	6	
From students	1	
From self	1	
Student Learning Styles	3	3%

About 36% of the reasons given for adjusting instruction were related to student deficiencies; 17% made a vague reference to student understanding; and 8% referred to specific student competencies. Based on the sources that teachers were using to detect students' thinking, it was easier to determine deficiencies than deep understanding or reasoning. Teachers reported that lessons were adjusted because high school students had misconceptions, a lack of foundational knowledge for the topic being taught, or a low level of mathematical understanding in general. Participants could easily identify errors on homework, class work, or tests and inferred associated misconceptions. A lack of foundational or prerequisite work in mathematics was often assumed to explain why students were having difficulty with a topic or making mistakes. Teachers reported adjusting lessons to accommodate groups of the students who continued to perform poorly and were assigned to low-level mathematics classes. Student teachers explained that the "low level of the students" was a surprise and that they had to bring the level of mathematics down so that students could understand. Frequently, student teachers valued the advice of their mentor teacher.

> My mentor teacher and I worked together to plan ahead for common misconceptions which also helped me learn about student thinking. When I would grade assessments, I tried to figure out why students made mistakes. I used assessments to judge whether or not it was okay for me to move forward. This helped me learn from my own teaching. If the entire class didn't do well on an assessment, I knew it reflected my teaching so I had to find another way to teach that concept. I talked with my colleagues to see how their students did on their assessments and we discussed alternate ways to teach these concepts. (ST)

Mentor teachers praised their student teachers for taking the responsibility of adjusting lessons to meet the perceived needs of students who have been unsuccessful in mathematics. They favored two common adjustments—reduction of the complexity of learning mathematics for unsuccessful students and transfer of responsibility for thinking and reasoning to the teacher from the student. Student teachers were eager to "meet the needs of their students" which were determined by the level of the class.

> (ST) did have some eye-opening experiences with regard to students who are slower to learn mathematics and students with little or no motivation to learn mathematics. She adjusted her instruction accordingly. For example, she developed note-taking guides for these students and gave notebook quizzes to encourage and reward the students for using her note-taking guides. She asked for guidance from me in finding some instructional activities that might be more likely to engage these students. (MT)

A student teacher shared a comparison of the ways she adjusted her instruction to accommodate students assigned to a basic mathematics class and students assigned to an advanced mathematics class.

Throughout student teaching I learned to adjust lesson plans to meet the needs of my students. Specifically in my Pre-Algebra class I would have to plan to work more examples and give the students time to practice in class to ensure that they understood the topics. On the other hand, my Algebra III class would move very quickly at times and I would have to be ready to move on in the lesson if they were bored. (ST)

A few student teachers challenged the notion that unsuccessful mathematics students did not think mathematically, but they struggled with how to adjust instruction based on the student's mathematical thinking. The following quote suggests that the student teacher recognized that all students can think about mathematics, but did not have a way elaborating on what "coming down to their level" might mean.

Starting out as a student teacher I was expecting the mathematics levels of the students to be higher than they were. I know, sounds very negative, but I soon learned that they were high, just needed a correct teaching method to draw out their thinking. I learned that by "coming down to their level," you are able to teach mathematics based on their mathematical thinking. (ST)

Approximately seventeen percent of the teachers reported adjusting lessons based on "student understanding" or "student thinking", but failed to elaborate on the nature of that student understanding or thinking. In some cases teachers referred to a variability of student competencies within the class, but did not provide descriptions.

Most of the adjustments of instruction were a result of assumptions made about students from homework completion, class performance, or the low level of the class. Only eight percent of the reasons given for adjusting instruction were based on probing students' thinking by analyzing individual student work, asking well-constructed questions, or carefully listening to student comments and explanations. Such teaching strategies are closely aligned with the goal "of learning to teach mathematics based on the mathematical thinking of students" endorsed in the teacher preparation program and promoted by the NCTM Standards. The following quotes from a university teacher and a student teacher illustrate significant efforts by student teachers to access students' mathematical thinking. Although this perspective was rare, it indicates that there are teachers who think that the role of students' thinking is to inform instructional decisions and contribute to good teaching.

Throughout her work (ST) worked hard to teach in accord with her students' thinking. This is evidenced throughout her notebook where she keeps a running dialogue of what the kids understood, what they didn't understand and how to address the misunderstandings in class in the future. For instance, she wrote after each quiz or test how the students did on the quiz or test, what major difficulties seemed to be, and how she might address these difficulties when going over the test with her students. (UT)

The mathematical thinking of the secondary students was the main focus of my student teaching experience. (MT) and I were constantly attempting to determine what the students were thinking, and also raise the level of that thinking. Perhaps more than anything else in my experience, I learned to base my instruction around student thinking. This meant changing the pacing of a lesson, changing how I presented the material, or sometimes changing the entire direction of a lesson or unit. MT helped me understand that student thinking should be the first thing on my mind in both planning a lesson, and teaching one. (ST)

Opportune student questions or comments were mentioned as reasons for adjusting instruction by about thirteen percent of the participants. These student questions were not a result of a teacher probing or setting up a situation that challenged students, but rather interesting questions and comments that came from practice problems or listening to a teacher explanation. A student teacher explained how student questions inspired her to adjust instruction.

I had two Advanced College Prep Geometry Classes that challenged me every day and taught me different ways of thinking about whatever we were doing at the time. They asked amazing questions which allowed me to think about these mathematical concepts in more depth than I had before. Not only did they show me how to think in different ways, they also challenged me to teach different ways. For instance, I learned how to explain different ideas in math in ways that they could understand. I also learned how to change my own plans in order to follow their thinking. (ST)

Teachers reported adjusting instruction based on previous lessons and especially lessons that did not go well. University teachers and mentor teachers frequently described the progress of student teachers in using students' thinking as adjusting instruction based on previous lessons. Several mentor teachers credited their feedback to student teachers as being influential in adjusting instruction, and some student teachers reported that they sought advice from mentor teachers when they were not sure how to adjust their instruction. When participants discussed learning from a previous lesson they referred to their perceptions about how well the lesson went or what the students misunderstood. Rarely, did they refer to evidence that explained why the lesson had not gone well. Rather than articulating a specific problem, they described efforts to just try something different. Several teachers mentioned the power of collaboration with colleagues as useful in adapting lessons and instruction in general. Students' thinking was rarely mentioned as a valuable source of information for improving a lesson. It appeared that students' thinking is perceived as something to be assessed rather than accessed.

As the semester progressed, she was able to self assess and make improvements or changes to her lessons throughout the day so that the students would better understand what she was talking about. She was able to critique me and watch me critique myself in order to better make these changes. (MT)

They (high school students) resisted at first but I learned that all of my students were able to learn mathematics at a high level. I learned from many people I worked with....Working with other teachers makes things easier for all parties, helps you stay creative in your classroom, and helps you catch mistakes before you bring them into the classroom. (ST)

Reflection on Teachers' Perspectives on the Role of Students' Thinking in Good Teaching

The sources that teachers used to access students' mathematical thinking were primarily assessments. By focusing primarily on homework, tests, and in-class responses to teacher questions, teachers were able to see solutions and answers but were not able to access the internal thinking that produced the solutions and answers. Consequently, the errors and misconception commanded their attention and they tried to *imagine* the thinking and confusion that led to the errors. They felt comfortable consulting experienced colleagues for their opinions, but very few reported that they actually asked students to explain their thinking. Teachers' limited use of questioning seemed to be the strategy that came closest to probing students' thinking, and teachers were well aware that good questioning techniques were hard to learn. With such limited access to students' thinking, it is reasonable that teachers focused on student misconceptions and their own analysis of those errors. These limitations influenced the way teachers could use their knowledge about students' thinking to inform instruction.

Our analysis of teachers' reasons for adjusting instruction and the actual adjustments suggest three insights into teacher's perception about effective instruction based on students' mathematical thinking. First, teachers may be equating students' thinking with students' knowledge. When they write about students' deficiencies they focused on things that students do not know. For example, teachers reported that students do not know how to work with fractions, they do not know characteristics of perpendicular lines, or they do not know how to solve a particular homework or test problem. We found relatively little discussion of how students were thinking, what strategies students were using, or what reasoning led to a specific error or solution. In particular, there was no discussion of adjusting lessons based on thinking that led to successful solutions and little discussion of adjusting lessons to encourage students to think about their errors. As educators we do not have a satisfactory vocabulary for talking about students' mathematical thinking. We inferred from the reports that teachers thought students who were assigned to low level classes were low-level thinkers. This may be evidence that a lack of mathematical knowledge was equated with a lack of the ability to think mathematically. We claim that young children, with relatively little formal mathematical knowledge, can think about mathematics, but high school students, who have more mathematical knowledge than elementary students but less than is expected at the high school level, are frequently considered to be incapable of mathematical thinking.

Second, teachers may be envisioning students' thinking as knowing how to perform procedures rather than developing mathematical habits of mind as proposed by Cuoco, Goldenberg & Mark (1997). References to understanding students' thinking were often in the context of completing a homework or test problem. The relative ease of assessing right and wrong answers has led to assessments that primarily measure students' abilities to solve mathematical exercises that require little reasoning. This makes it difficult to measure to what degree students have developed habits of mind that enable them to solve more complex problems by reasoning and integrating mathematical skills. Students and teachers value what is most often assessed, and this contributed to reducing the concept of student thinking to something that is easily measured and evaluated. Although we do not have observational data on how much instruction emphasized procedural mathematics, we do know that when teachers discussed students' thinking it was often in terms of whether or not students could complete a problem correctly. We found no evidence that teachers reflected on what students knew in order to see mathematics in terms of the students' constructions of mathematical ideas as Schifter (1998) advocated.

Third, teachers were referring to students' thinking as something that they were responsible for fixing or accommodating. When a teacher adjusted a lesson based on a student deficiency, the most popular strategies involved the teacher explaining the mistake, reteaching the topic, or structuring the lesson to avoid or prevent similar misconceptions. Although an error may have served as a stimulus for a lesson in the next class or the next day, no one proposed using the error to investigate how students' thinking led to an incorrect solution or how the mathematical thinking was on target but calculation errors had led to an incorrect solution. When teachers wrote about adjusting a lesson to take advantage of student understanding, they sought to challenge students by going faster or providing harder problems rather than encouraging students to make their thinking explicit. Experienced teachers have developed a highly respected knowledge about how to avoid or minimize specific mathematical mistakes. This expertise may be interfering with adjusting instruction based on the ways students think about the mathematics. Student teachers respected the advice of experienced teachers who made suggestions about how to bring the level of mathematics down to the student. Lessons were adjusted to reduce the complexity of the mathematics by requiring less student thinking and more attention to how to prevent mistakes or common errors. Teachers who wrote about trying to challenge students were working with students in higher-level mathematics classes, and they felt the responsibility to cover more mathematics.

HEARING THE ECHOES FROM RESEARCHERS AND THE FIRST STUDY

The second study confirmed and reiterated the tremendous dedication that teachers bring to their work and their students. The participants in the second study included not only practicing teachers, as in the first study, but also novice student teachers and experienced doctoral students serving as university teachers. The comments from all participants reflected the responsibility that they felt for helping students to learn mathematics. Like the teachers in the first study, they wanted students to understand the mathematics; they believed in varying their instruction; and they argued that you needed to know your students. Their comments confirmed the perspectives on effective instruction identified in the first study. Their comments were consistent with Polya's (1965) emphasis on understanding mathematics, and they were well aware of the NCTM documents and were dedicated to teaching for understanding. Also like the teachers in the first study, we found their comments portrayed a teacher-centered classroom.

Unlike the teachers in the first study, there was much more discussion of students' mathematical thinking and using that thinking to inform their instruction. We are convinced that the emphasis on students' mathematical thinking in the methods course and in the survey instruments forced the use of the term "students' thinking" and required all participants to address how students' thinking influenced their teaching. Teachers embraced the NCTM's emphasis on students and their learning. They found these ideas consistent with their strong beliefs that good teaching involves knowing your students. However, teachers talked about knowing students in personal terms and in knowing what mathematical content they understood. The purpose of knowing students' mathematical level was to make judgements about whether to remediate, review, or to move on to new topics. Even with a focus on students' mathematical thinking, we were unable to detect a desire in teachers to understand the way students were constructing their own mathematics. They were sincerely interested in understanding student reasoning or misconceptions that led to errors, because they could use that information to fix the problem and get students back on the right track. This is a different interpretation of students' mathematical thinking than researchers like Schifter (1998), Doyle (1988), or Stein et al. (2000) had in their work encouraging mathematical thinking. We saw many creative ways to assess students' knowledge and many efforts by teachers trying to interpret their assessments to inform instruction. We had evidence of student teachers using questioning, journals, and interviews to try to "get inside of students' heads", but it appeared they were trying to locate errors in thinking. We did not find a shift toward trying to understand the ways students think mathematically and especially how they reach creative solutions. The visions of curriculum developers like Cuoco et al. (1996) and framers of the NCTM Standards remain on the horizon. Our analysis of teachers' evaluations of student teachers indicated that teachers in the second study viewed good mathematics teaching in ways that were similar to the first group of mentor teachers. Effective teaching continued to be defined in terms of what teachers could do as an activity in itself rather than as an activity based on students' thinking. Although they talked about students' mathematical thinking, they thought about it in terms of how it could help teachers to correct or avoid mistakes and set the appropriate level of mathematics instruction. Teachers' comments continued to suggest that learning relies on the teacher's knowledge and decisions, and effective teaching takes place in a teacher-centered classroom.

LESSONS FOR MATHEMATICS TEACHER EDUCATION

Our studies suggest that teachers care about good teaching and they are listening to scholars and paying close attention to professional groups such as NCTM. We found a significant alignment between teachers' perspectives on good teaching and what researchers are advocating. However, there are substantial differences that remain, and it is the responsibility of mathematics teacher education to concentrate on these areas. We have uncovered two major areas that need attention. First teachers remain wedded to a teacher-centered classroom. Second, many teachers think of focusing on students' mathematical thinking as assessing errors and then correcting or preventing them. Both of these positions may grow out of teachers' incredible dedication to helping students learn mathematics that can be demonstrated on formal assessments. We need to help teachers distinguish between *assessing* students' knowledge and *accessing* students' thinking. Although both can inform instruction, the latter is a resource that it is not being utilized fully.

The evidence from the original study and the extended investigation suggests that teachers' notions of good mathematics teaching are grounded more in their experiences as teachers than as participants in teacher education programs. These teachers did not want to have lecture-dominated lessons but, nevertheless, it was clear that their orientation toward teaching was grounded in a teacher-centered classroom. When they focused on their students, their attention was drawn to misconceptions, but the teacher-centered classroom did not provide opportunities for students to share their thinking.

In other studies of pre-service secondary teachers, Eggleton (1995) and Chauvot (2000) found that pre-service teachers' beliefs about teaching became more reform-oriented as they progressed through their teacher education program but in the crucible of the classroom their teaching remained traditional. Thus, it is perhaps not surprising that Hiebert, et al., (2003) found that teachers across seven different countries talked, on the average, 90% of the time when teaching mathematics – thus ensuring a teacher-centered classroom.

Efforts to reform the teaching of mathematics are seldom all or nothing affairs. Wubbels, Korthagen, and Broekman (1997) conducted a teacher-education project in the Netherlands that helped prepare student teachers to: reflect on their own mathematical experiences and share those reflections with a colleague; reflect on the thinking and feelings of fellow students; shift their reflection emphasis to pupils in the classroom; and learn how to repeat this cycle and direct their own professional development. In short, the researchers found that the student teachers' views of mathematics education became more inquiry based but that only a few of the teachers used the principle of teaching mathematics that is based on pupils' mathematical construction.

The preceding analyses suggest that teacher educators who promote a reform-oriented style of teaching are, in fact, swimming upstream. This phenomenon is not news. What perhaps is news is that these studies demonstrate that the obstacles encountered in most reform-oriented teacher education programs are deeply embedded in the beliefs of experienced and professionally active teachers. The challenge is to enable teachers to see how their notions of good teaching, notions grounded in experience, do mirror those of scholars past, and that student-centered instruction does not negate what they believe constitutes good teaching but rather can enhance their notions of good teaching.

Teacher educators take their cues from scholars or from proclamations such as the NCTM documents, which, it could be argued, are essentially a reflection of what those scholars advocated. Teachers, on the other hand, point directly to experience and interaction with colleagues as the primary sources for their becoming good teachers. Although these two perspectives are not necessarily inconsistent, there is a certain tension that exists between them, a tension that often leads to limited change as indicated in the research previously cited. Teacher-centered classrooms are organized to help teachers fulfill the enormous responsibilities they feel. Student-centered classrooms are organized to let students assume some of that responsibility. If we want teachers to relinquish some control and enter into the risky endeavor of student-centered classrooms, we need better ways of accessing and discussing students' mathematical thinking. We need to be able to articulate ways that students' thinking can inform instruction and lead to the good teaching described by teachers. It is a circumstance that necessitates the kind of awareness of which Jaworski (1998) speaks in which each party strives better to understand the other. Therein lies the real challenge of teacher education.

NOTES

[1] Throughout this paper, the term NCTM documents designates the National Council of Teachers of Mathematics 1989 Curriculum and Evaluation Standards for School Mathematics, the 1991 Professional Standards for Teaching Mathematics, the 1995 Assessment Standards for School Mathematics, and the 2000 Principles and Standards for School Mathematics.

[2] Yvonne is a pseudonym, as are all the participant names. The number that follows the pseudonym indicates from which interview (1, 2, or 3) the statement was extracted, and as we present the participants' transcribed interview data, we often omit conversational pauses such as "you know," "like," "ah," and so forth for reading ease. Furthermore, throughout the data reporting ellipsis points represent omitted data, not pauses in the participants' speech.

[3] Statements from the survey data indicate whether the statement came from a mentor teacher (MT), a university teacher (UT), or a student teacher (ST).

REFERENCES

Chauvot, J. (2000). *Conceptualizing mathematics teacher development in the context of reform.* Unpublished Doctoral Dissertation. Athens, GA: University of Georgia.

Cooney, T. (1980). Research on teaching and teacher education. In R. Shumway (Ed.), *Research in mathematics education* (pp. 433–474). Reston, VA: National.

Cuoco, A., Goldenberg, P., & Mark, J. (1996). Habits of mind: An organizing principle for mathematics curricula. *Journal of Mathematical Behavior, 15*, 375–402.

Davis, P., & Hersh, R. (1981). *The mathematical experience.* Boston: Birkhäuser.

Dewey, J. (1916). *Democracy and education.* New York: The Free Press.

Doyle, W. (1988). Work in mathematics classes: The context of students' thinking during instruction. *Educational Psychologist, 23*(2), 167–180.

Eggleton, P. (1995). *The evolving mathematical philosophy of a preservice mathematics teacher.* Unpublished Doctoral Dissertation, University of Georgia, Athens, GA.

Fennema, E., & Nelson, B. (Eds.). (1997). *Mathematics teachers in transition.* Mahwah, NJ: Lawrence Erlbaum Associates.

Franke, M. L., & Kamezi, E. (2001). Learning to teach mathematics: Focus on student thinking. *Theory in Practice, 40*(2), 102–109.

Glesne, C. (1999). *Becoming qualitative researchers: An introduction* (2nd ed.). New York: Longman.

Good, T., Grouws, D., & Ebmeier, H. (1983). *Active mathematics teaching.* New York: Longman.

Hiebert, J., Gallimore, R., Garnier, H., Givvin, K., Hollingsworth, H., Jacobs, J., et al. (2003). *Teaching mathematics in seven countries: Results from the TIMSS 1999 Video Study.* Washington, DC: U.S. Department of Education. National Center for Education Statistics.

Jaworski, B. (1998). Mathematics teacher research: Process, practice and the development of teaching. *Journal of Mathematics Teacher Education, 1,* 3–31.

Lather, P. (1986). Issues of validity in openly ideological research: Between a rock and a soft place. *Interchange, 17*(4), 63–84.

Leinhardt, G. (1988). Expertise in instructional lessons: An example from fractions. In D. Grouws, T. Cooney, & D. Jones (Eds.), *Perspectives on research on effective mathematics teaching* (pp. 47–66). Reston, VA: National Council of Teachers of Mathematics.

Ma, L. (1999). *Knowing and teaching mathematics: Teachers' understanding of fundamental mathematics in China and the United States.* Mahwah, NJ: Lawrence Erlbaum Associates.

McKinney, K. (1986). *How the experts teach math. In research in brief.* Washington, DC: U.S. Department of Education. Office of Educational Research and Improvement.

National Council of Teachers of Mathematics. (2000). *Principles and standards for school mathematics.* Reston, VA: Author.

National Council of Teachers of Mathematics. (1995). *Assessment standards for school mathematics.* Reston, VA: Author.

National Council of Teachers of Mathematics. (1991). *The professional standards for teaching mathematics.* Reston, VA: Author.

National Council of Teachers of Mathematics. (1989). *Curriculum and evaluation standards for school mathematics.* Reston, VA: Author.

Polya, G. (1965). *Mathematical discovery: On understanding, learning, and teaching problem solving* (Vol. II). New York: John Wiley and Sons.

Raymond, A. (1997). Inconsistency between a beginning elementary school teacher's mathematics beliefs and teaching practice. *Journal for Research in Mathematics Education, 28*(5), 550–576.

Rosenshine, B., & Furst, N. (1971). Research in teacher performance criteria. In B. O. Smith (Ed.), *Symposium on research in teacher education.* Englewood Cliffs, NJ: Prentice Hall.

Schifter, D. (1998). Learning mathematics for teaching: From a teachers' seminar to the classroom. *Journal of Mathematics Teacher Education, 1,* 55–87.

Schön, D. (1983). *The reflective practitioner: How professionals think in action.* New York: Basic Books.

Sharp, J. M., & Hoiberg, K. B. (2001). And then there was Luke: The geometric thinking of a young mathematician. *Teaching Children Mathematics, 7*(7), 432–439.

Skott, J. (2001). The emerging practices of a novice teacher: The roles of his school mathematics images. *Journal of Mathematics Teacher Education, 4,* 3–28.

Stein, M. K., Smith, M. S., Henningsen, M. A., & Silver, E. A. (2000). *Implementing standards-based mathematics instruction: A casebook for professional development.* New York: Teachers College Press.

Wilson, M., & Goldenberg, M. (1998). Some conceptions are difficult to change: One middle school mathematics teacher's struggle. *Journal of Mathematics Teacher Education, 2,* 269–293.

Wilson, P. S., Cooney, T. J., & Stinson, D. W. (2005). What constitutes good mathematics teaching and how it develops: Nine high school teachers' perspective. *Journal of Mathematics Teacher Education, 8*, 83–111.

Wubbels, T., Korthagen, F., & Broekman, H. (1997). Preparing teachers for realistic mathematics education. *Educational Studies in Mathematics, 32*(1), 1–28.

Patricia S. Wilson
University of Georgia

Kanita K. DuCloux
University of Georgia

CHAP SAM LIM

IN SEARCH OF EFFECTIVE MATHEMATICS
TEACHING PRACTICE: THE MALAYSIAN
MATHEMATICS TEACHERS' DILEMMA

INTRODUCTION

To situate the context of this study, this chapter will begin with a brief introduction of the Malaysian school system and students' mathematics achievement in public examinations.

The Malaysian School System

The Malaysian school system is divided into four levels: Primary (6 years), Lower Secondary (3–4 years), Upper Secondary (2 years), and Form Six or Matriculation (2 years). At the primary level, due to the multi-ethnic characteristics of Malaysia, there are three choices of primary schools available, depending upon the medium of instruction. These are (a) Malay medium national schools (SK); (b) Chinese medium national type schools (SRJKC); and (c) Tamil medium national type schools (SRJKT). At the secondary levels, all schools are conducted in a common medium of instruction, the Malay language, which is also the official language of Malaysia. However, since the latest curriculum reform in 2003, the medium of instruction for mathematics curriculum has progressively been changing to using English as a medium of instruction from primary through secondary schools. By the year 2008, all primary and secondary school mathematics will be taught in English. This drastic change poses a great challenge to both mathematics teachers and students. This is because English is neither the first language nor the second language of most mathematics teachers, parents, or students. Nonetheless, the Malaysian government has put in great effort and allocated a huge budget in meeting these challenges.

In Malaysia, all public schools follow a standardized national mathematics curriculum as well as having national public examinations. There are four major public examinations conducted at each level. At the primary level, there is the Primary School Assessment Test (UPSR); at the lower secondary level, the Lower Secondary Assessment (PMR); at the upper secondary, the Malaysian Certificate of Education Examination (SPM); and at Form Six, the Malaysian Higher Education Certificate Examination (STPM). Nonetheless, the most decisive examination is the SPM. Based on the SPM results, a student may choose to enter Form Six or

J. Cai, G. Kaiser, B. Perry and N.-Y. Wong (eds.), Effective Mathematics Teaching from Teachers'
Perspectives: National and Cross-National Studies, 123–140.
© *2009 Sense Publishers. All rights reserved.*

matriculation, polytechnic or teacher training institutes, private colleges or local universities, or overseas institutions.

Students' Mathematics Achievement in Public Examinations

In view of the significant roles of mathematics in students' future careers and daily lives, mathematics is a compulsory subject for every Malaysian student from primary through secondary schools. A brief analysis of the annual results of student performance in the most crucial national examinations, the Malaysian Certificate of Education (SPM), shows that on average only 70% of these students (after 11–12 years of schooling) scored a pass or achieved the minimum competency in the SPM Mathematics paper (see Table 1). If the national goal is to have all students achieve at least minimum competency, then this result is far from satisfactory. It indicates that out of every 10 secondary school leavers, three of them have not yet achieved the minimum competency in mathematics. Even though Additional Mathematics is a higher-level mathematics subject that is taken optionally by mostly science stream students or those higher-ability students who intend to enter higher institutions, the overall annual student performance in this subject is far from satisfactory. Indirectly, these results might imply that mathematics teaching in schools is still not as effective as desired.

Table 1. Percentage of student passes in Malaysian national examination (SPM) in Mathematics and Additional Mathematics

Year	Mathematics	Add. Mathematics
1997 [a]	74.6%	86.8%
1998 [b]	72.0%	87.3%
1999 [b]	71.1%	89.9%
2000 [c]	72.1%	81.5%
2001 [d]	70.0%	76.5%
2002 [d]	71.2%	76.7%
2003 [e]	74.6%	77.2%
2004 [e]	74.6%	73.8%
2005 [e]	76.2%	74.5%
2006 [f]	76.5%	NA

Source: [a] The Star, 31 March 1998; [b] The Star, 5 April 2000; [c] The Star, 27 Feb 2001; [d] The Star, 27 March 2003; [e] The Star, 14 March 2006; [f] Berita Harian, 14 March 2007
NA= Not available

Possible Factors

Various factors—for example, school, teacher, student, social, and cultural as well as language factors—might have led to the unsatisfactory student performance in mathematics. Among these, teacher factors which include teachers' philosophical perspectives toward mathematics (such as formalistic versus fallibilistic, argued by Cooney & Wiegel, 2003); beliefs and values about mathematics (Bishop, 1991;

Chin, 1995; Ernest, 1989; Thompson, 1992; Seah, 2005); teachers' conceptions about lesson structure (Shimzu, 2007), teachers' specialized knowledge of mathematics (Ball, Hill, & Bass, 2005; Hill, Rowan, & Ball, 2005), as well as teachers' personality and rapport with students (Lim, 2001) were found to have significant impacts on teacher effectiveness.

For example, Hill, Rowan, and Ball (2005) studied a sample of 334 first grade and 365 third grade teachers (and 1190 first graders and 1773 third graders). Their findings show that teachers' mathematical knowledge about teaching was significantly related to student achievement gains in both first and third graders. Their findings suggested that "knowledgeable teachers can positively and substantially affect students' learning of mathematics, and the size of this effect, at least in the present sample, is in league with the effects of student background characteristics" (p.396).

Lim (2001) studied the teachers' influence on 62 adults' images of mathematics, especially in terms of liking and disliking mathematics. She compared the characteristics of mathematics teachers who claimed to like with those who claimed to dislike mathematics. Her findings show three main aspects: (i) teachers' teaching approaches such as "explain well" and "making learning interesting and enjoyable"; (ii) teachers' personality such as "inspiring and encouraging" and "has a lot of patience"; and (iii) teachers' rapport with students such as "give individual attention or time to pupils" and "get along with pupils". Even though Lim's study looked into the characteristics of mathematics teachers on adults' liking of mathematics, these findings might have indirect implications on teacher effectiveness. This is because students who claimed to like mathematics might be more likely to learn and achieve better in mathematics. Conversely, those who claimed to dislike mathematics might not do well and that would reflect the ineffectiveness of mathematics teachers.

Review of Local Studies on Characteristics of Effective Mathematics Teachers

A review of local literature shows that there are still very few studies (e.g. SEAMEO-RECSAM, 1990; Mohd Majid Konting, 1997; Lim, 2006) that looked into the characteristics of effective mathematics teachers and mathematics teaching.

The first one was a workshop report on the "Thinking in Science and Mathematics (TISM) Project" published by SEAMEO-RECSAM in 1990. During the workshop, seven teacher researchers from a local school were asked to list their perceptions of good teaching and good learning. Table 2 displays a summary of both lists.

In tune with our earlier discussion, Table 2 depicts teachers' perception of good (or effective) teaching as related to two major aspects: (a) teachers' aspect in terms of good planning and teaching presentation; and (b) students' aspect that focus on active participation of students that ensure a positive change in students' behaviours and attitudes towards the learning of mathematics.

Table 2. Perception of teacher researchers on good teaching and learning

Perception of good teaching	Perception of good learning
1. Achievement of objectives in that goal of lessons was attained.	1. That the students are happy at the end of the lesson and that they want more of the lesson taught.
2. Good delivery and presentation.	2. That the students participate by asking more questions and are thinking hard.
3. Good planning of student activities.	3. That the students understand what is being taught and can apply what they have learned to solve problems.
4. Keep students busy.	4. Good learning results in ability to apply knowledge to new situations.
5. Involving participation of students.	5. A good learner is not satisfied with what he knows at the moment. He constantly questions the "truth" of what the teacher says. He also tries to relate what he learns to his previous knowledge.
6. Involving positive changes in students.	
7. Resulting in long periods of retaining the knowledge acquired.	
8. Resulting in students' ability to understand, analyze, and internalize new knowledge.	
9. Resulting in change of behaviours, attitudes toward learning.	
10. Resulting in good learning on the part of students.	

Source: SEOMEO-RECSAM (1990, page 6–7).

The second study by Mohd Majid Konting (1997) observed 58 lessons of 16 effective mathematics teachers from one district. His assumption was that these teachers were nominated as "effective mathematics teachers" by those in authority (including the principal, assistant principal, and head of department), thus their classroom practice might reflect "good practice." Findings of his study show that:

The effective mathematics teachers were inclined to use traditional whole-class teaching strategies and to dominate classroom interaction. There was little group work and little evidence of pupil-centeredness. Their actions were associated with high levels of on-task activity and good pupil behaviour. But the differences are not, to some extent, parallel with the KBSM's recommended pedagogies of pupil-centeredness (p. 17).

Thus, his findings reflected a mismatch between effective teaching practice as recommended by the intended Malaysian mathematics curriculum (KBSM, 1990) and that which was practiced in the mathematics classroom.

With the aim of promoting good practices in mathematics teaching and learning, Lim (2006) described a lesson collaboratively planned by a Lesson Study group of mathematics teachers. The research lesson was taught by one of the teacher members and observed by all the others. On reflection, all these teachers were rather happy with the lesson because it fulfilled many of the characteristics of effective mathematics teaching. These characteristics include:

1. *Student-centred activities that encourage conceptual understanding*
2. *Related to students' daily life experiences*
3. *The students understand what is being taught and can apply what they have learned to solve problems*
4. *Good planning of student activities*
5. *Active participation of students in fun and meaningful activities*
6. *Use of teaching aids that enhance student understanding* (p.210).

Likewise, Lim's findings highlighted the two major similar focuses: first, on the teacher (such as good planning and effective use of teaching aids) and second, on the student (for example, student-centred activities that encouraged active participation and related to students' daily life experiences).

In brief, all three local studies seem to shed some light on the characteristics of effective mathematics teaching practices; nevertheless, most of these findings were inferred indirectly from mathematics teachers attending a workshop (SEAMEO-RECSAM, 1990) or from teaching observations (such as Mohd Majid Konting, 1997 and Lim, 2006). Hence, this chapter aims to draw out the characteristics of effective mathematics teaching practice as explicitly espoused by the Malaysian mathematics teachers and the possible challenges and dilemma faced.

DEFINITION OF EFFECTIVE MATHEMATICS TEACHING

The word "effective" is defined in the Oxford Advanced Learner Dictionary (2000) as "having an effect; producing the intended result" (p.569). It implies that whether something is effective or not is very much dependent upon the intended aims or goals. Hence, effectiveness could be relative and subjective, as well as context-dependent. Very often, effectiveness in mathematics teaching is taken to have reflected from its outcome such as students' achievement in examinations or assessment tasks.

Nevertheless, the definition of effective mathematics teaching is also very much dependent upon one's definition of mathematics. How teachers view school mathematics and mathematics learning will determine how they teach mathematics. For example, if school mathematics is viewed as a collection of formulae and procedures to be memorized and mastered, then teaching methods such as considerable drill and practice, and instrumental or procedural teaching (Skemp, 1976) will be considered as effective. Conversely, if mathematics is viewed as a structure of concepts and relationships and a mental abstraction of the world around us, then mathematics teaching should emphasize relational understanding (Skemp, 1976), problem solving, and mathematical thinking.

In this study, the phrase "effective mathematics teacher" is used instead of "good mathematics teacher." As discussed above, the word "effective" refers more to producing the intended result and is very much dependent upon a person's beliefs about mathematics and mathematics learning while the word "good" tends to cover more general meaning of "high quality," "enjoyable," "helpful," "nice," "skilful," etc. Nevertheless, there were studies that looked into pupils' perceptions of "good mathematics teacher" (see Jules & Kutnick, 1997 and Beishuizen, Hof, van Putten, Bouwmeester & Asscher, 2001) that found similar constructs of good mathematics teachers as described by the teacher's personality, ability, quality of the teaching process, and expected educational outcome obtained by pupils due to the teacher's effort. Findings from these studies were drawn from the pupils' perspective. Hence, for this study that aims to gain the perspective of teachers, the participants will be first asked to define what they perceived to be effective mathematics teaching.

CONCEPTUAL FRAMEWORK OF EFFECTIVE MATHEMATICS TEACHING

The conceptual framework of this study is based on two assumptions. First, quality teaching comes from quality teachers, hence effective teaching is assumed to be displayed by effective teachers. This assumption is derived from the process-product research. For example, the oft-quoted mathematics teaching experiment research project by Good and Grouws (1979) implemented in fourth-grade classrooms in the U.S. In that study, 40 mathematics teachers were divided into two groups. One group of teachers underwent the training with the list of effective mathematics behaviours while the other group of teachers was a control group. A comparison of pre- and post-test results showed that pupils taught by the trained teachers generally outperformed pupils in the control group. This result indirectly indicated that providing proper training of effective teaching behaviors could result in an effective teacher and consequently display effective teaching.

Second, a number of mathematics educators (see e.g. Stigler & Hiebert, 1999; Zaslavsky, Chapman, & Leikin, 2003) share the same view that "teachers teach as they were taught, not how they were taught to teach" (Cooney & Wiegel, 2003, p. 798). Hence, asking teachers to reflect upon who and how their effective mathematics teachers taught may elicit the kind of effective mathematics teaching practice they are most likely to follow. Even for those who could not recall any mathematics teachers that they perceived as effective, it is assumed that they have their ideal set of characteristics of what an effective mathematics teacher should be. Based on these assumptions, this study has been set up to explore the characteristics of effective mathematics teaching as perceived by Malaysian mathematics teachers. In addition, this study asks several questions: what kind of effective mathematics teaching practice are they following in actual practice? Do they have conflicts between what is practiced and what is intended/ideal? Do they face any constraints and dilemmas? These research questions will be addressed in this study.

PARTICPANTS

Ten mathematics teachers participated in this study on a voluntary basis. All except two novice teachers were pursuing their postgraduate studies, either at the master or doctoral level in mathematics education at a university. The two novice teachers had recently graduated with a bachelor degree from the same university and had taught in school for about a year. Thus, these teachers had experiences of mathematics teaching varying from one year to more than 20 years. They were either teaching primary or secondary level mathematics in urban or rural schools. Table 3 displays the background of the participants. Efforts were taken to include mathematics teachers of both genders and the three main ethnic groups in Malaysia (namely, Malay, Chinese, and Indian) to see if there might be some cultural differences in their perceptions of effective mathematics teaching. Nevertheless, analysis of the data shows no observed differences in these participants' views; hence the findings were discussed as a whole and no comparisons were made. It is acknowledged that the limited number of participants in this study might limit the variety and generalizations of the findings.

Table 3. Background of participants

Teacher	Gender	Ethnicity	Years of teaching mathematics	School level	School location	Degree pursuing
TG	Female	Chinese	20	primary	urban	M.Ed.
TJ	Female	Chinese	1	secondary	urban	
TC	Female	Indian	14	primary	urban	M.Ed.
TK	Female	Malay	10	secondary	urban	PhD
TM	Female	Malay	4	secondary	rural	M.Ed.
TE	Male	Chinese	21	secondary	urban	EdD
TO	Male	Chinese	24	secondary	urban	PhD
TH	Male	Malay	1	secondary	rural	
TS	Male	Indian	10	primary	rural	M.Ed.
TU	Male	Malay	21	secondary	rural	PhD

METHOD OF DATA COLLECTION AND ANALYSIS

The qualitative data were collected through one-time, in-depth interviews with the 10 mathematics teachers. All interviews were conducted by the researcher in her office, at a time that was most convenient for the participants. Hence, most interviews were conducted on weekends or in the evenings. The average interview time ranged from 20 minutes to one hour. The data collection period took place over about one month. A list of questions (as explained below) was drafted as a guide for each interview.

To make it more contextual, the interview began by asking participants to reflect and recall the name of one of their mathematics teachers that they considered an effective mathematics teacher. Some could still remember their teachers' name, but a few could not. There were sudden sparks of delight in their eyes when they talked about their effective mathematics teachers. They were also asked to list all the characteristics of their effective mathematics teachers and their teaching practices. Subsequently, the participants were asked to define the conception and characteristic of effective teaching practice. They also self-assessed to see if they considered themselves to be effective mathematics teachers. Lastly, the participants were asked to name the characteristics of their ideal effective mathematics teaching as well as any challenges and constraints they faced in their effort to practice as effective mathematics teachers.

All interview data were transcribed and analyzed qualitatively using the software NVivo 2.0. Data were coded according to the emerging themes, such as a definition of effective mathematics teacher, characteristics of an effective mathematics teacher, as well as the challenges and constraints faced in the pursuit of becoming an effective mathematics teacher. These themes are discussed as follows.

FINDINGS AND DISCUSSION

The Word "Effective" as Perceived by Malaysian Mathematics Teachers

When the participants were asked to define the word "effective" in mathematics teaching, the majority of them (such as teachers: TG, TE and TO) refer to an effective mathematics teacher as someone who is "able to help students to do well in exam." This is a common perception as the ultimate goal of school mathematics learning is often influenced by the examination-oriented culture. Malaysian teachers, students, parents, and the society alike, viewed public examination results as the best indicator of effective teaching and learning.

Another proposed indicator is active participation of students. One participant, TG, explained that active participation is particularly important for mathematics learning. She argued that only when students participated actively in solving mathematical problems and understood the concepts that they could do well in examination, which is consequently considered as effective learning. Her view was supported by another participant, TE, who said that an effective teacher is the one who can make complicated concepts or problems easier for students to understand and the best indicator of the effectiveness is reflected in her/his students' performance or achievement in examinations.

Characteristics of an Effective Mathematics Teacher

The participants were first asked to list the characteristics of an effective mathematics teacher that they had experienced when they were learning mathematics in school. This aims to provide context as well as to gauge participants' perception of effective mathematics teaching from their perspective as students. Analysis of the interview data highlighted the following three major characteristics:

i) A Lot of Practice

All of the participants recalled that their teachers gave them a lot of exercises or mathematical problems to solve. They did not feel bored, instead they found the practices interesting and challenging. This is because, as TO stated, "my teacher gave us practice [with] a lot of previous years' questions. He/she gave relevant examples and worked [with the] examples that ensured me to excel in examination." Another participant, TK, added that, "lessons were interesting because he [his teacher] asked us to challenge each other to see who can do the most number of sums and who can solve faster." This finding indicates there is a strong belief of "practice make perfect" among the participants and their teachers.

ii) Extra Time and Individual Attention

Another significant characteristic expressed by all participants is the extra time and individual attention given by their mathematics teachers. For example:

"She gave me extra time and attention. I [could] see her any time even after school. I rented a room which was near to her home." (TG)

"He gave extra coaching during weekends." (TC)

"He gave extra class [time]. He always [made] sure we [knew] how to answer..."(TU)

Clearly the extra care and attention given by their teachers encouraged them to be interested in mathematics and this further improves their mathematics achievement. This characteristic seems personal and related more to teachers' personalities rather than their teaching practices. However, this positive personality trait of caring and concern for students could have a significant impact on making mathematics teaching effective, as revealed in the participants' experiences.

iii) Clear Explanation

In terms of teaching approaches, all of them claimed that their teachers have "[made] mathematics [easy to] understand," as stated by TG, and according to TC, "he show[ed] every step, from basic to difficult." In addition, some participants stated that their teachers always used clear innovative teaching aids. Consequently, this enhanced the students' understanding and interest in learning mathematics.

Besides the above three characteristics, some participants also pointed out that the importance of rewarding, such as with simple verbal praise (good) or small gifts given by their teachers could have motivated them to learn better. Other characteristics include being patient and helpful, well-prepared and caring. For example, one participant recalled of his teacher, "He never scolded the students who failed in [the] exam but tried to improve the students' knowledge."

Characteristics of an Ideal Effective Mathematics Teacher and Mathematics Teaching

Perhaps it is not a surprise to notice that the above three characteristics resemble some of the characteristics the participants named when they were asked to give their own perspective as effective mathematics teachers. Below are the ideal characteristics of an effective mathematics teacher and mathematics teaching described by the participants:

a) Interesting Lesson

The lesson needs to be interesting to attract students' attention. One primary school mathematics teacher participant (TG) explained, "I do not like to follow the textbook because it usually has a lot of text, makes students very [bored]. I usually use pictures or analogies to explain to them. Put into stories…usually I find my students like to learn mathematics in this way." Another secondary mathematics teacher (TE) shared a similar view, "I always link to daily life situations. I try to catch their attention by telling stories related to their daily life or environment." Another participant (TK) added that she often links the mathematical concepts to the students' experience that they are familiar with.

All of these participants believed that attracting students' interest in learning is the first step to effective mathematics teaching. By linking teaching to students' everyday life as well as to what is happening in the classroom makes students feel mathematics learning is meaningful and interesting. Consequently, they will be motivated to continue learning and attain better achievement and continue this positive cycle.

B) Competent in Content Knowledge and Language Proficiency

Teachers need to be competent in mathematical knowledge and proficient in the language of instruction so that they are able to give clear explanations of concepts. Two participants noted that language competency, especially in English, is particularly important at the present time. This is because there was a switch in the medium of instruction from the Malay language to the English language for teaching mathematics and science in all Malaysian schools in 2003.

Besides language, some participants emphasized the importance of competence in mathematical content knowledge. One of them, an Indian mathematics teacher (TS) related his experience of teaching mathematics in a Chinese school, where nearly 95% of the students were Chinese. He recalled that when he was first posted to the Chinese school, he was asked to teach two classes of upper secondary mathematics.

Teacher S (TS): Some students were prejudice[d] about me because I am an Indian teaching them.

Interviewer (I): Why Indian?

TS: The first classes [students] ask[ed] me, "Sir, you can teach mathematics-kah?" Many times they will ask me [questions] like this. Because the first class majority [students] are Chinese. They are very good at mathematics. They will test me first.

I: How did they test you?

TS: They will find difficult questions and ask me to solve [them]. Then I solved and gave them the solutions and ha-ha, I also gave them harder questions to challenge them. Sometimes they could not solve [these problems], and I provided them with answers. After a few times like this, [only] then they were convinced.

The above case might be unique and linked to cultural prejudice. Nevertheless, to convince students to trust and learn with the teachers, the teachers need to be confident and competent in mathematical content knowledge that they are teaching.

In addition, another participant, TO, added that an effective mathematics teacher is someone who masters the content knowledge and knows how to select a relevant set of questions. These questions should promote mathematics thinking as well as allow students to understand better and to be able to apply this thinking to new problems or situations.

C) Teaching Approach

To produce an effective lesson, all participants agreed that teachers have to use "multiple teaching methods, not only chalk and talk" (TC). For example, another participant, TE, proposed to "use a lot of teaching aids in multiple ways such as ICT and concrete objects." TE believed that using teaching aids would help students understand mathematical concepts easily and hence make teaching more effective. He gave example of using concrete objects (such as models) and computer programs (e.g. Geometer's Sketchpad) to provide students with visual images of three-dimensional concepts. By encouraging his students to participate actively in hands-on and mind-on activities like these, he found even the weak classes became attracted to the teaching and were willing to explore further.

The youngest participant, TJ proposed recycling waste materials such as boxes and cans to create mathematical models. She found many innovative teaching ideas and useful resources from the internet and mathematics journals. TJ acknowledged that it takes a lot of time and effort for teachers and students to recycle and to surf the internet for information. However, she found these efforts are fruitful as both teachers and students could learn a lot from and enjoy these experiences.

d) Classroom Control and Management

Several participants stressed the importance of classroom control and management to ensure an effective teaching and learning classroom climate. TE described in his experience that his school practiced "streaming." Hence, it is a great challenge teaching the weak classes because they are not only weak in academics but also poor in discipline and lack of interest in schooling. According to TE, "these students are usually very weak in mathematics. They tend to talk a lot in class. Indirectly, this constrains the effectiveness of class teaching. So I usually tried to catch their attention by telling stories."

TJ agreed that "teachers need to be strict so that students will hand in their homework punctually." She found that many of her students were lazy about doing homework because they were distracted by many outside activities such as surfing the web at internet cafés, playing internet or video games, as well as loitering at shopping complexes. TG, who taught in a primary school, also faced similar problems with her students. To solve these, she always spent time checking her pupils' homework and ensured class control by using various teaching aids such as pictures, analogies, or stories to attract the attention of her pupils.

e) Personality – Caring, Approachable, and Helpful.

Similar to what they have experienced with their favorite teachers, the majority of the participants agreed that to be an effective mathematics teacher, one has to be "caring" (by TK, TC, and TU); "patient and polite" (TC) ; "good at making jokes" (TK); "motivating and close rapport (like parent) with students" (TU). This was specially the case for teacher TU, who teaches in a residential school where all his students live away from their family. He expressed the importance of caring for his students and was like a parent to them. He related his experience of teaching a class of students who were weak in mathematics. Because he managed to set up a very close relationship with them by giving extra tutoring after school hours and by helping them to resolve their problems like a parent, at the end of the year, he was very happy to see them improve in their mathematics exam results.

CONSTRAINTS, CHALLENGES, AND DILEMMA

Ideally, these teachers would like to practice the characteristics of effective teaching as they mentioned and discussed above. However, in reality or in practice, they faced a number of constraints and challenges. At times, they also faced conflicts and dilemmas that they had to resolve. Below are some examples as described by the participants.

Time Factor

Time constraint is the key factor proposed by all participants. One participant, TE, lamented that, "We have to finish the syllabus according to [a] certain time frame, which was instructed by the State Department of Education. Every school has to follow the schedule strictly so that the students are ready for the examinations set by the state department. We have no choice." It seems as if the scheduling of subject content is controlled or practically dictated by the State Education Department.

Another participant, TG, echoed the same constraint by stating, "We just rush through the syllabus. We hardly have time to try new thing or to teach new ways. Yes, my school fixed the time to finish certain topics, so it is always very rush[ed]."

Probing further, TE reckoned that it was not the problem of too much content but a lot of time wasted due to school holidays and examinations. His description on the usage of time allocated for teaching per year is summarized in Table 4 below.

As shown in Table 4, one year has 52 weeks. After taking away 10 weeks of school holidays, eight weeks of school tests and examinations, as well as two weeks of significant public festivals such as the Chinese New Year and Hari Raya Puasa, there were 32 weeks left for proper teaching. However, according to TE, the final or end-of-the-year examination must always be two to three weeks before holidays so that the teachers have enough time to mark the papers and discuss the results with their students before the long holidays begin. After accounting for that, only 29 weeks were left for real teaching and learning. If there are 14 topics per year, then on average, only two weeks or 10 periods (or 40 min $\times$ 10 = 400 minutes) is allocated for each topic. Four hundred minutes to cover the content of a mathematical topic such as transformation is clearly not sufficient. Consequently, most teachers resort to procedural teaching, which is deemed effective since one can cover a lot of content within a short period of time.

Table 4: Time allocation in a school year calendar

1 year calendar		52 weeks
School holidays per year	March – 1 week May/June – 2 weeks August – 1 week Nov/Dec – 6 weeks	10 weeks
Monthly test	4 times × 1 week each	4 weeks
Mid-semester exam	2 weeks	2 weeks
Final exam	2 weeks	2 weeks
Public festivals:		2 weeks
Chinese New Year	1 week	
Hari Raya Puasa	1 week	
Number of weeks left for teaching		52 – 20 = 32 weeks

Another participant, TO, also agreed that in the present school situation, procedural teaching and drill and practice are the most effective ways of teaching. This is because "With this method, we can be sure to cover the syllabus, and get the students ready for examinations. This is what the school principal and the parents want. As long as students can pass and score in the examinations, everybody is happy."

However, he further stated that most teachers acknowledge that procedural teaching often leads to instrumental understanding which, in the long term, might not be effective for students' mathematics understanding and learning. Ideally, most teachers would like to try different kinds of teaching approaches such as group activities, group projects, investigating and modelling that can promote relational understanding and mathematical thinking. However, all these approaches and activities not only take time to prepare, but they also take a lot of time to carry out. In view of the time constraint, most teachers are often in the dilemma of "teachingto test" or "teaching for understanding."

Administrative Support

In relation to the use of alternative teaching approaches such as student-centred activities and the use of ICT, one participant, TK, complained that sometimes there is a lack of support from the school administrators. For example, when students are actively participating in a student-centred activity, their excitement in the class-room might be considered as too noisy for some administrators. Furthermore, some schools might not have sufficient facilities such as the number of computers, LCDs, classroom space, or teaching aids to support some of these activities. Consequently, this lack of administrative and facility support has forced many teachers to opt for the easy way out, that is, the use of chalk and talk and a lot of drill and practice.

Student Factor

Another significant factor mentioned by the majority of participants is students' predisposition to learning, their interest, motivation as well as foundation in mathe-matical knowledge and skills. For example, TJ found that many of her students lacked interest in learning because they were more attracted to a lot of outside school activities such as sports, internet and computer games, window-shopping, and motorcycle racing. She added, "Students need to have interest, if not, they will not learn. But students nowadays are more interested in outdoor activities, which they find more interesting than learning mathematics in class." Hence, it is a big challenge for teachers to ensure that every student has an interest in learning before the teaching can be effective.

Two other teachers, TG and TE, also shared the same experience that some of their students were so weak in their mathematics foundation that teaching has to start from the very basics. These weak students were often the discipline problem students too because they could not pay full attention in class, and they found mathematics learning difficult and boring. They would not do their homework. This created problems as mentioned by TE that, "Every morning I have to check if they have done their homework and this takes time. Sometimes I have to punish them. All these things just take too much teaching time, so sometimes, I just ignore them. They don't want to study, [so I] let them be. I will focus on those who want to study."

TG added another problem that she faced: "Some kids can talk very well but cannot write it in a proper mathematical way." TG was teaching in a Chinese primary school. She found that some of her students could answer very well orally but they could not express them mathematically in their written work. For example, after teachers explained a word problem, some bright students could answer immediately what kind of operations to use. However, when it came to writing, they jumbled up the sequence of the operations, such as "3 + 15 = 18 – 4 = 14." Hence, these students tended to score better in multiple choice questions in which they did not need to show their algorithm or work. Subsequently, TG said that she would like to give more examples to illustrate and explain the concepts. She would also like to give more written activities for the pupils to practice. Yet, due to time constraints, teachers just rush through to complete the syllabus and to ensure students are ready for examination. This is again another case that depicts the teachers' dilemma of teaching to test or teaching for understanding.

PROPOSED FRAMEWORK OF EFFECTIVE MATHEMATICS TEACHING

Based on a synthesis of the related literature on effective mathematics teaching and the above findings, I propose the framework of effective mathematics teaching as depicted in Figure 1. As shown in Figure 1, effective mathematics teaching comes from effective mathematics teachers. To be an effective mathematics teacher, one needs to possess a certain kind of personality, content knowledge, language competency, and experience in mathematics teaching. However, to ensure effective mathematics teaching, other factors such as class control and management, teaching approaches, curriculum needs, and students' participation also need to be considered. Besides these factors, to produce an effective outcome or high student achievement, a teacher needs to have other supporting conditions such as administrative and parental support.

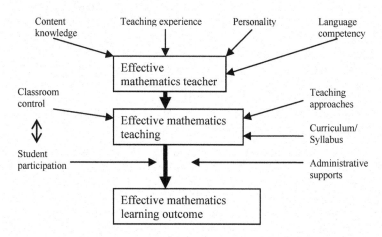

Figure 1. Proposed framework of effective mathematics teaching

Interestingly, a review of the latest studies on characteristics of effective mathematics teachers and teaching (see Cai, Perry, Wong, & Wang in this volume) also revealed a very similar list of characteristics, such as

    (i)   Strong background in mathematics;
    (ii) Adept in instructional skills;
    (iii) Knowing and caring for the students;
    (iv) Classroom management;
    (v) Active engagement of students; and
    (vi) Cultivating students' interests.

Their research compared experienced mathematics teachers' perspectives of effective mathematics teaching from four nations, namely the United States, Australia, the Chinese mainland and Hong Kong. Their findings further support the above framework and imply that the characteristics of effective mathematics teaching are rather universal though there might be differences in emphasis across nations.

IMPLICATIONS AND CONCLUSION

Malaysian mathematics teachers could be effective mathematics teachers. They recognized all the theories and practical experiences of making a mathematics lesson effective. They recognized the importance of relational understanding and mathematical thinking. They would like to promote student-centred and activity-based learning as well as an innovative use of ICT; however, due to time cons-traints and the rigid time frame, the teachers have to resort to procedural teaching and a lot of drills and practices. Hence, the results of this study imply that to ensure effective mathematics teaching, the following changes are needed:

1.   All parties – school administrator, teachers, students and parents, need to change their perception of effectiveness. Effective teaching should not just focus on examination results or mathematics achievement but also on other constructs such as mathematical thinking, relational understanding, and applications of mathematical content knowledge.
2.   There needs to be a change in the present school assessment system which focuses not only on procedural and algorithmic thinking, but also on problem solving and mathematical thinking.
3.   There needs to be a change in students' predisposition and motivation towards learning mathematics.

To conclude, time constraint should not be taken as an excuse anymore. It is high time for us (all Malaysians) to change the mindset of all parties – society, school, parents, teachers and students. To ensure our future generations who are mathematically able so as to be useful in the global society, we have no choice, but to change. We, especially the teachers and the mathematics educators, might have to take the first step to change ourselves and to make our future teachers change, too. As we all understand, in the era of globalization and rapid advancement of information technology and communication, a good foundation of mathematical knowledge is vital, but more importantly, we need to prepare our young generation to be analytical, systematic, logical, and critical as well as to have the ability to solve mathematical problems in daily situations. These are the goals or objectives that have been spelled out explicitly in the Malaysian KBSM mathematics curriculum (MOE, 2000). To achieve these goals, we, Malaysian mathematics teachers and educators, not only must be in search of effective mathematics teaching practices but also ensure that these practices could be actualized.

REFERENCES

Ball, D. L., Hill, H., & Bass, H. (2005). Knowing mathematics for teaching: Who knows mathematics well enough to teach third grade, and how can we decide? *American Educator, 14*, 46. Retrieved from <http://www.aft.org/pubs-reports/american_educator/issues/fall2005/BallF05.pdf>

Bishop, A. J. (1991). Mathematical values in the teaching process. In A. J. Bishop, S. Mellin-Olsen, & J. van Dormolen (Eds.), *Mathematical knowledge: Its growth through teaching* (pp. 195–214). Dordrecht: Kluwer.

Chin, C. (1995). *Mathematics teachers' beliefs, their classroom practices and influences on student learning: Four case studies*. Unpublished Ph.D. Thesis, University of Cambridge, Cambridge, UK.

Cooney, T. J., & Wiegel, H. G. (2003). Examining the mathematics in mathematics teacher education. In A. J. Bishop, M. A. Clements, C. Keitel, J. Kilpatrick, & F. K. S. Leung (Eds.), *Second international handbook of mathematics education* (pp. 795–828). UK: Kluwer Academic Publishers.

Ernest, P. (1989). The impact of beliefs on the teaching of mathematics. In P. Ernest (Ed.), *Mathematics teaching: The state of the art* (pp. 249–254). London: Falmer Press.

Good, T. L., & Grouws, D. A. (1979). The Missouri mathematics effectiveness project: An experimental study in fourth-grade classrooms. *Journal of Educational Psychology, 71*(3), 355–362.

Hill, H., Rowan, B., & Ball, D. L. (2005). Effects of teachers' mathematical knowledge for teaching on student achievement. *American Education Research Journal, 42*(2), 371–406.

Lim Chap Sam. (2001). Teachers' influence on adults' images of mathematics. *Jurnal Pendidik dan Pendidikan (Educators and Education), 17*, 57–67. Penang: PPIP, USM.

Lim Chap Sam. (2006). In search of good practice and innovation in mathematics teaching and learning: A Malaysian perspective. *Tsukuba Journal of Educational Study in Mathematics, 25*, 205–220.

Mohd. Majid Konting. (1997). In search of good practice: A case study of Malaysian effective mathematics teachers' classroom practice. *Journal of Science and Mathematics Education in South East Asia, XX*(2), 8–20.

Seah, W. T. (2005). Negotiating about perceived values differences in mathematics teaching: The case of immigrant teachers in Australia. In H. Chick & J. L. Vincent (Eds.), *Proceedings of the 29th Conference of the International Group for the Psychology of Mathematics Education* (Vol. IV, pp. 145–152). Melbourne: PME.

SEAMEO-RECSAM. (1990). *Workshop on Thinking in Science and Mathematics (TISM) Project: A report*. Penang: SEOMEO Regional Centre for Education in Science and Mathematics.

Shimizu, Y. (2007). Mathematics lesson planning based on cultural scripts: An analysis of teachers' conceptions of lesson structure. In Lim Chap Sam, et al. (Eds.), *Proceedings of the 4th East Asia Regional Conference on Mathematics Education [EARCOME4]* (pp. 553–560), 18–22 June 2007, Universiti Sains Malaysia, Penang, Malaysia.

Skemp, R. R. (1976). Relational understanding and instrumental understanding. *Mathematics Teaching, 77*, 20–26.

Stigler, J. W., & Hiebert, J. (1999). *The teaching gap: Best ideas from the world's teachers for improving education in the classroom*. New York: The Free Press.

Thompson, A. G. (1992). Teachers' beliefs and conceptions: A synthesis of the research. In D. A. Grouws (Ed.), *Handbook of research on mathematics teaching and learning* (pp. 127–146). New York: Macmillan.

Zaslavsky, O., Chapman, O., & Leikin, R. (2003). Professional development of math educators: Trends and Tasks. In A. J. Bishop, M. A. Clements, C. Keitel, J. Kilpatrick, & F. K. S. Leung (Eds.), *Second international handbook of mathematics education* (pp. 877–917). UK: Kluwer Academic Publishers.

Chap Sam LIM
Universiti Sains Malaysia

KATJA MAASS

WHAT ARE TEACHER'S BELIEFS ABOUT EFFECTIVE MATHEMATICS TEACHING?

A Qualitative Study of Secondary School Teachers in Germany

INTRODUCTION

The improvement of mathematics education and the introduction of innovative aspects into day-to-day classroom teaching are some of the major aims of research and design in education. However, it is often difficult to achieve these. Despite the efforts of researchers and curriculum designers, changes in mathematics education take place rather slowly. One factor influencing these changes is teachers' beliefs. It is evident that what is regarded as effective teaching from a teacher's perspective has a huge influence on what goes on in mathematics classrooms. In order to gain a deeper insight into teachers' beliefs about mathematics and its teaching and possible connections between different groups of beliefs, a qualitative study has been carried out that will be described here. The relevant research questions of the study were:

- What beliefs can teachers have about mathematics as a science?
- What beliefs about effective mathematics teaching can teachers have?
- Can a relationship among the various types of beliefs be established?
- Can different types of teachers be identified according to their beliefs about effective teaching?

This paper will focus on teachers' beliefs about effective teaching as indicated by the title of the book.

THEORETICAL BACKGROUND

Beliefs

Definition. Teachers' beliefs about mathematics and mathematics education are thought to have a major influence on the way in which innovative ways of teaching are implemented into day-to-day mathematical lessons (Bishop, Seah, & Chin, 2003; Chapmann, 2002; Llinares, 2002; Ponte et al., 1994; Gellert, 1998). The importance of taking a closer look at teachers' beliefs is highlighted by the results of research. Kaiser (2006) shows that innovations required by the curriculum can be interpreted by the teacher in such a way that they fit into their belief system.

J. Cai, G. Kaiser, B. Perry and N.-Y. Wong (eds.), Effective Mathematics Teaching from Teachers' Perspectives: National and Cross-National Studies, 141–161.
© *2009 Sense Publishers. All rights reserved.*

The same holds true for the tasks chosen (Kaiser 2006). Additionally, Lloyd (2002) found that teachers' beliefs about mathematical education have a strong connection to the mathematics lessons they experienced themselves as children.

However, different definitions of beliefs and different concepts are used within the discussion about mathematics education (Pehkonen & Törner, 1996; Op't Enyde, de Corte, & Verschaffel, 2002). Furinghetti and Pehkonen (2002) compare these various definitions and point out the differences among them, discussing as they do so the question of whether beliefs are incontestable personal knowledge and whether a relationship can be found between beliefs and knowledge. From an epistemological point of view, they suggest differentiating between objective and subjective knowledge, to regard beliefs as subjective knowledge and to take into consideration affective components as well. They also differentiate between deeply rooted beliefs and surface beliefs, the first of which are regarded as harder to be changed.

Following on from Törner, the term "beliefs" will be used here. According to Törner and Pehkonen (1996), beliefs will be defined as follow:

Beliefs are composed of a relatively long-lasting subjective knowledge of certain objects as well as the attitudes linked to that knowledge. Beliefs can be conscious or unconscious, whereby the latter type are often distinguished by an affective character (p.6).

Features

Green (1971) named three dimensions that characterize beliefs:
The cluster structure: Both beliefs and knowledge are organized in clusters. A belief can never exist completely independently of other beliefs. Beliefs are always organized in groups. Aguirre and Speer (2000) used a similar concept, namely "belief bundle."

The Quasi-logical Structure.   Closely related to the cluster structure of beliefs is their quasi-logical structure. The way in which beliefs are connected means that some beliefs can be derived from others or are closely related. However, whereas in the case of knowledge one can talk of there being a logical relationship which is comprehensible and arises by definition from premises, the relationship among beliefs is described as being quasi-logical. Everyone recognizes a connection among their own beliefs that is unique to the individual and is therefore not necessarily logical.

The Psychological Significance.   For many people, some beliefs are more important than others. Consequently, the most important beliefs are referred to as central, the less important ones as peripheral. This distinction is of particular significance in relation to the convertibility of beliefs: one assumes that peripheral beliefs are easier to change than central ones (Furenghetti & Pehkonen, 2002).

A person can have central beliefs that are contradictory (Green 1971, Abelson 1979). Green (1971) gives as a reason for this the organization of beliefs into clusters, which are separated and protected from each. The cluster structure, the quasi-logical structure and psychological significance are connected to one another and come together to form a whole, which distinguishes beliefs and can also serve to explain individual belief systems and changes to beliefs.

Altogether, beliefs are believed to be hard to change (Törner, 2002). Some studies, however, indicate that it can be possible under certain circumstances (Kaasila, Hannula, Laine & Pehkonen, 2006; Maass, 2004).

Categories

While beliefs are of a very complex nature, certain types of beliefs about mathematics can be distinguished (Törner, 2002). These are, for example, beliefs about mathematics as a science, beliefs about mathematics as a subject at school, beliefs about the learning of mathematics, beliefs about the role of the mathematics teachers and beliefs about the role of students.

A further means of distinguishing between certain categories of teachers' beliefs was developed by Grigutsch (see Grigutsch, 1996 or Grigutsch, Raatz, & Törner, 1998). The following categories of teachers' mathematical beliefs could be reconstructed: the aspect of scheme (mathematics is a fixed set of rules); the aspect of process (in mathematics, problems are solved); the aspect of formalism (mathematics is a logical and deductive science); and the aspect of application (mathematics is important for our lives and for society). Similar categories can be found within the international discussion. Ernest (1991) and Dionne (1984) differentiate between a traditional perspective, a formalist perspective and a constructivist perspective, which seem to correspond to the aspect of scheme, of formalism and of process.

These beliefs, however, mainly refer to mathematics as a science and not to mathematics education. In addition to the categories stated above, further categories for teachers' beliefs can be reconstructed. In a study of the teaching of probability, categories referring to effective mathematics teaching and the usefulness of mathematics lessons for students (Eichler, 2006), and categories referring to students and the general framework of school have been identified (Eichler, 2002).

However, concerning the distribution of the various aspects in teachers' beliefs, there are different results. Grigutsch, Raatz, and Törner (1998) discovered that the majority of teachers taking part in a teacher training course seem to have many application-oriented and process-oriented beliefs. In contrast, a group of teachers investigated by Kaiser (2006) had mainly formalist and scheme-oriented beliefs.

The widespread scheme of belief-categories described above was used as a basis for data evaluation in this study. In order to obtain information about teachers' beliefs regarding effective mathematics teaching, within Grigutsch's system, a difference was made between beliefs referring to mathematics education and those referring to mathematics as a science (Törner, 2002). Finally, beliefs referring to the general framework and beliefs about students were also taken into account. With the intention of finding a possible relationship between groups of beliefs, data collection was not restricted to beliefs about effective teaching. It included all

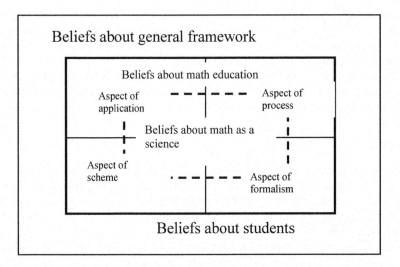

Figure 1. Categorization based on the theoretical framework

beliefs related to mathematics and its teaching and thus took care of the cluster structure and the quasi-logical structure of beliefs. Fig. 1 shows the categorization that was used at the beginning as a theoretical framework.

The German School System

In Germany, there are three kinds of secondary schools. Students are separated at the age of 10–11 according to their ability. Those with low abilities go to the *Hauptschule* for another 5 years, those with average abilities go to the middle *Realschule* for another 6 years, and those with high abilities go to the *Gymnasium* for another 9 years.

All three types of schools are intended to give students a general education. Students of the *Hauptschule* and the *Realschule* are prepared to learn a profession afterwards. The focus, however, is not on practical skills but on general education.[1] The main difference between the three schools, therefore, is the learning level. Additionally, students of the *Hauptschule* tend to have more social problems than the students of the *Realschule* and *Gymnasium*.

Teacher training for the three types of schools is very different. Teachers for the *Hauptschule* are trained together with Primary School teachers and partly with *Realschule* teachers. The mathematical education they get – especially in comparison with the teachers at the *Gymnasium* – is of a low level. In addition, a lot of teachers who teach mathematics at the *Hauptschule* are not educated to be mathematics teachers. However, they do get a lot of pedagogical instruction. By contrast, those who want to teach mathematics at a *Gymnasium* (up to higher secondary level) get a scientific education in mathematics, whereas their pedagogical education is often not regarded as important.

Since 2004, new standards for mathematics education have been in place throughout Germany that are based on the current discussion about mathematics education. These standards have the same focus for all types of schools. Within these standards, six main competencies are named which are supposed to be taught within six main areas of content. These main competencies are mathematical modelling, problem solving, reasoning, communicating, using mathematical representations and using formal mathematical symbols. Based on these standards, there are now new curricula in some parts of Germany. These new curricula differ enormously from the older ones.

Nevertheless, it is still possible for teachers not to change their style of teaching because regional comparative tests still do not include very open tasks or modelling tasks, although there have been changes towards more open and more realistic tasks. Additionally, the new curricula leave a lot of leeway for personal interpretation. Altogether, this has led to a new situation in Germany whereby many teachers just continue with business as usual while others try to change the way they teach.

METHODOLOGICAL BACKGROUND

The study described here is mainly a qualitative study. A basic goal of qualitative research is to explain complex relations within a day-to-day context, rather than explaining individual relationships in isolation (Flick, Kardorff, & Steinke, 2002). It would rather discover new things than prove things that have already been discovered. In this study, teachers' beliefs about mathematics and its effective teaching are to be explored in detail.

An essential characteristic for the selection of sample survey and evaluation methods was the principle of openness: since not much is known about teachers' beliefs about effective teaching and their reasoning patterns, hypotheses should not be brought to the study but rather developed while dealing with the data and then be formulated as results (Flick 2000).

The sample group in this study included 20 *Gymnasium* teachers and 20 *Hauptschule* teachers. Teachers of both school types were chosen in order to have as wide a variety as possible. Additionally, teachers were chosen according to the following criteria: sex, location of the school, and teaching experience. To obtain information about teachers, the heads of various schools were asked by means of a brief questionnaire. From those teachers willing to take part in an interview (about 100), 40 were chosen who together provided as great variation as possible (Flick, 2000).

In order to minimize the risk of just getting answers teachers might think a researcher would like to hear, interviews were carried out by student assistants specially trained for this project. In this way, a more informal, relaxed atmosphere was guaranteed.

In this study, semi-structured interviews were used to collect data about teachers' beliefs. The interview questions should leave enough space for a wide range of teachers' answers, and at the same time the questions should elicit as much information as possible about teachers' mathematical beliefs (Flick 2000). In order to obtain information about their beliefs about effective mathematics teaching and about mathematics as a science, questions concerning both aspects were chosen and clearly distinguished (see Appendix).

Fundamental to this evaluation of the study are procedures for creating types (Kelle & Kluge, 1999) and the qualitative content analysis according to Mayring (2003); on the other hand, elements of the quantitative content analysis were also employed (Bortz & Döring, 2005). If one understands the dichotomy "quantitative vs. qualitative" as a continuum, then this study integrates some aspects which are assigned more to the qualitative pole and some assigned more to the quantitative (for the integration of qualitative and quantitative aspects in content analysis, see Groeben & Rustemeyer, 1994).

Overall, a coded evaluation of the interviews was carried out, whereby the relevant approach to reality was always seen in terms of the situational context and to the subjective relationship between meanings. The basis for the evaluation is the categories model illustrated in the chapter entitled "Theoretical Background", (following on from the quantitative content analysis of Bortz & Döring, 2005). In addition, to aid differentiation, in-vivo codes were used, which means codes based directly on the words of teachers (Mayring, 2003). The evaluation was, on the one hand, deductive, using the named theory-based categories, and on the other hand, inductive, based on the material. The synthesis of both through this deductive-inductive methodology led to a clear specification of the categories.

As part of the evaluation process, three approaches from the qualitative content analysis (Mayring, 2003) were used:

1. *Summary content analysis*: First of all, the source text is summarized into a short text by means of paraphrasing and reduction of similar phrases. A more thorough investigation of the qualitative content analysis follows.

2. *Explanatory content analysis*: To help elucidate passages that are still not clear, other statements and information from the interviewee are used (e.g. other passages from the interview, behaviour during the interview, teacher biography). Thus, between the different statements a fabric of relationships is created from which certain tendencies emerge, thereby presenting an overall picture of the interview.

3. *Structural content analysis*: With the final synopsis of the material, standard structuring can be carried out in a last step in which cases are compared or evaluated under certain criteria. One possible result of this analysis can be a typology.

Procedures for creating types and comparing and contrasting cases play an important role in qualitative research, because in this way the complex reality is reduced and made concrete (Kelle & Kluge, 1999). A typology is the result of grouping processes in which one or more characteristics are used to allocate objects to groups in such a way that the objects within the groups are as similar as possible and the actual groups are as different as possible. The newly formed groups are called types. According to Kelle and Kluge (1999), the process of creating types is carried out in four steps:

A. Finding relevant dimensions of comparison: finding and defining categories of beliefs that help to compare the individual cases.

B. Grouping of cases: the individual cases are grouped according to the dimensions found in the step described above. The aim is to group such cases which are as similar as possible while differences between groups should be as big as possible. At the same time, the groups can have partial overlap (Kelle & Kluge 1999). This means that on a continuum, types can also represent characteristics that show only a gradual change from one to the next.

C. Analysis of contextual relationships: The groups and their characteristics should not only be described; also contextual relationships should be searched for. This analysis normally leads to a reduction of types.

D. Characterisation of the created types.

The evaluation process in this study followed a combination of the steps described by Mayring (2003) and by Kelle and Kluge (1999).

I. Each case (teacher) was first of all analyzed individually with the help of codes. A summary content analysis was written for every case. Using the explanatory content analysis, unclear passages were clarified. Both steps resulted in a case description of every case (Mayring, 2003). In carrying out these analyses, categories which helped to compare individual cases (step A of Kelle & Kluge, 1999) were also looked for. Initially, the categories used for this step were those described in Fig. 1. In-vivo codes lead to new codes and thus a new categorisation for analysis (see Fig. 2 p. 149 and the description in "results of the study – categorisation of beliefs"). Changing the codes of analysis from the beginning to the end of data evaluation naturally leads to a circular process of data-analysis.

II. Grouping of cases: This step refers to step B of Kelle and Kluge (1999). In this step, cases were grouped according to the categorisation found in step I.

III. This step followed steps C and D as described by Kelle and Kluge (1999). Steps II and III of this method together also represent step 3, as defined by Mayring (2003). An analysis of contextual relationships was carried out which led to a characterization of types. Within the chapter "results of the study," some results of the analysis of contextual relationships will be described.

In the end, two main groups of teachers out of the whole cohort of teachers (see chapter results) could be identified. Each of these could be further divided into two subgroups. The two case studies described below are two cases that are very typical for the two main groups. They are in some way situated at two opposing ends of a long continuum, starting off with transmission teaching and ending with an open style of teaching. Within the chapter "results of the study," the characterisation of types will be given. Each case from the whole cohort of 40 cases was adjusted to the types created. Although not every case matches completely the description of types given below, the two groups could be identified very clearly. A diagram showing the frequencies will be also given below.

The objectivity of the approach was ensured through group analyses and discussions and the independent analyses of several people. Regarding the overall description of a certain teacher in the study, it was observed that the individual analyses often produced the same results. In the case of single statements, however, the analyses often differed. Therefore, the relevant statements were discussed in the group and interpreted accordingly as part of consensus building. The few people whose overall descriptions had led to different results were discussed again at the end of the evaluation before finally being classified.

RESULTS OF THE STUDY

The description of the results aims, on the one hand, to describe the results as clearly as possible, and, on the other hand, tries to elucidate the process of data evaluation.

In the following, we will first describe the categorization of beliefs used to carry out step I in data evaluation as described within the chapter "methodological background." The reconstructed categorisation of mathematical beliefs of teachers forms a first important result of study. The result of step I being case descriptions taken from the whole random sample of teachers, we will then turn to a description of two example cases, giving insight into two specific cases and into how all the individual cases where analyzed. These two cases are also prototypes for the created types. Afterwards, we will turn to the grouping process and the creation of types. We will first look at the groupings we expected and that did not turn out to be relevant, which is another important result of the study. Following this, we will look at contextual relationships as described in step III above, which is required in order to create the typology. Finally, we will describe the created types as the most important result of the study.

Categorization of Beliefs

Using Grigutsch's categorization (1996) as a starting point and its extension as described in the theoretical background (see Fig. 1), the analysis of data leads to a categorization of teachers' beliefs about effective mathematics teaching and beliefs related to these beliefs (see Fig. 2). While the scheme proposed in Fig. 1 focuses on beliefs about mathematics as a science, it turned out that most teachers who were interviewed focus on mathematics teaching. Categories that have not been considered in Fig. 1 arose. Additionally, it became clear that many types of beliefs are interrelated and thus have a cluster structure (see theoretical background).

The following categories of beliefs about effective teaching could be reconstructed in the whole cohort of teachers:
– *Beliefs about the teaching style*: While some teachers seemed to regard the explanation of rules and standard exercises (transmission teaching) as effective and chose their tasks accordingly, others regarded independent solving processes of the students as effective (learning process teaching) and chose open problems as tasks. Differences could also be found concerning context-free or context-related teaching.
– *Beliefs about teaching methods and media:* Teachers regarded using different teaching methods such as teacher-student-talk or group work effective.

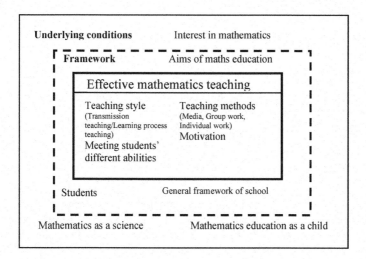

Figure 2. Categories of beliefs about effective teaching

The following categories seemed to be closely related to the beliefs about effective teaching (details about the relationships will be explained later):

– *Beliefs about the aims of mathematics education*: Aims identified by the teachers were the development of logical or spatial thinking, learning to calculate or learning to solve or apply mathematics. Some teachers named special mathematical contents as an aim.

– *Beliefs about how to meet students' different abilities within one class*: Some teachers referred to additional tasks they give to higher achieving students and others seemed to prefer open tasks as a means of coping with students' different abilities.

– *Beliefs about their own mathematics education at school*: Some teachers regard their mathematics education – which seemed to have been mainly transmission teaching – as highly effective; others disliked it.

– *Beliefs about the general framework of school*: While some teachers regarded the framework (lack of time, curriculum) as an important reason for not integrating open problem- solving tasks; others did not regard this as an obstacle.

– *Beliefs about students*: While some teachers regarded the students' abilities or their expectations as an important reason for not integrating open problem-solving tasks, others did not regard this as an obstacle.

– *Beliefs about mathematics as a science*: Beliefs according to the categorization of Grigutsch (1996) could be reconstructed.

The categories described above were used to evaluate all the individual cases and to carry out comparisons between cases. In the following, we will describe two cases as a examples, both of which are prototypes of the two types described later (see below). The case descriptions elucidate the results of the analysis of all 40 individual cases. The final evaluation of the case examples is based on the whole interview, but for reasons of space, we will only describe here the results of this evaluation and give some quotations as an illustration.

Case Example Claus (Male)

Claus is a teacher at the German Gymnasium. He studied mathematics and physics at university. He has been teaching for decades.

Claus regards the training of students' logical thinking as a main goal of mathematics education.

> *"Mathematics education is first and foremost an education in basic logic, an exercise in logical thinking."*

He names further aims, such as making mathematics a basis for other sciences or calculating in daily life. These aspects, however, do not seem to be very important for him because he keeps coming back to logical thinking. This aim seems to influence his beliefs about effective mathematics teaching.

> *"Logical thinking can be exercised in many areas of mathematics. You must not think that the current curriculum is the only way to exercise logical thinking."*

This aim appears to determine what he regards as effective teaching. He explains how he exercises logical thinking effectively.

> *"[When choosing tasks] it is very important to proceed in tiny little steps, from simpler tasks to more difficult tasks, [so] that you are not too hasty [...] you have to proceed in very tiny steps."*

In his lessons he clearly distinguishes between explanation and exercise.

> *"One lesson clearly determines what I do in the following lesson: whether I have to do exercises or whether I can proceed with content."*

In this system of exercises and proceeding with content he regards his own explanations as highly effective.

> *"An explanation of mathematics is the most important thing; the teacher must be able to do this; [...] this comes first!"*

He is even of the opinion that students cannot really work without explanations.

> *"It is, of course, great if you can support students in understanding independently, but of course explanation is always necessary."*

He seems to regard problem solving as highly ineffective, if not impossible.

> *"The teacher cannot conduct mathematics lessons as some optimistic pedagogical experts may wish. [...] Mathematics has been developed over hundreds of years. How can students invent this by themselves every year?*

This [mathematics education] is only possible if the teacher directs the lessons and [...] explains the things."

In his opinion, open tasks and mathematics do not belong together, and for this reason he does not choose them for his lessons. Additionally, context-related tasks do not seem appropriate to him for mathematics lessons.

"[Context-related tasks] are not really important in my lessons because the most important aim I see is an education in logic."

He regards context-related tasks as too complicated for his students because here students have to proceed from the level of the context to a more abstract level. The teaching methods he prefers relate to his way of proceeding.

"Students have to be able to write down something in the place where they are sitting [...], and they need a direct view to the blackboard because there everything is explained. So they cannot sit around a big table like in conferences. [...] The most important media is the blackboard. [...] The work at the blackboard with chalk is the most efficient way to explore things with a large number of students."

Additionally, he regards group work as highly inefficient.

"Normally, groups are put together by chance. This means there are groups where there is one good student with two or three weak students who show no interest in the tasks. Then nothing happens, because the good student loses interest and the weak students do not want to engage themselves."

Apart from this explanation as to why he does not use group work, he otherwise does not appear to differentiate between the different levels of his students' ability. Furthermore, it would seem he does not use explicit means to motivate students; he only briefly refers to motivation created by the subject itself and the grades students get.

In conclusion, for Claus, effective teaching seems to consist of explanations given by the teacher and of exercises. In his opinion, students are not able to solve given problems, and he regards context-related mathematics as not necessary to teach students logical thinking.

Case Example Peter (male)

Peter studied physics and mathematics to become a teacher at *Gymnasium*. He has 13 years' teaching experience and is involved in teacher training. Peter's beliefs about effective mathematics teaching differ greatly from those of Claus. First of all, he sees totally different aims for mathematics education.

"The most important aspect is fun. [...] You have to make students see that mathematics is fun. And this is possible also for low achieving students. [...] And it is one big aim for me that my students say [...] 'Okay, this is a problem, I will try to solve it.' [...] That is all I want."

He obviously wants to enable students to solve problems and this aim seems to be significant for his beliefs about effective mathematics teaching.

"Just imagine you didn't allow a child to make any mistakes [when trying to learn to walk] or you would say, 'You have to do it exactly as I do.' You can be assured that no child in the world would be able to walk [...], and this is how we do mathematics education."

In his opinion, students need to experience things themselves when trying to learn mathematics.

"I not always but often try to find situations where students can discover things on their own and where they also have the chance to make mistakes. [...] The aspect 'mistakes' is one of the most important in mathematics education. It is a huge misconception of mathematics teachers that mistakes should be banned from mathematics education. In this way we lose students."

Peter obviously regards making mistakes as a relevant part of learning mathematics effectively. In order to give the students the opportunity to make mistakes he often uses group work.

"I divide students into groups, without saying anything, and then they have to work on a problem I give them. Afterwards, the groups present the solutions. Some of them may be correct, some brilliant, others will be a catastrophe and others will have interesting mistakes."

References to reality are also important for Peter.

"In the old days, first mathematics was taught and then applications of the respective topic were shown. My way of teaching is the other way round. [...] I start off from the situation [...] and develop mathematics out of it. And it is a real application which has relevance to life [...], and very often it is an application which is not only has relevance to life but is also of interest to the students."

He believes that applications do not discriminate against low achieving students.

"If you give the students a context-related task, then some students of course have difficulties. If I give them other tasks [...], other students have difficulties [...] You cannot say that especially low achieving students have problems."

Additionally, he regards it as effective for the improvement of student understanding if they explain mathematics content to each other. By doing so, the students who explain, as well as those who need explanations, learn.

"Anna explains something to her [...] in a language which may not be exact in a mathematical sense, maybe even wrong, but which Paula understands. [...] Not only Paula but also Anna learns from this. [...] Learning by teaching."

In Peter's opinion, it is very important and effective if students work together without the teacher and if he only has to help in cases of serious problems In order to support these aims, he names a wide range of methods. He emphasizes the necessity of selecting a method that fits the chosen task. So, in his view, group work, for example, is appropriate when the students need to cooperate in order to discover new things.

> *"When students are supposed to discover things, I choose group work to make the students inspire [one another]."*

Additionally, he uses several media, such as calculators, computers, the overhead projector and, of course, the blackboard. If students are asked to present their group work, they have to use posters. He also makes the students write articles about mathematics.

> *"I like to have students write articles about mathematics, from age 10 to age 19. They get a certain mathematical topic which they have to deal with at their level, and they like it. [When] [t]hey are allowed to write [about] mathematics or fairy tales, they do the craziest things, this is really good, very good. And these things help to make students like mathematics."*

In his view, the most important way to motivate students is to show them that mathematics can be fun.

Altogether, Peter's belief-system about effective mathematics teaching focuses on giving the students the opportunity to work independently and to have fun discovering things. In light of these aims, he seems to select tasks and teaching methods.

Peter's and Claus' beliefs about effective mathematics teaching are rather contrasting and mark in some way the two opposing ends of a long scale of belief-systems about mathematics education. Peter and Claus are case-studies for two big groups that could be identified (see below).

Grouping of Cases

During the grouping process, we looked first for groups which appeared obvious, e.g. groups according to the type of school or the teaching experience. The analysis of data showed no relevant differences between teachers' beliefs in terms of their gender or how much teaching experience they had. Additionally, differences between teachers of the *Hauptschule* and the *Gymnasium* concerning effective mathematics teaching were relatively small or almost non-existent. Considering the different forms of teacher training and the different types of students, this result is remarkable and forms an important outcome of the study.

Differences between the teachers at the *Gymnasium* and the *Hauptschule* related mainly to beliefs about mathematics as a science, as well as some other differences. Some of these beliefs seem to be related to beliefs about effective mathematics teaching. However, in general, the differences in these beliefs highlight the fact that the similarity of teachers' beliefs about effective teaching is an important result. Therefore, these differences will be described here briefly.

Beliefs about Mathematics as a Science. The mathematical beliefs of many *Gymnasium* teachers seem to consist of formalism-oriented beliefs. Furthermore, the teachers seemed to have a strong sense of the usefulness of mathematics for the development of society and also for day-to-day life. Concrete examples, however, were seldom given. Few process-oriented beliefs could be identified and almost no scheme-oriented beliefs. The teachers of the *Hauptschule* seemed to have less pronounced beliefs about mathematics as a science than the others did. Most of the answers they gave referred to mathematical education. They described mathematics as logical and structured but were not more explicit. Although stressing a usefulness of mathematics in daily life and professions, they apparently only saw the use for elementary mathematics.

Interest in Mathematics. All teachers of the *Gymnasium* showed a high interest in mathematics. *Hauptschule* teachers did not express any particular interest in mathematics as a science but were merely interested in teaching mathematics.

Beliefs about the Aims of Mathematics Education. Most Gymnasium teachers seem to regard the preparation of the students for university as an important aim of their lessons, regardless of the fact that only some of the students will go to university. In contrast, *Hauptschule* teachers often named calculating as preparation for life.

Beliefs about Motivation. Student motivation did not seem to be very important for *Gymnasium* teachers. Students were expected to be motivated simply because they are at a *Gymnasium*. In contrast, the issue of motivation was regarded as very important by *Hauptschule* teachers in terms of making teaching effective. These differences between the two types of teachers may be seen in connection with their education at university and their teaching experience at school. However, neither the different types of teacher training nor the different beliefs about mathematics as a science that teachers of both schools have (pronounced vs. no pronounced beliefs) seem to have a major impact on what teachers regard as effective mathematics teaching. The reasons for this could be further influential factors, such as their own experience with mathematical lessons (see theoretical framework) or, despite all differences, similar features in their teacher education.

In contrast to these first grouping efforts, the grouping process based on the categories described above suggest that teachers' beliefs can be distinguished mainly according to two aspects of the dimension "teaching style": the aspect "transmission teaching or learning process teaching" and the aspect "context-free or context-related teaching." All other dimensions seemed to be more or less connected to these aspects, as the analysis of contextual relationships and connections showed. The main results of this analysis will be described in the following section. More details will become clear in the description of types given afterwards.

Contextual Relationships

Teachers who preferred highly pre-structured lessons and regarded teacher explanations as the most effective way of teaching (transmission teaching) gave reasons for not integrating open problem solving tasks or modelling tasks. These reasons either referred to the students or the general framework of school. Concerning the students, they were of the opinion that students are not able to solve these tasks, do not like solving these tasks or to not understand long texts. Referring to the framework, they named a lack of time in lessons, a lack of applications of mathematics, a lack of tasks, too many students per class, and an overlapping with other subjects.

In contrast, teachers who apparently regard the integration of open and reality-based tasks and independent learning as effective (learning process teaching) did not view these aspects as critical, or even referred to problem solving as a means to differentiate between students of different levels of competencies.

Reasons for this different perception of students and framework may be found in the different aims seen for mathematics education and in their application-orientated beliefs. Case-comparing and case-contrasting analysis showed that teachers who referred to mathematics education as a learning process named as aims of mathematical education the ability to solve problems, to apply mathematics to real life, to see the various characteristics of mathematics and to see mathematics as a cultural heritage. Apparently they did not expect the students to be able to apply mathematics or solve problems without dealing with these issues in class. When asked about the relevance of mathematics, they were able to give various examples. Additionally, a huge variety of teaching methods was named and seen as a means to support the ideas of applications and problem solving.

In contrast to these teachers, a different focus concerning the aims of mathematics education could be reconstructed for those teachers referring to transmission teaching. They named as aims the ability to calculate, the development of a spatial sense, knowledge of mathematics, and the education in logical thinking. Those who named the ability to apply mathematics to daily life seemed to expect students to do the transfer themselves. Whilst some of them did consider context-related mathematics to be an important aspect of mathematics education, others seem to regard applications as not belonging to mathematical lessons. They could name very few situations in daily life where mathematics is applied and did not seem to know appropriate reality-related tasks. Teaching through group work or through student explanations was considered to be too difficult for the students. Some teachers were disappointed because initial efforts to change their way of teaching were unsuccessful.

These contextual relationships again show the cluster structure and the quasilogical structure of beliefs (see theoretical background). We will now look at the final types created based on the insights of the steps I – III, some of which have been described above. In the end there seemed to be two main groups (types), both of which could be further divided into two sub-types.

Types of Teachers Concerning their Beliefs about Effective Mathematics Teaching

Type I. – Transmission teacher: Logical thinking, calculation, spatial thinking and knowledge of mathematics are seen as the most important aims in mathematics education. With the intention of reaching these goals, both teacher explanation and standard exercises are considered as highly effective. Mathematics lessons that are highly pre-structured by the teacher and leave little leeway for the student to work independently are considered highly successful. In contrast, open tasks and problem solving tasks are seen as ineffective. Different levels of student ability seem to be met with different amounts of tasks while doing exercises. The teacher seems to prefer the blackboard and the textbook to other media, and the main teaching methods chosen are teacher-student talk in plenary and individual work.

To explain why they did not integrate open problem-solving tasks or modelling tasks, the teacher referred to the students or the general framework of school or mathematics as a subject as described above. This teacher believes the lessons he experienced as a child as were good. If he teaches at a *Gymnasium*, he has formalism-oriented beliefs about mathematics as a science. If he teaches at a *Hauptschule*, he has no pronounced beliefs about mathematics as a science but focuses on mathematics education.

Two subtypes could be identified:

I.a: Transmission teacher with focus on context-free mathematics: The teacher focuses on context-free mathematics. Context-related mathematics is regarded as not effective in relation to his aims (see Claus).

I.b: Transmission teacher with focus on context-related mathematics: The teacher wants the students to learn how to apply mathematics later in life. To reach these aims, tasks that are related to daily life are regarded as important. However, they have to be directly connected to certain mathematics content; emphasis is put on finding an exact solution. Open context-related tasks and modelling tasks are not considered important.

Type II. – Learning process teacher. According to the beliefs of this teacher, mathematics teaching is effective when the thinking processes of students are initiated. He names as aims of mathematical education the ability to solve problems, to apply mathematics to real life, to see the various characteristics of mathematics and to see mathematics as a cultural heritage. To reach these goals, open tasks and problem solving tasks are regarded as important and methods where students work independently– such as group work – are chosen. Explanations by the teacher are not regarded as effective. The teacher tries to meet the students' various levels of ability by letting students work on open tasks independently and on their own level. Several media are used.

He did not enjoy the mathematics lessons he experienced as a student and became a teacher to improve mathematics education. If he teaches at a *Gymnasium*, he has process and application-oriented beliefs about mathematics as a science. If he teaches at a *Hauptschule*, he has no pronounced beliefs about mathematics as a science but focuses on mathematics education.

Two subtypes could be identified:

II.a: Learning process teacher with focus on context-free mathematics: The teacher mainly focuses on context-free mathematics. He seems to use context-related tasks only occasionally to make mathematics more meaningful.

II.b: Learning process teacher with focus on context-related mathematics: One aim of the teacher is to show how mathematics can be applied in life. To fulfil this aim, open context-related tasks and modelling tasks are chosen as often as possible. Emphasis is put on tasks that start with the experience of the students (see Peter).

The data evaluation showed a relationship between groups of beliefs: the beliefs about effective teaching seem to be strongly related to the beliefs about the aims of mathematics education and beliefs about methods. Additionally, there seems to be a connection between the mathematics education the teacher experienced as a child, the beliefs about his students and organizational constraints. For those teachers, having pronounced beliefs about mathematics as a science, they seem to be closely related to the beliefs about effective teaching.

Although, of course, not every teacher matches exactly one of the types, the two groups of teachers can be identified very clearly. In the chosen sample, mostly type I could be identified, both in the *Hauptschule* and in the *Gymnasium*. In both types of schools, teachers of type II could be identified more rarely (see Fig. 3). The results as given in Fig. 3 are not to be seen as representative because the random sample was not representative. They are only meant to give a deeper insight into the results of the study.

Despite these similarities, however, some small differences could be established between the teachers from the different types of schools. Within type I, teachers of the *Hauptschule* seemed to put even more emphasis on transmission teaching. Unlike the teachers for high achieving students, they pointed out the importance of *repeated* explanations, of exercising *a lot*, of having an special exercise book only filled with rules, and the importance of explaining *only one way* of solving a task

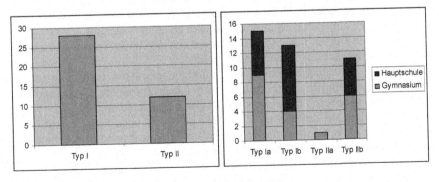

Figure. 3. Absolute frequency of types

in order to give the weak students a clear structure. Whereas in the *Gymnasium* type Ia could be reconstructed quite often, it was type Ib in the *Hauptschule*. Considering these differences and the different educational backgrounds, the agreement concerning the beliefs about effective mathematical education is interesting.

CONSEQUENCES

The results of the study show that beliefs about effective mathematics teaching can be very different. However, the majority of all investigated teachers seem to have very similar beliefs about effective teaching, which were all related to transmission teaching – irrespective of their teaching experience, their gender, and the type of school at which they teach.

The results indicate an interrelation between beliefs about effective mathematical teaching and the beliefs about mathematics as a science – mainly for teachers at the *Gymnasium* – and are in concord with the results of Kaiser (2006). Additionally, there seems to be an interrelation between the beliefs about teaching and the aims of mathematical education seen by the teacher. In cases where the beliefs about the aims of mathematics education do not seem to meet the beliefs about effective mathematics teaching, it may be due to the fact that the teacher does not reflect on how to reach these aims.

Furthermore, teachers of Type I simply do not seem to know enough reality-related or open tasks. Often they regarded students as not being able to work independently in groups. Altogether, this could be not only a question of beliefs but also a question of the educational and mathematical competency of the teacher.

A further hypothesis for these similar beliefs about effective mathematics teaching could be that the mathematics education the teachers experienced as students has a very heavy impact on the beliefs about effective mathematics teaching (see also theoretical background, Lloyd 2002). This could be an explanation why transmission teaching still has huge relevance today. The data show that mainly those who liked their mathematics lessons felt encouraged to become teachers, while only a few of those who do not like their mathematics lessons became teachers in order to change the situation. A reason for this may be that school often is the only place where students learn about mathematics.

Concerning the aims of integrating innovation into day-to-day teaching practice, these are important aspects of teacher education:
- The aims of mathematical education should be discussed with prospective teachers (as well as with in-service teachers in a teacher training course) and the question of how to reach these goals should also be reflected on.
- Methods to find and develop reality-related tasks and open tasks should be a further issue. Links between the content of mathematical lessons and methods should be highlighted (e.g. Peter sees these links.)
- The positive benefits of letting students work on open tasks independently should be highlighted. It has to be made clear that strong guidance of weak students leads to dependence, as Peter explains.
- Teacher training should include reflections about the nature of mathematics and its usefulness on a meta-level, as well as reflections on the mathematics

education they experienced as students, in order to create an awareness which might allow beliefs about mathematics teaching developed during school time to change.

These aspects seem to be relevant for pre-service and in-service training. As beliefs need a long period of time to be changed, in-service teacher training has to mean long-term training. Pre-service training has to start with these aspects from the very beginning.

Some of these demands do not seem to be new. Firstly, however, the results of the study validate them empirically. Secondly, the details of the beliefs reconstructed in the study as well as the described interrelations show the importance of paying attention to details, such as the aims of mathematical education or reflection about mathematics, and not only postulating on the integration of problem solving into teaching education.

The results of this study may also produce changes in terms of future research:

− In mathematics education, whether or not teachers' beliefs about effective mathematics teaching can be changed by long-term intervention needs to be assessed.
− In order to identify important key variables within a possible development from former student to teacher, a long-term study that takes into account the beliefs of students, student teachers and young teachers has to be carried out.
− Under what conditions a change in teachers' beliefs about effective teaching might lead to a change in classroom practice also needs to be evaluated.
− Studies comparing the training of prospective teachers for the *Gymnasium* and the *Hauptschule* could help to identify the best components of both systems and lead to an optimization of the training.

All together, the relationship between different beliefs about effective mathematics teaching identified in this study gives a deeper insight into teachers' thinking. This insight may help to develop a more detailed concept for teacher training which concerns itself with these beliefs. However, in order to acquire more information about how to change teachers' beliefs, more research is necessary as was pointed out above.

NOTES

[1] Practical skills related to the chosen profession are taught in a vocational school which all students have to attend after they have left the system of general education.

REFERENCES

Berger, P. (2000). Zur Theorie mathematischer Weltbilder. *Beiträge zum Mathematikunterricht 2000*, 101–104.

Bishop, A., Seah, W., & Chin, C. (2003). Values in mathematics teaching – the hidden persuaders? In A. Bishop, M. A. Clements, C. Keitel, J. Kilpatrick, & F. Leung (Eds.), *Second international handbook of mathematics education* (pp. 717–765). Dordrecht: Kluwer Academic Publishers.

Blum, W. (1996). Anwendungsbezüge im Mathematikunterricht − Trends und Perspektiven. *Schriftenreihe Didaktik der Mathematik, 23*, 15–38.

Chapmann, O. (2002). Belief structure an inservice high school mathematics teacher growth. In G. Leder, E. Pehkonen, & G. Törner (Eds.), *Beliefs: A hidden variable in mathematics education?* (pp. 177–193). Dordrecht: Kluwer Academic Publishers.

Dionne, J. (1984). The perception of mathematics among elementary school teachers. In J. Moser (Ed.), *Proceedings of 6th conference of the North American chapter of the international group for the psychology of mathematics education (PME-NA)* (pp. 223–228). Madison, WI: University of Wisconsin.

Eichler, A. (2006). Individuelle Stochastikcurricula von Lehrerinnen and Lehrern. *Journal für Mathematik-Didaktik, 27*(2).

Eichler, A. (2002). Vorstellungen von Lehrerinnen and Lehrern zum Stochastikunterricht. *Der Mathematikunterricht, 4–5,* 26–44.

Ernest, P. (1991). *The philosophy of mathematics education.* Hamshire: The Falmer Press.

Flick, U., von Kardorff, E., & Steinke, I. (2002). Was ist qualitative Forschung? Einleitung and Überblick. In U. Flick, E. von Kardorff, & I. Steinke (Eds.), *Qualitative Forschung, Ein Handbuch* (pp. 13–29). Reinbek bei Hamburg: Rowohlt.

Flick, U. (2000). *Qualitative Forschung.* Reinbek bei Hamburg: Rowohlt Taschenbuch Verlag GmbH.

Mayring, P. (2003). Qualitative content analysis. In U. Flick, E. von Kardorff, & I. Steinke (Eds.), *Qualitative Forschung, Ein Handbuch* (pp. 468–475). Reinbek bei Hamburg: Rowohlt.

Furinghetti, F., & Pehkonen, E. (2002). Rethinking characterisations of beliefs. In G. Leder, E. Pehkonen, & G. Törner (Eds.), *Beliefs: A hidden variable in mathematics education?* (pp. 39–57). Dordrecht: Kluwer Academic Publishers.

Gellert, U. (1998). *Von Lernerfahrungen zu Unterrichtskonzeptionen, eine soziokulturelle Analyse von Vorstellungen angehender Lehrerinnen und Lehrer zu Mathematik and Mathematikunterricht.* Berlin: Verlag für Wissenschaft and Forschung.

Gerhardt, U. (1991). Typenbildung. In U. Flick, et al. (Eds.), *Handbuch qualitative Sozialforschung. Grundlagen, Konzepte, Methoden und nwendungen* (pp. 435–439). München: Beltz/PVU.

Grigutsch, S., Raatz, U., &. Törner, G. (1998). Einstellungen gegenüber Mathematik bei Mathematiklehrern. *Journal für Mathematikdidaktik, 19,* 3–45.

Grigutsch, S. (1996). *Mathematische Weltbilder von Schülern, Struktur, Entwicklung, Einflussfaktoren.* Duisburg: Dissertation, Gerhard-Mercator-Universität, Gesamthochschule Duisburg.

Kaasila, R., Hannula, M., Laine, A., & Pehkonen, E. (2006). Faciliators for change of elementary teacher student's view of mathematics. In J. Novotaná, H. Moraová, M. Krátká, & N. Stehliková (Eds.), *Proceedings 30th conference of the international group for the psychology of mathematics education* (Vol. 3, pp. 385–392). Prague: PME.

Kaiser, G. (2006). The mathematical beliefs of teachers about application and modelling – results of an empirical study. In J. Novotaná, H. Moraová, M. Krátká, & N. Stehliková (Eds.), *Proceedings 30th conference of the international group for the psychology of mathematics education* (Vol. 3, pp. 393–400). Prague: PME.

Kelle, U., & Kluge, S. (1999). *Vom Einzelfall zum Typus.* Opladen: Leske + Budrich.

Llinares, S. (2002). Participation and reification in learning to teach: The role of knowledge and beliefs. In G. Leder, E. Pehkonen, & G. Törner (Eds.), *Beliefs: A hidden variable in mathematics education?* (pp. 195–209). Dordrecht: Kluwer Academic Publishers.

Lloyd, G. (2002). Mathematics teachers' beliefs and experiences with innovative curriculum materials. In G. Leder, E. Pehkonen, & G. Törner (Eds.), *Beliefs: A hidden variable in mathematics education?* (pp. 149–159). Dordrecht: Kluwer Academic Publishers.

Maass, K. (2004). *Mathematisches Modellieren im Unterricht.* Hildesheim: Franzbecker.

Op't Eynde, P., de Corte, E., & Verschaffel, L. (2002). Framing students' mathematics related beliefs. A quest for conceptual clarity and a comprehensive categorization. In G. Leder, E. Pehkonen, & G. Törner (Eds.), *Beliefs: A hidden variable in mathematics education?* (pp. 13–37). Dordrecht: Kluwer Academic Publishers.

Pehkonen, E., & Törner, G. (1996). Mathematical beliefs and different aspects of their meaning. *ZDM,* 101–108.

Ponte, J., Matos, J., Guimaraes, H., Leal, L., & Canavarro, A. (1994). Teachers' and students' views and attitudes towards a new mathematics curriculum: A case study. *Educational Studies in Mathematics, 26*, 347–365.

Tietze, U. (2002). Zur Einführung. *Der Mathematikunterricht, 4–5*, 3–6.

Törner, G. (2002). Epistemologische Grundüberzeugungen – verborgene Variablen beim Lehren and Lernen von Mathematik. *Der Mathematikunterricht, 4–5*, 103–128.

Wilson, M., & Cooney, T. (2002). Teacher change and development. The role of beliefs. In G. Leder, E. Pehkonen, & G. Törner (Eds.), *Beliefs: A hidden variable in mathematics education?* (pp. 127–148). Dordrecht: Kluwer Academic Publishers.

Katja Maass
University of Education Freiburg

APPENDIX

Questions for the Interview

1. Which subjects did you study?
2. How many years' teaching practice do you have?
3. Can you explain what mathematics is in your opinion?
4. In which areas of life can mathematics be used?
5. Why did you study mathematics?
6. What are the main aims of mathematics education?
7. What should a mathematics lesson look like?
8. What criteria are relevant for choosing tasks?
9. How important are context-related tasks for your lessons? Are they more complicated or easier for students?
10. How important are open tasks for your lessons? How important is problem solving in your lessons?
11. Which media do you use?
12. How important is it for you to motivate students?
13. Which ways of working do you use?
14. How do you deal with the different levels of performance students show?
15. Describe the mathematics lessons you experienced as a child. How did they influence your choice of profession?

RONGJIN HUANG AND YEPING LI

EXAMINING THE NATURE OF EFFECTIVE TEACHING THROUGH MASTER TEACHERS' LESSON EVALUATION IN CHINA

INTRODUCTION

At a time when we acknowledge the importance of effective teaching for improving students' learning, it is also important to realize that we do not know much about the nature of effective teaching (e.g., Krainer, 2005). The difficulty in defining effective teaching reflects the fact that the quality of teaching can be measured in terms of different aspects, including students' achievement, students' classroom involvement, the use of specific teaching approaches, and/or the cognitive demands of the mathematical tasks selected and used (Martin, 2007). However, the difficulty in defining what counts as effective teaching does not decrease the enthusiasm in identifying and developing effective teaching. Rather, worldwide efforts to improve students' learning of mathematics have led to the ever increasing interest in searching for quality teaching especially from high-achieving education systems, including China. When compared to U.S. mathematics classroom instruction, the quality of teaching practices observed in East Asia is generally acknowledged (e. g., Stevenson & Lee, 1995; Stigler & Hiebert, 1999). Yet, much still remains to be understood about the nature of effective teaching that is viewed and valued in East Asia (e.g., Li & Kaiser, 2008).

In this study, we aimed to examine and understand the nature of effective teaching that is viewed and valued in Mainland China. Although mathematics classroom instruction in China has not been focused on in large-scale cross-national studies, the quality of classroom instruction in China is positively reported in sporadic cross-national studies (see Clarke, Keitel, & Shimizu, 2006; Li, Kulm, Huang, & Ding, 2008). A focus on China is especially interesting because teaching in China is taken as a shared professional activity that is also open to public scrutiny and examination. High-quality classroom teaching is identified and culturally valued through frequent classroom observations and exchange of teaching ideas in and out of the school. Such a professional communication and exchange process makes it very possible for Chinese teachers to identify both effective teaching practices and who may be a better teacher. In particular, master teachers in China are often identified as the ones who bear most of the culturally valued moral character and expertise for others to follow (e.g., Li & Huang, 2008). Examining master teachers' teaching or their views about mathematics teaching

J. Cai, G. Kaiser, B. Perry and N.-Y. Wong (eds.), Effective Mathematics Teaching from Teachers' Perspectives: National and Cross-National Studies, 163–181.
© *2009 Sense Publishers. All rights reserved.*

should provide a plausible approach for understanding the nature of effective teaching valued in China (e.g., Huang, Chen & Zhao, 2005; Zhao & Ma, 2007). Thus, we aimed to take this approach to develop a better understanding of the effective teaching valued in China. Specifically, we examined Chinese master teachers' views of effective teaching based on video-stimulated, semi-structured interviews with ten secondary master mathematics teachers.

RESEARCH BACKGROUND

Research on Good Teaching

Although there has not been a consensus about what can be considered good mathematics instruction, great efforts to search for good classroom practice have been made over the past decades (Hiebert, et al., 2003; Martin, 2007; National Mathematics Advisory Panel [NMAP], 2008; RAND Mathematics Study Panel, 2003). It is generally accepted that teaching is a cultural activity (Stigler & Hiebert, 1999), and its quality evaluation needs to be based on the feasibility of establishing a classroom practice norm (Krainer, 2005). Franke, Kazemi and Batter (2007) argued that three aspects of classroom practice, namely discourses, norms, and building relationships, were crucial for establishing the quality of classroom practice. Students also need opportunities in the classroom to share their mathematical thinking, discuss alternative approaches to solve problems, use mathematical tools flexibly, and so on. A high quality mathematics experience is not determined simply by the presence of the latest technological tools, the use of small groups, manipulatives, students' discussions (Martin, 2007), or the exclusive use of either teacher-centered or student-centered instruction approaches (NMAP, 2008). Rather, it depends on whether the teachers are able to select worthwhile mathematical tasks, create a challenging and nurturing classroom environment, and facilitate meaningful discourses that can lead to socially negotiated understanding (e.g., Martin, 2007; NCTM, 2000).

Some researchers further suggested specific frameworks for assessing classroom teaching. For example, Carpenter and Lehrer (1999) argued that five forms of mental activities helped students to develop understanding, which included (a) constructing relationships, (b) extending and applying mathematical knowledge, (c) reflecting upon experiences, (d) articulating what one knows, and (e) making mathematical knowledge one's own. Likewise, Artzt and Armour-Thomas (2002) described a model for classroom observation and self-assessment, which consisted of the following three dimensions: instructional task (representation, motivation, sequence/difficult levels), learning environment (social/academic atmosphere, teaching model, and classroom arrangement), and discussion (interaction between teacher and student, interaction among students, and questioning).

In China, there are also numerous models developed and used for evaluating mathematics lessons by researchers and institutes. For example, Ma and Zhang (2003) described a model of evaluating mathematics lessons which included teaching objectives, teaching content, teaching method, psychological environment in teaching, teaching behavior, students' behavior, teaching achievement. Recently, many frameworks were suggested to encourage innovative teaching and learning ideas. For instance, Ma (2006) proposed to pay specific attention to students' active participation, effective interaction between teacher and students, interaction among students, quality of learning materials and proper time for exploration, students' understanding of knowledge, students' development of self-control and reflection ability, and students' positive attitudes towards mathematics learning, as crucial aspects in improving mathematics instruction.

As described above, there are many studies that either focus on the quality of mathematics classroom practice or propose frameworks for assessing classroom instruction. In contrast, a very limited number of studies are available that investigated teachers' opinions on effective mathematics teaching and their ways of evaluating mathematics lessons. Understanding the nature of effective teaching from the teachers' own views are important as they are the agents in the classroom setting who carry out classroom instruction and negotiate classroom instruction norms with their students.

Master Teachers in China

Stewart (2006) observed that China has a coherent teacher development system. Chinese teachers developed their professional competence through extensively observing others' classroom instruction and being observed and evaluated by experienced teachers. What teachers can learn from others is the type of knowledge and skills that are publically valued and often locally proven as effective. Teachers' professional development in China is also supported with a professional promotion system, starting from primary to intermediate (two levels), senior (advanced rank), and finally to exceptional class (special rank). Chinese teachers are being promoted from one rank to another through a systematic appraisal of practice at each level based on the teachers' education background, teaching experience, teaching performance, publications and so on (Li, Huang, Bao, & Fan, 2008). In particular, exceptional class rank is an honorary title given at the secondary school level and is regarded as equivalent to the rank of full professor in University (Ministry of Education, 1995). Master teachers in this chapter refer to the teachers who are of advanced rank or exceptional rank. In China, it is also an expected responsibility for master teachers to help other teachers improve their teaching skills and knowledge needed for teaching (Li & Huang, 2008).

With the recent release of new curriculum standards (Ministry of Education, 2001, 2003) in China, both novice and experienced teachers have met many challenges in implementing reform oriented new curriculum standards in classroom settings. The new curriculum standards advocate the use of an innovative instructional approach that emphasizes students' active learning through manipulatives, collaborative communications, and independent explorations. To accommodate these challenges, many different in-service teacher professional development programs have been developed and implemented. For example, the development of exemplary lessons based on action research is one of the most popular strategies. Typically in the application of this strategy, master teachers took an even more crucial role in the joint endeavour to design, teach, reflect, and improve lessons than what had been the case in traditional teaching research activities. Thus, master teachers in China are respected as experts in developing high quality teaching even in the context of school mathematics reform. Examining their views of effective teaching should provide a insightful window to understand the nature of the effective teaching valued in China.

Investigating teachers' conceptions of effective mathematics teaching is a relatively new endeavour in mathematics education research (e.g., Cai, 2007; Correa, Perry, Sims, Miller, & Fang, 2008; Wilson, Cooney, & Stinson, 2005). Nevertheless, researchers also try to explore teachers' views of effective mathematics teaching through examining their evaluation of mathematics lessons (Huang et al., 2005; Zhao & Ma, 2007). For example, Huang et al. (2005) explored what five Chinese master mathematics teachers valued about effective lessons through video-taped lesson stimulated interviews. It was found that these master teachers evaluated mathematics lessons in terms of the following aspects: (1) students' participation, (2) the teacher's skills of questioning, (3) the teacher's construction of learning situation, (4) use of innovative students' learning methods, (5) room for exploration, (6) organization of teaching content, (7) the design and quality of in-class exercises, and (8) in-class summary and evaluation of the lesson. Adopting a similar research method, Zhao and Ma (2007) also interviewed five master teachers at the elementary school level and found three common standards for a good mathematics lesson, which included (1) the clarity of the lesson's instructional goals and objectives, (2) the extent of students' participation, and (3) the extent of fulfilling the lesson's instructional goals and objectives.

The results from the previous video-stimulated interview studies for investigating teachers' notions of effective classroom teaching were promising. However, the small number of interviewees may limit the findings of these studies. Therefore, we decided to extend the previous study by Huang et al. (2005) to collect five more master teachers' data and conduct a more thorough analysis of all the data. This study was thus designed to answer the following questions:

– What dimensions do Chinese master teachers value in identifying and developing effective teaching?
– Are there certain patterns present in these master teachers' evaluations?

METHOD

Data Collection

The data of this study consists of two parts. One part is the existing data collected by Huang et al. (2005), which included five master secondary mathematics teachers' interviews. By following the same method (the same video-taped lessons and modified interview questions extending beyond the previous ones), we collected five more master teachers' written responses to several interview questions. One local mathematics education professor helped us identify and contact interviewees. Then, we sent the videotaped lessons and interview questions to interviewees. Two types of questions were used. One was the teachers' opinions or comments about these two videotaped lessons, as follows: (1) Do you like these two lessons overall? If any, what are the impressive parts of each of these two lessons, and why? Be sure to provide some specific examples to illustrate your points; (2) If any, what may be your suggestions on the improvement of these two lessons? The other question was the teachers' opinions and/or suggestions about effective mathematics teaching and learning in general, such as (a) in your opinion, how should mathematics best be taught and learned? and (b) in your opinion, what dimensions are important to consider in evaluating the effectiveness of mathematics classroom instruction?

All the written responses of the interviewees were collected in October 2006. The background information of all ten master teachers is shown in Table 1.

Table 1. Background information of the master teachers

Code of teacher*	Professional rank	Highest degree	Teaching experience	Job nature
EMT1	Exceptional	Bachelor	20 years	High school teacher
EMT2	Advanced	Bachelor	31 years	Middle school teacher
EMT3	Exceptional	Bachelor	32 years	Teaching researcher
EMT4	Exceptional	Bachelor	30 years	High school teacher
EMT5	Exceptional	Bachelor	35 years	High school teacher
NMT1	Exceptional	Master	20 years	High school teacher
NMT2	Advanced	Bachelor	24 years	Teaching researcher
NMT3	Advanced	Bachelor	16 years	High school teacher
NMT4	Exceptional	Bachelor	27 years	High school teacher
NMT5	Advanced	Bachelor	14 years	High school teacher

Note (*): EMT 1~5 denotes existing master teachers numbered 1~5, while NMT1~5 denotes newly sampled master teachers numbered 1~5.

Table 1 indicates that all master teachers were very experienced, each with at least 14 years of teaching experience. They all had a bachelor's degree or above in mathematics and taught at secondary schools or supervised secondary school teachers.

Video-taped Lessons

We deliberately selected two videotaped lessons related to geometry at grade eight. One lesson (hereafter, L1) is about the relationship between two circles. The lesson was taught by a young teacher who was awarded the first prize in a national instruction contest in 2002. This lesson demonstrated a successful reform-orientated teaching style. The other lesson (hereafter, L2) is about the theorem of medial line (segment connecting the middle points of two sides), which was taught by an experienced teacher who has more than thirty years of teaching experience. The teacher tried his best to adopt an innovative teaching approach, but he eventually demonstrated many traditional features of teaching. The contrasting features of these two lessons are intended to stimulate and broaden interviewees' opinions on effective teaching. The basic stages of these two lessons will be introduced briefly in the next section.

Lesson one (L1) consists of the following phases: (a) construction of the learning situation, (b) questioning and discussion, (d) exploration of new knowledge, (e) exercise with variation, (f) consolidation and familiarity of new knowledge, and (g) summary and assignment. At the beginning of the lesson, the teacher showed a set of dynamic pictures related to annular eclipse by means of the modern multimedia technology, followed by the questions: "After you have seen these pictures, do you recognize any questions related to mathematics?" and "Can you state any relation between the positions of the circular shapes of the moon and the sun?" Through discussions between the teacher and students, students realized that the relationship between the moon and sun can be represented by the positions of the two circles with the help of demonstrating two different sized circular plate models. After that, the students were asked to use two prepared circular models placed on transparent paper, and experiment to find the relationships of their positions when they were moved toward or away from each other along the line that passes through the centers of the two circles. Furthermore, students were asked to explore the quantitative relations in line with the position relations of two circles by investigating and analyzing the positions of the two circles. Then the teacher assigned the class a set of exercises related to the position relations and relevant quantitative relations of two circles. Finally, the students were invited to share their experience and attainment in the lesson, and some homework was assigned to the students at the end.

Lesson two (L2) includes the following stages: (a) reviewing and introduction, (b) exploring and proving the properties of medial line, (c) application of the properties, (d) summary and assignment. The teacher first asked students the properties and definition of median and then presented an instructional task to introduce the new learning content. After that, students were grouped to explore the properties of the medial line of a triangle by doing another instructional task: drawing a special triangle, such as a right triangle, an obtuse-angled triangle or an acute-angled triangle, measuring lengths of sides and medial lines, and make conjectures on the relationships among sides. Then, students found that the properties, namely, the medial line was parallel to the third side and equal to half of the length of the third side of the triangle. One proof of the properties of the medial line was introduced with the help of *Sketchpad* software, and was written formally on the blackboard. After completing the proof, the the teacher presented a set of varying exercises based on the same diagram. Finally, the teacher summarized the lesson and asked students to create a set of questions as homework according to the last problem they discussed in the last part of the lesson.

Data Analysis

After a detailed reading of all ten interview transcripts, more than thirty tentative codes were developed to capture the features of assessing mathematics instruction by these master teachers. Then, based on extensive discussions between authors and consulting with other mathematics educators, these codes were classified into five categories: instructional objective, instructional design, instructional procedure, teaching/learning environment, and teacher quality. The instructional objective consists of three items concerning the intended and achieved goals in knowledge and skills, mathematical thinking, and emotions and attitudes. Instructional design includes the aspects of retrieved teaching planning based on the observation of the lesson such as dealing with crucial and difficult knowledge points, knowledge connection, organization and development of knowledge, readiness of students' knowledge and cognition level, appropriateness of teaching method, etc. Instructional procedure is concerned with the process of unfolding a lesson such as introduction and development of the new topic, practicing the new content, summarizing, and assignment. Teaching and learning environment refers to the classroom interaction and contribution made by teacher and students. Teacher quality includes the teacher's subject knowledge, teaching skills, and personality. Based on this tentative category system, the first author and a mathematics education professor coded three master teachers' interviews separately and got an inter-rater reliability of 86%. Through extensive discussion, a final code system was formed as shown in the first two columns of Table 2.

After that, one coder carefully completed all the other coding. For example, EMT2 said that it is important to have teaching objectives including "knowledge and skills, process and ability, attitudes and emotion"; they were then coded as having three *instructional objectives* (IO1, 2, 3). For another example, EMT1 mentioned that "inducing the new topic through lunar eclipse is in line with the [psychological] characteristics of middle school students"; it was coded as *instructional design* (ID5, readiness of students' preparation).

The number of teachers and frequency of each item used by teachers are presented in the third and fourth columns of the Table 2. Because a teacher could mention one item multiple times in her/his evaluation of the two lessons, the frequencies of occupancy of some items in column four can be larger than the number of teachers given in column three. The characteristics of teachers' lesson evaluation are basically depicted in a qualitative way.

Table 2. Frequency of teachers' comments classified in different categories

Category	Items	No. of teachers	Frequency
Instructional objective [IO]	1. Knowledge and skill	10	17
	2. Mathematical thinking	10	15
	3. Attitude and emotion	9	17
Instructional design	1. Quantity of content	3	4
	2. Dealing with important and difficult points	8	14

Category	Items	No. of teachers	Frequency
[ID]	3. Connection among topics	6	12
	4. Organization and development of topics	8	21
	5. Readiness of students' preparation	6	10
	6. Selection of proper teaching methods	6	10
	7. Use of teaching aid tools/media	8	20
	8. Scientific and reasonable design	8	15
Instructional procedure [IP]	1. Introduction to new topic	10	27
	2. Developing new topic	9	43
	3. Practicing new topic	4	12
	4. Summarizing and evaluation	6	8
	5. Assignment	4	6
Learning environment [LE]	1. Classroom atmosphere	7	12
	2. Students' motivation and interest	8	20
	3. Students' participation	10	38
	4. Students' initiative of questions and opinions	9	24
	5. Students' self-exploration and learning	8	31
	6. Listening to students and giving feedback	5	14
	7. Stimulating students' thinking	10	35
	8. High order thinking and exploration time	10	32
	9. Collaborative discussion in group	8	20
Teacher quality [TQ]	1. Reflecting modern education ideas	7	7
	2. Mathematical foundation	8	22
	3. Fostering students' mathematical thinking	10	55
	4. Catering to individual needs and development	5	9
	5. Assisting students to develop their generalization and synthesis ability	10	22
	6. Teaching appearance /language/drawing	6	16
	7. Enthusiasm and passion for teaching	9	13

RESULTS

The results are presented in two sections. First, the main features of teachers' lesson evaluation will be described after combining the frequencies of teachers' comments for all items and categories. Then, patterns of lesson evaluation with regard to specific content or teachers, if any, will be charted respectively.

Main Features of Evaluating Mathematics Lesson

Table 2 shows that all ten master teachers emphasize instructional design, instructional procedure, learning environment and teacher quality overall. At the same time, there are different emphases placed on different items. In the following subsections, we describe how much teachers value these items.

Comprehensive instructional objectives. Regarding the instructional objective, almost all the teachers (9 or more) emphasized the importance of multiple intended and obtained objectives of the lesson. Particularly, it is more fundamental to achieve the intended instructional goals. For example, some teachers (EMT1, EMT2, and NMT1) indicated that the first priority in evaluating a lesson was to examine if the instructional objectives were achieved and the instructional objectives should include not only knowledge but also ability and emotion.

Reasonable and smooth lesson planning. Eight of the ten master teachers emphasized dealing with important knowledge points and difficult knowledge points (mentioned 14 times), organization and development of content (21 times), use of teaching aid tools and media (20 times), and scientific and reasonable design (15 times). There were six master teachers who appreciated connection of topics (12 times), readiness of student preparation (10 times), and selection of proper teaching method (10 times). Only three master teachers mentioned the quantity of content in a lesson.

To address the important and difficult knowledge points, master teachers emphasized the importance of dealing with difficult points successfully and ensuring students' correct understanding of important points. Sometimes master teachers pointed out the improper way of dealing with difficult points and provided improvement suggestions.

With regard to organization and development of content, ways to build new knowledge on students' previous knowledge and daily experiences, and ways to develop concepts through certain activities were emphasized. For example, one master teacher believes a good lesson should explore the internal connection of mathematics:

> The new topic should be connected to relevant previous knowledge. When designing a lesson, the teacher should consider how to develop new knowledge based on existing knowledge, but not to relate it to artificially non-mathematical situations. When creating a situation, we should keep mathematics in the center of the learning situation…Teachers should consider where the concept is derived from, and how it has been formed and developed [EMT5]

In addition, it was appreciated that teachers used *Sketchpad* to show students how to make conjectures through changing figures systematically. These kinds of activities not only deepen students' understanding of the theorem and its application, but also make sense of mathematical ideas: finding invariable principles within changing phenomena.

Regarding the readiness of students, some master teachers believed that it was important to understand students, their knowledge preparation and psychological readiness in order to set reasonable instruction aims (including knowledge and skills, process and ability, attitude and emotion) within the *zone of proximal development*. This means that students can achieve set teaching goals with the help of teachers. With reference to instruction methods, it was emphasized that there were certain instruction methods, but there was no fixed or best one. It is crucial to adapt certain methods to fit classroom instruction reality and highlight teacher's own personality and learn from students.

Developmental procedure of lessons. Ten master teachers emphasized the introduction to new topics (27 times), and nine teachers emphasized the development of the new topic (43 times). Six master teachers mentioned classroom instruction summarization and evaluative feedback (8 times). In addition, four teachers commented on the classroom practicing (12 times) and assignment (6 times).

With regard to the introduction of the new topic, it was highlighted to establish proper learning (daily life or mathematical) situations to motivate students' interest, build connection among concepts, and expose the mathematics thinking embedded within. One teacher explained how impressively the teacher used the eclipse situation to introduce the relationship between two circles:

> It was impressive that the teacher motivated students and exposed the varying thinking from qualitative to quantitative through demonstrating a dynamic movie about annular eclipse, and the relationship between the positions of two circles and their radii and the distance between the centers of the two circles [NMT2].

Knowledge development is most often mentioned by these master teachers. It includes the introduction, exploration, clarification, and application of the new concepts. One teacher explained how to fully develop new knowledge through observation, manipulatives, and synthesis:

> Starting with the daily life situation of annular eclipse moves, the teacher helped students develop initial perception and then further such experience with hands-on drawing and activities with manipulatives. After that, the relevant concepts were developed and finally defined. This process of learning is accorded to students' cognitive levels, and should be an effective and scientific method of learning. [EMT1].

Regarding the importance of summarizing and evaluating comments, one teacher explained the ways and functions of summarizing:

> Classroom summarizing should be the phase for advancing students' ability, thinking methods and assessment, etc. The students' process of mathematical thinking could be reified by students' self-evaluation. According to the reform curriculum standards, at the end of a lesson, students should assess their performance by themselves. In the last five minutes, summarization could be done in many different ways. For example, students can give their own opinions on the questions raised by the teacher or students [EMT3].

With classroom practicing, multiple formats and proper difficulties of problems, varying problems – with internally mathematical connection, multiple solutions, and mathematical thinking underlying the solutions – were emphasized. For example, one master teacher [NMT4] not only emphasized the quality of the problems in question and the ways to present them, but also appreciated the teacher's positive comments on students' creative thinking and solutions.

Interactive and social learning environment. All ten master teachers emphasized students' participation (38 times), stimulating students' thinking through questioning and problem posing (35 times), and providing students with high-order thinking problems and proper time to explore (32 times). Nine of them appreciated students' problem posing and opinion expression (24 times). Eight of them referred to students' motivation and interest (20 times), students' self-exploratory learning (31 times), and collaborative discussion in-groups (20 times). Seven teachers mentioned classroom atmosphere (12 times), and five of them paid attention to listening to students and giving them evaluative feedback (14 times).

Students' participation (38 times), stimulating students' thinking (35 times), and providing students with high-order thinking problems to explore (32 times) were mentioned most often. Mainly, it was appreciated that teachers got students actively involved in the activities of exploring, inquiring, discovering, conjecture and justification, and synthesis to develop new knowledge. One teacher explained the importance of self-exploratory learning:

It is a teacher's basic skill to provide a clear explanation that is easy to understand. In fact, some knowledge does not need a teacher's lecture because students can learn by themselves. In the innovative classroom, students should actively engage themselves in the process of learning rather than just following the teacher to achieve the instructional objectives [EMT1].

With regard to the importance of exploring high-order thinking problems with plentiful time, they explained how to facilitate and lead students to think actively through scaffolding, problems solving, and questioning. One teacher pointed out the disadvantage of the lack of providing students with enough time to think in L1:

When discussing quantitative relationship between radii of two circles and the distance of the centers of these two circles, the teacher only let the students observe dynamic movement, and give results. Thus, it may reduce the thinking level of the students. Moreover, the time for students to think is limited. [NMT3]

With regard to students' problem posing and opinion expression, students' active and systematic presentations were encouraged. It is important to listen to students' voice and build on students' ideas, but not to stick to the teacher's pre-determined track. In particular, one teacher explained why it was important to ask students to present their ideas:

Students' expressions could be relatively primitive because they never learn it. However, the students' expressions in this lesson are right. Students have their own ideas and pose one problem about the relationship between two same-sized circles. The relationships between two circles such as apart from each other, tangency, and intersection are presented by the students but not the teacher [EMT2].

Moreover, active, harmonious, and joyful relationships between the teacher and students were appreciated. Various ways to motivate students and stimulate their interests, such as creating situations, questioning, and problem solving were described. One teacher particularly explained how teachers could use varying problems with the help of a computer to arouse students' interest:

> The last set of problems with variation, namely, judging the shape of quadrilateral which consists of connecting four mid-points in any quadrilateral is wonderful. The proper use of the computer motivates students' interest [EMT4].

Profound subject knowledge and skillful instructional strategies of teachers. All ten of the master teachers emphasized the importance of enlightening and leading students to abstract and synthesize (22 times), and foster students' mathematical thinking (methods) and learning ability (55 times). Nine of them appreciated the teacher's interest in and passion for teaching (13 times). Eight of them emphasized profound subject knowledge and broad mathematical literature (22 times). Seven of them referred to the innovative instruction ideas and behaviors (7 times). Six teachers emphasized the teacher's appearance/language/drawing design (16 times), and five of them mentioned catering for individual needs and development (9 times).

Regarding abstraction and synthesis, some master teachers emphasized abstracting mathematical concepts and thinking based on observation and manipulative activities. One teacher emphasized the roles of mathematizing and synthesizing in developing mathematical propositions:

> First, based on a daily life situation of annular eclipse, mathematics problems were abstracted. Then, based on the numbers of intersecting points of two circles, the position relationships between two circles were preliminarily classified. Finally, the position relationships between two circles were expressed quantitatively by radii of two circles and the distance between the centers of the two circles [EMT1].

Some master teachers appreciated the effort to develop students' mathematical thinking methods.

> During the process of lecturing, the teacher advanced students' logical thinking based on their activities. The process reflects the scientific thinking and philosophical thinking ways. It provides students with more space of thinking to develop their scientific thinking methods. In this lesson, classification and analogy are two main mathematics thinking methods to be explored [NMT3].

Some master teachers valued profound and broad subject knowledge, which is a prerequisite for unfolding a lesson smoothly and flexibly. Critically, some inaccurate or improper expressions and explanations were pointed out below:

Mathematical foundation is not strong enough, and the mathematical context and mathematical connection are not handled properly. Thus, the mathematical demanding level is not high enough [NMT1].

In addition, teaching skills and teacher personality, such as attractive mathematics language, passionate eye contact, skillful presentation and writing and drawing were emphasized. One master teacher appreciated the L2 teacher's quality:

The magnetic mathematics language, profound mathematics foundation, frequent eye contact with students, fluent writing and drawing, and proper enlightening are impressive to me [NMT4].

Summary. The ten master teachers provided comments distributed in all five categories as summarized in Table 3.

Table 3. Frequency in terms of different categories

Categories	Frequency	Percent (%)
Instructional objective	49	8
Instructional design	106	17
Instructional procedure	96	15
Learning environment	226	36
Teacher quality	144	23

Table 3 shows that master teachers put much attention on the learning environment (36%), such as students' participation, self-exploratory learning, and collaborative exchanges. It was emphasized that a certain amount of time should be allocated for students to think and express. The teacher's quality was the second-most important aspect to examine (23%). Profound and broad subject knowledge, sound teaching skill, and nice personality were also valued. Instructional design (17%) and lesson delivery procedure (15%) were the third-most important factors to evaluate. Content connections within and across lessons, and knowledge development were also emphasized. Additionally, in evaluating the lesson, practice and summarization were emphasized to a certain extent. Comprehensive (both intended and obtained) instructional objectives of a lesson (8%) were the least frequently mentioned issue.

Does Specific Topic Have an Impact on Teachers' Evaluation?

In order to examine if there are differences between evaluating particular lessons (responses to the first two interview questions) and talking about the ways of evaluating lessons in general (responses to the latter two questions), we separated the data into two groups. One is called "evaluation of specific lessons" (L1 and L2), and the other refers to "evaluation in general" (i.e., beliefs concerned with effective lesson and ways of evaluating lessons in general). The distribution of teachers' comments concerning different aspects of the five dimensions is shown in Table 4.

Table 4. Frequency of categories with regard to specific lessons and general views

Categories	Evaluation of Specific Lessons		Evaluation in General	
	No. of Teacher	Frequency (percent)	No. of Teacher	Frequency (percent)
Instructional objective	4	12(3%)	10	37(15%)
Instructional design	10	60(16%)	10	46(19%)
Instructional procedure	10	72(19%)	6	24(10%)
Learning environment	10	147(38%)	10	79(33%)
Teacher quality	10	90(24%)	9	54(23%)

Table 4 shows that all of the teachers mentioned each of the five aspects with different emphases. When talking about particular lessons, they referred to learning environment most frequently (147 times, 38%), followed by teacher quality (90 times, 24%), and instructional procedure (72 times, 19%). The instructional objective was least mentioned (3%). While discussing evaluating a lesson in general, they mentioned learning environment most often (33%), then teacher quality (23%) and instruction design (19%). The instructional procedure was least referred to (10%). Thus, learning environment and teacher quality are two common factors to be valued when evaluating lessons. When talking about particular lessons, teachers emphasized instructional procedures more than instructional design while it is a reversed situation when evaluating lessons in general. It is quite strange that all the teachers mentioned the importance of instructional objectives (37 times, 15%) when evaluating lessons in general but only four of them referred the importance of instructional objective (12 times, 3%) when evaluating specific lessons.

DISCUSSION AND CONCLUSION

Based on the above results, these Chinese mathematics master teachers seem to evaluate the lesson from five aspects: instructional objectives, instructional design, instructional procedure, learning environment, and teacher quality. However, the emphases placed on different dimensions are varied. The learning environment is the first priority to consider. Students' participation, self-exploratory learning, independent thinking, collaboration and exchange are appreciated. Teacher's quality is the second priority to examine. Teacher's subject knowledge, teaching skill, and personality are highly emphasized. Connections within a lesson and across lessons and well-developed knowledge are emphasized when designing and delivering a lesson. Comprehensive instructional objectives are important factors to consider when evaluating a lesson.

In addition, the ways of evaluating a particular lesson and evaluating a lesson in general have some differences. Moreover, the ways of evaluating different specific lessons are also different. There is no unified pattern of evaluating lessons that emerged in this study.

Are Some Characteristics of Evaluating Mathematics Lessons Culturally Specific?

This study shows some features of classroom instruction that were valued by Chinese master mathematics teachers. Some features revealed in this study, such as having clear teaching objectives, emphasizing students' participation, and organizing and developing content, support and extend what was reported in existing studies on Chinese master mathematics teachers' lesson evaluation (Huang et al., 2005; Zhao & Ma, 2007). Meanwhile, some of the findings are also in line with some other studies. For example, emphasizing teachers' profound and broad subject knowledge was well reflected in Ma's (1999) book. For another example, emphasizing mathematical thinking and methods was revealed to be justified in China in some studies (Huang & Leung, 2004; Leung, 2001, 2005), while emphasizing connection and coherence in Chinese mathematics lessons were supported by others (Huang & Wong, 2007; Leung, 2005; Wang & Cai, 2007; Wang & Murphy, 2004). These consistent findings may reflect some unique features of mathematics classroom instruction in China such as highly demanding content, emphasizing mathematical thinking and reasoning, emphasizing connections and coherence of lessons, emphasizing introduction and development of knowledge and so on (Huang & Wong, 2007; Leung, 2005; Stevenson & Lee, 1995; Wang & Lin, 2005) .

Compared to what the U.S. teachers may consider as good mathematics teaching (Wilson, Cooney, & Stinson, 2005), we found that there are some aspects not commented on by these Chinse master teachers. In Wilson et al.'s (2005) study, experienced mathematics high school teachers in the U.S. emphasized the importance of (1) teachers' knowledge of mathematics and their students, (2) promoting mathematical understanding, (3) motivating and engaging students, (4) effective classroom management, and so on. In contrast, the Chinese teachers did not mention classroom management at all. Is it not important? Or is it not an issue to be concerned about? As many studies have shown, Chinese students are well disciplined when compared with their Western counterparts (Leung, 1995; Stevenson & Stigler, 1992), so classroom management may not be a matter to mention from the master teacher's perspective.

Are Some Characteristics of Lesson Evaluation Universal?

Surprisingly, these Chinese master teachers greatly emphasized student-centered teaching, such as student participation, student mathematical thinking and method, student self-exploratory learning, and student problem-posing and opinion-expressing, collaborative discussions which were advocated by Western documents (e.g., NCTM, 2000) . These notions were also manifested in other studies on mathematics classroom instruction in China (Huang & Leung, 2004; Huang & Wong,

2007; Mok, 2006), which were hardly demonstrated in an explicit way in traditional mathematics classrooms. Some studies have shown that the teacher-dominated teaching did not necessarily result in a teacher-centered and passive students' learning. Rather, there were many elements of student-centeredness in Chinese classrooms (Cortazzi & Jin, 2001; Huang & Leung, 2005; Mok, 2006; Mok & Ko, 2000). Partially, it may reflect the evolution of the mathematics classroom instruction in China. Over the past two decades, particularly after the recent release of the new mathematics curriculum standards in 2001, authorities and educators have paid great attention to improving classroom teaching by learning from Western theories and practices, which emphasized more student-centered, exploratory learning. It is important to note that in the Chinese setting, while learning from the West, its own tradition still has remained in essence. As argued by Zheng (2006), the evolution of modern education in China "is mainly a process of assimilation. That is to say, rather than being alienated by foreign factors, the foreign values were absorbed and assimilated into the Chinese culture" (p. 382). Instead of going to the extremes, Chinese mathematics educators prefer to get balances between various extremes in education, which is the central idea of "*Zhong yong*", a spirit of Chinese culture. Thus, it may be possible to develop some unique features of mathematics classroom instruction by adopting some innovative notions from Western theories while keeping some good Chinese traditions alive. If this is the case, then some dichotomies to capture classroom instruction developed by Western researchers such as student-centered versus teacher-centered, telling versus not telling, and listening versus speaking, should be deconstructed, and certain new perspectives should be developed (Clarke, 2006; Huang, 2002; Huang & Leung, 2005).

In addition, the framework of evaluating mathematics lessons emerging from this study seems to enrich those models developed by both Western and Chinese scholars. In the Western tradition, student understanding, learning environment, and knowledge representation were usually emphasized (Artzt & Armour-Thomas, 2002), while in Chinese tradition, the teaching objective, lesson planning, teaching procedure, and teaching effectiveness were often appreciated. The results obtained from this study seem to suggest that a complementary model with negotiated notions from both the East and the West is possible, which may shed light on identifying effective mathematics teaching in different contexts (Franke, Kazemi, & Batter, 2007).

What Can We Learn from this Study with Regard to Methodology?

Although studying teachers' beliefs about mathematics teaching and learning is not a new endeavour, case study methodology may be the most commonly used approach to provide a detailed description of teachers' beliefs by relying on rich data sets that include a combination of classroom observation, interview, stimulated-recall interview, response to vignettes or videotape, and so on (Philipp, 2007). The video-taped lesson-stimulated, structured interview used in this study shows certain advantages in investigating teachers' view on classroom teaching and learning. However, as demonstrated in this study, the ways of evaluating specific lessons and the beliefs concerning effective lessons in general are also not closely related to each other. The finding should alert researchers to be cautious in selecting particular situations or video-taped lessons. Moreover, due to the nature of qualitative studies, all the findings of this study could not be generalized arbitrarily. We should be prudent when interpreting the findings of this study.

ACKNOWLEDGEMENTS

We would like to thank Professor Xiaoya He from South China Normal University, China, for his help in data collection and pilot coding. We are also grateful to the master teachers for their time and sharing their views.

REFERENCES

Artzt, A. F., & Armour-Thomas, E. (2002). *Becoming a reflective mathematics teacher: A guide for observation and self-assessment.* Mahwah, NJ: Lawrence Erlbaum Associates.

Cai, J. (2007). What is effective mathematics teaching? A study of teachers from Australia, Mainland China, Hong Kong SAR, and the United States. *ZDM-The International Journal on Mathematics Education, 39*(4), 265–270.

Carpenter, T. P., & Lehrer, R. (1999). Teaching and learning mathematics with understanding. In E. Fennema & T. A. Romberg (Eds.), *Mathematics classroom that promote understanding* (pp. 19–32). Mahwah, NJ: Lawrence Erlbaum Associates.

Clarke, D. (2006). Deconstructing dichotomies: Arguing for a more inclusive approach. In D. J. Clarke, J. Emanuelsson, E. Jablonka, & I. A. C. Mok (Eds.), *Making connections: Comparing mathematics classrooms around the world* (pp. 215–236). Rotterdam, The Netherlands: Sense.

Clarke, D., Keitel, C., & Shimizu, Y. (2006). *Mathematics classrooms in twelve countries.* Rotterdam, The Netherlands: Sense.

Correa, C. A., Perry, M., Sims, L. M., Miller, K. F., & Fang, G. (2008). Connected and culturally embedded beliefs: Chinese and U.S. teachers talk about how their students best learn mathematics. *Teaching and Teacher Education, 24*(1), 140–153.

Cortazzi, M., & Jin, L. (2001). Large class in China: "Good" teachers and interaction. In D. A. Watkins & J. B. Biggs (Eds.), *Teaching the Chinese learner: Psychological and pedagogical perspectives* (pp. 115–134). Hong Kong/Melburne: Comparative Education Research Centre, the University of Hong Kong/ Australian Council for Education Research.

Franke, M. L., Kazemi, E., & Battey, D. (2007). Mathematics teaching and classroom practice. In K. Frank & Lester, Jr. (Eds.), *Second handbook of research on mathematics teaching and learning* (pp. 225–256). Charlotte, NC: Information Age Publishing.

Hiebert, J., Gallimore, R., Garnier, H., Givvin, K. B., Hollingsworth, H., & Jacobs, J. (2003). *Teaching mathematics in seven countries: Results from the TIMSS 1999 video study* (NCES 2003-013). U. S. Department of Education. Washington, DC: National Center for Education Statistics.

Huang, R. (2002). *Mathematics teaching in Hong Kong and Shanghai: A classroom analysis from the perspectives of variation.* Unpublished Doctoral Dissertation, The University of Hong Kong, Hong Kong.

Huang, R., & Leung, F. K. S (2004). Cracking the paradox of the Chinese learners: Looking into the mathematics classrooms in Hong Kong and Shanghai. In L. Fan, N. Y. Wong, J. Cai, & S. Li (Eds.), *How Chinese learn mathematics: Perspectives from insiders* (pp. 348–381). Singapore: World Scientific.

Huang, R., & Leung, F. K. S. (2005). Deconstructing teacher-centeredness and student-centeredness dichotomy: A case study of a Shanghai mathematics lesson. *The Mathematics Educators, 15*(2), 35–41.

Huang, R., & Wong, I. (2007). A comparison of mathematics classroom teaching in Hong Kong, Macau and Shanghai. *Journal of Mathematics Education, 16*(2), 77–81.

Huang, R., Chen, Y., & Zhao, X. (2005). How do expert teachers evaluate mathematics lessons? [in Chinese]. *Journal of Mathematics Education, 14*(1), 52–56.

Krainer, K. (2005). What is "good" mathematics teaching, and how can research inform practice and policy? (editorial). *Journal of Mathematics Teacher Education, 8*(2), 75–81.

Leung, F. K. S. (1995). The mathematics classroom in Beijing, Hong Kong and London. *Educational Studies in Mathematics, 29*, 197–325.

Leung, F. K. S. (2001). In search of an East Asian identity in mathematics education. *Educational Studies in Mathematics, 47*, 35–51.

Leung, F. K. S. (2005). Some characteristics of East Asian mathematics classrooms based on data from the TIMSS 1999 video study. *Educational Studies in Mathematics, 60*(2), 199–215.

Li, Y., & Huang, R. (2008). *Learning about and from a master mathematics teacher in China.* Paper presented at the research pre-session, National Council of Teachers of Mathematics annual conference (NCTM), April 7–9, 2008, Salt Lake City, UT.

Li, Y., & Kaiser, G. (2008). RF: Pursuing excellence in mathematics classroom instruction in East Asia. In O. Figueras, J. L. Cortina, S. Alatorre, T. Rojano, & A. Sepúlveda (Eds.), *Proceedings of the joint meeting of 32nd annual conference of the international group for the psychology of mathematics education and the 30th of the North American chapter* (Vol. 1, pp. 155–188). Morelia, Mexico: PME.

Li, Y., Huang, R., Bao, J., & Fan, Y. (2008). *Facilitating the development of mathematics teachers' expertise through professional promotion practices in Mainland China.* Paper presented at the 11th International Congress on Mathematical Education (ICME 11), July 6–13, 2008, Monterrey, Mexico.

Li, Y., Kulm, G., Huang, R., & Ding, M. (2008). On the quality of mathematics lesson: Do elementary mathematics teachers have similar views as students and their school? In J. Cai, G. Kaiser, B. Perry, & N. Wong (Eds.), *Effective mathematics teaching from teachers' perspectives: National and international studies (this volume).* Rotterdam, The Netherlands: Sense.

Ma, L. (1999). *Knowing and teaching elementary mathematics: Teachers' understanding of fundamental mathematics in China and the United States.* Mahwah, NJ: Lawrence Erlbaum Associates.

Ma, Y. (2006). *Teaching and learning of primary mathematics* [in Chinese]. Beijing: People's educational press.

Ma, Y., & Zhang, C. (2003). *Mathematics educational evaluation* [in Chinese]. Beijing: Higher Educational Press.

Martin, T. S. (2007). *Mathematics teaching today: Improving practice, improving student learning* (2nd ed.). Reston, VA: National Council of Teachers of Mathematics.

Ministry of Education, P. R. China. (1995). *Regulation of teacher's qualification* [In Chinese]. Retrieved April 22, 2008, from http://www.moe.edu.cn/edoas/website18/info5919.htm

Ministry of Education, P. R. China. (2001). *Mathematics curriculum standard for compulsory education stage* (experimental version) [in Chinese]. Beijing: Beijing Normal University Press.

Ministry of Education, P. R. China. (2003). *Mathematics curriculum standards for normal senior high schools* [in Chinese]. Beijing: People's Educational Press.

Mok, I. A. C. (2006). Teacher-dominating lessons in Shanghai: The insider's story. In D. Clarke, C. Keitel, & Y. Shimizu (Eds.), *Mathematics classrooms in twelve countries* (pp. 87–98). Rotterdam, The Netherlands: Sense.

Mok, I. A. C., & Ko, P. Y. (2000). Beyond labels - Teacher-centered and pupil-centered activities. In B. Adamson, T. Kwan, & K. K. Chan (Eds.), *Changing the curriculum: The impact of reform on primary schooling in Hong Kong* (pp. 175–194). Hong Kong: Hong Kong University Press.

National Council of Teacher of Mathematics. (2000). *Principles and standards for school mathematics*. Reston, VA: Author.

National Mathematics Advisory Panel. (2008). *Foundations for success: The final report of the national mathematics advisory panel*. Washington, DC: U.S. Department of Education.

Philipp, R. A. (2007). Mathematics teacher's beliefs and affects. In F. Lester, Jr. (Ed.), *Second handbook of research on mathematics teaching and learning* (pp. 257–315). Charlotte, NC: Information Age Publishing.

RAND Mathematics Study Panel. (2003). *Mathematical proficiency for all students: Towards a strategic development program in mathematics education*. Santa Monica, CA: RAND Corporation MR-1643.0-OERI.

Stevenson, H. W., & Lee, S. Y. (1995). The East Asian version of whole-class teaching. *Education Policy, 9*, 152–168.

Stevenson, H. W., & Stigler, J. W. (1992). *The learning gap: Why our schools are failing and what we can learn from Japanese and Chinese education*. New York: Summit Books.

Stewart, V. (2006). China's modernization plan: What can U.S. learn from China? *Education Week, 25*(28), 48–49.

Stigler, J. W., & Hiebert, J. (1999). *The teaching gap: Best ideas from the world's teachers for improving education in the classroom*. New York: The Free Press.

Wang, J., & Lin, E. (2005). Comparative studies on U.S. and Chinese mathematics learning and the implications for standards-based mathematics teaching reform. *Educational Researcher, 34*(5), 3–13.

Wang, T., & Murphy, J. (2004). An examination of coherence in a Chinese mathematics classroom. In L. Fan, N. Y. Wong, J. Cai, & S. Li (Eds.), *How Chinese learn mathematics: Perspectives from insiders* (pp. 107–123). Singapore: World Scientific.

Wang, T., & Cai, J. (2007). Chinese (Mainland) teachers' views of effective mathematics teaching and learning. *ZDM-The International Journal on Mathematics Education, 39*(4), 287–300.

Wilson, P. S., Cooney, T. J., & Stinson, D. W. (2005). What constitutes good mathematics teaching and how it develops: Nine high school teachers' perspectives. *Journal of Mathematics Teacher Education, 8*, 83–111.

Zhao, D., & Ma, Y. (2007). A qualitative research on evaluating primary mathematics lessons [in Chinese]. *Journal of Mathematics Education, 16*(2), 71–76.

Zheng, Y. X. (2006). Mathematics education in China: From a cultural perspective. In F. K. S. Leung, K. D. Graf, & F. J. Lopez-Real (Eds.), *Mathematics education in different cultural traditions - a comparative study of East Asia and the West, the 13th ICMI study* (pp. 381–390). Dordrecht/Boston/ London: Springer.

Rongjin Huang
Texas A&M University

Yeping Li
Texas A&M University

CATHERINE P. VISTRO-YU AND ROSEMARIEVIC VILLENA-DIAZ

TEACHERS' BELIEFS, INSTRUCTIONAL PRACTICES, AND CULTURE: UNDERSTANDING EFFECTIVE MATHEMATICS TEACHING IN THE PHILIPPINES

INTRODUCTION

For a country that has long struggled in many areas of life – political, economic, cultural, and educational – a deep and purposeful inquiry into how beliefs and the belief systems of its people influence day-to-day living, particularly in the educational arena, is imperative but frustratingly futile. The Philippines' struggle to raise achievement scores in international mathematics surveys such as the Third (Trends) in International Mathematics and Science Study (TIMSS) leaves many mathematics educators and stakeholders in the country perplexed. We wonder how else we could improve mathematics teaching and learning in our schools. In the area of mathematics teacher education, increasing teaching effectiveness has been the utmost concern. But, even the definition of effectiveness is unclear to many. What is it based on? What indications are there? Is teaching effectiveness readily visible or measurable? An equally important question to ask is, "What influences or contributes to mathematics teaching effectiveness?"

One area that has been investigated in recent years is mathematics teachers' beliefs and belief systems and their effects on teaching practices and on how teachers make the day-to-day instructional decisions. Several studies abroad have indicated the critical role that mathematics teachers' beliefs play in their teaching (Iida & Yamaguchi, 1998; Perry, Howard, & Tracey, 1999; Thompson, 1992). Following the lead of international researchers, Philippine mathematics education researchers have likewise, embarked on several studies about mathematics teachers' beliefs and attitudes about the nature of mathematics, mathematics teaching and learning, and the use of technology in mathematics, among others (see Villena, 2004; Vistro-Yu, 2001, 2002). A cross-national study of elementary mathematics teachers' beliefs conducted by Perry, Vistro-Yu, Howard, Wong, & Fong (2002) indicated that both Singaporean and Philippines teachers made significantly different responses not only to each other but to all other groups on the transmission-labeled belief statement: "*Being able to memorise facts is critical in mathematics learning.*" Both countries reported high percentages of elementary teachers who agreed with the statement. The same study also reported high percentages of teachers from Singapore, Taiwan, and Australia agreeing with the child-centered labeled statement:

J. Cai, G. Kaiser, B. Perry and N.-Y. Wong (eds.), Effective Mathematics Teaching from Teachers' Perspectives: National and Cross-National Studies, 183–201.
© *2009 Sense Publishers. All rights reserved.*

"Mathematics learning is enhanced by activities which build upon and respect students' experiences" suggesting that teachers may have heard the rhetoric of reform.

One cannot help but ask if beliefs could really influence one's actions or practices. Theoretically, they should. Thus, when mathematics teachers agree, for example, to the statement that *"Effective mathematics teachers provide an opportunity for the students to discover concepts and procedures for themselves"* (Villena, 2004), one would anticipate that they actually practice discovery learning in their classes. However, as Leatham (2006) pointed out in his discussion of beliefs as sensible systems, a person may not necessarily be aware of a belief that is held nor is the person able to articulate that belief. Furthermore, Herbel-Eisenmann, Lubienski, and Id-Deen (2006) showed in their case study of a secondary school mathematics teacher that local and global contexts, not one single belief, are taken into consideration when teachers decide on certain classroom practices. Therefore, teachers who agree to a belief statement may not necessarily act accordingly.

Drawing from the Philippine experience based on results from local research as well as studies from other countries, this chapter is an attempt to understand effective mathematics teaching in the country by pulling together articulated ideas about teachers' beliefs, instructional practices, and culture. While some studies have shown that beliefs do exert a certain amount of influence on teaching, the Philippine experience adds to a large body of literature that suggests otherwise, for reasons that seem larger than the teachers' espoused beliefs (Handal, 2003; Herbel-Eisenmann et al., 2006). Likewise, the variety of instructional practices by this country's mathematics teachers does not provide a clear recipe for achieving teaching effectiveness. Finally, culture plays a crucial role in understanding what effectiveness means.

The chapter highlights some issues that involve effective mathematics teaching and mathematics teachers' beliefs and belief systems. The cross-national study by Perry et al. (2002) and local studies by Bernardo and colleagues (Bernardo, Clemena, & Prudente, 2000; Bernardo, Prudente, & Limjap, 2003) dichotomized beliefs statements as those that encourage traditional, transmissive learning as opposed to child-centered or inquiry-based learning. One issue that must be resolved lies in the stereotypic view of transmissive or traditional beliefs statements. Are these beliefs inferior and therefore must be discouraged? Who says they are inferior and why would they be inferior? It can be argued that these dichotomies are undemocratically labeled and are problematic. The Philippine experience challenges the stereotypic views of some of the beliefs statements used in the recent studies. Beliefs that support reform are not necessarily superior to those that encourage transmissive learning. Another important issue that must be addressed relates to what effective mathematics teaching is. Are teachers who hold beliefs that are inquiry-based or child-centered necessarily effective? Are teachers who hold beliefs that are transmissive ineffective?

The chapter includes a brief historical and cultural background of the Philippine educational system to give light to certain peculiarities in the culture of Philippine schools. It proceeds to discuss the varying notions of teaching effectiveness in mathematics as expressed in studies and other literature in mathematics education and defined by the current practices in the system. However, it is the mathematics teachers that are at the heart of teaching effectiveness. Thus, a portion of the chapter discusses teachers' perceptions of effective mathematics teaching based on their espoused beliefs and teaching practices. A critical examination of what influences mathematics teachers' perceptions of effective mathematics teaching and of the issues put forth earlier is in order. Finally, the chapter concludes with some thoughts and questions that might help both local and foreign researchers and educators reconcile disparate ideas about teaching effectiveness in mathematics and more importantly, understand the dynamics of mathematics teaching in a country like the Philippines.

HISTORICAL, CULTURAL, AND EDUCATIONAL BACKGROUND

The system of education in the Philippines has undergone several changes from pre-Spanish times to the present. Changes occurred as the country struggled from its colonizers and adjustments were implemented in the hope of addressing the needs of the society. It is believed that education was informal and unstructured during the pre-Spanish era. The children were trained and taught by their parents and by their tribal tutors. Passing on the culture, norms, and traditions from one generation to the next was most important.

The priests replaced the tribal tutors when the Spaniards colonized the Philippines. These priests had to undergo professional training under the tutelage of the older clergy. Education was for the elite, and religious beliefs and practices were given emphasis in the curriculum. It was only on December 20, 1863 that a complete system of education was established through the promulgation of the Educational Decree of 1863. Primary schooling was free, and the teaching of Spanish was compulsory. In the 1900s, the Americans, who defeated the Spaniards, established a public school system patterned after the educational system of the United States. Elementary education was free and compulsory. The public schools together with the private institutions established by Spain worked side by side and eventually grew into the educational system that the Philippines has today.

The Management Structure

The basic education in the Philippines consists mainly of six years in elementary school and four years in secondary school. However, many children also have a pre-school education before enrolling in first grade. All public and private schools offering basic education (pre-, elementary, and secondary) are regulated and super-vised by the Philippine Department of Education (DepEd). The DepEd prescribes the minimum requirements for elementary and secondary schools. All public schools, except the special schools (e.g. science high schools) follow the same basic educa-tion curriculum while the private schools usually add more subjects depending on their particular thrust. A National Achievement Test (NAT) for each level is given every year to all students finishing that year.

The Organizational Structure

The DepEd is organized into two major structural components (Department of Education, n.d). The DepEd Central Office maintains the overall administration of basic education at the national level. The DepEd Field Offices are responsible for coordinating and administering DepEd's activities at the regional (16 Regional Offices) and local levels (150 Provincial and City School Divisions). Orders and directives, usually containing pointers on how the curriculum should be implemented, come from the Central Office. The Field Offices take charge of the dissemination and implementation of the orders and directives.

The Teacher Education Program

In 2004, the Commission on Higher Education (CHED), the government body that takes care of the regulation and supervision of tertiary and higher education in the country, released the guidelines for the "New Teacher Education Curriculum (NTEC)," (CHED, 2004), which took effect in the first semester of 2005-2006. The offerings were as follows:

Table 1. The New Teacher Education Curriculum
(Bachelor of Elementary Education, Bachelor of Secondary Education)

	For BEEd	For BSEd
General Education	63 units	63 units
Professional Education	54 units	51 units
Content/ Specialization	57 units	60 units
TOTAL	174 units	174 units

Prior to the 2004 NTEC, the teacher education curriculum offered 9 units of mathematics under the General Education component. The universities and colleges were given the freedom to decide what mathematics courses were to be offered. The usual consideration is the mathematics content being included in the licensure examination such as Basic Mathematics, College Algebra and Geometry although, again, these courses varied from one university to another.

In the 2004 NTEC, 6 units of mathematics are included in the General Education component and 12 more units of mathematics are added to the Content component of the Bachelor of Elementary Education (BEEd) program, indicating the serious move of the government to prepare the BEEd students thoroughly in content, should they be assigned to teach mathematics in the elementary level.

Practice teaching, which was previously offered as a 12-unit course, now offered as a 6-unit course is an important component of the teacher education programs in the country along with a 1-unit Field Study course. In each of these courses, the students are provided practical learning experiences where they are engaged as observers in a classroom. The Field Study course gives the students opportunities to verify and reflect on the different components of the teaching and learning process in the actual classroom setting before they undertake the practice teaching. In the 6-unit practice teaching course, the future teachers are given one quarter (approximately 9 weeks) to serve as apprentices in a school.

A graduate of a teacher education program needs to pass a Licensure Examination for Teachers (LET) before being allowed to teach in a public school. The LET is administered by the government through the Philippine Regulation Commission (PRC) and is composed of the following knowledge areas: general education, professional education, and content specialization.

The PRC issues a common license to all LET passers. There is no difference in the license of a BEEd major and a Bachelor of Secondary Education (BSEd) major LET passer. Similarly, there is no difference in the license between one who passes the LET with mathematics as the specialization from someone with English as the specialization. Hence, it is not unusual to see a non-mathematics major, albeit a licensed one, handling mathematics classes in the high school level because of lack of qualified (i.e. licensed) teachers in the field.

WHAT DOES IT MEAN TO TEACH MATHEMATICS EFFECTIVELY?

It is important to understand what teaching mathematics effectively means. There are several ways that researchers and professional groups define or characterize effective mathematics teaching. On the whole, there are some common ideas that need to be highlighted.

Research from Other Countries

In their review of research on the effective teaching of mathematics, Reynolds and Muijs (1999), identified the major ideas that define effective mathematics teaching or that characterize an effective mathematics teacher. Based on research studies in the United States, they suggest that the following elements constitute effective mathematics teaching:
– High opportunity to learn
– Teacher's high academic orientation
– Effective classroom management
– Teacher's high expectations of pupils
– A high proportion of whole-class teaching
– Heavily interactive teaching

Based on the Oracle Study, teachers labelled as Class Enquirers appeared to be more effective in teaching mathematics and language (Reynolds & Muijs, 1999, p. 273). Furthermore, correlations indicate that teachers who highly utilize whole class instruction with or without the use of other teaching strategies generate high academic gains among their students (Croll, 1996, cited by Reynolds & Muijs, 1999). The study by Mortimore et al. (1988, cited in Reynolds & Muijs) reported 12 factors associated with effectiveness in specific subjects such as mathematics. These factors include:
– Structured sessions
– Use of higher-order questions and statements

- Frequent questioning
- Restricting sessions to a single area of work
- Pupil involvement and whole class interaction by the teacher

Reynold & Muijs (1999) noted that the use of whole class instruction benefited pupils in their academic achievements, but these were limited to gains in the learning of basic skills. Peterson (1988, cited in Reynolds & Muijs, 1999) suggested that whole class instruction alone is not sufficient in developing students' higher-order thinking and problem solving skills, principal end goals in mathematics learning, and that other classroom processes may be needed.

In their study of effective mathematics teachers of numeracy, Askew, Brown, Johnson, Rhodes, and Wiliam (2006) identified factors that enable teachers of numeracy to become effective. Numeracy is the ability to process, communicate and interpret numerical information in a variety of contexts (Askew et al., 2006). The study considered 90 teachers from 11 schools, that were categorized as *highly effective, effective,* or *moderately effective* based on average gains of their pupils in a specially designed numeracy test that was administered twice. The study specifically gathered data on the teachers' beliefs, pedagogical and content knowledge of mathematics, professional development experiences, and instructional practices.

Results showed that some of the characteristics of highly effective teachers of numeracy include the following:

- Highly effective teachers know, understand, and are aware of conceptual connections within and between the areas of primary mathematics curriculum which they teach.
- Highly effective teachers believe that being numerate requires having a rich network of mathematical ideas and the ability to select and use both effective and efficient strategies.
- In support of such belief, highly effective teachers utilize teaching approaches that:
  - connect different ideas of mathematics using a variety of words, symbols, and diagrams;
  - use pupils' descriptions of their methods and their reasoning to help establish and emphasize connections and address misconceptions;
  - emphasize the importance of using mental, written, and electronic methods of calculation; and
  - emphasize the development of mental skills.

Askew et al. (2005) were also able to establish that highly effective teachers of numeracy are able to mentor and assist other teachers to become effective after working with them closely over a period of time. Moreover, highly effective teachers are more likely to have undertaken mathematics-specific professional development over an extended period. These teachers generally believed in the significance of their professional development.

Wilson, Cooney, and Stinson (2005) gathered nine high school teachers' perspectives of what constitutes good mathematics teaching using audio-recorded interviews. The two questions that guided the study were (p. 89):

- What constitutes good mathematics teaching?
- How do the skills necessary for good mathematics teaching develop?

Wilson et al. were able to identify what these nine teachers believed about good mathematics teaching. To these teachers, good teaching:
− requires extensive knowledge of both mathematics and their students;
− aims to develop students' understanding of mathematics beyond the instrumental level;
− engages and motivates students to learn mathematics; and
− utilizes effective management techniques.

Furthermore, the nine teachers indicated that experience, education, personal reading and reflection, and working with colleagues are what enable them to develop good teaching skills.

Lim (2007) observed mathematics teachers from five schools in Shanghai. Based on class observations and interviews with the teachers, Lim identified, with a possible unintended bias, major characteristics that she observed to be possibly contributing to high mathematics achievement amongst Shanghai students. Lim noted that Shanghai mathematics teachers:
− tended to use different kinds of examples that vary in connotation and/or difficulty level in one lesson;
− asked questions that emphasize higher order thinking skills (Questions such as why, how, or what if were not uncommon);
− emphasized the use of precise and elegant mathematical language;
− were able to establish good rapport with their students, despite a serious and orderly classroom atmosphere most of the time; and
− often collaborated with one another, meeting and discussing lessons to be taught the following week.

Lim (2007) also noted that Shanghai teachers and students both strongly believe in the value and importance of mathematics in developing reasoning and thinking skills. Moreover, there appeared to be a strong coherence between mathematics teachers' teaching philosophy and their students' beliefs about mathematics learning.

A Local Benchmarking Study

Vistro-Yu and Rivera (2004) observed several practices of mathematics teachers that contribute to a highly successful delivery of mathematics and science education in seven schools that have been judged by a panel of experts as model schools in science and mathematics in the Philippines. These are practices mostly by teachers within the classroom but also outside of the classroom setting. Two-week intensive classroom observations showed that the following were very effective teaching practices:
− drawing out ideas from students;
− giving out more than enough exercises;
− covering of high levels of content material;
− using a significant amount of visual aids;
− teachers doing most of the talking and writing on the board or the acetates;
− using group work that put students on task; and
− instilling classroom discipline at all times.

Further analyses of other data that included notes from focus group discussions, responses to teacher and student questionnaires, and teachers' class notes highlighted two components that contributed to the notion of effective mathematics teaching. These are classroom teaching strategies and classroom management styles. Elementary mathematics teachers used teaching strategies that are student-oriented. They respond to students' individual needs while still maintaining control of the flow of the class. On the other hand, secondary school mathematics teachers' lessons are very formal, highly organized, and coherent. They maintain a well-disciplined and orderly class.

A Local Framework Document

The recently published Working Draft of the *Framework for Mathematics Teacher Education* by the Science Education Institute and the Philippine Council of Mathematics Teacher Educators (MATHTED & SEI, 2006) stated their vision of a competent mathematics teacher:

A fully competent mathematics teacher possesses a strong *mathematical content knowledge,* is armed with *mathematical pedagogical knowledge* as well as *general pedagogical knowledge and management skills,* displays an appropriate *mathematical disposition* and values one's own *professional development.* (MATHTED & SEI, 2006, p. 11)

Furthermore, for each type of knowledge, domains and performance indicators have been identified that make up the specific competencies expected of a mathematics teacher. Some of these competencies are:
- The teacher can arrange mathematics topics following their logical sequential order.
- The teacher is able to generalize results of problems and extends them to other problem situations.
- The teacher is able to pose problems that provoke, engage and challenge students.
- The teacher selects, evaluates and uses appropriate technologies as aids to effective mathematics teaching and learning.
- The teacher analyzes and evaluates the mathematical thinking of students using varied methods of inquiry.
- The teacher displays knowledge of group work, practical work, investigative studies, and class presentations as different ways of teaching mathematics to students.

The framework expresses the groups' notion of effective mathematics teaching. Essentially, to these two groups, effective mathematics teaching means satisfying the competency demands of mathematics teachers as outlined in the said document. An important question to ask is how these competencies truly relate to teaching effectiveness. MATHTED and SEI (2006) appears to equate a competent mathematics teacher to an effective mathematics teacher. With the way competency in mathematics teaching has been characterized, the two concepts seem to be one and the same.

Prevailing Concept of Effective Mathematics Teaching

School evaluation practices in the Philippines suggest the following: *a teacher is effective if he/she has succeeded in fulfilling the objectives for which her/his lessons are designed with the given resources and if he/she was able to address problems confronting the school community.* The first condition, sadly trans lates to, "if the students of this teacher obtain acceptable scores in the national examinations." School administrators, mathematics teachers, and the mathematics education community generally agree that the results of TIMSS, the National Elementary Achievement Tests, the National Secondary Achievement Tests and the Division Achievement Tests are the indicators of whether lesson or curriculum objectives were achieved or not. The results of these tests are used as national measures, to determine if mathematics teachers are effective or not in delivering their lessons.

In 1991, results of the Project for Decentralized Education (PRODED) National Evaluation and Impact Study placed the mathematics education sector in a very precarious situation. The study showed that the achievement of grade school pupils in mathematics was the lowest among five areas tested (Ibe, 1991a). Concerned people in the mathematics education sector were constantly alarmed when follow up studies of the PRODED, as well as of other national and internationally administered examinations yielded the same results (Ibe, 1991b; Ibe & Ogena, 1998).

According to the Philippine Education Sector Study (PESS) (1998) and Philippine Education Commission Report (Presidential Commission on Educational Reform [PCER], 2000) which closely examined the state of mathematics education in the country, the poor performance of the students could be attributed to the poor and ineffective performance of teachers. Many educators have highlighted the important role of mathematics teachers in improving the achievement of students in mathematics.

To address the problem of teachers' inadequate performance, several in-service programs and short-term courses for mathematics teachers were conducted. One of these massive intervention programs is the project *Rescue Initiatives in Science Education* (RISE), launched in 2000 by the Department of Science and Technology-Science Education Institute (DOST-SEI) and the Department of Education.

"Project RISE is being implemented in view of the dismal performance of Filipino students in the Third International Mathematics and Science Study (TIMSS) in 1995 (sic) and the TIMSS-Repeat in 1999 (sic)..." (Cristobal, 2006, p. 1). Similarly stated in the Department of Education, Culture, and Sports (DECS, now DepEd) Memo No. 194, s. 2000 entitled *Implementation of the Intensive Science and Mathematics Teacher Training Program of Project RISE*: "The project aims to improve/enhance the capabilities of the science and mathematics teachers in both elementary and secondary levels to empower them to teach more *effectively* and efficiently. ..."

These two public documents clearly show that effective mathematics teaching is associated with high or satisfactory performance of students in the TIMSS and in other national or division achievement tests. Looking at it from the other end, poor performance of students in mathematics achievement tests indicates ineffective teaching. This impression is affirmed when after five years, due to a re-alignment of the budget, the DOST-SEI stopped funding the Project RISE, and yet, the DepEd still continued the project, now on its own.

The continuous poor showing of Filipino students in the Trends in Math and Science Study (TIMSS) in 2003, in which Filipino Grade 8 students ranked 42nd out of 46 countries and Grade 4 students ranked 23rd out of 25 participating countries, and in the National Achievement Tests, as reflected in the table below, prompted the DepEd to continue the project (RISE), but this time, called it "Project Upgrading." The DepEd now funds the project but seeks the assistance of the DOST-SEI in implementing it through its Regional Science Teaching Centers (RSTC). The following data reveal the trend in students' performance in the National Achievement Tests.

Table 2. Mean Scores (Mathematics) in the National Achievement Tests

Exam	2002–2003	2003–2004	2004–2005	2005–2006
elementary (NEAT)	44.84	59.45	58.73	54.66
high school (NSAT)	32.09	46.20	50.70	47.82

This practice of using the results of national and international achievement tests as indicators of effective teaching is also evident in other locally or internationally funded intervention programs. These programs have the same objective – to upgrade and update teachers' competencies to effect better students' performance in the said exams. A vicious cycle began when two major programs- the Third Elementary Education Project (TEEP), a mass training for elementary school teachers in some selected deprived regions nationwide, and the Secondary Education Development Improvement Program (SEDIP), the TEEP version for high school students – used students' mathematics scores in the NEAT and NSAT exams to assess the effectiveness of the program. After five years, the TEEP is perceived to be effective because of the tremendous increase in students' scores in the 2004 National Achievement Test (Nuqui, Doronila, Bautista, Aquino, Catibog, & Ducanes, 2006).

While there are similar views about what effective mathematics teaching is across countries, there are also a few differences. One striking difference is the way the Philippine educational leaders view effectiveness. This might be the only nation that consistently uses national achievement scores as the main gauge for determining teaching effectiveness in mathematics and designing professional upgrading programs for mathematics teachers. While there are attempts by local researchers to introduce a wider vision of teaching effectiveness, the prevailing concept by the country's educational leaders remains, perhaps, due more to pragmatic reasons (e.g. straight-forward – give a test, grade the test then compute mean scores) than what seems to be complete disregard for contemporary ideas or reform.

MATHEMATICS TEACHERS' BELIEFS AND EFFECTIVE TEACHING

Studies have shown that mathematics teachers' beliefs are strongly associated with the day-to-day decisions teachers make about their teaching, their students, or the curriculum they teach, and these may influence changes in their teaching or their instructional practices in complex ways (Arbaugh, Lannin, Jones, & Park-Rogers, 2006; Grootenboer & Lowrie, 2002; Handal, 2003; Iida & Yamaguchi, 1998; Lloyd, 2005; Thompson, 1992). Many studies, however, fall short of making definite conclusions about how teachers' beliefs specifically affect their actions inside the classroom. Recent studies about mathematics teachers often investigate teachers' beliefs, including their attitudes, perceptions, and articulated philosophies about the nature of mathematics, the goals of mathematics education, specific pedagogical approaches, the use of technology, and the role of teachers in the classroom, among others. This indicates that in spite of inconclusive studies, researchers continue to acknowledge the value of studying the role that beliefs play in mathematics teaching and learning.

Local Studies on Mathematics Teachers' Beliefs

Philippine studies of mathematics teachers and mathematics teacher education generally focus on the cognitive aspects of developing teachers. These include developing methods to improve content knowledge and teaching methods. Recent research in the country, however, has slowly integrated investigations about mathematics teachers' beliefs, attitudes, and perceptions about mathematics, as well as their philosophical inclinations about the nature of mathematics. Investigations of teachers' beliefs mostly use surveys that purport to identify belief statements to which mathematics teachers adhere. Sometimes, interviews are conducted in order to make sense of the survey results. From these survey results, categorizations of teachers' beliefs and implications on their understanding of mathematics or instructional practices are drawn up and discussed. Eventually, connections are made with respect to what mathematics teachers need to develop themselves further.

Some of these investigations on mathematics teachers' beliefs have certainly enhanced the results of the main studies. For example, Salazar (2007) found that preservice teachers' beliefs about mathematical proofs (what they are, how they are constructed, etc.) explained several errors that they made while writing their own proofs. In her study, Vistro-Yu (2005) understood mathematics teachers' decisions about their teaching because of the beliefs, perceptions, and attitudes about teaching and the mathematics classroom that they revealed through a questionnaire and interviews.

On the other hand, there are those studies that focus solely on mathematics teachers' beliefs as the main object of investigation. In these types of studies, results are often analyzed in order to characterize the teacher as an entity whose actions are influenced not just by cognitive knowledge but also by affective factors such as beliefs and attitudes. For example, Vistro-Yu (2001) categorized secondary school mathematics teachers' beliefs about the nature of mathematics and about mathematics teaching and learning according to Ernest's (1988, cited in Vistro-Yu, 2001) framework on philosophical orientations in mathematics – the instrumentalist, Platonist, and problem-solving orientations. She found that secondary school mathematics teachers tend to hold beliefs consistent with the problem-solving view much more strongly than the other two orientations. Ernest describes the problem-solving view of mathematics as one that sees mathematics as a dynamic, continually expanding field of human creation. Mathematics from this view is a process of inquiry, not a finished product (Ernest, 1988, cited in Vistro-Yu, 2001). In the same study, Vistro-Yu also found that teachers who obtained relatively low scores in the Licensure Exam significantly tend to hold more strongly beliefs that are associated with the instrumentalist view, which sees mathematics as an accumulation of facts, rules, and formulas (Ernest, 1988, cited in Vistro-Yu, 2001).

Some studies on affect yield significant results while others do not. Dingal (1980) studied the relationship between elementary mathematics teachers' perceptions of their difficulties in teaching with their actual teaching performance. Her study showed a negligible relationship between the teachers' perceptions of their difficulties and their actual teaching difficulties. In particular, she found that the teachers' difficulties reflected in their actual performance did not relate to what these teachers perceived to be difficult for them.

Relating Beliefs to Teaching: The Philippine Experience

Bernardo and colleagues (Bernardo et al., 2000; Bernardo, Limjap, Clemena, & Prudente, 2004; Bernardo et al., 2003) explored the beliefs of mathematics teachers from schools in four different regions in the Philippines. These teachers had been participating in the DepEd initiated project "School Based Training Program" (SBTP) since 1999. Results showed that these teachers' beliefs about the goals of mathematics education do not tend to either one of the two divergent systems: *transmissive* or *inquiry-oriented*.

The studies (Bernardo et al., 2000, 2003, 2004) suggest that although the mathematics teachers appreciate the more contemporary view of the goals of mathematics education, which is consistent with the inquiry-oriented system, they could not let go of the traditional view, which is consistent with the transmissive system. Based on self-reports and students' reports, the teachers' teaching practices are more consistent with the inquiry-oriented than transmissive systems. The statement of objectives in their lesson plans, when analyzed, indicated that the lessons are directed towards the development of higher-order thinking skills.

Bernardo and Limjap (2002) and Villena (2004) considered beliefs and teaching practices of mathematics teachers from five regions, yielding more revealing results. In both studies, the participating schools were categorized as High Performing and Low Performing, based on the results of the national achievement tests. The studies showed that mathematics teachers from the High Performing schools held beliefs consistent with the inquiry-oriented system while mathematics from the Low Performing schools held beliefs that are consistent with the transmissive system. Results of their self-reported teaching practices revealed the same results.

Statistical analyses, however, revealed that the beliefs of teachers are not related significantly to their practices. Based on the observations of the mathematics teachers' actual teaching performance, Bernardo and Limjap (2002) and Villena (2004) found that those who claimed that they were using the inquiry-based approach were actually not teaching in that manner. The kind of questions asked by some of these teachers were not geared towards building concepts, but rather, towards checking how well students were able to follow instruction or whether they could focus their learning on the application of concepts that were presented and demonstrated.

Interviews with the teachers whose practices were observed to be consistent with the inquiry-oriented system, likewise gave interesting results. These teachers did not feel comfortable with what was happening in their mathematics classes. While some of them admitted to lacking confidence in answering questions and problems posed by their students, others were worried about spending so much time preparing lessons that would allow students to explore or discover concepts on their own. When asked what made them do what they were doing, the common answer was that their supervisor, principal, and subject area coordinator expected to see those activities being conducted in class. This suggests that the teachers' primary consideration when planning and implementing lesson plans is what would please their supervisors.

CRITICAL ISSUES

There are issues that emerge from the earlier discussions that need to be addressed.

Dichotomizing Mathematics Teachers' Beliefs

Perry et al. (2002) classified belief statements as *child-centered* or *transmissive*. Child-centered belief statements basically stem from a teaching philosophy that places the student in the heart of teaching. Transmissive belief statements work from a teaching philosophy that emphasizes the principal role of the teacher as transmitter of knowledge. As a result, teaching is one-directional and hardly acknowledges the knowledge that the child brings to the classroom. The two types of belief statements appear to be opposites of each other. What is problematic in the dichotomy is how belief statements are classified as one versus the other type. School mathematics traditions in some countries, most especially in the West, consider statements that imply belief in the importance of memorizing facts and formulas as a transmissive belief statement as opposed to child-centered. Why? Why does the importance of memorizing facts and formulas in mathematics evoke an anti-child belief as if memorization is not a skill that must be taught or learned by everyone? In his exposition on the differences between the mathematics teaching practices of East Asian (of Confucian tradition) and Western countries, Leung (2001) noted that for East Asians, "memorization has always been an accepted way of learning, even when committing to memory things not totally understood" (p. 39). To the contemporary Western point of view, such is called rote learning. Leung (2001) explains that to the Chinese, memorization is part of the process of understanding the material to be learned. To the Chinese, discouraging memorization is tantamount to discouraging understanding, truly a disservice to the child. Thus, to the East Asians the above belief statement is not anti-child.

Locally, Bernardo et al. (2000, 2003, 2004) and Villena (2004) used a very similar dichotomy, except that their labels are based on which end of the spectrum teachers ended up. For example, the belief statement "Effective mathematics teachers give students many exercises so they can perfect the important skills" (Villena, 2004, p. 162), reflects the transmissive (school mathematics tradition) orientation. However, giving students the opportunity to practice skills does not contradict the child-centered philosophy. How could it when "East Asian students who engage in diligent practice in mathematics often top the list in international assessments in mathematics and in mathematics competitions" (Li, 2004, p. 175)? What could be contradictory is the frequency and manner with which the teacher gives the pupil the exercises needed. Drills could be ineffective and downright heartless if given in excess. Once again, the Western viewpoint appears to dominate the categorization. Li (2004) sums it up:

> Most mathematics educators in the West ... adopt an attitude of negating drill and practice and regard imitative practice as an actually (*sic*) purely behavioural manipulation. (Li, 2004, p. 176)

Indeed, some belief statements are not fairly categorized principally because the contexts and in most case, the culture, within which these statements are espoused could be different from one teacher to another. In the Philippines, for example, drill and practice is important and must be given to school children. But, certainly, these should be given judiciously, as needed by students and not simply because drill and practice just have to be done. Certainly, what we in the Philippines would like to encourage is what the Chinese understand as practice, i.e. *to familiarize with* and *be proficient at* (Li, 2004, p. 180). Categorizing belief statements is not as easy as what past studies seem to assume.

Superior vs. Inferior Beliefs

Another issue that needs to be addressed also relates to the labeling of belief statements. There seems to be a universal understanding that transmissive oriented beliefs are inferior to the so-called child-centered beliefs. Child-centered- oriented beliefs speak of reform while transmissive-oriented beliefs do not. But, again, the value of reform is relative. Would it be so bad if teachers of high performing schools hold transmissive-oriented beliefs and also practice transmissive-oriented teaching methods? The study of Vistro-Yu and Rivera (2004) showed that the "giving of more than enough exercises" in mathematics is effective for students in the model schools that have been identified. Because this practice is proven to be effective, teachers would believe in its value. Does that make the teachers inferior because they hold transmissive-oriented beliefs? Certainly, belief statements must not be viewed as inferior or superior to others because these are beliefs that have some basis for adherence. Teachers have reasons for holding on to such beliefs and must be respected for such, without judgment.

On the other hand, perhaps, it is not so much whether these beliefs are inferior or superior but whether these beliefs support curricular reforms. Certainly, some belief statements that teachers hold do not match the orientation that is needed for curricular reform to flourish and even if they do, often the traditional systems make it difficult for teachers to act on the reforms (Handal, 2003). To minimize possible prejudices, it might be worthwhile for researchers to reconsider the labelling of beliefs and, instead, work towards reconciling differing viewpoints about the implications of beliefs.

Effective Mathematics Teaching as Culture Bound: The Role of Values

The Philippine experience showed that beliefs and teaching practices do not seem to be related or are inconsistent. Villena's (2004) study showed that although the beliefs and practices of mathematics teachers of high performing schools are more consistent with the inquiry-based orientation and those of the low performing schools are more consistent with transmissive orientation, it cannot be said that beliefs really influence their practice. In addition, although there was an indication that teachers' beliefs and practices associated with high performing schools were consistent with inquiry-based orientation, it cannot also be said that the beliefs and practices of the teachers in these schools resulted in effective mathematics teaching.

What is evident so far is that teachers do what their superiors expect them to do. This makes translation of beliefs into practice a fuzzy concept to Philippine educators. It is obvious that teachers' beliefs are influenced by external factors such as an authority figure. It is not that these teachers are coerced but that teachers seem to value their job and working relationships with their superiors very much. It would seem that these mathematics teachers are inconsistent as seen by the decisions they might make that are in conflict with their espoused beliefs. However, in reality, there is no conflict, but there are just some factors that are far more important to them, which result in seemingly conflicting beliefs and practices. This is precisely what Leatham (2006) pointed out. Teachers' beliefs are developed into organized systems, and when conflict arises the beliefs that make more sense to them are the ones acted on. Green (1971, cited in Leatham, 2006) suggested that one dimension to be considered to describe the relative importance that individuals attach to their beliefs is psychological strength. Identifying beliefs as central rather than peripheral (Rokeach, 1968; Green, 1971, cited in Leatham, 2006) could explain why in the end, for Philippine mathematics teachers, although reform-oriented in their beliefs and, possibly, in their practices, it is what their superiors dictate that they follow. To these teachers, the belief that keeping a healthy relationship with superiors and keeping their job are more valuable is a central belief, one that is resistant to change (Rokeach, 1968 cited in Leatham, 2006).

Furthermore, it would seem that these teachers lack philosophical bases on which to ground their beliefs. However, in recalling the historical background of the Philippine educational system, one could surmise that culture has cultivated the values that teachers primarily hold. The differences between mathematics teachers' beliefs and practices could be attributed to the prevailing school culture which is dominantly paternalistic and encourages an acquiescent attitude. The prevailing concept of effective mathematics teaching among educational leaders is high mean scores in achievement tests. Thus, whether a mathematics teacher's beliefs are consistent with inquiry-based or transmissive orientation does not matter much nor does using teaching methods that are inquiry-based because in the end, this teacher will be evaluated based on his or her students' performance in the national tests. In other words, what is still most important is how teachers' educational leaders evaluate teaching effectiveness, which in this country is performance-based and defined as students obtaining a high mean score in national and international assessments.

CONCLUDING REMARKS

Two things clearly stand out:
- Effective mathematics teaching (or even teaching, in general) in the Philippines means higher achievement scores in national and international assessments.
- Whether Philippine mathematics teachers hold transmissive or child-centered/inquiry-based beliefs and use instructional practices consistent with either set of beliefs, ultimately, it is what their supervisors tell them to do that is more important.

In order to understand how effective mathematics teaching is pursued in this country, one has to understand the factors that come into play: how the educational leaders understand effectiveness, how this goal of mathematics teaching effectiveness is articulated within the educational system, how mathematics teachers are trained to become effective, how mathematics teachers' beliefs may or may not influence their teaching practices, and the prevailing culture in the Philippine school system. Like most Asian countries, we wish to see our students rank high in international mathematics comparative studies. Until we show a marked improvement in our rank, there will surely be the continued use of mean scores in national and international assessments as a measure of effectiveness in teaching mathematics. Until we have reached a decent rank, it would be very difficult to integrate reforms that could be viewed as confusing teachers and distracting them from this goal.

What is left for us to do? Local mathematics educators and researchers need to work together to combine reform-oriented goals and practices with the implied national goal of raising mean scores. Reforms that come from abroad will have to be carefully examined and contextualized in order for us to obtain their maximum effects while at the same time keeping to our goal. Raising mean scores as a goal is not bad at all. What might be appalling is the means to achieve it. Ultimately, the well-being of Filipino students is more important.

As for Philippine mathematics teachers, there is much to be done. Given that mathematics teachers adhere to seemingly opposing sets of beliefs and conflicting teaching practices, we would do well to reflect on Beswick's (2006) argument to shift the focus of mathematics teachers' professional development from improving teaching practices to helping teachers examine and change their beliefs. Recent research on teacher change (Clarke & Keitel, 2006; Herbel-Eisenmann et al., 2006; Wilson et al., 2005) have elicited many thoughts on how we could help mathematics teachers change their ways. These include attending to historical contexts, understanding pupil and parent effects, and encouraging personal reading and reflection. Using some of these ideas would definitely help us identify new and better ways to provide for improved professional development programs for Philippine mathematics teachers.

REFERENCES

Arbaugh, F., Lannin, J., Jones, D. L., & Park-Rogers, M. (2006). Examining instructional practices in core-plus lessons: Implications for professional development. *Journal of Mathematics Teacher Education, 9*, 517–550.

Askew, M., Brown, M., Johnson, D., Rhodes, V., & William, D. (2005). *Effective teachers of numeracy: Summary of findings.* London: Teacher Training Agency.

Bernardo, A. B. I., Clemena, R. M. S., & Prudente, M. S. (2000). *The contexts and practices of science and mathematics education in the Philippines: Foundations of responsive science and mathematics teacher education programs.* Manila: DLSU- Lasallian Institute for Development and Educational Research (DLSU- LIDER).

Bernardo, A. B. I., & Limjap, A. A. (2002). *Mathematics teachers' pedagogical beliefs: Implications for mathematics achievement in primary and secondary education.* Manila: DLSU- LIDER.

Bernardo, A. B. I., Limjap, A., Clemena, R. M. S., & Prudente, M. S. (2004). *Endline study for SBTP schools.* Manila: JICA Philippines and DLSU-LIDER.

Bernardo, A. B. I., Prudente, M. S., & Limjap, A. A. (2003). *Exploring mathematics and science teaching in the Philippines.* Manila: JICA Philippines and DLSU-LIDER.

Beswick, K. (2006). The importance of mathematics teachers' beliefs. *Australian Mathematics Teacher, 62*(4), 17–22.

CHED. (2004). *CHED memorandum order number 30.* Manila: Author.

Clarke, D., & Keitel, C. (Eds.). (2006). *Mathematics classrooms in twelve countries.* Rotterdam: Sense Publishers.

Cristobal, R. (2006). *Education: 248 Tutors learn to teach science and math better.* DOST Media Service. Retrieved August 20, 2007, from http://www.dost.gov.ph

Department of Education. (DepEd). (n.d.). *Welcome to DepEd.* Retrieved August 20, 2007, from http:///www.deped.gov.ph

Dingal, E. V. (1980). *The relation between perceived teaching difficulties and actual performance scores of teachers in mathematics.* Unpublished Thesis, University of the Philippines, Diliman.

Grootenboer, P., & Lowrie, T. (2002). Preservice primary school teachers' views on mathematics and mathematics education. In D. Edge & B. H. Yeap (Eds.), *Mathematics for a knowledge-based era, Volume II* (pp. 232–239). Singapore: National Institute of Education.

Handal, B. (2003). Teachers' mathematical beliefs: A review. *The Mathematics Educator, 13*(2), 47–57.

Herbel-Eisenmann, B. A., Lubienski, S. T., & Id-Deen, L. (2006). Reconsidering the study of mathematics instructional practices: The importance of curricular context in understanding local and global teacher change. *Journal of Mathematics Teacher Education, 9*, 313–345.

Ibe, M. (1991a). *Teacher education in the Philippines: State of the art and state of practice: A report on a study commissioned by EDPITAF.* Quezon City: University of the Philippines.

Ibe, M. (1991b). *A follow-up evaluation of pupil achievement under PRODED in five regions.* Quezon City: DECS-BEE and UP College of Education.

Ibe, M., & Ogena, E. (1998). Science education in the Philippines: An overview. In E. Ogena & F. Brawner (Eds.), *Science education in the Philippines: Challenges for development.* Manila: NAST-SEI.

Iida, S., & Yamaguchi, T. (1998). The analysis of teachers' views on teaching and learning mathematics from the constructivist perspective. In H. S. Park, Y. H. Choe, H. Shin, & S. H. Kim (Eds.), *Proceedings of the ICMI-East Asian regional conference on mathematical education* (Vol. 2, pp. 433–446). Chungbuk, Korea: Korea Society of Mathematical Education.

Leatham, K. (2006). Viewing mathematics teachers' beliefs as sensible systems. *Journal of Mathematics Teacher Education, 9*, 91–102.

Leung, F. K. S. (2001). In search of an East Asian identity in mathematics education. *Educational Studies in Mathematics, 47*(1), 35–51.

Li, S. (2004). Does practice make perfect? In J. Wang & B. Xu (Eds.), *Trends and challenges in mathematics education* (pp. 175–183). Shanghai: East China Normal University.

Lim, C. (2007). Characteristics of mathematics teaching in Shanghai, China: Through the lens of a Malaysian. *Mathematics Education Research Journal, 19*(1), 77–89.

Lloyd, G. (2005). Beliefs about the teacher's role in the mathematics classroom: One student teacher's explorations in fiction and in practice. *Journal of Mathematics Teacher Education, 8*, 441–467.

MATHTED, & SEI. (2006). *Mathematics framework for teacher education: A working draft.* Taguig, Philippines: SEI & MATHTED.

Nuqui, H. G., Doronila, M. C., Bautista, M. B., Aquino, R. A., Catibog, V. L., & Ducanes, G. M. (2006). *Transforming basic education: Lessons and recommendations from the third elementary education project, final report, executive summary.* Quezon City: University of the Philippines. Unpublished manuscript.

Perry, B., Howard, P., & Tracey, D. (1999). Head mathematics teachers' beliefs about the learning and teaching of mathematics. *Mathematics Education Research Journal, 11*(1), 39–53.

Perry, B., Vistro-Yu, C., Howard, P., Wong, N.-Y., & Fong, H. K. (2002). Beliefs of primary teachers about mathematics and its teaching and learning: Views from Singapore, Philippines, Mainland China, Hong Kong, Taiwan, and Australia. In B. Barton, K. C. Irwin, M. Pfannkuch, & M. O. J. Thomas (Eds.), *Mathematics in the south pacific* (pp. 551–558). Sydney: Mathematics Education Research Group of Australasia.

Philippine Education Sector Study. (PESS). (1998). *Philippines education for the 21st century.* Manila: Republic of the Philippines.

Presidential Commission on Educational Reform. (PCER). (2000). *Philippine agenda for educational reform: The PCER report.* Manila: Republic of the Philippines.

Reynolds, D., & Muijs, D. (1999). The effective teaching of mathematics: A review of research. *School Leadership & Management, 19*(3), 273–288.

Salazar, D. (2007). *Enhanced-group Moore method: Effects on Van Hiele levels of geometric understanding, proof construction performance, and beliefs.* Unpublished Dissertation, University of the Philippines, Diliman.

Thompson, A. G. (1992). Teachers' beliefs and conceptions: A synthesis of the research. In D. A. Grouws (Ed.), *Handbook of research on mathematics teaching and learning* (pp. 127–146). New York: Macmillan.

Villena, R. G. (2004). *Exploratory investigation of the beliefs and practices of elementary mathematics teachers of high and low performing schools in Metro Manila.* Unpublished Dissertation, De la Salle University, Manila.

Vistro-Yu, C. P. (2001). Implications of teachers' beliefs about mathematics for classroom and teacher education reform. *Loyola Schools Review, 1*(1), 103–121.

Vistro-Yu, C. P. (2002). Teachers' beliefs about the use of technology in the mathematics classroom. In D. Edge & B. H. Yeap (Eds.), *Mathematics for a knowledge-based era* (Vol. II). Singapore: National Institute of Education.

Vistro-Yu, C. P. (2005). On pedagogical knowledge in mathematics: How secondary school mathematics teachers face the challenge of teaching a new class. *International Journal for Mathematics Teaching and Learning.* Retrieved August 20, 2007, from http://www.cimt.plymouth.ac.uk/journal/vistroyu.pdf

Vistro-Yu, C. P., & Rivera, F. D. (2004). The effective learning environment: The delivery modes of model schools. In M. D. Ibe, E. B. Ogena, & F. G. Brawner (Eds.), *Effective practices in science and mathematics education: A benchmarking project* (pp. 41–58). Quezon City: Department of Science and Technology, Science Education Institute.

Wilson, P. S., Cooney, T. J., & Stinson, D. W. (2005). What constitutes good mathematics teaching and how it develops: Nine high school teachers' perspectives. *Journal of Mathematics Teacher Education, 8*, 83–111.

Catherine P. Vistro-Yu
Ateneo de Manila University

Rosemarievic Villena-Diaz
Philippine Normal University

RAIMO KAASILA AND ERKKI PEHKONEN

EFFECTIVE MATHEMATICS TEACHING IN FINLAND THROUGH THE EYES OF ELEMENTARY STUDENT TEACHERS

INTRODUCTION

The main task of mathematics educators could be considered to improve mathematics teaching in school. There are at least two ways to implement this: to improve the written curriculum and its implementation, e.g. mathematics text books, or to improve mathematics teaching itself in order to develop good mathematics teaching. And thus we come to the concept "effective mathematics teaching" that is similar to "good mathematics teaching." Actually, we think that the former is an American term, whereas in Europe we are not so happy with the term "effective" and usually use the latter term.

Effective Mathematics Teaching

The topic of effective teaching was already raised by NCTM about 20 years ago. In the first part of the NCTM book *Effective Mathematics Teaching*, the editors stated that "it becomes especially important that we develop a conceptually rich under-standing of what effective mathematics teaching is and how to foster it" (Grouws & Cooney 1988, p. 1). Furthermore, they emphasized that the focus must be in the teaching process, but should include certain linked ideas, like how pupils learn mathematics, the nature of school mathematics, social conditions, and outside expectations on the teacher.

Teachers' conceptions about effective mathematics teaching have recently been considered in ZDM theme number 4/2007. According to this, there doesn't seem to be any agreement about the characterization of effective mathematics teaching, and the main reason for this is that teachers' views of mathematics vary from one another in different countries. For example, in Mainland China and Hong Kong, teachers generally hold a Platonic view and emphasize very much the abstract structure of mathematics knowledge in their teaching. Practice plays a central role in their lessons, and memorization can come before or after understanding. In contrast, teachers from the United States and Australia are stressing the "functional view" of mathematics: they see that mathematics is a useful way to solve everyday problems. For Australian and US teachers, memorization is reasonable only after understanding. They emphasize flexibility so that their teaching fits the individual

J. Cai, G. Kaiser, B. Perry and N.-Y. Wong (eds.), Effective Mathematics Teaching from Teachers' Perspectives: National and Cross-National Studies, 203–216.
© *2009 Sense Publishers. All rights reserved.*

student's needs in contrast to teachers from China and Hong Kong (Bryan, Wang, Perry, Wong, & Cai, 2007). In three European countries, it is not easy to classify teachers' views: Teachers' conceptions in France lie rather on the East Asian side with emphasizing mathematical structure and logic as principal elements. Teachers in England promote a pragmatic understanding of mathematics in line with Australian and U.S. teachers. Views of teachers in Germany can be located somewhere in the middle (Kaiser & Vollsted, 2007).

One way to go about studying this phenomenon is to use an indirect definition. For example, according to Schoenfeld (1985), if teaching a concept begins with simply pointing out the definitions or rules and is followed by the teacher stating procedures, the natural process of learning the concept can be reversed, potentially limiting students' mathematical power. Such an instructional approach provokes some students to view mathematics as an unrelated set of rules and procedures. Many students experience difficulty when applying their knowledge and skills because the knowledge and skills are, at large, fragmented, isolated, and mechanical.

In addition, we cannot say that certain teaching methods are effective or ineffective: More likely the effectiveness or ineffectiveness of certain methods depends on what kind of learning goals we set (McNaught & Grouws, 2007). Thus, when discussing effective mathematics teaching, it is reasonable to separate development of basic skills and problem solving competence, for example.

Reynolds & Muijs (1999) have collected characteristics of the effective mathematics teaching, dealing particularly with the evidence of the British professional knowledge based on the Office for Standards in Education. When teaching basic skills effectively, the characteristics are as follows: A clear structure for lessons is provided when the teacher

– includes sessions of direct teaching, is involved pro-actively and not just when pupils are stuck;
– involves regular interaction with pupils, using perceptive questioning, giving careful attention to misconceptions, and providing help and constructive responses;
– rehearses existing knowledge and skills in order to enhance them and encourages quick recall of as many number facts as possible;
– uses a variety of activities on a topic in order to consolidate and extend understanding.

If our goal is to teach conceptual understanding, the characteristics of effective teaching are different than when teaching basic skills. From the research literature, McNaught & Grouws (2007) found two features of instruction that can help students develop conceptual understanding: (a) explicitly attending to connections among facts, procedures, and ideas, and (b) encouraging students to wrestle with important mathematical ideas in an intentional and conscious way.

Here we will give our characterization for effective mathematics teaching as follows: mathematics teaching is *effective* when pupils' mathematical performance is promoted as much as possible, i.e. when their calculation skills and understanding in mathematics will optimally develop.

Finnish School System

In Finland, we have a nine-year comprehensive school that begins at the age of seven. After the comprehensive school there are two options: the upper secondary school (grammar school) and vocational school. In the comprehensive school, mathematics is taught with 3–4 lessons per week, and in the upper secondary school there two selective courses: advanced mathematics and general mathematics. The amount of mathematics taught in vocational schools varies according to the career, but it usually is combined with situations of the career in question.

In Finland, students in elementary teacher education take a higher academic degree (usually five years of university studies), and the subject of their master's thesis is education. The goal of the scientific elementary teacher program is to produce reflective teachers who can combine knowledge of educational sciences with knowledge of subject pedagogy, e.g. mathematical pedagogy.

For more details about the Finnish school mathematics and teacher education, one may read the published book *How Finns learn mathematics and science* (Pehkonen, Ahtee, & Lavonen, 2007).

Focus of the Paper

In Finland there is not much research on effective mathematics teaching. The only research project we know of is the so-called EMU project (Effektiv matematikundervisningen) implemented in Vaasa, but there seems to be very few papers written about it (Burman, 2003).

Therefore, we describe effective mathematics teaching with the help of Finnish elementary student teachers. The data are based on three different research projects concerning elementary student teachers' conceptions of teaching and learning mathematics and the change in these conceptions. From these studies we have selected the parts in which they – explicitly or implicitly – tell their conceptions about effective mathematics teaching. Our research question is: What kinds of conceptions do elementary student teachers have about effective teaching in mathematics?

METHOD

The ideas about effective mathematics teaching that will be presented in the following paragraphs are based on elementary student teachers' statements in the interviews and in the teaching portfolios of three studies implemented recently in Finland. Our data were collected after the mathematics method course and the second year's teaching practice. Teaching portfolios were based on the mathematics lessons in the students' practice teaching. We have re-analyzed parts of the data for this paper.

The Three Studies

The first study was the dissertation of the first author about eight years ago (Kaasila, 2000). It involved 60 elementary student teachers in their second year of studies at the University of Lapland (Rovaniemi) in autumn 1997 and spring 1998. Based on the questionnaire (especially school time memories), Kaasila selected 14 student teachers for interviews and for more detailed observations in the practicing school during the practice period known in Finland as Subject Didactics 2 (SD 2) in November and December of 1997.

The second study draws on the data of the research project, "Elementary teachers' mathematics" (for more details, see Hannula, Kaasila, Laine, & Pehkonen, 2005; Kaasila, Hannula, Laine, & Pehkonen, 2008), financed by the Academy of Finland (project #8201695). The research participants included 269 student teachers at three Finnish universities (Helsinki, Turku, Lapland). Two questionnaires were administered in autumn 2003 to assess teacher students' knowledge, attitudes and skills in the beginning of their mathematics education course. The aim of the questionnaires was to measure student teachers' experiences of mathematics, their views of mathematics, and their mathematical skills. In this paper we focus on 57 student teachers at the University of Lapland because they taught mathematics during teaching practice in spring 2004 and wrote teaching portfolios based on their experiences. The student teachers in Helsinki and Turku came later in teaching practice, and therefore, we did not collect data about their teaching experiences.

The third study focuses on the interactionist perspective of teacher knowledge in mathematics and other subjects. The data consists of 40 student teachers' teaching portfolios in their second year practice of teaching (SD 2) at the University of Lapland in autumn 2006 and spring 2007. In addition, four of them were selected for interviews and more detailed observation in the practicing school during SD 2 (Kaasila & Lauriala, 2008a; Kaasila & Lauriala, 2008b).

Data Dealing Methods

When dealing with our data, we applied the phenomenographical approach (Marton, 1994). Its aim is to find out the different ways in which people experience, interpret, understand, perceive, or conceptualize a phenomenon. Our goal is to find out the different ways in which student teachers interpret and understand effective mathematics teaching. The aim of phenomenographical research is not to define how common different conceptions are among research persons, but to describe the variety of conceptions. Therefore, we did not report the frequency of each conception.

Since we had our own ideas about effective mathematics teaching in the beginning, the study is neither purely data-driven nor theory-driven. On the one hand, it is theory-driven in the sense that we developed a preconception of four components of effectiveness as teacher educators (Pehkonen, 2006a). On the other hand, the study is data-driven since re-analyzing the interviews of the three studies partly changed our understanding of effectiveness. In one phase of the study, there were eight components that were finally merged into seven features.

Our study is also a narrative study (Lieblich, Tuval-Mashiach, & Zilber, 1998; Kaasila, 2007a). In keeping with a narrative approach, we are interested here in the content of the narratives; that is, we are interested in the themes, especially pre-service teachers' conceptions of effective mathematics teaching which the protagonist has invoked in her/his story. It is important to note that during the interviews or in the instructions of teaching portfolios, we did not explicitly ask student teachers to discuss their conceptions about effective mathematics teaching. On the contrary, we looked afterwards at our data for the kind of statements where these conceptions were manifested. Furthermore, we were interested in the forms, i.e., the different ways in which student teachers relate changes that take place in their conceptions.

RESULTS

From the student teachers' answers, we were able to contract central ideas for effective mathematics teaching that are grouped here under the subheadings: goal-orientedness, listening to and understanding pupils' thinking, flexibility, a mixture of different elements, problem-centeredness, connections to everyday experiences, and assessment. In each case, we will give some basis or our conclusions in the form of direct quotes from the student teachers' interviews.

Goal-orientedness

The student teachers emphasized a lot that teaching must be *goal-oriented*. From the interviews, we may determine the following: Teachers must figure out what their goals are in teaching. In order for mathematics teaching to be effective, teachers' main goals should be to develop pupils' understanding and calculation skills. Only following the textbook and to working through it is not enough. The goals should direct all of the teachers' actions: their planning of mathematics lessons, their practice of teaching, and the ways they are assessing their teaching.

A student teacher has internalized this goal-orientedness if he/she, in the self-evaluation, always relates her/his implementation of the lesson to the goals of the lesson. Cognitive objectives are connected to the development of conceptual and procedural knowledge. In mathematics, affective objectives are also very central. This aspect of goal-orientedness can be easily seen, e.g. in the statements of Kati and Sirpa:

Kati: *"I reached well the objectives of my own lessons. My pupils learned the concept of the decimal number and its different ways of notion. Almost all pupils got full points in the quizzes of the first week measuring these topics. The connection between decimal number and fraction was more difficult, but locating a decimal number on a number line and recognition of a decimal number corresponding a certain point was very easy* " (Kaasila et al., 2008).

Sirpa: *"We succeeded in reaching the objectives [of the teaching period]. Every pupil in the class surely knows the basics of division. Using different lesson structures, we were able to maintain the motivation, and the practices used were such that mathematics does not stay outside a child's world, but it has really some connection with reality. Learning division helps a pupil in her/his every-day life, for example in doing shopping"* (Kaasila, 2000).

Listening to and Understanding Pupils' Thinking

Student teachers should *focus on their pupils' thinking* and actions. It is important to *listen to pupils* as well as to try to understand their ideas. To listen to pupils is an attitude that can be influenced during teacher pre-service and in-service training. Additionally, a teacher needs information on her/his pupils' beliefs, on strategies they are mainly using, and on their systematic errors, i.e. mini-theories, in order to make pupils' listening as effective as possible. If the teacher doesn't have this information, there is a danger that he/she can't correctly understand pupils' utterances.

Examples of such situations are given in the following paragraphs, in which two student teachers (Heli and Pirjo) emphasize pupil-centeredness in their lesson observations:

Heli: *"An interesting observation that I made during my teaching practice was that the focus of the teacher's interest should lie more in pupils' wrong answers than in their correct answers. The pupils who answer correctly have understood the topic in question, and the teacher should no longer pay so much attention to them. The teacher's interest should lie in those pupils who give a wrong answer. Special attention should be given on the processes and mini- theories that are behind wrong answers"* (Kaasila & Lauriala, 2008b).

Pirjo: *"I noticed during my own teaching week how important it is to ask a pupil how you will calculate the task. Then the teacher gets a picture how each pupil thinks about the task and the way of calculation, and thus it is easier for the teacher to help her/his pupil, since he/she is familiar with the way of thinking. Also pupils learn, when listening to each other's different solution methods and learn to listen to others"* (Kaasila & Lauriala, 2008b).

In what follows, we describe how Sirpa's conceptions of mathematics teaching changed during teaching practice. Her case is described in a more detailed way in Kaasila (2007b). Sirpa's reflection, when considering her first lesson, shows that she could not yet analyze the phases of her lesson from the pupils' perspective: "You must think beforehand of how to give instructions to the pupils and control your tone. Think how long every phase of the lesson lasts." Her focus was clearly on her own actions. The turning point can be seen in her self-evaluation of the second lesson:

Sirpa: *"My second lesson, the topic of which was the measurement of length, could have been good if I had given the pupils more opportunities to measure objects by themselves. Now I showed them different kinds of measures, and they thought about what they could measure with them. I should have let them explore the measures independently and look for things to apply them to"* (Kaasila, 2000).

This reflection emphasizes a criticism of teacher-centered teaching. Many linguistic features, especially the sentences beginning with the word "if" and "but" and the use of a negative sentence and conditional, show that Sirpa's conceptions are changing: she realized that it is useful to analyze the lesson from the pupils' perspective, and she presented concrete suggestions for what could be done differently. Sirpa wrote that her third lesson was the best one:

> Sirpa: *"I made six different posts for the pupils and everyone visited them in turn in groups of three. At every post, the pupils at first estimated the volume of an object and then measured the object. At the end of the lesson, they thought about why the result of the estimation and the result of the measurement possibly differed from each other"* (Kaasila, 2000).

Sirpa summed up the process of change:

> Sirpa: *"It would have been easy to prepare the lessons as teacher-centered instead of pupil-centered. It is a sure way. However, during the school practice, I realized how effective such active learning is and how important it is to teach pupils to learn. … My lessons improved themselves all the time towards the end, when I gave pupils more opportunities to experiment, and was not only talking before them, and they listened"* (Kaasila, 2000).

A central role for Sirpa's change process seemed to be concrete advice given by the mentor teacher: try to take the position of a pupil when elaborating your lesson plan, i.e. the importance of role-taking: "Think always also what pupils are doing when you do something." Sirpa showed with her actions that she had also internalized these rules (Kaasila, 2000).

Flexibility

The third feature of effective mathematics teaching in the student teachers' interviews was *flexibility*. We see that flexibility is a useful feature when analyzing teachers' classroom decision-making (Calderhead 1984). When we consider teaching practice, which in Finland is an important part of teacher education, we know that many pre-service teachers do not have the courage to change their lesson plan in order to adapt it according to what is happening in the class. A student teacher Sari, was an exception to that rule. In the following she explains how she flexibly changed the lesson plan she had made beforehand:

> Sari: *"We began the lesson with the checking of subtraction tasks pupils have invented. Here I gave pupils a work sheet where there were a lot of tasks that they were asked to calculate, and then to check with addition. For some pupils, beside the subtraction tasks, there was a table where the corresponding checking task was given. For the more advanced pupils there was an empty table beside the subtraction tasks. This practice seemed to be very demanding for all pupils: most of the pupils asked for help, and some of the pupils were frustrated, and they invented their own addition tasks. Therefore, I decided to do a couple of easier tasks on the blackboard as examples*

of checking subtraction, so that we could continue with the work sheet. However, I noticed that differentiation with these work sheets was successful without problems, since all pupils could reflect problem solving on their own level" (Kaasila & Lauriala, 2008b).

An aspect of a teacher's flexibility is *individualization* in teaching. According to constructivism, knowledge-building is a personal process, and knowledge cannot be given from outside. Every pupil has her/his own way of understanding and building knowledge. Therefore, one key idea is the individualization of learning, thus individualization of teaching. This is a very demanding task for the teacher. In the following Sirpa explains her solutions:

> Sirpa: *"The teacher has to take into account differentiation in teaching, and to remember that for some pupils a certain method is a more proper one, whereas some others prefer another method. Differentiation is necessary especially in a class where there are big differences in learning ... Differentiation happens naturally if a pupil has learned to ponder, he/she will search for new challenges. When a teacher gives more freedom to pupils and opportunities to realize themselves, they will do differentiation themselves"* (Kaasila, 2000).

A Mixture of Different Elements

In teaching, there should be a *mixture of constructivist and behavioristic* elements. It is important that teachers master different kinds of teaching methods. What is the most effective method in a specific situation is very situation-dependent. Among others, it depends on the goals of teaching, on the teacher in question, and on the class in question. If the teaching goal is that pupils understand mathematical concepts and rules, the constructivist approach might be the most effective way. If the goal is that pupils master calculation skills, the behavioristic approach is useful. In Finnish education, constructivism, especially socio-constructivism, has been emphasized and the role of behavioristic teaching methods has stayed marginal. This trend can be seen in the student teachers' statements.

Sirpa's conception on mathematics teaching that follows constructivist principles is flexible and partly critical. She emphasizes the role of a teacher "as a person who creates security and best possible frames for learning."

> Sirpa: *"The teacher thinks about the base of the class and the topics to be learned, what kind of approach is proper for a new topic. It is good to use many different approaches, since pupils are very different in their level and learning abilities.... Constructivism demands from a teacher a little more in planning of lessons, just in getting of materials, but it gives much more to pupils and the results of this are clearly seen. It would be the best solution that the teacher stays only as an action guide, and would check that pupils have materials needed. ... In behaviorism there are good sides, too, and one must remember that constructivism is not closing out other learning views"* (Kaasila, 2000).

Thus Sirpa emphasized the meaning of pupils' preconceptions, and stressed that "*a teacher cannot begin to change a pupil's thoughts with a knock-out method, but reflections and discussions with the teacher and other pupils can lead thoughts into a better direction*" (Kaasila, 2000).

Problem-centeredness

In mathematics teaching, the problem solving approach is emphasized in teacher education. Teaching should be organized as *problem-centered* whenever possible and sensible. This means that a problem or a problem situation is in the center of the teaching unit.

Especially, a teacher should use open problems and even complex situations. In problem-centered learning (or teaching), pupils are conducted towards a new mathematical content by solving one or more so-called key problems in which the main characters of the new content (e.g. a concept or an algorithm) are represented. When pupils solved these key problems in groups or alone, they presented their solutions to their classmates, and compared these and the strategies they used. Teachers have an important role in problem-centered learning (teaching): they organize a proper problem environment—i.e. they select or construct problems, guide pupils' discovery process—by giving hints how to solve problems and directing the phase of a lesson in which pupils are presenting their solutions.

In the following quote, one student teacher (Kati) comments on her solutions in the case of problem-centered teaching:

> Kati: "*During my own lessons, I tried strongly to use problem-centered teaching because I think that it is a rewarding and reasonable way to approach mathematics. A pupil experiences the strong feeling of success when solving a problem, whether it happened with the help of a teacher's hints, in pairs, in groups, or independently. When reflecting afterwards I should have put all pupils to work, since now the problem solving process might not be finalized by many pupils or even not begun. ... According to my understanding, problem solving is one of the most fascinating dimensions in mathematics. Suddenly, mathematics is no more a mere repetition of rigid schemata, but creative thinking and many-sided mind gymnastics of different answer alternatives*" (Kaasila et al., 2008).

In the following, there are two examples showing how student teachers have implemented problem-centered mathematics teaching. Both Heli and Raija discuss the problem-centered lessons they have implemented, and emphasize what they have learned in their lessons.

> Heli: "*The topic of the lesson was subtraction and borrowing in hundreds. My idea was to implement the lesson with the help of place value materials. Some of the pupils understood at once that a hundred flat should be changed into ten rods, but the problem was that pupils took an arbitrary amount of ten rods. Then we discussed and pondered together how many ten rods might be in a hundred flat The pupils were allowed to check themselves, and then they*

understood that one hundred flat was equal to ten ten rods" (Kaasila & Lauriala, 2008b).

Raija: "*To each pair of pupils a cardboard parallelogram was given. Firstly, the pupils calculated the area of the parallelogram. After that, the teacher asked how they calculated the area of parallelogram and what answers the pairs hade. The teacher used the cardboard parallelograms in the way that the pupils' task was to think in pairs how they could divide a cardboard parallelogram into two equal-size triangles. Then the pupils got the following task: What might be the area of one triangle? I was surprised that after this thinking period some of the pupils could tell the rule for the area of an triangle. ... I had a feeling that I was rather successful in teaching, and additionally that most of the pupils understood the rule for the area of an triangle, and were able to use it in different tasks*" (Kaasila & Lauriala, 2008b).

Connections to Everyday Experiences

The connections between mathematics and everyday experiences were emphasized in student teachers' conceptions. This means that to connect pupils' informal experiences to more formal mathematical ideas, their world would be used as a context for the problems and tasks. In the following excerpts, Leila and Sirpa recognize that these connections are also an important way to add all pupils' motivation towards learning mathematics.

Leila: "*During my lesson I wanted to handle such tasks which have connections to everyday, real life experiences. ... Pupils solved addition problems. Pupils told what kinds of things they had bought during this winter It was very nice to discuss also a little bit other things – evocative life*" (Kaasila, 2000).

Sirpa: "*The practices used were such that mathematics does not stay outside a child's world, but it has really some interface with reality. Learning division helps a pupil in her/his everyday life, for example in doing shopping*" (Kaasila, 2000).

Assessment

It is important to *assess* pupils' learning in mathematics continuously and using various ways. The ways in which teachers assess their pupils' learning guide their pupils' beliefs, and they also thus develop socio-mathematical norms in a class, i.e., normative aspects of interactions that are specific to mathematics (Yackel & Cobb, 1996). These aspects are important when learning mathematics. Teachers' teaching methods do not change if the ways they assess pupils' learning do not change. It is important to focus in assessment on the process of learning, not only on the products of learning, for example, the strategies the pupils are using. It is also useful that pupils learn to assess their own learning, and reflect upon the strategies they are using when solving problems or other tasks. It is clear that assessment overlaps with all other features presented, but assessment needs to be mentioned as a separate point, since teachers easily forget that assessment is also a tool for teaching.

Two student teachers (Sirpa and Kati) describe their many-sided assessment procedures: For example, Sirpa assessed pupils' learning several ways: a diagnostic test in the beginning, continuous observation, pupils' self-assessment in the middle and at the end of the period, a short test in the middle of the period, and at the end, a summative test compounded of pupils' own tasks.

Sirpa: *"According to curriculum, pupils' assessment should be flexible and take into account a pupil's readiness as well as the relativity and changing of knowledge"* (Kaasila, 2000).

Kati: *"When assessing tests, a teacher should reward both a successful solving process and a correct answer. Then pupils would get the picture that getting a correct answer is not a value in itself, but the process, ideas and insights leading to the solution are equally important"* (Kaasila et al., 2008).

DISCUSSION

The ideas about effective mathematics teaching are gained from the elementary student teachers' statements in the interviews of three different studies. Since student teachers easily repeat what they have learned, these ideas about effective mathematics teaching reflect the common way of thinking and understanding teaching and learning mathematics in Finnish teacher education.

With the results, we were able to abstract seven features that are typical, according to elementary student teachers, for effective mathematics teaching: goal-orientedness, listening to and understanding pupils' thinking, flexibility, a mixture of different elements, problem-centeredness, connections to everyday experiences, and assessment. We could structure these ideas in many ways. The most evident grouping might be: We begin with considering the goals of mathematics teaching, because the goals should be the starting point for all meaningful actions. Then the five following aspects are related to how we are implementing our teaching in practice. The assessment mentioned in the last feature relates to every aspect mentioned before. Therefore, these aspects are overlapping, and they all come out in most examples.

An additional aspect that is emphasized in Finnish teacher education is net-like planning. A teacher's good *planning is net-like*, not linear, so that he/she could easily change her/his mind according to the class situation. This kind of planning is stressed in teaching methods courses, but student teachers are not writing about the planning phase of their lessons in their portfolios. This might be the reason why net-like planning is not seen in teacher students' conceptions.

Connecting Our Results with Literature

When comparing Finnish elementary student teachers' conceptions of effective mathematics teaching to studies done earlier in other countries, we found similarities and differences. In Finland, student teachers emphasize flexibility and connections to everyday experiences, but not to the abstract structure of mathematical knowledge. So we can say that Finnish conceptions of effective mathematics teaching are clearly closer to Australian, American, and German teachers' pragmatic conceptions than to more formalist conceptions of teachers in Mainland China, Hong Kong, and France (Bryan & al. 2007; Kaiser & Vollsted 2007). Our findings support the view that conceptions of effective mathematics teaching are culture-based.

Reynolds & Muijs (1999) listed four characteristics of effective teaching when teaching basic skills (direct teaching, communication, repetition, and variety of methods). McNaught & Grouws (2007) found two features that help students develop conceptual understanding (connections, persistence). There are some connections between these and the features we compiled in our study: Listening and understanding pupils' thinking and flexibility are connected with communication. A mixture of different elements is about the same as a variety of methods. And problem-centeredness trains students in their persistence. The two remaining features (goal-orientedness and assessment) do not seem to have any clear correspondence in the literature. Similarly, two characteristics (direct teaching, repetition) were not found in our study. Therefore, we may say that Finnish elementary student teachers include in their teaching both basic skills and conceptual understanding.

Our results imply that when learning effective teaching methods, the student teachers profit a great deal from research that adheres to theoretical understanding of daily activities in learning and teaching. They seemed to be explicitly concerned with pupils' learning as they tried to enhance pupils' active role in learning and help them to become creative thinkers and problem solvers (Kaasila & Lauriala, 2008a).

Teacher Change

It is good to take into account some reservations when considering our results. Firstly, pre-service teachers know well that teacher education has built-in expectations of change, and this can steer their beliefs and actions. This rhetorical dimension should be taken into account when analyzing teacher students' narration (Brown, 2003; Kaasila, 2007b). Secondly, it is a well-known fact that when the researcher leaves the class, it usually follows that teachers are folding back to their old"good"practices, and teachers'beliefs seem to be unaffected (Cobb, Wood, & Yackel, 1990). An interpretation of this fact is that teachers have not internalized new beliefs and practices, and on a deep surface their beliefs have not yet changed. Therefore, the view of effective mathematics teaching gained here might not reflect the reality, i.e. what actually happens in Finnish mathematics classes.

Although Finnish pupils have been successful in all three PISA comparisons (2000, 2003, 2006), there seem to be severe gaps in the mathematical knowledge, especially in understanding, of even our best students. This can be seen in national studies where we have tried to single out pupils' (Hannula, Pehkonen, Maijala, & Soro, 2006, Hellinen & Pehkonen 2008) and teacher students' (Merenluoto & Pehkonen 2002) understanding of number concepts as well as more general understanding and mathematical thinking (Huhtala, 2000). In order for the level of pre-service teachers' understanding to be raised, we should convey at least some features of effective mathematics teaching in school instruction in mathematics. We consider the use of problem solving and the follow-up in promoting student teachers' thinking to be the most critical factors, the latter especially in the development of their practical strategies.

The process of teacher change is a very complex phenomenon and not yet clarified with research (Pehkonen, 2006b). On the one hand, teachers need some external facilitators or support to change their beliefs and practices into a more effective direction. On the other hand, teachers must develop themselves in order to be autonomous actors who will reflect their beliefs and practices. Without autonomy of thinking, the changes usually are not longlasting. The mastery of art of tolerating uncertainty in teaching can be one of the key phenomena that promote autonomy and further teacher change. This mastery also helps teachers to change their lesson plans flexibly.

REFERENCES

Brown. T. (2003). Mathematical identity in initial teacher training. In N. Pateman, B. Dougherty, & J. Zilliox (Eds.), *Proceedings of the 27th conference of the international group for the psychology of mathematics education* (Vol. 2, pp. 151–156). University of Hawaii. Retrieved from http://onlinedb.terc.edu/PME2003/PDF/RR_brown_T.pdf

Bryan, C., Wang, T., Perry, B., Wong, N.-Y., & Cai, J. (2007). Comparison and contrast: Similarities and differences of teachers' views of effective mathematics teaching and learning from four regions. *ZDM – International Journal of Mathematics Education, 39*, 329–340.

Burman, L. (2003). Effektiv matematikundervisning i gymnasiet [Effective mathematics teaching in upper secondary school]. In *Utvickling av matematikkundervisning i samspill mellom praksis og forskning*. Nordic conference in mathematics teaching, 18.–19.11.2002. Skriftserie for Nasjonalt Senter for Matematikk i Opplaeringen, N. 1., 85–90.

Calderhead, J. (1984). *Teachers' classroom decision-making*. London: Holt, Rinehart & Winston.

Cobb, P., Wood, T., & Yackel, E. (1990). Classrooms: A learning environment for teachers and researchers. In Davis, et al. (Eds.), *Constructivist views on the teaching and learning of mathematics* (pp. 125–146). JRME Monograph Number 4. Reston, VA: NCTM.

Grouws, D. A., & Cooney, T. J. (Eds.). (1988). *Effective mathematics teaching. Research agenda for mathematics education* (Vol. 1). Lawrence Erlbaum: NCTM.

Hannula, M. S., Kaasila, R., Laine, A., & Pehkonen, E. (2005). Structure and typical profiles of elementary teacher students' view of mathematics. In H. Chick & J. Vincent (Eds.), *Proceedings of the 29th conference of the international group for the psychology of mathematics education* (Vol. 3, pp. 89–96). University of Melbourne.

Hannula, M. S., Pehkonen, E., Maijala, H., & Soro, R. (2006). Levels of students' understanding on infinity. *Teaching Mathematics and Computer Science, 4*(2), 317–337.

Hellinen, A., & Pehkonen, E. (2008). On high school students' problem solving and argumentation skills. In T. Fritzlar (Ed.), *Problem solving in mathematics education. Proceedings of the ProMath conference Aug 30–Sept 2, 2007 in Lüneburg* (pp. 105–120). Hildesheim: Verlag Franzbecker.

Huhtala, S. (2000). *Lähihoitajaopiskelijan oma matematiikka* [Practical nursing student's own mathematics]. Dissertation, University of Helsinki. Department of Teacher Education. Research Report 219.

Kaasila, R. (2000). *"Eläydyin oppilaiden asemaan"* [An insight into the role of pupils. The significance of school recollections in the formation of the conceptions and teaching practices of mathematics for preservice teachers]. Dissertation. Acta Universitatis Lapponiensis 32, University of Lapland, Rovaniemi.

Kaasila, R. (2007a). Using narrative inquiry for investigating the becoming f a mathematics teacher. *ZDM – International Journal of Mathematics Education, 39*(3), 205–213.

Kaasila, R. (2007b). Mathematical biography and key rhetoric. *Educational Studies in Mathematics, 66*(3), 373–384.

Kaasila, R., Hannula, M. S., Laine, A., & Pehkonen, E. (2008). Socio-emotional orientations and teacher change. *Educational Studies in Mathematics, 67*(2), 111–123.

Kaasila, R., & Lauriala, A. (2008a). Interactionistic perspective on student teacher development during problem-based teaching practice. To be published in E. Ollington (Ed.), *Teaching strategies, innovations and problem solving.* New York: Nova Science Publisher.

Kaasila, R., & Lauriala, A. (2008b). *Pre-service teachers' reflection skills.* Unpublished Manuscript.

Kaiser, G., & Vollstedt, M. (2007). Teachers' views on effective mathematics teaching: Commentaries from a European perspective. *ZDM – International Journal of Mathematics Education, 39,* 341–348.

Lieblich, A., Tuval-Mashiach, R., & Zilber, T. (1998). *Narrative research. Reading, analysis and interpretation.* London: Sage.

Marton, F. (1994). Phenomenography. In T. Husén & T. Postlethwaite (Eds.), *The international encyclopedia of education* (2nd ed., Vol. 8, pp. 4424–4429). Pergamon.

McNaught, M., & Grouws, D. (2007). Learning goals and effective mathematics teaching: What can we learn from research? *Taiwan Journal of Mathematics Teachers, 10*(6), 2–11.

Merenluoto, K., & Pehkonen, E. (2002). Elementary teacher students' mathematical understanding explained via conceptual change. In D. Mewborne, P. Sztajn, D. Y. White, H. G. Wiegel, R. L. Bryant, & K. Nooney (Eds.), *Proceedings of the PME-NA XXIV* (pp. 1936–1939). Columbus (OH): ERIC.

Pehkonen, E. (2006a). On teachers' mathematical beliefs. *A presentation in the PME Prague in Working Group.*

Pehkonen, E. (2006b). What do we know about teacher change in mathematics? In L. Häggblom, L. Burman, & A.-S. Röj-Lindberg (Eds.), *Kunskapens och lärandets villkor. Festskrift tillägnad professor Ole Björkqvist* (pp. 77–87). Åbo Akademi, Pedagogiska fakulteten, Specialutgåva Nr 1/2006. Vasa.

Pehkonen, E., Ahtee, M., & Lavonen, J. (Eds.). (2007). *How Finns learn mathematics and science.* Rotterdam/Taipei: Sense Publishers.

Reynolds, D., & Muijs, D. (1999). The effective teaching of mathematics: A review of research. *School, Leadership & Management, 19*(3), 273–288.

Schoenfeld, A. H. (1985). *Mathematical problem solving.* Orlando, FL: Academic Press.

Yackel, E., & Cobb, P. (1996). Sociomathematical norms, argumentation, and autonomy in mathematics. *Journal for Research in Mathematics Education, 27*(4), 458–477.

Raimo Kaasila
University of Lapland

Erkki Pehkonen
University of Helsinki

YEPING LI, GERALD KULM, RONGJIN HUANG,
AND MEIXIA DING

ON THE QUALITY OF MATHEMATICS LESSON: DO ELEMENTARY MATHEMATICS TEACHERS HAVE SIMILAR VIEWS AS STUDENTS AND THEIR SCHOOL?

INTRODUCTION

Efforts to pursue high-quality classroom instruction worldwide have led to an increased interest in exploring teachers' instructional practices in high-achieving education systems in East Asia, including China. Although it is now common knowledge that some Chinese mathematics teachers have a profound under-standing of the mathematics they teach (An, Kulm, & Wu, 2004; Ma, 1999), the quality of Chinese classroom instruction may just be assumed but not well understood (e.g., Watkins & Biggs, 2001). Much less is known about Chinese mathematics teachers' perceptions of effective classroom instruction. As educational researchers have discovered that mathematics teaching is a cultural activity (Stigler & Hiebert, 1999), examining Chinese mathematics teachers' views of effective teaching becomes increasingly important for understanding what may happen in Chinese classrooms and why.

Although mathematics classroom instruction in China (Mainland) has not been a focus of large-scale cross-national studies, educational researchers can gain some knowledge about Chinese classroom instruction from some small-scale cross-national studies. In studies that focused on elementary mathematics classrooms, it was revealed that Chinese mathematics classroom instruction is coherent and polished (Stigler & Stevenson, 1991) in the form of well-organized whole-class teaching (Stevenson & Lee, 1997). In particular, Stigler, Lee, and Stevenson (1987) found that Chinese teachers make increasingly good use of class time for academic activities over grade levels. Classroom activities focus on discussing and solving mathematically challenging problems (Stigler & Stevenson, 1991), and engage students in solving problems with multiple solutions and justification (Fan, Wong, Cai, & Li, 2004). Recent research has further revealed a teaching gap between American teachers and their counterparts in high-achieving education systems such as Japan and Hong Kong (e.g., Stigler & Hiebert, 1999, 2004). It is reported that teachers in Japan (Stigler & Hiebert, 1999, 2004) and Hong Kong (Stigler & Hiebert, 2004) tend to develop mathematical concepts and procedures and maintain high cognitive demands in the mathematical tasks. Along with the

J. Cai, G. Kaiser, B. Perry and N.-Y. Wong (eds.), Effective Mathematics Teaching from Teachers' Perspectives: National and Cross-National Studies, 217–234.
© 2009 Sense Publishers. All rights reserved.

development of cross-national studies on mathematics classroom instruction, there is also a growing research interest in understanding Asian teachers' reasons for their practices (Correa, Perry, Sims, Miller, & Fang, 2008; Fernandez & Cannon, 2005; Wang & Cai, 2007). However, much still remains to be understood about Chinese mathematics teachers' thinking about the quality of mathematics instruction.

Although effective teaching can take many different forms, especially when examined cross-culturally (e.g., Cai, Perry, & Wong, 2007; Stigler & Hiebert, 2004), teachers play a key role in making what can become effective teaching in their own classrooms in a particular cultural context. A better understanding of teachers' perspectives behind their own teaching practices is of great importance to those who care about ways of making possible classroom instructional changes. Thus, the present study aimed to explore Chinese teachers' views on the quality of mathematics classroom instruction. Moreover, as the quality of classroom instruction also matters to students as learners and their school as quality control stake-holder, possible similarities and differences between Chinese teachers' views and those of students and their school are fundamentally important but largely unknown. Therefore, this study examined views held by Chinese students and their school to provide a base for a comparison with mathematics teachers' views in the same school.

RESEARCH BACKGROUND

Research on the Quality of Mathematics Instruction

The quality of classroom instruction has long been recognized as a key to the improvement of students' learning outcomes (e.g., National Commission on Teaching & America's Future [NCTAF], 1996; National Council of Teachers of Mathematics [NCTM], 1991). Efforts to pursue high-quality classroom instruction have also led to some on-going studies about and recommendations for the 'best practices' (Li, 2004). In particular, existing publications and documents have attempted to summarize and provide examples of the best practices for mathematics classroom instruction at various grade levels (e.g., NCTM, 2000; Zemelman, Daniels, & Hyde, 1993). The suggested approaches include the use of cooperative group learning, the use of manipulative materials, a problem-solving approach to instruction, and the integration of technology in classroom instruction. Experts from the Math Connections (2007) project developed a comprehensive list of nine broad categories of "Best Practices for Mathematics Instruction," with each category containing one to six sub-categories. The presentation of these recommendations conveys a belief that some practices have better potential than others in improving the quality of classroom instruction.

Although some suggestions have been made for best practices, best practices may exist only at a theoretical level and can be recommended. The implementation process for achieving a "good" mathematics lesson should take into account many other factors that are often social-culturally situated. In fact, there has not been a consensus about what can be considered "good" mathematics instruction. According to Krainer (2005), the question of whether we can define "good" mathematics teaching assumes the feasibility of establishing a norm. The complex nature of the teaching process leaves researchers uncertain about choosing the options of refusing norms, establishing norms, or negotiating norms, not to mention the difficulty of defining the norms itself. For example, in the process-product research paradigm, students' test performance is taken as an ultimate measure of the effectiveness of classroom instruction. However, students' performance itself does not spell out the nature of classroom instruction. In fact, just as students' test performance can be affected by many more factors than classroom instruction, the quality of classroom instruction can be examined from many more aspects than students' performance alone.

The selection and use of certain aspects for judging classroom instruction as "good" or "bad" is also a value-laden interpretation that goes beyond the description of what is going on in a classroom setting. For example, Schoenfeld (1988) visited a tenth-grade geometry class that was taught by an experienced teacher. From one point of view, the class was well-taught in terms of its instructional design and its content delivery in the classroom as planned. On the other hand, Schoenfeld argued that the class actually led to "bad" learning outcomes for students. The classroom instruction failed to provide students with opportunity to learn mathematics as a connected body of knowledge, rather they learned "at best a fragmented sense of the subject matter" (p. 145). The interpretation of classroom instruction clearly bears the researcher's criteria for "good" mathematics instruction. However, over the years, various criteria have been used implicitly or explicitly by scholars in specifying the features of good teaching (Wilson, Cooney, & Stinson, 2005). These criteria include the broader goals of educating students, the process of teaching, teacher's role in the process of classroom instruction, connections with students' understanding of mathematics, and/or instructional focus on fostering students' problem-solving and thinking. The lack of a clear agreement, on the criteria for what can be counted as good teaching in the past, points to both the difficulties and the need to understand the nature of teaching.

Methodological Considerations

Some studies have focused on expert teachers' classroom instruction (e.g., Borko & Livingston, 1989; Leinhardt, 1987) or their evaluation of others' classroom instruction (e.g., Huang, Chen, & Zhao, 2005). In these studies, expert teachers' performance in classroom instruction or their evaluation were implicitly taken as indicators of "good" mathematics instruction. For example, Huang et al. (2005) interviewed five middle and secondary expert mathematics teachers to explore their evaluations of two video-taped mathematics lessons. Their results suggested that participating Chinese expert teachers evaluated mathematics lessons from the following aspects: (1) students' participation, (2) teacher's skill of questioning, (3) teacher's construction of the learning situation, (4) classroom use of innovative students' learning methods, (5) room for exploration, (6) organization of the lesson's teaching content, (7) the design and quality of in-class exercises, and (8) in-class summary and evaluation of the lesson. The results provided a glimpse at several aspects that Chinese expert teachers would value as "good" mathematics teaching. This approach has been undertaken by Huang and Li in this book to further explore Chinese expert teachers' views on mathematics teaching.

Research directly addressing the issue of "good" classroom instruction from teachers' perspectives is a relatively new endeavour in mathematics education (Wilson, Cooney, & Stinson, 2005). In their study with nine experienced U.S. mathematics teachers about their perspectives on good teaching, Wilson et al. (2005) reported that all these participating teachers emphasized the importance of (1) teachers' knowledge of mathematics and their students, (2) promoting mathematical understanding, (3) motivating and engaging students, and (4) effective classroom management. There were four additional aspects emphasized by some teachers but not others: (5) connecting mathematics, (6) visualizing mathematics, (7) assessing students' understanding, and (8) moving away from telling. In a more recent study with Chinese experienced teachers, Wang and Cai (2007) conducted semi-structured interviews with nine experienced teachers. In one set of questions about teaching, they probed teachers about their views on the nature of an effective teacher and an effective lesson. These nine teachers perceived that a common feature of an effective lesson is to develop students' understanding of mathematical concepts through active participation. In particular, these experienced teachers all emphasized instructional coherence and the use of concrete examples as two important features of an effective lesson, plus eight other features shared by some of these teachers. Likewise, Zhao and Ma (2007) interviewed three mathematical instruction supervisors and two expert mathematics teachers at the elementary school level. The interviews contained two parts: (a) the five participating experts' views on "good" mathematics lesson, (b) their evaluations of two video-taped mathematics lessons. The results indicated that these five participants shared three common standards but differed on 10 others. The three common standards for a "good" mathematics lesson are: (1) the clarity of the lesson's instructional goals and objectives, (2) the extent of students' participation, and (3) the extent of fulfilling the lesson's instructional goals and objectives. The diversity is evidenced in their choices that are spread out on 10 other standards, including the design of instruction, teaching content, teacher's guidance, fostering mathematical thinking, teacher's basic teaching skills, and the use of multi-media, etc. The results led the researchers to conclude that there are some common understandings of what is important for a "good" mathematics lesson, but variations are also large from one expert teacher to another. However, it still remains to be explored what views about the quality of classroom instruction normal mathematics teachers in China may hold and how their views may differ from their students and school.

In our study on the perspective of "good" teaching held by Chinese teachers with various teaching experiences, it becomes necessary for us to avoid possible subjective pre-judgement by adopting or creating pre-specified criteria. Thus, we tended not to use an approach with any pre-specified criteria. Instead, we decided to use a research method that can allow teachers and students themselves to tell us what constitutes a "good" mathematics lesson from their own understanding. Other studies have shown the feasibility of the free-essay writing method for eliciting participants' thinking, especially in a cross-cultural setting (e.g., Beishuizen, Hof, van Putten, Bouwmeester, & Asscher, 2001; Jin & Cortazzi, 1998; Kutnick & Jules, 1993). So we adopted this method to collect Chinese elementary teachers' and students' essays in an open-ended question. Content analysis method was then applied to extract cognitive constructs used by teachers and students in their descriptions of a good mathematics lesson, a method that is feasible to explore participants' thinking from their writing (e.g., Kutnick & Jules, 1993).

THE CURRENT STUDY

The present study aimed to explore views on the quality of mathematics classroom instruction held by elementary teachers, students, and their school from one elementary school in China. Because elementary school teachers in China are specialized in the major content area they teach, this study only invited elementary mathematics teachers from the same primary school. Moreover, as younger students in an elementary school may not be mature enough to articulate "good" mathematics instruction, only sixth graders were invited to participate in this study. In particular, the following research questions were asked:

– What are the characteristics of Chinese elementary mathematics teachers' views of a good mathematics lesson?
– What are Chinese students' views of a good mathematics lesson? What are possible similarities and differences in describing a good mathematics lesson between mathematics teachers and students?
– What is the school's view of the quality of mathematics classroom instruction? What are possible similarities and differences on viewing the quality of classroom instruction among teacher, students, and their school?

METHOD

Participants

One elementary school located in an eastern province of mainland China partici-pated in a larger research project that aims to investigate Chinese mathematics classroom teaching. This is one of seven elementary schools that participated in the larger research project. With Chinese mathematics education experts' help, the seven schools were selected to represent a wide spectrum of school quality and reputations. However, we were able to collect a school's evaluation sheet of classroom teaching only from this elementary school, and this school was judged as having an average quality level in that province. The quality level is evaluated in terms of the school's location, the community it serves, the school's students' test scores and perceived teachers' quality. In particular, the school is located in a small city and serves a student population mainly from the rural areas adjacent to the city. This elementary school has about 1200 students enrolled in grades one to six.

The selected school was invited to join the project and received an explanation of the objectives, the procedure, and the instruments used to collect the data. The school, participating teachers, and students were all informed that the data collection was only for research purposes. As part of the research project, the assignment of writing a free-essay about a good mathematics lesson was given to all mathematics teachers and the participating two sixth-grade classes from the same school. A total of 11 mathematics teachers and 84 sixth graders from this elementary school completed and turned in their essays. The teachers' and students' responses represent 85% and 78% returning rate, respectively. Moreover, the evaluation sheet used by the school for judging the quality of mathematics classroom instruction was also collected.

Procedure

In the essay assignment given to the teachers and students, all participants were asked to write a free-essay with the following instructions.

Write an expository essay entitled: 'What is a good mathematics lesson?'
Note: In this essay, you describe in your own words what a good mathematics lesson should be. Do not mention names of teachers and do not describe one particular teacher, but the good mathematics lesson in general. There is not a word limit, so just put on paper what you consider the most important points.

One teacher in the school helped distribute the assignment sheet to all mathematics teachers and collected all completed essays. Teachers were asked to complete the essays voluntarily and anonymously. There was no time limitation on completing the essays. Some teachers turned in their essays the same day while many others the next day or so.

To collect students' essays, mathematics teachers for the two sixth-grade classes helped distribute the writing assignment sheet to their students. Students' essays were then collected by a pre-appointed student two days later.

Data Coding and Analysis

Content analysis of participants' essays was carried out to extract conceptual constructs used by teachers and students (e.g., Kutnick & Jules, 1993). In particular, the data coding consisted of a process of one step (only the following first step) for teachers' essays and three steps for students' essays: (1) a full-content analysis of 10% of students' essays (100% for teachers' essays) to generate a list of conceptual items, (2) a preliminary review of the remaining students' essays to check whether there were any other new conceptual items, and (3) coding the remaining 90% of students' essays.

In the case of coding teachers' essays, all of the teachers' essays were analyzed by two coders and all differences were resolved through discussions. This procedure resulted in a list of 28 conceptual items from the 11 teachers' essays, such as students' learning cognitive outcomes (knowledge, ability development), students' active thinking and reasoning, fulfilling instructional objectives, and using different teaching methods flexibly. The following is part of a teacher's essay that was identified as containing eight conceptual items.

1. A good mathematics lesson should be valuable and benefit students in terms of <u>knowledge acquisition, increasing interactions and experience</u>, and <u>opening their minds</u>. 2. It should be scientific as <u>meeting students' learning and psychological development</u>. 3. It should have its own characteristics as <u>meeting the students' needs</u>, and well connecting <u>the instructional environment</u> with <u>the curriculum content requirements</u>. 4. It should be an <u>innovative lesson as resulted from the teacher's continued pursuit</u>. ......
[T10]

(Note: Each underlined phrase represented one conceptual item. The numbers in the text were used originally by the teacher.)

In the first step of coding students' essays, all of the essays were first randomly put together. Then one student's essay was randomly selected from every 10 students' essays to generate 10% of all students' essays as a representative sample of students' essays to be analyzed. Two content coders who are fluent in both the Chinese and English language read through the same selected essays and identified every conceptual item of each essay independently. The two coders then cross-checked and discussed their self-identified conceptual items for consistency and agreement for each selected essay. This led to sets of conceptual items that were agreed upon by the two coders. After checking possible replications and overlap, this analysis and discussion resulted in a total of 45 distinct conceptual items that were identified from the selected essays. Sample items include: student actively raised hands to answer questions; student enjoyed learning with confidence; teachers' clear and detailed lecturing and explanation; joyful classroom atmosphere. This process also established the follow-up coding procedure that allowed any single conceptual item to be applied only once for each essay, although a participant may have mentioned something essentially the same repeatedly or at length.

With this list of 45 identified conceptual items, the second step was carried out first with one content coder going through the rest of all students' essays to check whether there are any new conceptual items. In the event that a new conceptual item was noticed, two coders would then have further discussion about the possible new item to decide whether it should be added to the list of conceptual items.

After identifying three new items, the complete list of 48 distinct conceptual items was obtained. Another 10% of the essays were then analyzed by the two coders independently. Intercoder reliability was 89%. After that, one coder finished the coding of the remaining 80% of students' essays. While all the coding was done in Chinese, the final list of 48 distinct conceptual items for these 84 sixth graders was then translated into English based on these two bilingual coders' discussion and consensus.

All coded data were then subjected to both qualitative and quantitative analyses to answer the research questions. In particular, the nature of all conceptual items identified from teachers' and students' essays was examined with extensive discussion for possible categorization (e.g., Kutnick & Jules, 1993). Four focus aspects were identified for classifying all conceptual items into (1) student and learning, (2) teacher and teaching, (3) instructional content, or (4) classroom context. The frequencies and percentages of teachers' and students' use of different conceptual items were then summarized at both the item and category levels. Moreover, the evaluation sheet from the school was also analyzed and compared with teachers' and students' responses. Special attention was given to find what relationships may exist among mathematics teachers, students and the school in their views on the quality of mathematics lesson.

RESULTS

The results show different patterns in teachers' and students' thinking about a "good lesson." In general, teachers used more conceptual items and mentioned students and their learning more frequently than other aspects including teaching. Students discussed students themselves most frequently, but used more conceptual items about teachers and teaching. In contrast, the evaluation sheet used in the school focused more on teachers and teaching than students and learning. The following five sections are structured to provide detailed findings related to research questions.

Elementary Mathematics Teachers' Views of a Good Mathematics Lesson

A total of 28 conceptual items in four categories were used by the elementary mathematics teachers in describing a good mathematics lesson. Table 1 summarizes the number of items classified into different categories and percentages of times that items in different categories were used in teachers' essays.

Table 1 shows that these teachers used more items related to student and learning than the other aspects. In fact, 13 out of 28 items focus on students and their learning. Sample items include: students motivated to participate, student-centered instruction, students' exploration and discovery, students' learning with understanding. There are 11 items that focus more closely on teachers and teaching, such as having innovative instruction concept (approaches, tools), effective teaching with low pressure, fulfilling instructional objectives, and using different teaching methods flexibly. For the other four items, two are on instructional content (i.e., rich and/or solid content in mathematics, connecting mathematics with real life) and the other two are on classroom context and interactions.

Table 1. Number of conceptual items classified into different categories and percentages of times that they were used in teachers' essays

Categories	Number of items	Percentage of usage
Teacher and teaching	11	28%
Student and learning	13	53%
Instructional content	2	13%
Classroom context	2	6%

Consistently, these teachers tended to describe students and their learning more frequently than the other three aspects mentioned above. Accumulatively, conceptual items focusing on students and their learning were used 42 times (or 53%), whereas items on teachers and teaching, instructional content, and classroom context were used 22 times (28%), 10 times (13%), and 5 times (6%), respectively.

In examining individual teacher's essays, the number of conceptual items used ranged from 4 to 16 with an average of about 7 items per essay. There were no specific patterns noticed in terms of the ways that these conceptual items were used together in these teachers' description of a good mathematics lesson. Across these individual items, relative high frequency use were all related to students and their learning (especially on students' engagement and learning interest, student-centered instruction, and students' overall development). Another high frequency item was on instructional content (i.e., rich and/or solid content in mathematics). The results present a consistent focus among these teachers on students and content, when considering what can be counted as a good mathematics lesson. For example, the following are part of two teachers' essays:

"[A good lesson] should let students enjoy the lesson, be motivated to think actively. It should have certain cultural substance, rooms for application, and is rich in mathematics" [T2].

"I think that a good mathematics lesson should first have a mathematical taste as its special character. Then, mathematics content should be connected to students' daily life. ......, displaying students' learning process. Finally, (the teacher) needs to design and use rich and challenge problems that can show the value of a mathematics lesson" [T7].

Although these two teachers used different conceptual items when describing a good mathematics lesson, it becomes apparent that both students and content were focused on in their description. In particular, T2 mentioned students and their learning first, then talked about the requirement on the lesson's content. In comparison, T7 placed even more attention on the lesson's mathematics content, and how it should be connected to students and their learning.

Chinese Sixth Graders' Views of a Good Mathematics Lesson

A total of 48 conceptual items were used by 84 sixth graders in their description of a good mathematics lesson. Table 2 summarizes the number of items classified into different categories and percentages of times that items in different categories were used in these students' essays.

Among these 48 items, Table 2 shows that teacher and teaching is the category that students used the most often, with 23 out of 48 items. Sample items include: teachers' kindness and humor, teacher not blaming students, teachers' clear and detailed lecturing and explanation. In comparison, there are fewer items (11 items) used that have a focus on students and learning, such as student listening attentively, student learning knowledge and developing mathematical ability,

Table 2. Number of conceptual items classified into different categories and percentages of times that they were used in students' essays

Categories	Number of items	Percentage of usage
Teacher and teaching	23	37%
Student and learning	11	46%
Instructional content	10	6%
Classroom context	4	11%

student actively raising hands to answer questions, and student enjoying learning with confidence. For the remaining 14 items, 10 items are on instructional content (e.g., not just for examination preparation, having both basic and difficult problems, mathematics as a dynamic and meaningful body of knowledge); the other four were on classroom atmosphere and interactions (e.g., joyful classroom atmosphere, frequent interactions between teacher and students).

In contrast to the item distribution in different categories, Table 2 shows that the students tended to describe students and their learning (not teacher and teaching) more frequently than the other three aspects mentioned above. Cumulatively, conceptual items focusing on students and their learning were used 157 times (or 46%), whereas items on teachers and teaching, instructional content, and classroom context were used 126 times (37%), 22 times (6%), and 37 times (11%), respectively.

In looking through individual student's essays, the number of conceptual items that students used ranged from 1 to 12 with an average of about 4 items per essay. There were no specific patterns noticed in terms of the ways that these conceptual items were used together in these students' description of a good mathematics lesson. Across the individual items, relative high frequency use were all related to students and their learning (especially on students' self-discipline and listening attentively – 41 persons mentioning that students learned knowledge and developed mathematical ability – 28 persons, students actively raised hands to answer questions – 24 persons). There was one high frequency item mentioned about teachers (i.e., teachers' kindness and humor – 31 persons). The results present a relatively focused agreement among these 84 students on specific aspects of students and teacher, when describing what can be considered a good mathematics lesson.

Differences and Connections between Participating Elementary Mathematics Teachers and Six Graders in Their Views of a Good Mathematics Lesson

By taking a closer look at these conceptual items used in teachers' and students' descriptions, we found an important dimension of differences. In particular, teachers tended to use more general terms in their descriptions, whereas students often pointed to specifics. For example, teachers mentioned students and their learning with phrases like "students motivated to participate/learn," "student-centered instruction," "students' exploration and discovery," and "students' learning with understanding." In contrast, 41 students (out of 84 respondents) indicated that students should be self-disciplined and listen attentively during classroom instruction, and 24 students mentioned that students should actively raise hands to answer questions. The same pattern applies to teachers' and students' descriptions related to teacher and teaching. For example, the teachers indicated the needs for innovative design of classroom instruction, teaching effectively with low pressure, and using the textbook adequately to meet instructional needs. The top four comments made by the students are (a) the teacher should be nice and have a sense of humor (31 out of 84 students), (b) the teacher should not blame students, even if they make a mistake (14 students), (c) the teacher should take the teaching seriously and explain clearly (13 students), and (d) the teacher should care about students and treat all students in a fair manner (12 students). The differences between students' and teachers' descriptions suggest that students and teachers developed their descriptions about a good mathematics lesson from different angles. Teachers paid close attention to the whole structure and general features of a lesson. Students were likely, perhaps based on their own experiences as learners in the classroom, to describe what may be desired features of a good mathematics lesson. The differences call for special attention to students' thinking and feeling in classroom instruction.

In examining teachers' and students' descriptions holistically, it seems that teachers and students developed varying perceptions about a good mathematics lesson. No single common picture is readily perceivable, except the more apparent difference in terms of specifics between teachers' and students' descriptions. None of these teachers described a good mathematics lesson from a perfectionist perspective, rather with a more reasonable attitude. In fact, one teacher specifically indicated that "I think that a lesson cannot be perfect, but not being perfect does not mean not a good lesson. ..." The case for students' descriptions of a good lesson is about the same, as most students have no clear idea about a good mathematics lesson beyond their own experience.

The School's Evaluation Sheet on the Quality of Mathematics Instruction

It is a common practice in Chinese schools to develop and use an evaluation sheet for judging the quality of mathematics classroom instruction. The school usually takes a gradual approach to continue revising and polishing the evaluation sheet based on teachers' use and feedback. The evaluation sheet thus presents a collective point of view about the important features to consider when evaluating a lesson in the school. In this study, the evaluation sheet was also developed and made available to all teachers in the elementary school. Every mathematics teacher knew what was important to consider when developing and delivering classroom instruction.

In this elementary school, seven aspects were specified in the evaluation sheet. They include (1) instructional objectives, (2) textbook use, (3) instructional method, (4) lesson structure, (5) instructional effects, (6) teacher's instructional skills, and (7) students' active participation. Specific explanations for each aspect were provided as criteria for judgement. For example, the seventh aspect on students' active participation included (a) let students raise their own questions, (b) let students explore by themselves, (c) let students discover patterns, (d) let students create their own methods, (e) let students expand their own learning area, (f) let students explore learning content by themselves, (g) let students use their own learning outcomes, and (h) let students develop their own learning interest. By taking each explanation as one conceptual item, the whole evaluation sheet would contain 34 items. Among these 34 items, 15 items focused on teachers and teaching, 15 on students and their learning, 3 on curriculum and content, and 1 on classroom atmosphere.

Each of the seven aspects stated on the evaluation sheet is specified with different pre-determined weights that can be used by evaluators in obtaining a numerical score for each mathematics lesson observed. In particular, while the aspects of (5) instructional effects and (7) students' active participations are given the highest weight of 20%, the aspects of (3) instructional method and (6) teacher's instructional skills are weighted as 15%. The remaining three aspects are all weighted at 10%. Thus, the sum of these seven aspects, if all fully credited, is 100%. If the four aspects used in analyzing teachers' and students' essays are re-distributed using the weights, the evaluation sheet assigns 48% to teachers and teaching, 38% to students and their learning, 10% to curriculum and content, and 4% to classroom context.

Emphases Placed on Viewing the Quality of Classroom Instruction among Participating Elementary Mathematics Teachers, Students, and Their School

The broad differences, when viewing the quality of classroom instruction, are more obvious than similarities among participating elementary mathematics teachers, students, and their school. Table 3 summarizes that the number of conceptual items used by teachers, students, and the school vary across four categories, i.e., teacher and teaching, student and learning, instructional content, and classroom context. It appears that teachers used relatively more conceptual items related to students and learning in describing a good mathematics lesson, whereas students used more conceptual items related to teacher and teaching, and the school had about the same number of items for teacher and teaching vs. student and learning. The results indicate that teachers and students had more variations in aspects of a good mathematics lesson than the school.

Table 3. Number and percentage of conceptual items with different focuses that teachers, students, and their school used

Item focus	Teachers	Students	School
Teacher and teaching	11 (39%)	23 (48%)	15 (44%)
Student and learning	13 (46%)	11 (23%)	15 (44%)
Instructional content	2 (7%)	10 (21%)	3 (9%)
Classroom context	2 (7%)	4 (8%)	1 (3%)

The number of conceptual items used only reveals one dimension of possible attention given to different aspects. Table 4, below, summarizes the percentages of times that conceptual items in different categories were used by different parties. The results indicate that teachers mentioned student and learning much more frequently than the other three aspects, a result that shows a similar pattern as the number of conceptual items used by teachers in Table 3. However, the pattern is very different in students' descriptions and in the school's evaluation sheet. In particular, students mentioned student and learning more frequently than the other three aspects, although students used many more different conceptual items in describing teacher and teaching than the other three aspects. In contrast, the school placed more weight on teacher and teaching in the evaluation sheet than the other three aspects, although it used about the same number of conceptual items for teacher and teaching versus student and learning.

Table 4. Percentage of times that conceptual items with different focuses were used by teachers, students, and their school

Item focus	Teachers	Students	School
Teacher and teaching	28%	37%	48%
Student and learning	53%	46%	38%
Instructional content	13%	6%	10%
Classroom context	6%	11%	4%

By putting the above two measures together, it becomes clear that these elementary mathematics teachers placed a consistent focus on students and their learning when describing a good mathematics lesson. They described not only more different aspects related to students and their learning, but also more frequently. The result suggests that these elementary mathematics teachers thought a great deal about students and their learning in the process of classroom instruction.

In contrast, the picture is different from the school's perspective where teacher and teaching received more attention in the evaluation sheet. However, the difference between teachers' descriptions and the school's evaluation sheet may not necessarily be a negative thing. It is understandable that observers and/or evaluators need to pay close attention to what a teacher does in mathematics classroom instruction. If the teacher can pay more attention to students and their learning in classroom instruction, it is less likely that something will go wrong than if the teacher focused on her/his own teaching.

What becomes more interesting is reflected in students' descriptions. Student participants seemed to have many more different things to say about teacher and teaching, but actually mentioned themselves more frequently in their descriptions of a good mathematics lesson. It is possible that students, who might not be able to view classroom instruction from an instructor's perspective, could not say more about teacher and teaching.

DISCUSSION AND CONCLUSION

What May We Learn about the Nature of Effective Teaching from Elementary Mathematics Teachers in Comparison to Their Students?

The results highlight several aspects in Chinese elementary mathematics teachers' views about a good mathematics lesson. In general, the results obtained from this study are in line with what has been reported by others (e.g., Wang & Cai, 2007; Zhao & Ma, 2007) in their study with Chinese experienced teachers. For example, expert teachers in Zhao and Ma's study took the extent of students' participation as one common standard. Two other common standards were reported, more from an evaluation point of view, as all related to instructional objectives and their fulfilment. There were also 10 other standards mentioned by these five expert teachers in Zhao and Ma's study. The diversity on what counts as a good mathematics lesson is thus evidenced in a way that is similar to what we found with these 11 Chinese elementary teachers in our study.

Although no single common picture about effective teaching can be extracted from these participating elementary teachers' essays in this study, it is through contrasting with their students' descriptions that we can learn something more about the nature of these mathematics teachers' views. In particular, because participating students had many different things to say about teacher and teaching, an examination of all related conceptual items used by students suggests that these items are specific in nature. It is very possible that most students can only talk about a good mathematics lesson based on their own experience and feeling, rather than from a sophisticated perspective. Students' descriptions and their use of specific items mirrored the teachers' tendency in their use of general and broad terms when describing a good mathematics lesson.

Because students likely focused their attention in ways different from their teachers, we can thus learn something beyond what we can gain from examining teachers' views about effective teaching alone. For example, the top two comments made by participating sixth graders about teacher and teaching in our study are (a) the teacher should be nice and have a sense of humor, and (b) the teacher should not blame students, even if they make a mistake. These popular comments suggest that students had concerns related to the teachers' treatment of students in classrooms. This result is in a direct contrast to teachers' extensive mentioning of student and learning in their descriptions of a good mathematics lesson. It is possible that these students, as human beings, hope to be cared about and respected by teachers, while the teachers may treat students as learners who need to be well-disciplined and care more about their learning. Thus, students may feel differently about their teacher's care given in a strict manner. At the same time, it is also possible that such concerns are specific to a special group of participating Chinese students in the study. It is a question that requires further investigation.

Another interesting difference between these teachers' and students' descriptions is revealed when students' classroom behavior is taken into consideration. None of the eleven elementary teachers mentioned anything about students' classroom behavior. Classroom management did not seem to be a concern at all to these elementary mathematics teachers in describing a good mathematics lesson, a result that is in line with our recent study on Chinese teachers' perceptions of students' classroom misbehavior (Ding, Li, Li, & Kulm, 2008). Surprisingly, students' classroom behavior was the highest concern for having a good mathematics lesson among these sixth graders. The differences between teachers' and students' concerns about classroom behaviour suggests the need for further research on this topic in the future, as well as the importance of examining both teachers' and students' views about effective teaching.

What May These Chinese Elementary Mathematics Teachers' Views Tell Us about Mathematics Classroom Instruction in China?

The results obtained from this study provide a glimpse of what is valued in mathematics classroom instruction in China. Although it is well-documented that Chinese classroom instruction can be characterized by large class size, teacher's lecture-oriented instruction, and examination-driven (e.g., Fan, Wong, Cai, & Li, 2004; Watkins & Biggs, 2001), the results from this study suggest that Chinese elementary mathematics teachers thought a great deal about students and their learning in the process of classroom instruction. This finding supports the observations that the teacher-dominated lecture style of traditional teaching in China does not mean decreased efforts to engage students in classroom teaching and learning activities, and that students still involve themselves heavily in the process of learning in classrooms (Cortazzi & Jin, 2001; Huang & Leung, 2004; Mok, 2006). To a certain degree, the result reflects a less-known side of Chinese teachers' thinking that has often been masked by the perception of teacher-lecture dominated teaching in China.

Cross-nationally, it is now well-perceived that mathematics classroom instruction in the U.S. is different from what is happening in mathematics classrooms in East Asia, including China (e.g., Hiebert et al., 2003; Stigler & Hiebert, 1999; Stigler, Lee, & Stevenson, 1987). As mentioned at the beginning of this chapter, Wilson et al. (2005) reported that teachers interviewed in their study emphasized the importance of (1) teachers' knowledge of mathematics and their students, (2) promoting mathematical understanding, (3) motivating and engaging students, and (4) effective classroom management. Although there are many differences between participating teachers in Wilson et al.'s study and those in our study, the results may provide a hint to some possible similarities and differences when compared to what we can find with Chinese teachers in our study. In particular, U.S. teachers in Wilson et al.'s study emphasized teachers' effective classroom management, which was not mentioned at all by Chinese elementary teachers in our study. The difference is actually interesting, because the typical U.S. class size is much smaller than the Chinese one. This difference suggests different considerations that U.S. and Chinese teachers may have in relation to students' classroom behavior. At the same time, it seems common between U.S. teachers and Chinese teachers, as reported in these two studies, to place their focus on students and their learning. The common focus placed on student and learning suggests the need to search for possibly more common ground cross-nationally in mathematics teachers' thinking and their teaching, an aspect that is often overlooked in cross-national studies.

Limitations and Future Directions

This study certainly has its own limitations. First of all, the data is restricted to 11 mathematics teachers and 84 sixth graders from one elementary school. Nevertheless, the study shows its unique value as it provides a better picture of what counts as a good mathematics lesson viewed by teachers, students, and their school. Extreme caution should be taken to interpret these results and compare them to elementary mathematics teachers and students in China. Further investigations become necessary to expand the sampling scope to include more participants from other schools in China. Moreover, the results obtained from this study have not been connected directly with what was happening in these participating students' classes. The interpretation of the results is thus restricted to what we can learn from literature about Chinese mathematics classroom instruction in general. Further investigation for making such a direct connection is also valuable to develop a better understanding of elementary classroom instruction in mainland China.

ACKNOWLEDGEMENTS

The research reported in this paper was supported in part by a research grant from the Spencer Foundation. However, any opinions expressed herein are those of the authors and do not necessarily represent the views of the Spencer Foundation. We would like to thank Jiansheng Bao, Yijuan Shao, Hong Jian, and Hongwei Zhu for their assistance in the process of collecting the Chinese data. We are also grateful to all the participants for sharing their thoughts.

REFERENCES

An, S., Kulm, G., & Wu, Z. (2004). The pedagogical content knowledge of middle school mathematics teachers in China and the U.S. *Journal of Mathematics Teacher Education, 28*(2), 145–172.

Beishuizen, J. J., Hof, E., van Putten, C. M., Bouwmeester, S., & Asscher, J. J. (2001). Students' and teachers' cognitions about good teachers. *British Journal of Educational Psychology, 71*, 185–201.

Borko, H., & Livingston, C. (1989). Cognition and improvisation: Differences in mathematics instruction by expert and novice teachers. *American Educational Research Journal, 26*(4), 473–498.

Cai, J., Perry, R., & Wong, N.-Y. (Eds.). (2007). What is effective mathematics teaching? A dialogue between East and West. *ZDM-The International Journal on Mathematics Education, 39*(4).

Correa, C. A., Perry, M., Sims, L. M., Miller, K. F., & Fang, G. (2008). Connected and culturally embedded beliefs: Chinese and US teachers talk about how their students best learn mathematics. *Teaching and Teacher Education, 24*, 140–153.

Cortazzi, M., & Jin, L. (2001). Large classes in China: 'Good' teachers and interaction. In D. A. Watkins & J. B. Biggs (Eds.), *Teaching the Chinese learner: Psychological and pedagogical perspectives* (pp. 115–134). Hong Kong: Comparative Education Research Center, The University of Hong Kong.

Ding, M., Li, Y., Li, X., & Kulm, G. (2008). Chinese teachers' perceptions of students' classroom misbehaviour. *Educational Psychology, 28*, 305–324.

Fan, L., Wong, N., Cai, J., & Li, S. (Eds.). (2004). *How Chinese learn mathematics – perspectives from insiders.* Singapore: World Scientific Publishing.

Fernandez, C., & Cannon, J. (2005). What Japanese and U.S. teachers think about when constructing mathematics lessons: A preliminary investigation. *Elementary School Journal, 105*(5), 481–498.

Hiebert, J., Gallimore, R., Garnier, Giwin, K. B., Hollingsworth, H., Jacobs, J., et al. (2003). *Teaching mathematics in seven countries: Results from the TIMSS 1999 video study.* U. S. Department of Education. Washington, DC: National Center for Education Statistics.

Huang, R., Chen, Y., & Zhao, X. (2005). How do expert teachers evaluate mathematics lessons? *Journal of Mathematics Education, 14*(1), 52–56.

Huang, R., & Leung, F. K. S. (2004). Cracking the paradox of the Chinese learners: Looking into the mathematics classrooms in Hong Kong and Shanghai. In L. Fan, N. Y. Wong, J. Cai, & S. Li (Eds.), *How Chinese learn mathematics: Perspectives from insiders* (pp. 348–381). Singapore: World Scientific Publishing.

Jin, L., & Cortazzi, M. (1998). Dimensions of dialogue: Large classes in China. *International Journal of Educational Research, 29*, 739–761.

Krainer, K. (2005). What is "good" mathematics teaching, and how can research inform practice and policy? (editorial). *Journal of Mathematics Teacher Education, 8*, 75–81.

Kutnick, P., & Jules, V. (1993). Pupils' perceptions of a good teacher: A developmental perspective from Trinidad and Tobago. *British Journal of Educational Psychology, 63*, 400–413.

Leinhardt, G. (1987). Development of an expert explanation: An analysis of a sequence of subtraction lessons. *Cognition and Instruction, 4*(4), 225–282.

Li, Y. (2004). Learning from curriculum materials for developing mathematical instruction. In *Proceedings of the seminar on best practices and innovations in the teaching and learning of science and mathematics at the secondary level* (pp. 134–144). Pennang, Malaysia, 18–22 July, 2004.

Ma, L. (1999). *Knowing and teaching elementary mathematics: Teachers' understanding of fundamental mathematics in China and the United States.* Mahwah, NJ: Lawrence Erlbaum Associates.

Math Connections Implementation Center. (2007). *Math connections* [On-line]. Retrieved June 25, 2007, from http://www.its-about-time.com/htmls/mc/mcbestpractices.html

Mok, I. A. C. (2006). Teacher-dominating lessons in Shanghai: The insiders' story. In D. J. Clarke, C. Keitel, & Y. Shimizu (Eds.), *Mathematics classrooms in twelve countries: The insider's perspective* (pp. 87–98). Rotterdam: Sense Publishers.

National Commission on Teaching & America's Future. (1996). *What matters most: Teaching for America's future.* New York: The Authors.

National Council of Teachers of Mathematics. (1991). *Professional standards for teaching mathematics.* Reston, VA: The Authors.

National Council of Teachers of Mathematics. (2000). *Principles and standards for school mathematics.* Reston, VA: The Authors.

Schoenfeld, A. H. (1988). When good teaching leads to bad results: The disasters of "well-taught" mathematics courses. *Educational Psychologist, 23*(2), 145–166.

Stevenson, H. W., & Lee, S. (1997). The East Asian version of whole-class teaching. In W. K. Cummings & P. G. Altbach (Eds.), *The challenge of Eastern Asian education* (pp. 33–49). Albany, NY: State University of New York.

Stigler, J. W., & Hiebert, J. (1999). *The teaching gap - best ideas from the world's teachers for improving education in the classroom.* New York: The Free Press.

Stigler, J. W., & Hiebert, J. (2004). Improving mathematics teaching. *Educational Leadership, 61*(5), 12–17.

Stigler, J. W., Lee, S.-Y., & Stevenson, H. W. (1987). Mathematics classrooms in Japan, Taiwan, and the United States. *Child Development, 58*, 1272–1285.

Stigler, J. W., & Stevenson, H. W. (1991). How Asian teachers polish each lesson to perfection. *American Educator, 15*(1), 12–20, 43–47.

Wang, T., & Cai, J. (2007). Chinese (mainland) teachers' views of effective mathematics teaching and learning. *ZDM-The International Journal on Mathematics Education, 39*, 287–300.

Watkins, D. A., & Biggs, J. B. (Eds.). (2001). *Teaching the Chinese learner: Psychological and pedagogical perspectives.* Hong Kong: Comparative Education Research Center, The University of Hong Kong.

Wilson, P. S., Conney, T. J., & Stinson, D. W. (2005). What constitutes good mathematics teaching and how it develops: Nine high school teachers' perspectives. *Journal of Mathematics Teacher Education, 8*, 83–111.

Zemelman, S., Daniels, H., & Hyde, A. (1993). *Best practice – new standards for teaching and learning in America's schools.* Portsmouth, NH: Heinemann.

Zhao, D., & Ma, Y. (2007). A qualitative research on evaluating primary mathematics lessons. *Journal of Mathematics Education, 16*(2), 71–76.

Yeping Li, Gerald Kulm, Rongjin Huang
Texas A&M University

Meixia Ding
University of Nebraska-Lincoln

QIAN-TING WONG, NGAI-YING WONG, CHI-CHUNG LAM,
AND QIAO-PING ZHANG[1]

BELIEFS ABOUT MATHEMATICS AND EFFECTIVE TEACHING AMONG ELEMENTARY MATHEMATICS TEACHERS IN HONG KONG

BELIEFS ABOUT EFFECTIVE TEACHING CREATE REALITY:
THE LIVED SPACE OF MATHEMATICS LEARNING

In his seminal paper, Snyder (1984) illustrated, with a number of experiments, how beliefs can create reality. Inevitably, teachers' beliefs[2] about mathematics teaching and their views on effective mathematics teaching play an important role in their teaching, which in turn makes an impact on students' learning outcomes (see, for example, Carpenter, Fennema, Franke, Levi, & Empson, 1999; Fennema et al., 1996; Furinghetti, 1997; Pehkonen & Törner, 1998; Perry, Wong, & Howard, 2006; Shirk, 1972; Thompson, 1992). For instance, some teachers think that mathematics is understood when students can successfully follow procedural instructions. Those who see mathematics as following sets of procedures invented by others will provide their students with little opportunity for making sense out of mathematics (Battista, 1994). Lerman (1983) also showed that a problem-centered view of mathematics resulted in different teaching when compared with a knowledge-centered view. Furthermore, teachers who believe that children learn mathematics by constructing their own understanding are more inclined to refrain from mere transmission of knowledge (Furinghetti, 1994; Peterson, Fennema, Carpenter, & Loef, 1989). These results were not just obtained through questionnaire surveys in which the participants' perceptions were tapped. In Stipek, Givvin, Salmon, and MacGyvers (2001), video analysis of the actual classroom teaching was also performed, which came up with consistent results. Though inconsistencies between teachers' beliefs and actions were occasionally found, as Philipp (2007) puts it "most researchers ... found that the inconsistencies that arose when documenting teachers' beliefs and action[s] ceased to exist after they better understood the teachers' thinking about some aspects of their contexts" (p. 276).

While teachers' beliefs about effective mathematics teaching influence their actual teaching behavior, these two in turn create an impact on students' learning and their learning outcomes. On the one hand, as Kember (1997) pointed out, teachers' beliefs and approaches to teaching would impose similar beliefs on students' beliefs on learning. In his paper, Kember (1997) put forth a model which was later revised by Watkins and Biggs (2001) into "teachers' conception[s] of

J. Cai, G. Kaiser, B. Perry and N.-Y. Wong (eds.), Effective Mathematics Teaching from Teachers'
Perspectives: National and Cross-National Studies, 235–257.
© *2009 Sense Publishers. All rights reserved.*

learning → teachers' conception[s] of teaching → teachers' approaches to teaching → students' conception[s] of learning → students' approaches to learning → students' learning outcomes" (p. 17). Research findings do support such an assertion: students' and teachers' beliefs about mathematics possess a lot of resemblances, though teachers could have more flexibility in their responses (Wong, 2000b, 2001a, 2002).

In other words, while students' beliefs about mathematics (and about how mathematics is learned) resemble the teachers', such beliefs impose great impact on students' approaches to mathematics learning and consequently their learning outcomes (Cobb, 1985; Crawford, Gordon, Nicholas, & Prosser, 1998a, 1998b; Leder, Pehkonen, & Törner, 2002; McLeod, 1992; Pehkonen & Törner, 1998; Underhill, 1988). It is the teacher who shaped the "lived space" of mathematics learning. Since less variation is associated with narrower ways of experiencing a phenomenon, and more variation is associated with wider ways of experiencing that phenomenon (Bowden & Marton, 1998; Marton & Booth, 1997), teachers' narrow conceptions of mathematics and their conservative views of effective mathematics teaching would lead them to create a restricted "lived space" for their students. Being brought up in such a space with limited experience, students would not only inherit their teachers' narrow conceptions of mathematics (such as taking mathematics as a set of absolute truths), but also be inclined to use surface approaches to tackle mathematical problems, thus leading to lower levels of learning outcomes (Lam, Wong, & Wong, 1999; Marton & Säljö, 1976; Wong, Chiu, Wong, & Lam, 2005).

This precisely coincides with what we have found in the Hong Kong context in a series of studies that were conducted in the past decade. Results revealed that students identified mathematics by its terminology and content and that mathematics was often perceived as a set of rules. To them, mathematics is a subject of calculables. With such a perception, they tend to tackle mathematical problems by the search for routines. In order to do so, they look for clues embedded in the questions, including the given information, what is being asked, the context (in which topic it lies), as well as the format of the question (Lam et al., 1999; Wong, 2000a, 2000b, 2001a, 2001b, 2002, 2004; Wong, Lam, & Wong, 1998; Wong, Marton, Wong, & Lam, 2002). When we analyzed more than 1,500 mathematical problems given by mathematics teachers to their students, it was found that these problems were stereotyped, lacked variation, possessed a unique answer, allowed only a single approach, and demanded only low cognitive skills (Wong, Lam, & Chan, 2002).

We proceeded to investigate views on effective teaching among expert teachers (Wong, 2007). Though their views were very much in line with the students,' naturally they possess a broader view. To them, effective mathematics teaching is one that sets a path of mathematization for the students that goes from the concrete to the abstract, that enhances understanding, and that allows students to acquire a flexible use of rules. To this end, well-organized practices (repetition with variation) may serve as a scaffold that leads from the basics to higher-order thinking skills (Wong, 2006). To actualize such a teacher-led, yet student-centered teaching, in which the teachers are believed to be most effective, teacher professionalism becomes the crux of the matter. Teachers must have strong professional knowledge, including the mastery of teaching skills and the ability to understand the students. These findings by and large are echoed by teachers in various regions (see Cai, Perry, & Wong 2007, or Chapter 1, this book).

If we put students' and teachers' beliefs into a single picture, teachers' beliefs about mathematics and mathematics learning affect their views of effective mathematics teaching and their approaches to mathematics teaching. These would affect not only their teaching behavior but also their shaping the "lived space" of their students, thus affecting students' learning and learning outcomes (Figure 1).

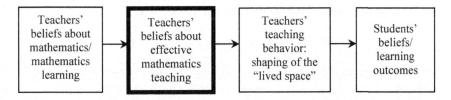

Figure 1. The lived space of mathematics learning

To date, though a voluminous body of research is devoted to the investigation of students' and teachers' beliefs about mathematics, mathematics learning and teaching (including teachers' views on effective mathematics teaching studies), there are not very many studies of these three beliefs among teachers in a single research effort, so as to delineate how one influences the other (Raymond, 1997, could be regarded as one of those). This is the purpose of this study. In this study, not only teachers' various beliefs are tapped, but these beliefs are also delineated in relation to their actual teaching.

METHODOLOGY

Qualitative Strategy

To answer the research questions, it is necessary to gather two sets of data: how teachers teach and what their beliefs about mathematics are – mathematics teaching and learning. Conducting a questionnaire survey may gather the views and self-reported teaching practices from a large sample. However, the deep nature of one's beliefs implies that such an approach is unlikely to provide quality data needed to answer the research questions. The research team therefore decided to follow the practices of other researchers (e.g., Kouba & McDonald, 1991; Lam et al., 1999; Lederman, 1999), and use qualitative methods such as interview and observations. In particular, on top of other methods, hypothetical situations similar to those in Kouba and McDonald (1991) were employed (see Appendix 1 for details), in which participants were asked to judge whether "doing mathematics" was involved in each case.

Taking into consideration the need to link the teachers' beliefs and their practices, we adopted the case study approach. Through revealing the beliefs of the teachers participating in the study and how they teach in classroom, the research team is in a stronger position to assert the linkage between beliefs and practices. As Yin (2003) has argued, multiple cases allow comparison and facilitate the exploration of the development of propositions from the data (see also Schoenfeld, 2002).

In light of the complexity of the research questions and the resources available, the research team invited seven teachers who were teaching Primary 5 mathematics to participate in the study. All of them had more than one year's experience of teaching Primary 5. Their backgrounds are given in Table 1.

Table 1. The backgrounds of the participants

Participant	Teaching experience	Professional qualifications related to mathematics
Teacher A	5 years	Teacher Certificate, B.Ed. (mathematics)
Teacher B	5 years	Teacher Certificate, B.Sc. (mathematics)
Teacher C	More than 10 years	Teacher Certificate (mathematics)
Teacher D	More than 10 years	Teacher Certificate (mathematics)
Teacher E	More than 10 years	Teacher Certificate not related to mathematics
Teacher F	5 years	Teacher Certificate not related to mathematics
Teacher G	More than 10 years	Teacher Certificate not related to mathematics

Data Collection Methods

To show how teachers carry out their work in the classroom, the teachers participating in the study were asked to be observed for three or four lessons, with each lesson lasting for 35 minutes. All the lessons were on the topic of inverse proportion. A member of the research team observed the lessons and noted the flow and special features – such as how teachers responded to students' questions. Moreover, the lessons were video-taped for more detailed analysis at the data analysis stage.

In the present research, the research team was interested in teachers' beliefs about effective mathematics teaching in relation to their beliefs about mathematics and mathematics learning. To reveal this set of beliefs, the research team involved the participants in a series of interviews. In these interviews, the two interview guides used were based on Wong, Lam, and Wong (1998) and Thompson (1991). The former included a set of hypothetical situations (see Appendix 1) that helped to focus the interview on what mathematics is. The latter covered not only what mathematics is but also what mathematics learning and what effective mathematics teaching are (for details, see Appendix 2).

Teachers were also invited to comment on a set of hypothetical situations concerning mathematics teaching. Here are some examples of these situations.
– For the following students' workings, how would you mark them?

a)
```
      3
  7 )2 1
    2 1
      0
```

b)
```
    2 0
  3 )6 1
    6
    1
    0
    1
```

c)
```
      4
  6 )2 9
    2 4
      5
```

d)
```
    1 1
  6 )6 8
    6 0
      8
      6
```

e)
```
    1 0 6
  7 )7 4 2
    7 4 2
```

f)
```
    2 1 4
  2 )4 2 8
        8
        2
        2
```

- Consider the following question: "Siu Fong spent $75 on dolls and snacks. Each doll sells for $59. How much did Siu Fong spend on snacks?" Which of the following expressions are acceptable to you? (a) $x = 75 - 59$; (b) $75 - x = 59$; (c) $59 + x = 75$; (d) $75 - 59 = x$
- Each apple costs $3. The total price of 2 apples should be expressed as $3 × 2, $ (3 × 2) or $ (2 × 3)?

These situations were designed to tap into teachers' beliefs about effective mathematics teaching. For example, a teacher responded to the third question in the following way:

In the beginning of the learning process, my marking will be rigid. Which one is the original number, what is the multiple and what is the multiplier should be stated clearly, and one should write the expression according to the question.

We can say that this teacher is fairly rigid and students are required to follow what teachers teach.

To tap into teachers' beliefs, the research team also asked the participants to explain their rationale behind the design of their lessons before the lesson observation, and discuss how and why, in the lessons observed, they delivered the lessons in the way that they did. These pre-observation and post-observation interviews were found to be very useful because they were based in a naturalistic setting. In the interviews, the interviewer and the interviewee were able to refer to the teaching and learning process they had gone through together.

In sum, each participant was interviewed four times. In the first interview, the interviewee was asked to provide some basic demographic data – such as years of service and classes taught by completing a simple one-page questionnaire – followed by a pre-observation interview focusing on the rationale behind their lesson plans. In the second interview, teachers were interviewed using the "what mathematics is" interview guide (i.e., Appendix 2). The third interview was the post-observation interview. In the fourth interview, the interview guide in Appendix 2 and the hypothetical situations concerning mathematics teaching were used.

Data Analysis

All the classroom observations and interviews were taped and transcribed. These transcripts were read carefully to identify themes. This practice is very similar to what Miles and Huberman (1994) recommended. For the classroom observation, the foci were laid on the flow of the lessons, the ways in which difficult concepts were introduced, the way in which classwork was carried out, the homework assigned, and the ways in which teachers and students interacted.

For the interviews, it is necessary to piece the data together from the four interviews to reconstruct the beliefs that the teachers were upholding. To achieve this, the research team went through all the interview transcripts, "cut and pasted" the "interview segments," and placed them under common themes. Through this, the belief system of each single interviewee was constructed. After this, teachers' beliefs were compared to identify commonalities and differences. When constructing the beliefs of teachers, the research team encountered the problem of contrasting views found in different interviews conducted to the same teacher. For example, when a teacher was asked about her/his preference of teaching methods, her/his response may reflect a more student-centered approach. But when s/he explained why s/he planned her/his lessons the way s/he did, s/he showed very strong inclination toward the transmission of knowledge and considered the dogmatic way more effective. When facing such contrasting signals, the research team would go through the interview data of the teacher to try to establish which reported vignettes were the valid and reliable ones.

TEACHERS' BELIEFS ABOUT MATHEMATICS

Though the focus of this book is on teachers' views of effective mathematics teaching, what is special in the present research is the attempt to delineate an entire picture on the linkage between teachers' beliefs about mathematics and their views of effective mathematics teaching. So we begin by giving a brief summary of the former, which can be seen as an antecedent of the latter.

First of all, consistent with the results of earlier studies on students, most teachers considered calculation as one of the most important aspects of mathematics. Again, similar to what was found in previous studies, mathematics needs understanding is unanimously agreed upon. Furthermore, a majority of the teachers took the view that mathematics and daily life are inseparable. However, one of the teachers (Teacher D) mentioned that there is a trend of making mathematics teaching more and more real-life and contextualized, and thus more sophisticated mathematics is overlooked.

Again, consistent with students' responses in earlier studies, thinking was seen as the heart of mathematics. Though thinking and understanding were emphasized very much, some teachers still identified mathematics by its content and terminologies (appearing in the curriculum). In brief, we see close resemblance between students' (as found in earlier studies) and teachers' beliefs about mathematics. It is reasonable to hypothesize that students' beliefs were actually teachers' beliefs imposed on them through long years of schooling.

TEACHERS' BELIEFS ABOUT EFFECTIVE MATHEMATICS TEACHING

As hypothesized, we will see in this section that the above beliefs about mathematics are closely related to teachers' beliefs about effective mathematics teaching.

Learning by Doing

The importance of practices (exercises) was again unanimously agreed upon. "Since [learning] mathematics needs to go through one's thinking, one can know how much one knows by working it out" [C-cm-1][3]. Yet there are discrepancies on the purpose of class work. Teacher G took classwork as a means of evaluation. She took it that if students can work them out, it is a clear indication that the students have learned [G-cm-11]. However, Teacher A only took classwork as a means of learning [A-cm-14]. There is a variety of classwork, but most rely on paper-and-pencil exercises. However, it should be worth noticing that many of the teachers emphasized the quantity of the exercises as they believe in the maxim "practice makes perfect." Teacher G even prepared a supplementary worksheet of harder word problems in addition to giving those found in the textbook.

Consistent with previous studies (see Chapter 1, this book), in the eyes of the teachers, the provision of a considerable amount of practice is one of the features of effective mathematics teaching. It is not the quantity that counts. Effective mathematics teaching implies a careful arrangement of such exercises so that students can progress from the simple to the complicated. These exercises also serve as diagnoses of learning in between. This is in line with what was found earlier in classroom practices in China (both in Hong Kong and Mainland) (Biggs & Watkins, 1996) and coherent with the anticipations of the students (Wong, Lam, Leung, Mok, & Wong, 1999).

From Rigidity to Flexibility

Teachers said that they would impose a more rigid format (of presenting one's solution, for example) in earlier grades but would become more relaxed as students grow up. As Teacher C said:

> In the beginning of the learning process, my marking will be rigid. Which one is the original number, what is the multiple and what is the multiplier should be stated clearly and one should write the expression according to the question. But the two expressions (2×3 or 3×2) are all allowable after they have learned the commutative law for multiplication. [C-ht-8]

We got a similar response from Teacher B:

> In the beginning, the emphasis is to get hold of the concept. They [students] need to understand the principles of long division. When they are at senior grades, I believe that students will know what they are doing. So I would not impose my methods [on] them. [B-ht-8]

While undoubtedly conformity and discipline are repeatedly stressed in schools, the teachers in the present study see both sides of the coin. Their views of effective mathematics teaching comprise the striking of a balance of formality and flexibility. The effective mathematics teacher should present formal mathematics on the one hand but would not suppress learning with lots of "red tape" on the other. Not only that, as in the case of the use of practice, effective mathematics teaching, in this aspect, should demonstrate a progress (or even a spiral) from rigidity in presentation to flexibility in mathematical thinking.

The Role of the Teacher

Different participants described different roles of the teacher. One of these roles is to demonstrate to the students the ways of calculation. For instance, Teacher G said: "If a student obtained the answer by another method, I will ask her/him to use my method to solve the problem. This could prove that s/he really understand[s] [what] to do" [G-ht-9]. Teacher G continued to say: "Once the teacher has taught it, the students should know [what] to do. If s/he does not understand that, it must be due to her/his carelessness" [G-ht-13].

Another role of the teacher is to enhance understanding. For instance, Teacher E mentioned clearly that "a good mathematics teacher should possess clear concepts and can let students understand" [E-cm-20].

Besides these, the teacher should also provide students with different learning experiences like discussion, problem posing, enquiries, and using of concrete objects. "If the teacher only lectures, well, this is only one mode [of delivery], [and] there would not be new discoveries later; one should encourage the students to think" [A-cm-9].

Teachers should encourage students to express what they think too. This is clear from the following response of Teacher B:

> I am not just a teacher, but also a navigator, an instructor, a learning partner, with which the students can share and discuss, and I am not just teaching the students directly how to calculate and manipulate. [B-cm-27]

As repeatedly revealed in the vast literature on the learning phenomenon among Confucian Heritage Cultures,[4] the effective mathematics teacher illustrates a mentor-mentee relationship rather than just someone holding the authority (Biggs, 1994). In the beliefs of the teachers who participated in the present study, the effective mathematics teacher is one who first demonstrates to the students the right way (or "rite") of doing mathematics and gradually passes the skills to the students, and finally these skills become the students' own skills. This could coincide with the notion of proceeding from "entering the Way" to "transcending the Way," common among Confucian Heritage Cultures (Wong, 2004, 2006).

Problem Solving

Problem solving has earned high regard in recent years, but teachers in our research reflected frankly that they do not know exactly what it is all about. So it is not surprising that they have different ways to address this issue. In brief, some treated problem solving separately and some incorporated it in daily teaching:

> There is one class each week that was devoted to teach problem solving."We do something [that] is different [from] the [formal] curriculum, something like mathematics palindrome. The contents are mainly open problems and [there are] multiple solutions to a single problem. The aim is to make students get used to the idea that mathematics involves thinking and understanding. [E-cm-17]

Another said:

> Problem solving is a thinking method. We should teach and learn synchronously during the day-to-day teaching. In order to make students get used to problem solving, we should implement it continually. Then when they encounter difficulties, they may know what is to be considered first and what is next. [A-cm-16]

We see from the above that while it is unanimously agreed upon that effective mathematics teaching is one which enhances problem solving, how this is achieved is not that clear. Basically, these teachers by and large believe that demonstrating standard ways of solving mathematical problems and doing practice helps. How these problem solving skills can be internalized is an issue awaiting further investigation.

Summary

The above results revealed that understanding and thinking were repeatedly stressed by teachers. Along this line, learning by doing and problem solving were emphasized among the participating teachers. In their eyes, the general picture of effective mathematics teaching is one that not only highlights the above two views, but also allows the students to move gradually from the rigid to the flexible, from solving standard problems to non-routine problems. This is in fact in line with the notion of entering/transcending the Way put forth by the second author (Wong, 2004). In other words, effective mathematics teaching is one that builds a path on which the students can go from the rigid to the flexible, from imitating the right way of solving mathematical problems to solving these problems on their own, and from the stereotyped to a variation of problems. Teachers' mentorship and partnership (in learning) definitely helps students in this transcendence. The progress in this path can further be enhanced by a careful arrangement of practices.

Also, this echoes our earlier findings on the views of effective teaching among elementary teachers in Hong Kong: teaching for understanding, enhancement of thinking skills, and the wise use of practices to arrange a scaffolding to proceed from the concrete to the abstract. All these require the professionalism of the teacher. Though it paints a teacher-led scenario, it can be at the same time student-centered (Wong, 2007; Chapter 1, this book), or even learning-centered (Watkins, 2008). In fact, Biggs and Watkins (2001) already summarized the belief of effective learning (not confined to mathematics) among the teachers and students in China (both in Hong Kong and the Mainland), in which the features of concentrated learning, vicarious learning, careful planning, timed questioning, and associated activity, and learner-trained learning were identified. "Good learning occurs when, to a Western eye, there is a repetitive, teacher-dominated script" (p. 285).

PROTOTYPES OF MATHEMATICS TEACHERS

To go for a more refined picture of teachers' beliefs about mathematics and effective mathematics teaching, three prototypes of beliefs were identified and analyzed separately. Teachers F and G repeatedly emphasized the relationship between mathematics and daily life. They used a lot of realistic examples in their teaching preparation and during their teaching, and first demonstrated with a lot of examples for students to follow. They are identified as the pragmatic-oriented. On the other hand, Teachers D and E held the view that mathematics learning should go beyond computation; one should understand the principles and concepts behind them. Students' mathematical thinking is once again stressed. They believed that mathematical knowledge should be constructed by the students. They frequently pointed at the connections among topics during their teaching so as to give the students a holistic picture of mathematics. We call them the understanding-oriented. Teachers A, B, and C opined that mathematics is a tool that helps to develop thinking skills. Through mathematics, abilities like spatial sense and logical reasoning are acquired. This was also reflected in their teaching. They would offer a variety of teaching methods and materials so as to stimulate students to think from different angles. We label them as the thinking-development-oriented.

The Pragmatic-oriented

Beliefs about mathematics. Teachers F and G belonged to this category. To them, determining whether something is mathematics was judged by the curriculum content. For instance, Teacher F pointed out that as long as it is included in the curriculum document, "absolutely it is doing mathematics. It includes various mathematics [concepts], such as subtraction, algebra, half, a third, assuming how many candies we have .... As long as there is mathematics manipulation in mind, it is mathematics" [F-hy-1]. They did not see a close connection among topics. For instance, though they vaguely saw a connection between the topics direct proportion and inverse proportion, Teacher G treated them as separate topics and deliberately asked the students to distinguish the two concepts clearly [G-ac-1].

However, they saw a close relationship between mathematics and daily life. As said by Teacher G, "Lots of what we are doing [is] concerned with mathematics. There are so many things that are associated with mathematics around us, such as the trapezium decorations on the wall. You see so many things relating to mathematics when you open your eyes" [G-hy-5]. However, it seems that they failed to see the special features of the discipline. They only regarded mathematics as something common with other subjects. "Knowledge is something in common. It exists in all disciplines and just now is situated in mathematics" [F-hy-8]. Teacher G also commented that "now there is a topic on the use of the calculator in the new mathematics curriculum...maybe one day that could be taken out from [the] mathematics [curriculum] and form a new subject called calculator" [G-hy-9].

When asked whether something is considered as mathematics, they felt inclined to rely on authority, such as the opinions of mathematicians and/or experts in mathematics education. "Once having a doubt, we will ask an authoritative person and wait for the correct answer" [G-ac-15]. "I have forgotten exactly whether it was the head teacher or an official of the Education Department who told us that unit is not necessary during the calculation" [G-ht-10].

Mathematics teaching. In mathematics teaching, the usual strategy employed by these two teachers is the use of examples. As said by Teacher G, "Examples are problems they may encounter in daily life. So I let them try to solve them. My view is: if students find the relevance, they would try to solve it. Of course there are many other teaching methods. I still think this [the use of examples] is the more direct one" [G-ac-6]. They emphasized the conformity of laid-down formats (e.g., of presenting a mathematics solution). For example, Teacher F showed hesitation when considering the following presentation:

$$
\begin{array}{r}
2\ \ 1\ \ 4 \\
2\ \overline{)4\ \ 2\ \ 8} \\
8 \\
\hline
2 \\
2 \\
\hline
4 \\
4 \\
\hline
\end{array}
$$

"... I am not sure, but it could [be a] mistake because it is not the format of long division. And this kind of expression may not work for all problems ... pause for hesitation) Well, though it may not be totally forbidden, students may get confused [in presenting in this way]. So I would consider it as wrong" [F-ht-6]. Students' ability to solve harder problems rather than the process of problem solving is stressed. "We call them 'Thinking Problems.' We give them one or two such problems in a week. The problems are concerned with the school curriculum or daily life. Students could use old methods to solve it. Drawing or table also could be used" [G-cm-16]. One such harder problem is:

Peter and Mary compete in a 100m running contest (assuming that their speed remains unchanged). When Peter passed 90m, Mary is still 25m from the end point. So when Peter reaches the end point, how far is Mary from the end point?

Though they said that they would accept different solutions from the students, they still wished that their students could ultimately arrive at the model answer. For instance, as shown in the class conducted by Teacher G, she did not accept all the solutions offered by the students. Though she allowed the students to offer different solutions, she hoped that ultimately their solutions could funnel to the standard solution in her mind.

Mathematics learning. To both Teacher F and Teacher G, practices are essential in mathematics learning. "Students must know whether they understand the knowledge. I also have to know if they understand it. So practice could be used for evaluation" [F-ac-10]. They believed in the maxim "practice makes perfect" and the most effective way is to imitate what teachers do. "If a student obtained the answer by another method, I will ask her/him to use my method to solve the problem. This could demonstrate that s/he really understands [what] to do" [G-ac-9].

Summary. From the above paragraphs, we come up with a clear portrayal of a pragmatic-oriented mathematics teacher. They possess, to a certain extent, an absolutistic view of mathematics. Conformity is emphasized, and thus, learning mathematics is essentially copying what teachers do and (re-)producing what is correct mathematically. It is clear from their responses that their view of an effective teacher is one with her/his lessons well-planned, gearing precisely to the curriculum standards, so that the students can imitate what the teachers do, coming up with correct solutions to problems. Clear and step-to-step explanation was anticipated by Hong Kong students as found in previous studies (Wong, Lam, Leung, et al., 1999). The delivery of mathematics under the view of effective mathematics teaching among these teachers is more or less of this type. The effective mathematics teacher is one who can, by the use of worked examples and practices, transmit this body of mathematics knowledge and skills to the students efficiently.

The Understanding-Oriented

Beliefs about mathematics. Teachers D and E fell into this category. Understanding was especially stressed. "Mathematics has a lot of variations, so not much hardship and not much recitation is required. What one needs most is to understand. The mathematics context and number may change, so you need not recite and cannot recite everything anyway. If you understand it, then you can vary [according to different contexts]. The hardship of learning mathematics in primary schools may come from not understanding" [E-cm-8]. At the same time, mathematics was seen as a tool of communication. "Sometimes we need to show the problem we solved to others. To make others understand, we need to conform to rules that others could understand [by] just making out of our free will. Just like the traffic lights, the rules have been fixed and you must follow [them]" [D-ht-6].

Furthermore, mathematics was also seen as a way of thought. "Mathematics consists of ways of thought, not just some calculation methods. It consists of mathematical thinking, understanding and concepts" [D-ac-25]. Mathematics is not confined to those found in the school curriculum and is an ever-evolving subject. "If the time allows, I would introduce fuzzy mathematics. For instance, rain can be forecast. I would illustrate by examples that estimation is also part of mathematics" [D-hy-17].

Mathematics teaching. In line with the above view, the formation of concept was seen as something of utmost importance with these two teachers. As Teacher D said, "I think the mathematical element of this lesson is mainly to look for the invariance and the relationships among different quantities. I believe that in the teaching of both primary and secondary mathematics, if a teacher could help students clarify the relationships among quantities, the students will benefit a lot from this" [D-ac-16]. Providing contrasts by examples and non-examples were commonly used. This is clear from the dialogues after attending Teacher D's class:

Researcher: Just now, I noticed that you used different non-examples (e.g., fixed sum, fixed quotient and fixed difference) in introducing inverse proportion. Can you tell me your purpose?

Teacher D: I wished to let the students have a holistic understanding, so I let them see different examples, and let them distinguish what are inverse proportions and what are not. I do not want my students merely picking up a formula freely and applying it. They should have a thorough understanding of the content, then perform meaningful operations [D-ac-17].

These teachers also employed a variety of teaching modes. Mathematical concepts were brought out through discussions, observation, and enquiries. Teacher D even said, "If the mathematics curriculum at the junior level can be made more relaxed [the time frame not that tight], we could conduct a lot of activities. For example, when teaching the divisibility of 3, we could explore the divisibility of other numbers immediately afterwards; when teaching the ten-line table, we could extend the observations on multiples to 12-line or 13-line tables. Of course, I will consider students' ability [before conducting these enrichment activities]" [D-ac-14].

Connecting with prior knowledge was seen as important. "When preparing for lessons we should know what students have known. That is the starting point of teaching. If we teach the new knowledge immediately, students could not connect it with old ones. That is just like a building hanging in the air without groundwork. Students may forget it soon" [D-ac-3]. These teachers also considered students' provision of different solutions as natural since everybody has different thinking mode. "A good mathematics teacher should accept other answers and different solutions to a single problem so that the students' thought is not suppressed. We need to encourage students to develop different thoughts. If there is only one thought and one solution, mathematics will not develop" [E-cm-21].

Mathematics learning. In this light, mathematics learning is not just imitating what the teachers do but requiring one to internalize and personalize what is learned. For instance, Teacher D took the following presentation as correct:

$$
\begin{array}{r}
2\ \ 1\ \ 4 \\
2\ \overline{)4\ \ 2\ \ 8} \\
8 \\
\hline
2 \\
2 \\
\hline
4 \\
4 \\
\hline
\end{array}
$$

"No marks should be deducted in all circumstances. If the student can tell me that the division starts from the unit digit, I will praise her/him in front of the class. Since the student knows that s/he can start doing from any digit, and not just merely following what was taught by the teacher. This shows that s/he can utilize the principles and concepts of division and internalize into her/his own strategies, that's why s/he should be praised" [D-ht-5]. In fact, the notion of students' self-invented strategies is repeatedly put forth in recent years (Tsang, 2005). And thus material must be presented to the students flexibly.

Summary. Again we see the close relationship between teachers' conceptions of mathematics and their views of effective mathematics teaching. To Teachers D and E, mathematics is basically seen as a way of thought. It is part of the human culture. Thus, their beliefs about effective mathematics teaching and learning are more inclined to those of the constructivists. They see understanding as a major outcome of mathematics learning, not just getting the correct answer to mathematical problems. In line with this, effective teaching is synonymous with teaching for understanding rather than the transmission of a static body of knowledge since mathematics itself is fluid and an evolving human cultural activity. The effective mathematics teacher is one who can create an environment conducive to mathematics understanding. Teachers should lead students into the mathematical world of enquiries and investigations. This is their image of effective mathematics teaching.

The Thinking-Development-Oriented

Beliefs about mathematics. The conceptions of Teachers A, B, and C have commonalities with the understanding-oriented category. What makes them different is their emphasis of the development of thinking skills. First of all, mathematics was seen as a tool to such a development. "Mathematics not only is applicable but also helps in our thinking. If one can do well in mathematics, one will be logical in both thinking and language [expressing]. Since mathematics is structured into layers, when one is considering mathematics concepts, one would think layer by layer. The more you think [in this way], the better structured your thinking and saying would be" [B-cm-4]. "In fact, the major purpose of mathematics is to develop among the students methods of thinking, such as ... logic, reasonableness, and so on. That is more crucial than [the] correct answer by calculating" [C-cm-24].

To these teachers, mathematics is rigorous and beautiful. On the one hand, mathematics is rigorous and objective. "Mathematics needs evidences and proofs. It could be taken as correct only through being proved. It is objective and not subjective like languages" [B-cm-1]. On the other hand, mathematics was seen as beautiful. Yet, besides that beauty of geometric shapes, the beauty also comes from precision and pattern, for instance, number patterns [A-cm-24; B-hy-3]. This coincides with what we found among primary and secondary mathematics teachers China (both in Hong Kong and the Mainland) in previous studies (Wong, 2002). In line with the teachers in the understanding-oriented category, they found mathematics as something evolving rather than static.

Mathematics teaching. The taste of mathematics was emphasized in the teaching of these teachers. "When we teach, we need to know what exactly we are teaching. [For instance] in teaching multiplication in junior grades, the purpose is to let students understand the meaning of multiplication. But in senior grades, the students familiarize themselves [with multiplication] in various kinds of contexts" [B-ht-17].

Understanding was also stressed in this category. As expressed by Teacher B, "I think understanding is the first thing. When one understands, then one can calculate it. If a student does not know how to calculate, certainly s/he has not understood completely. As long as s/he has the clear concept, then s/he can compute even if her/his method is not the same as yours or your teaching" [B-ac-18]. Though teachers from both categories showed high regard for understanding, the structure of what is to be presented was seen as something important for teachers in this category. Teachers even reflected that they would re-structure the textbook contents to make it more systematic before delivering to their students. "When we prepare our lessons, the selection of materials and teaching methods depends on the students' abilities. To do so, one could arrange the teaching content to adapt to the students' ability, interest and learning goal" [A-cm-5].

As indicated above, a variety of teaching modes, "one problem, multiple solutions," and the connection with prior knowledge were considered in teaching.

"If students introduce other ideas or methods, I will discuss the advantages and disadvantages of different methods with them. I would let them judge in order to broaden their views" [B-ac-15].

Mathematics learning. These three teachers encouraged students to express their views. "When students are discussing problems, they could learn from [one another]. The better students could organize their knowledge when they express their ideas; at the same time, the average students could use them for reference" [A-ac-13]. However, the subtle difference (with the understanding-oriented category) is that it is taken as a means to enable students to judge what is mathematically correct. As Teacher B said, "The ability to judgie right or wrong needs to be developed with the help of the teacher. I would discuss the whole problems with the students and make them explain their methods. When explaining their methods, they may find if there is anything wrong" [B-cm-29].

Summary. Obviously the last two categories have a lot in common. Yet in this category, the knowledge structure of mathematics and mathematical rigor is repeatedly stressed. Though there are differences in the responses of teachers in this category, their picture of the ultimate outcome is the acquisition of a mathematical way of thought and the construction of an objective mathematical knowledge structure in the students' minds. Another major difference is the emphasis of working on harder mathematical problems so as to upgrade students' problem solving skills. The image of effective mathematics teaching in the eyes of these teachers could be the provision of a well-organized spectrum of problems so that the students can acquire various mathematical skills.

SUMMARY AND DISCUSSION

After decades of investigations of students' and teachers' beliefs about mathematics and effective mathematics teaching (Leder et al., 2002), more effort still needs to be invested to dig out the ghost hidden in mathematics education (Furinghetti, 1994, 1997). What is special in this study is that we tried to investigate teachers' views of effective mathematics teaching in relation to their beliefs about mathematics. These data were also triangulated with classroom observation on the teachers' actual teaching. Results reveal that teachers' beliefs about mathematics play a crucial role in their views of effective mathematics teaching.

On the other hand, because beliefs are too deeply buried to be explored by usual methodologies, in this study, multiple methods were employed to explore teachers' conceptions from different angles. While the use of hypothetical situations has been successful in belief studies among students, this is probably one of the first attempts to apply it among teachers, which yielded fruitful results.

Similar to what was found among students in general (Wong, Lam, & Wong, 1998; Wong et al., 2002), teachers identify mathematics by its content and terminology, and regard mathematics as a subject of calculables and that involves thinking. Yet teachers also see mathematics as requiring understanding and connection to daily life. This coincides with what we have found earlier in a study of teachers' views of effective mathematics teaching (Wong, 2007). Though they possess a broader conception when compared with the students, we see a close resemblance between the two. This reinforces our premises that teachers' conceptions of mathematics have much influence on students' conceptions of mathematics, probably through their construction of the students' lived space.

The results of teachers' views of effective mathematics teaching found in the present and previous studies are quite consistent. Similar to the expectations of students (Wong, 1993), teachers also see themselves as the key figure in the mathematics classroom. Since understanding is the heart of mathematics learning and teaching, the enhancement of problem-solving abilities was seen as crucial. This is in line with what was stated in the 1977 NCSM position statement that "learning to solve problems is the principal reason for studying mathematics" (National Council of Supervisors of Mathematics, 1977, p. 2). To the participants of the present study, learning by doing is an effective means. One needs to be equipped with the ability to apply their mathematical skills to a variety of context, thus mathematics teaching should move from being rigid (conformed to required formats) to flexibility.

In sum, understanding, thinking, and problem solving are generally highly regarded by the teachers. Their views of effective mathematics teaching are some that enhance all these, which can be done through learning by doing. An effective mathematics teacher is one who can organize such experiences (including the provision of suitable mathematical problems) for the students so that one can be gradually moved from the rigid to the flexible, from solving standard problems to non-routine problems.

If we compare the results of the present study with those of another study on teachers' conceptions of effective mathematics teaching among another group of primary mathematics teachers in Hong Kong (Wong, 2007), we will find similarities and differences. Though we get consistent themes between these two studies, obviously the responses of teachers from the latter study are more refined, and those from the former are more conservative. This is expected since the participants from the latter study are expert teachers while those from the former are general ones. We see that as teachers become experienced, there is a difference.

Ernest (1991) identified three views of mathematics: instrumental, Platonic, and problem solving. By analyzing the teaching of our participants, we came up with three slightly different prototypes, namely the pragmatic-oriented, the understanding-oriented, and the thinking-development-oriented. We think that the difference is not the issue, and what is most interesting is the delineation of a linkage between teachers' beliefs about mathematics to their views of effective mathematics teaching in each of these prototypes. The pragmatic-oriented mathematics teacher possesses, to a certain extent, an absolutistic view of mathematics. Conformity is emphasized and thus learning mathematics is essentially copying what the teacher does and (re-)producing what is correct mathematically. These are their views of effective mathematics teaching. For the understanding-oriented mathematics teacher, mathematics is seen as a way of thought. Thus their view of effective mathematics teaching is understanding instead of getting the correct answer, which is the major learning outcome. Every means should be employed to enhance students' understanding. The thinking-development-oriented category could have some overlappings with the second category, yet the knowledge structure of mathematics and mathematical rigor are repeatedly stressed. Their picture of the ultimate outcome is the acquisition of a mathematical way of thought and the construction of an objective mathematical knowledge structure in the student's mind.

In brief, for the pragmatic-oriented teachers, effective mathematics teaching is one in which mathematics is delivered to the students efficiently through well-planned and structured teaching, with clear and step-by-step explanation. For the understanding-oriented teachers, effective mathematics teaching is realized by the creation of a learning environment in which students can investigate and explore and finally come up with their own way of mathematical thinking. The solving of problems is emphasized by those thinking-development-oriented teachers and so their views of effective mathematics teaching are some that can upgrade students' thinking skills and strategies.

With the limited number of participants, we do not aim to arrive at a conclusive picture of beliefs about mathematics – mathematics learning and teaching among Hong Kong mathematics teachers. However, we see consistent evidence of how teachers' beliefs about mathematics affect their views of effective mathematics learning and teaching, which, in turn, affect their actual teaching. We also see a resemblance of teachers' and students' conceptions, and there is likelihood that such collective societal belief is passing from generation to generation (Pehkonen, 1998b; M. K. Siu, 1995; Zheng, 1994). Without the professionalism of teachers, there is a possibility that teachers' narrow conceptions of mathematics will impose narrow conceptions of mathematics among their students. Lampert (1990) sums up this undesirable trend by saying: "These cultural assumptions are shaped by school experience, in which doing mathematics means following the rules laid down by the teacher; knowing mathematics means remembering and applying the correct rule when the teacher asks a question; and mathematical truth is determined when the answer is ratified by the teacher" (p. 32). In contrast, a scholar-teacher should be able to reverse such a trend (F. K. Siu, Siu, & Wong, 1993).

Finally, in this study, we made a new attempt of using multiple methods to unfold teachers' beliefs. Besides conventional interviews and observation of actual classroom teaching, hypothetical situations, both in the contexts of doing mathematics and of mathematics teaching, were used. This went beyond earlier studies of using hypothetical situations among students and is shown to be effective in unfolding the hidden beliefs among teachers. It is our belief that this methodology has its potential in disclosing beliefs.

NOTES

[1] The chapter is based on the thesis of the first author's M. Phil. study at The Chinese University of Hong Kong under the supervision of the second and the third authors. The thesis was originally written in Chinese. The fourth author helped in the translation from Chinese into English. He also helped in the review of literature. The chapter is dedicated to the good health of the first author.

[2] Though there had been extensive discussions on the distinctions among terminologies like "conception," "belief," "view," "image," ... (see, e.g., Kember, 1997; Pehkonen, 1998a, 1998b; Philipp, 2007), in this chapter, we used them quite interchangeably.

[3] This symbol carries the structure of T-m-n, where T refers to the code of the teachers (e.g., "A" represents Teacher A), n refers to the quotation number. As for m, "hy," "cm," "ht," "ac" mean that the responses were collected through hypothetical situations, interviews on conceptions of mathematics, hypothetical situations of teaching, and after-class interviews respectively.

⁴ The Confucian Heritage Cultural regions usually refer to East Asian regions like the China (Mainland), Taiwan, Macau, Japan, Korea and probably Singapore. It is commonly believed that these regions are influenced by Confucian values. See Wong (2004) for details.

REFERENCES

Battista, M. T. (1994). Teacher beliefs and the reform movement in mathematics education. *Phi Delta Kappan, 75*(6), 462–463, 466–468, & 470.

Biggs, J. B. (1994). What are effective schools? Lessons from East and West (The Radford Memorial Lecture). *Australian Educational Researcher, 21*, 19–39.

Biggs, J. B., & Watkins, D. A. (2001). Insights into teaching the Chinese learner. In D. A. Watkins & J. B. Biggs (Eds.), *Teaching the Chinese learner: Psychological and pedagogical perspectives* (pp. 277–300). Hong Kong: Comparative Education Research Centre, The University of Hong Kong; Melbourne, Australia: The Australian Council for Educational Research.

Bowden, J., & Marton, F. (1998). *The university of learning.* London: Kogan Page.

Cai, J., Perry, R., & Wong, N. Y. (2007). What is effective mathematics teaching? A dialogue between East and West. *ZDM — International Journal of Mathematics Education, 39*(4).

Carpenter, T. P., Fennema, E., Franke, M. L., Levi, L., & Empson, S. (1999). *Children's mathematics: Cognitively guided instruction.* Portsmouth, NH: Heinemann.

Cobb, P. (1985). Two children's anticipations, beliefs, and motivations. *Educational Studies of Mathematics, 16*, 111–126.

Crawford, K., Gordon, S., Nicholas, J., & Prosser, M. (1998a). Qualitative different experiences of learning mathematics at university. *Learning and Instruction, 8*, 455–468.

Crawford, K., Gordon, S., Nicholas, J., & Prosser, M. (1998b). University mathematics students' conceptions of mathematics. *Studies in Higher Education, 23*(1), 87–94.

Ernest, P. (1991). *The philosophy of mathematics education.* London: Falmer Press.

Fennema, E., Carpenter, T. P., Franke, M. L., Levi, L., Jacobs, V. R., & Empson, S. B. (1996). A longitudinal study of learning to use children's thinking in mathematics instruction. *Journal for Research in Mathematics Education, 27*, 403–434.

Furinghetti, F. (1994). Ghost in the classroom: Beliefs, prejudices and fears. In L. Bazzini (Ed.), *Proceedings of the fifth international conference on systematic cooperation between theory and practice in mathematics* (pp. 81–91). Pavia, Italy: Istituto Superiore di Didattica Avanzata e di Formazione.

Furinghetti, F. (1997). On teachers' conceptions: From a theoretical framework to school practice. In G. A. Makrides (Ed.), *Proceedings of the first Mediterranean conference on mathematics* (pp. 277–287). Cyprus: Cyprus Pedagogical Institute and Cyprus Mathematical Society.

Kember, D. (1997). A reconceptualisation of the research into university academics' conceptions of teaching. *Learning and Instruction, 7*(3), 255–275.

Kouba, V. L., & McDonald, J. L. (1991). What is mathematics to children? *Journal of Mathematical Behavior, 10*(1), 105–113.

Lam, C. C., Wong, N. Y., & Wong, K. M. P. (1999). Students' conception of mathematics learning: A Hong Kong study. *Curriculum and Teaching, 14*(2), 27–48.

Lampert, M. (1990). When the problem is not the question and the solution is not the answer: Mathematical knowing and teaching. *American Educational Research Journal, 27*(1), 29–63.

Leder, G. C., Pehkonen, E., & Törner, G. (Eds.). (2002). *Beliefs: A hidden variable in mathematics education?* Dordrecht, The Netherlands: Kluwer.

Lederman, N. G. (1999). Teachers' understanding of the nature of science and classroom practice: Factors that facilitate or impede the relationship. *Journal of Research in Science Teaching, 36*(8), 916–928.

Lerman, S. (1983). Problem solving or knowledge centered: The influence of philosophy on mathematics teaching. *International Journal of Mathematical Education in Science and Technology, 14*, 59–66.

Marton, F., & Booth, S. (1997). *Learning and awareness*. Mahwah, NJ: Lawrence Erlbaum Associates.

Marton, F., & Säljö, R. (1976). On qualitative differences in learning — I: Outcome and process. *British Journal of Educational Psychology, 46*, 4–11.

McLeod, D. B. (1992). Research on affect in mathematics education: A reconceptualization. In D. A. Grouws (Ed.), *Handbook of research on mathematics teaching and learning* (pp. 575–596). New York: Macmillan.

Miles, M. B., & Huberman, A. M. (1994). *Qualitative data analysis — An expanded sourcebook* (2nd ed.). Thousand Oaks, CA: SAGE.

National Council of Supervisors of Mathematics. (1977). *Position paper on basic mathematical skills*. Washington, DC: National Institute of Education.

Pehkonen, E. (1998a). International comparison of pupils' mathematical views. In E. Pohkonen & G. Törner (Eds.), *The state-of-art in mathematics-related belief research: Results of the MAVI activities* (Research Report 195) (pp. 249–276). Helsinki, Finland: Department of Teacher Education, University of Helsinki.

Pehkonen, E. (1998b). On the concept "mathematical belief." In. E. Pohkonen & G. Törner (Eds.), *The state-of-art in mathematics-related belief research: Results of the MAVI activities* (Research Report 195) (pp. 11–36). Helsinki, Finland: Department of Teacher Education, University of Helsinki.

Pehkonen, E., & Törner, G. (Eds.). (1998). *The state-of-art in mathematics-related belief research: Results of the MAVI activities* (Research Report 195). Helsinki, Finland: Department of Teacher Education, University of Helsinki.

Perry, B., Wong, N. Y., & Howard, P. (2006). Beliefs about mathematics, mathematics learning and mathematics teaching: A comparison of views from primary and secondary mathematics teachers in Hong Kong and Australia. In F. K. S. Leung, G.-D. Graf, & F. J. Lopez-Real (Eds.), *Mathematics education in different cultural traditions: The 13th ICMI study* (pp. 435–448). New York: Springer.

Peterson, P. L., Fennema, E., Carpenter, T. P., & Loef, M. (1989). Teachers' pedagogical content beliefs in mathematics. *Cognition and Instruction, 6*(1), 1–40.

Philipp, R. A. (2007). Mathematics teachers' beliefs and affect. In F. K. Lester, Jr. (Ed.), *Second handbook on research on mathematics teaching and learning: A project of the national council of teachers of mathematics* (pp. 257–315). Charlotte, NC: Information Age Publishing.

Raymond, A. M. (1997). Inconsistency between a beginning elementary school teacher's mathematics beliefs and teaching practice. *Journal for Research in Mathematics Education, 28*, 550–576.

Schoenfeld, A. H. (2002). Research methods in (mathematics) education. In L. English (Ed.), *Handbook of international research in mathematics education* (pp. 435–488). Mahwah, NJ: Lawrence Erlbaum Associates.

Shirk, G. B. (1972). *An examination of conceptual framework of beginning mathematics teachers*. Unpublished Doctoral Dissertation, University of Illinois.

Siu, M. K. (1995). Mathematics education in ancient China: What lessons do we learn from it? *Historia Scientiarum, 4*(3), 223–232.

Siu, F. K., Siu, M. K., & Wong, N. Y. (1993). Changing times in mathematics education: The need of a scholar-teacher. In C. C. Lam, H. W. Wong, & Y. W. Fung (Eds.), *Proceedings of the international symposium on curriculum changes for Chinese communities in Southeast Asia: Challenges of the 21st century* (pp. 223–226). Hong Kong: Department of Curriculum and Instruction, The Chinese University of Hong Kong.

Snyder, M. (1984). When belief creates reality. In L. Bertowitz (Ed.), *Advances in experimental social psychology* (Vol. 18, pp. 247–305). San Diego, CA: Academic Press.

Stipek, D. J., Givvin, K. B., Salmon, J. M., & MacGyvers, V. L. (2001). Teachers' beliefs and practices related to mathematics instruction. *Teaching and Teacher Education, 17*(2), 213–226.

Thompson, A. G. (1991). The development of teachers' conceptions of mathematics teaching. In R. G. Underhill (Ed.), *Proceedings of the 13th annual meeting of the North American chapter of the international group for the psychology of mathematics education* (Vol. 2, pp. 8–14). Blacksburg, VA: Virginia Tech.

Thompson, A. G. (1992). Teachers' beliefs and conceptions: A synthesis of the research. In D. A. Grouws (Ed.), *Handbook of research on mathematics teaching and learning* (pp. 127–146). New York: Macmillan.

Tsang, K. W. F. (2005). Invented strategies versus standard algorithms, creativity versus formality. In N. Y. Wong (Ed.), *Revisiting mathematics education in Hong Kong for the new millennium* (pp. 141–155). Hong Kong: The Hong Kong Association for Mathematics Education.

Underhill, R. (1988). Mathematics learners' beliefs: A review. *Focus on Learning Problems in Mathematics, 20*, 55–69.

Watkins, D. A. (2008, February). *Learning-centered teaching: An Asian perspective.* Keynote address at the 2nd international conference onlLearner-centered education. Manila, the Philippines.

Watkins, D. A., & Biggs, J. B. (2001). The paradox of the Chinese learner and beyond. In D. A. Watkins & J. B. Biggs (Eds.), *Teaching the Chinese learner: Psychological and pedagogical perspectives* (pp. 3–23). Hong Kong: Comparative Education Research Centre, The University of Hong Kong; Melbourne, Australia: The Australian Council for Educational Research.

Wong, N. Y. (1993). The psychosocial environment in the Hong Kong mathematics classroom. *The Journal of Mathematical Behavior, 12*(3), 303–309.

Wong, N. Y. (2000a). Investigating conceptions of mathematics by the use of open-ended mathematical problems. In E. Pehkonen (Ed.), *Problem solving around the world — proceedings of the topic study group 11 (Problem solving in mathematics education) at the ICME-9 meeting August 2000 in Japan* (pp. 141–149). Turku, Finland: University of Turku.

Wong, N. Y. (2000b). The conception of mathematics among Hong Kong students and teachers. In S. Götz & G. Törner (Eds.), *Proceedings of the MAVI-9 European workshop* (pp. 103–108). Duisburg, Germany: Gerhard Mercator Universität Duisburg.

Wong, N. Y. (2001a). The lived space of mathematics learning: From conception to action. In L. Sun (Ed.), *Proceedings of the international conference on mathematics education* (pp. 6–19). Changchun, China: Northeast Normal University.

Wong, N. Y. (2001b, June). *The shaping of the lived space of mathematics learning.* Paper presented at the third Nordic conference on mathematics education, Kristianstad, Sweden.

Wong, N. Y. (2002). Conceptions of doing and learning mathematics among Chinese. *Journal of Intercultural Studies, 23*(2), 211–229.

Wong, N. Y. (2004). The CHC learner's phenomenon: Its implications on mathematics education. In L. Fan, N. Y. Wong, J. Cai, & S. Li (Eds.), *How Chinese learn mathematics: Perspectives from insiders* (pp. 503–534). Singapore: World Scientific.

Wong, N. Y. (2006). From "entering the Way to "exiting the Way": In search of a bridge to span "basic skills" and "process abilities." In F. K. S. Leung, G.-D. Graf, & F. J. Lopez-Real (Eds.), *Mathematics education in different cultural traditions: The 13th ICMI study* (pp. 111–128). New York: Springer.

Wong, N. Y. (2007). The conceptions of mathematics and of effective mathematics learning/teaching among Hong Kong elementary mathematics teachers. *ZDM — International Journal of Mathematics Education, 39*(4), 301–314.

Wong, N. Y., Chiu, M. M., Wong, K. M., & Lam, C. C. (2005). The lived space of mathematics learning: An attempt for change. *Journal of the Korea Society of Mathematical Education Series D: Research in Mathematical Education, 9*(1), 25–45.

Wong, N. Y., Lam, C. C., & Chan, C. S. (2002). The current state of the "lived space" of mathematics learning. *Hiroshima Journal of Mathematics Education, 10*, 27–52.

Wong, N. Y., Lam, C. C., Leung, F. K. S., Mok, I. A. C., & Wong, K. M. P. (1999). Holistic reform of the mathematics curriculum — The Hong Kong experience. *Journal of the Korea Society of Mathematical Education Series D: Research in Mathematical Education, 3*(2), 69–88.

Wong, N. Y., Lam, C. C., & Wong, K. M. (1998). Students' and teachers' conception of mathematics learning: A Hong Kong study. In H. S. Park, Y. H. Choe, H. Shin, & S. H. Kim (Eds.), *Proceedings of the ICMI-East Asia regional conference on mathematical education* (Vol. 2, pp. 375–404). Seoul, Korea: Korean Sub-Commission of ICMI; Korea Society of Mathematical Education; Korea National University of Education.

Wong, N. Y., Marton, F., Wong, K. M., & Lam, C. C. (2002). The lived space of mathematics learning. *Journal of Mathematical Behavior, 21*(1), 25–47.

Yin, R. K. (2003). *Case study research: Design and methods* (3rd ed.). Thousand Oaks, CA: SAGE.

Zheng, Y. (1994). Philosophy of mathematics, mathematics education and philosophy of mathematics education. *Humanistic Mathematics Journal, 9*, 32–41.

APPENDIX 1

Are they doing mathematics if:
- Siu Ming said that half a candy bar is better than a third;
- your younger brother added 3 and 2 on the calculator and got 5;
- Ah Kap had 3 candy bars and Ah Yuet had 2 candy bars. Ah Bing said that together they had 5;
- one day the classmate sitting next to you took out a ruler and measured her/his desk;
- elder sister lifted her younger brother and said that he must weigh about 30 pounds less than she;
- one day Siu Wan made a Valentine card in the shape of a heart by paper folding;
- Siu Ming loved cycling and he kept track each day of how many miles he rode on his bike;
- your elder brother loves drawing. Everyday when he wakes up, he draws a picture to show how many hours he sleeps each night;
- Siu Ping loves to play with dogs so he often runs over to Siu Wan's house to see her dog;
- one day when it was raining heavily, Alan was sitting in a car and looking at the rain through the window;
- Siu Ming went to the canteen for lunch and found that he could choose from 4 dishes for the day. These dishes could be served together with rice, spaghetti, or a vegetable;
- Dai Keung and Siu Chun went to take a photo at the spiral staircase at the City Hall. When the photo was processed, Dai Keung discovered that the staircase looked like a sine curve;
- each day when Mr. Ho goes out, he listens to the weather forecast to see if he needs to take an umbrella;
- your school ran a 300m race (which is a non-standard distance) in the athletic meet, and your Physical Education teacher fixed the starting points of the lanes when he inspected the field;
- you like reading newspapers and one day you bought a newspaper and you estimated the number of words on the front page.

APPENDIX 2

The interview questions that were based on the framework given in Thompson (1991) (see also Pehkonen, 1998b) were as follows:
1. What is mathematics?
   - When you see the word "mathematics," what do you think about?

- Please use some adjectives to describe mathematics.
- Do you think mathematics today is the same as mathematics in the past and in the future?
- Where do you think mathematics comes from?

2. What does it mean to teach/learn mathematics?
   - What should be taught/learned when you are teaching/learning mathematics?
   - What is the aim of teaching/learning mathematics?
   - If you were observing a mathematics lesson, what rules would you use to evaluate it?

3. What should the roles of the teacher and the students be?
   - What are the characteristics of an effective mathematics teacher?
   - What do you think an ideal mathematics teacher should be?

4. What constitutes evidence of student knowledge and criteria for judging correctness, accuracy, or acceptability of mathematical results and conclusions?
   - Do you agree "An answer is either right or wrong in mathematics?"
   - If a student asks you how s/he would know her/his answer is right or wrong, what would be your response?
   - Do you think a student could get the right answer without understanding?

5. What is problem solving?
   - In your view, how would you enhance students' problem solving ability?
   - What would you do to include problem solving in teaching mathematics?

Qian-Ting Wong
The Chinese University of Hong Kong

Ngai-Ying Wong
The Chinese University of Hong Kong

Chi-Chung Lam
The Hong Kong Institute of Education

Qiao-Ping Zhang
The Chinese University of Hong Kong

WILL MORONY

"EFFECTIVE TEACHING OF MATHEMATICS" BY TEACHERS, FOR TEACHERS: AN AUSTRALIAN CASE STUDY

INTRODUCTION

This chapter[1] discusses the work of the Australian Association of Mathematics Teachers (AAMT) and others over the past decade to develop "a consensus view, by the profession for the profession, describing the knowledge, skills and attributes required for (effective) teaching of mathematics" (AAMT, 2006, p. 1) and of the uses to which the resulting materials have been put. Promoting and supporting effective teaching of mathematics is the *raison d'être* for mathematics teacher associations around the world, and the AAMT has a proud record of achievement in this area. Hence, in retrospect, it is surprising that until 10 or so years ago the idea that there could be a description of 'effective' teaching of mathematics had not arisen. If effective teaching was our aim, surely we should have known what we were aiming for?

Clearly, the individuals who wrote articles for AAMT journals, those who presented at our conferences and other professional development sessions; those who reviewed and recommended teaching resources, and so on, did have their own views on the matter. Their definitions of effective teaching were evident in what they did as authors, presenters and reviewers, but were held internally. Achieving an explicit consensus view on effective teaching of mathematics presented three key challenges:

– Feasibility—is it possible to develop such a statement in a form that clearly communicates the expectations to teachers and others?
– Usefulness—can such a statement be useful to the profession?
– Difficulty—is the effort worth it?

This chapter is a case study of what the AAMT has done in responding to these challenges. It begins with an outline of the broader educational context in Australia —aspects of this have provided powerful external drivers for the work. An outline of the research project to develop the AAMT's *Standards for Excellence in Teaching Mathematics in Australian Schools* (the *Standards*) and a description of the materials developed follows. There is discussion of two of the main ways in which the *Standards* can and have been used, including descriptions of pilot projects. This is followed by an outline of current initiatives, some of which signal

J. Cai, G. Kaiser, B. Perry and N.-Y. Wong (eds.), Effective Mathematics Teaching from Teachers' Perspectives: National and Cross-National Studies, 259–280.
© *2009 Sense Publishers. All rights reserved.*

external valuing of this work. The chapter concludes with some reflections and speculation on the future.

Within Australia, the fact that an association of teachers has made substantial and widely lauded progress with an important agenda without deferring to the authority of employers or the government is a significant break-through. Associations have tended to be reactive rather than proactive in these sorts of major policy areas. The AAMT's work on professional standards provides a model and a precedent that professional associations can lead educational debates and developments.

Internationally, the work has relevance when considering the seemingly intractable issue of 'distance' between research/researchers and practice/teachers in mathematics education. This work is a series of research and development initiatives owned and undertaken by teachers under the auspices of a teacher organisation. Mathematics education researchers have been 'invited in' to support the work. This essentially reverses the situation found in most research initiatives in mathematics education. However the research questions and the project are formulated, conventionally conceived and conducted research sees the researcher with a key leadership role. This leadership may be shared through a partnership with teachers—seldom do teachers have the philosophical and practical control that the AAMT maintains in this case. The distance mentioned above may well be diminished if teachers' groups took proactive control of agendas that matter to themselves and their members. Defining and promoting effective practice is clearly one of these.

THE EDUCATIONAL CONTEXT OF THE WORK

At the broadest level, it is necessary to outline the way in which education is organised in Australia. The eight states and territories have the constitutional responsibility for the delivery of school education. Each state and territory has the functions associated with running school systems—curriculum development, teacher employment and support, selection of students for university entrance, facilities and so on. The setting and monitoring of professional standards of teachers has been seen to fit with these responsibilities.

Some national collaboration designed to have an impact on school education is fostered by the national government which, although it does not have direct responsibility for any schools, does have significant influence as the source of the majority of funds for schooling.

Professional Teaching Standards

In 1998 the Australian Senate Employment, Education and Training References Committee released *A Class Act,* a report of an inquiry into the status of teaching. In commenting on the issue of standards of professional teaching practice, "the Committee insists that establishing... standards of professional teaching practice is possible, unavoidable and absolutely necessary" (Australian Senate Employment,

Education and Training References Committee, 1998, p. 16; see also Commonwealth of Australia, 2003). The AAMT takes the view that there is a special set of knowledge, skills and attributes that distinguishes effective teaching of mathematics from other teaching, and that teachers themselves are best placed to identify these unique characteristics.

This approach was supported by two further contextual factors. Firstly, the National Council of Teachers of Mathematics (NCTM) in the USA published its *Professional Standards for Teaching Mathematics* (NCTM, 1991). This work of the NCTM was further developed by the National Board of Professional Teaching Standards, the body in the USA that has developed and implemented a system of credentialing high-achieving teachers in a comprehensive set of discipline and age related areas (National Board for Professional Teaching Standards, 1989, 1996). The NCTM continued its promotion of expectations for 'effective teaching' in 2000 with the publication of its *Principles and Standards for School Mathematics*. This single volume "buil[t] on the foundation of the original *Standards* documents" and "integrated the classroom-related portions of *Curriculum and Evaluation Standards for School Mathematics* (NCTM, 1989), *Professional Standards for Teaching mathematics* (NCTM, 1991) and *Assessment Standards for School Mathematics* (NCTM, 1995)" (p. x).

The Australian Science Teachers Association had been keen to work in the area of professional teaching standards for several years (Ingvarson, 1998) and this helped persuade the AAMT that the development of subject-specific teaching standards by professional associations was both feasible and essential in the growing climate of interest from employers and others in the development of professional teaching standards.

Importantly, *A Class Act* made a commitment "that [the standards] are [to be] determined by the profession itself" (Australian Senate Employment, Education and Training References Committee, 1998, p. 17). This suggests that professional associations should play an important role. The AAMT resolved to do so in the case of effective teaching of mathematics and formally commenced its work in 1999.

Since that time there has been a growing interest in 'professional standards' in teaching in Australia. Significantly, the states and territories have now established statutory bodies with responsibilities in this area. These boards, institutes and councils[2] have responsibilities for enhancing the status of teaching. Most have arrangements through which teachers are registered—this is a legal requirement for employment as a teacher in the jurisdictions. A number are developing arrangements for credentialing teachers at levels beyond basic registration. In all cases the intention is for the awarding of credentials (registration or at some higher level) based on some sort of assessment against statements of professional teaching standards that have been developed by the authority. All this work has occurred in parallel with the work of the AAMT. Whilst it is likely that these other initiatives have seen the AAMT's work as an irrelevance that would eventually be subsumed into or overtaken by their work, this has never been the Association's view.

All the sets of teaching standards developed by the various state and territory bodies are generic in nature. That is, they do not specify expectations in relation to specialisations, whether these are in terms of subjects (mathematics, history, physical education etc.), levels of schooling (early childhood, primary, middle years, senior secondary) or particular groups of students (special education, English as a Second or Further Language etc.). The contrasting approaches—specialist (by the AAMT and some other professional associations) on the one hand, and generic (by the authorities)—remains a tension to be resolved.

The Importance of the Teacher and the Quality of Teaching

It is clear that a range of factors can have an impact on students' learning. Hattie (2003) identifies factors associated with students; their homes; their schools, the principal; peers; and their teachers as having the potential to cause variance in students' achievement. Through synthesis of the findings of other studies, he estimates that student factors "account for about 50% of the variance of achievement" (p. 1). Of the other factors, he finds that teacher factors are responsible for a further 30%. The rest have minimal impact—in Hattie's view, less than 10% for any of them. Hattie concludes: "It is what students bring to the table that predicts achievement more than any other variable." The task for schooling is "to improve the trajectory of all (students)" and "[i]t is what teachers know, do, and care about which is very powerful in this learning equation" (p. 2) . His findings and those of others such as Rowe (2003) stress the importance of teacher quality as a key determinant of students' experiences and outcomes of schooling. These findings have been echoed by many researchers outside Australia.

In recent years, the quantification of the importance of the quality of teaching has been influential in bringing greater focus by governments on improving the work of teachers in Australia. In this context, the question posed at the start of this chapter arises again. It can be slightly restated as: "If there are to be efforts (by governments and others to 'improve the teaching of mathematics' should there not be clear targets for that improvement?" The AAMT's view on this is clear. Our work on describing effective teaching of mathematics provides those targets.

DEVELOPING THE AAMT *STANDARDS*

Purposes

It was clear from observations of the work of the National Board of Professional Teaching Standards that developing a description of effective teaching of mathematics would be difficult and time-consuming. To make the effort worthwhile there needed to be real gains for teachers of mathematics. In the context of the generalist approaches to the credentialing of accomplished teachers and efforts to 'improve the quality of teaching,' the AAMT's aim was to provide alternatives that are more in tune with the interests and aspirations of teachers of mathematics.

Fundamental to this aim was the development of the AAMT *Standards* as the profession's statement of what effective teachers of mathematics know, do and are like. Three main uses for the *Standards* were identified:

- **Recognition**—a process for awarding a credible and recognised AAMT credential to those teachers who present themselves for assessment by their peers and who successfully demonstrate that their professional work is at the standard set by the AAMT *Standards*.
- **Professional development**—the AAMT *Standards* were seen as the framework for teachers' career-long professional development.
- **Influence**—for the AAMT's leading edge work to inform and influence wider efforts to enhance teacher professionalism through the development and use of professional teaching standards.

The first two of these purposes are discussed in detail in later sections of this chapter. Although the third purpose (influence) is not of direct value to teachers of mathematics, it was seen to be of strategic importance as it provided a way of encouraging more professional associations to undertake similar work (see Ingvarson & Kleinhenz, 2006, pp. 40–49 for a survey and summary of the significant progress by 10 or more national professional associations) as well as providing opportunities for constructive dialogue with the educational authorities working in the area of professional standards.

The Excellence in Teaching Mathematics: Professional Standards Project

The AAMT and colleagues from the Education Faculty at Monash University (Melbourne) successfully bid for government funding of a research and development project entitled *Excellence in Teaching Mathematics: Professional Standards Project*. The project was conducted over the triennium 1999–2001. The partnership with the university was critical as it provided the necessary expertise in research that was needed to ensure the academic credibility and integrity of the work and its outcomes.

The source of the funding was a program designed to promote industry-focussed applied research in Australia, the Strategic Partnerships with Industry for Research and Training (SPIRT)[3]. The AAMT was the 'industry partner' in the research and, under the terms of the grant, was required to commit funds to match those provided to support the university researchers' work. The AAMT contribution was largely the dollar equivalent of the 'in kind' volunteer time spent on project activities by teachers. The formal recognition of teachers' out of hours work on professional activity is seen as a major achievement, and, in Australia, something of a precedent in the acknowledgement of this work.

The aims of the research project were to:
- determine consensual views on national professional standards for excellence in teaching mathematics in Australian schools (i.e., the *Standards*); and
- develop an assessment scheme and protocols for certifying this excellence.

Teacher Focus Groups (TFG) were established in four states (New South Wales, Victoria, Tasmania and South Australia). The mathematics teacher associations in these states nominated people to be members of the TFG. Members were predominantly classroom teachers, with one or two teacher educators in two states (Victoria and NSW). Each group included teachers from K–12. The members of the TFGs (approximately 50 in all) were seen by the researchers as part of the research team. As such, their role in this project was as 'practitioner/researchers.' The TFGs met in their state groups on up to 8 weekends over the duration of the project. The Preparing summaries of the TFG discussions and synthesising views from the different groups, and other tasks such as sourcing readings and preparing draft materials for public release were undertaken by a Project Team consisting of representatives of the TFGs, the university researchers and key officers of the AAMT with responsibility for the project. There was also a Steering Committee consisting of representatives of a wide range of education stakeholders including employers, unions, principals, teacher educators and others. This committee met annually and provided a forum that enabled the AAMT to make its work known to the broader educational community and to seek advice from their perspectives[4].

The project used a grounded theory approach (Glaser and Strauss, 1967) that continually sought the views of teachers in the TFGs, synthesised these and reflected the synthesis back to those teachers for confirmation or modification. A range of prompts and other strategies were used with the TFGs to initiate the discussion of "What makes for a good effective teacher/teaching of mathematics?" and "How would you know/what would it look like in the classroom?". For example, at one time the TFGs discussed and analysed the strengths and weaknesses of different metaphors for teaching. Another activity involved teachers in the TFGs bringing an artefact from their classroom that they believed represented an aspect of effective teaching of mathematics. These examples serve to illustrate another dimension of the work undertaken by the TFGs. Many of the teachers involved in the TFGs commented on the professional development that was part of the experience for them. It would seem that this was an important factor in maintaining their commitment to the task—around three-quarters of the teachers remained actively involved throughout what was a time-consuming and extended duration (3 years) project, undertaken completely in their own time.

The raw material from the TFG sessions was notes taken by the Project team, and audio tapes that were subsequently transcribed and summarised. A key task for the Project Team was to develop a structure for the material, and the final version of this structure—the domains and standards themselves—is described below. After several iterations with the TFGs, a draft document was developed that reflected the views of the practitioner/researcher team. This was made available in late 2000 to the full membership of the AAMT who were encouraged to provide comments and feedback. Whilst a range of matters were raised and suggestions made by members, it was clear at that time that the draft *Standards* were well on the way to being acceptable within the profession. Further work and checking saw the AAMT *Standards for Excellence in Teaching Mathematics in Australian Schools*[5] approved and adopted by the AAMT Council in January 2002. The *Standards* were published in hard copy and distributed to members and key educational organisations including the national, state and territory education authorities, the faculties of education in all universities and other professional societies.

During the remainder of the project (i.e., after the draft *Standards* were developed and revised), the attention of the TFGs moved to the second of the project purposes—developing an assessment scheme and protocols. This work formed the basis for a project on assessing teachers against the *Standards* that is described later in this chapter.

One of the core intentions of the project was to ensure that the *Standards* embrace diversity in teaching mathematics in matters such as teaching approaches, level of schooling (i.e., age of students), type or location of school. The slogan "*Standards* not standardisation" was adopted within the project as an indication of the commitment to this diversity. The approach adopted in the *Standards* development tried to ensure that voices representing this diversity were included in the TFGs, although restricted funding limited the direct involvement of teachers from regional and remote locations. The inclusivity of the *Standards* is constantly being monitored, and to date no teachers have reported that they do not see themselves reflected in them. To that extent it is reasonable to claim that the *Standards* do represent a consensus view, not just of the AAMT Council, but of the profession more broadly.

An example of the primacy of the views and input of practising teachers (the TFGs) in the project is the approach to the issue of different statements for different levels of schooling. The National Board of Professional Teaching Standards identifies four overlapping levels of schooling (Early Childhood, Middle Years, Early Adolescent, and Adolescent and Young Adult) and has developed different standards and credentials across these in order to reflect the different contexts of teaching. TFGs were consistently determined that these kinds of distinctions did not fit their views and experiences, despite the opposite approach taken by the National Board of Professional Teaching Standards, and the reservations of some of the non-teachers in the project. The commitment to the principle that these were to be 'standards by teachers, for teachers,' has resulted in the AAMT *Standards* being K-12 in scope.

At the commencement of the project the TFGs expressed the strong opinion that the document itself needed to be brief—"if we write a book no-one will read it!" As a result of this advice from the teachers involved, the *Standards* document is a little over 1000 words in length—it can be displayed on one piece of A3 paper. This adds greatly to the potential for it to be considered and used by teachers, its primary audience.

THE AAMT *STANDARDS* MATERIALS

The AAMT Standards Document

There are ten professional teaching standards, arranged in three domains (see Table 1).

Table 1. The AAMT Standards arranged into the three domains

Domain 1 — Professional Knowledge	Domain 2 — Professional Attributes	Domain 3 — Professional Practice
1.1 Knowledge of students 1.2 Knowledge of mathematics 1.3 Knowledge of students' learning of mathematics	2.1 Personal attributes 2.2 Personal professional development 2.3 Community responsibility	3.1 The learning environment 3.2 Planning for learning 3.3 Teaching in action 3.4 Assessment

The domains are fairly logical categories for *Standards* that describe what excellent teachers of mathematics know and do—knowledge, attributes and skills. Within each of the domains the actual standards that were identified are also reasonably unsurprising. This is certainly true of the Professional Knowledge and Professional Practice domains in which it would be difficult to imagine other components from those included.

The standards in the Professional Attributes domain were more challenging to categorise into the three standards. The first standard in this domain (*2.1 Personal attributes*) needed to be crafted to avoid any suggestion of stereotyping the personality required by effective teachers. The identification of a standard for Community responsibility relies on multiple meanings for the term 'community.' The AAMT *Standards* take the view that effective teachers react to and lead in several communities simultaneously. Some of these are 'professional'—teaching colleagues within and beyond the school—whilst others are broader and include parents and the wider community, as well as specific groups (e.g., local employers) within the wider community. This aspect of the *Standards* has aroused some commentary as it challenges the common perception that teachers of mathematics have a narrow focus.

The following examples illustrate the style of the AAMT *Standards*. The first example shows how the critical matter of teachers' knowledge of mathematics is specified in the *Standards*.

Standard 1.2: Knowledge of mathematics
Excellent teachers of mathematics have a sound, coherent knowledge of the mathematics appropriate to the student level they teach, and which is situated in their knowledge and understanding of the broader mathematics curriculum. They understand how mathematics is represented and communicated, and why mathematics is taught. They are confident and competent users of mathematics who understand connections within mathematics, between mathematics and other subject areas, and how mathematics is related to society.

The requirement that the *Standards* be applicable for teachers K–12 makes it impossible to identify specific mathematics content that they should know as this is highly dependent on the 'student level[6] they teach.' Moreover, this needs to be 'situated in their knowledge and understanding of the broader mathematics curriculum.' In other words, they need to know 'what came before for their students, and what comes after,' to paraphrase the language used by the teachers in the TFGs—they saw this as a critical aspect of knowledge, in recognition that students develop at vastly different rates. The standard on Knowledge of mathematics is also clear that teachers should know their mathematics in a 'connected' way that mirrors the findings of Askew, Brown, Rhodes, Wiliam and Johnson (1997) in their UK study on the effective teaching of numeracy. Other critical ideas in this standard are about:

– representations;
– communications;
– the rationale for teaching mathematics ('why mathematics is taught');
– teachers also being 'users' of mathematics;
– uses of mathematics; and
– how mathematics is related to society.

The economy of words in the *Standards* is therefore not an indication of lack of coverage of the key elements of effective teaching of mathematics.

The second example of a standard is from the Professional Attributes domain. The standards in this domain proved to be the most challenging for teachers to express in clear, explicit and helpful ways. The example illustrates that this work— by teachers, for teachers—has been able to capture the essence of what it means to be an excellent teacher of mathematics.

Standard 2.1: Personal attributes

The work of excellent teachers of mathematics reflects a range of personal attributes that assists them to engage students in their learning. Their enthu-siasm for mathematics and its learning characterises their work. These teachers have a conviction that all students can learn mathematics. They are commit-ted to maximising students' opportunities to learn mathematics and set high achievable standards for the learning of each student. They aim for students to become autonomous and self-directed learners who enjoy mathematics. These teachers exhibit care and respect for their students.

The term "enthusiasm for mathematics" is used in this statement to convey what the TFGs meant when they used the term "passion for mathematics." This idea of "passion" was common to all the TFGs, but was not used in the final document as it was judged to be open for misinterpretation. In retrospect, it could be that this was a mistake and that the essence of excellent teaching of mathematics is characterised by passion for the subject and its learning.

There was an opinion amongst some in the various TFGs that the standards in the Professional Practice domain were all that really counts. That is, 'excellent' teaching of mathematics is about practice. The consensus was, however, that practice needs to be underpinned by high levels of knowledge about teaching (Professional Knowledge) and the range of commitments identified as Professional Attributes.

Other Materials

A range of other materials is included on the AAMT website www.aamt.edu.au. These materials are designed to 'fill-out' the picture provided by the *Standards*.

Elaborations

Feedback on the *Standards* identified a number of phrases in each of the standards that required further elaboration. This material (Elaborations) is provided in the electronic version of the materials. For example, in Standard 1.3 (Teachers knowledge of students' learning of mathematics), the phrase "understanding of current theories" is elaborated by the statement shown below.

understanding of current theories:

Research in mathematics education is, for the most part, designed to explore and understand issues relating to the teaching and learning of mathematics. 'Theories' about students' mathematical learning emerge from this work. These range from the grand (social constructivism, SOLO taxonomy) through to smaller scale suggestions about novel and improved ways of introducing or assessing a particular topic. Through their commitment to their own ongoing professional development, excellent teachers of mathematics maintain a currency with research that is relevant to them and their teaching context. They are able to discuss this with colleagues, and critically appraise new, research-based information for adaptation or adoption in their work in the classroom, given the opportunities and constraints of the context.

Teacher Stories

The Teacher Stories are another means used to exemplify the *Standards*. They have been designed to be both engaging and informative. An example is given below. Note that like most of the stories and examples, this example relates to several of the standards—in this case those relating to Knowledge of students (1.1) and Assessment practices (3.4), as well as illustrating an understanding of the importance of students developing strategies for the various phases of problem solving (i.e., Knowledge of students learning of mathematics; 1.3)

What does Eric know?

During the first two weeks of the year, I have a diverse range of maths activities and investigations for the purpose of finding out what the students know and can do in mathematics. This year by the end of the first week, I knew nothing about what Eric knew or could do. Eric was in Year 5 in a Year 5/6 composite. Every time I observed him he was "preparing" to start. All of his work was incomplete. I decided to frequently observe and note Eric's behaviour for a lesson. My observations confirmed that Eric never actually engaged in the mathematics activity. I was relatively new to the school and asked some other teachers about Eric. Their comments described Eric as "lazy", "not very bright", "slow" and "unobtrusive". During a relief from teaching time, I decided to interview Eric as we worked collaboratively on a construction task. He revealed to me that he could not do very much mathematics and was very slow to do it. Also he preferred to be thought of as "lazy" rather than "stupid". Therefore, he had developed a whole range of strategies so that he never disrupted the class but was always "getting ready" to start whenever the teacher might question him. If he didn't start, he couldn't be called "dumb" for not finishing. I changed my tasks for the following two weeks. Rather than give the students a set of tasks that they could choose from, I organised for every student to start every investigation. They were given insufficient time to finish. I also explained to them that we would be focussing on how we start solving problems, and at the end of the first week each student would choose one investigation to undertake for a week. As that next week progressed and Eric noticed that no-one was finished, I noted that he was getting more involved in the investigations and doing more mathematics.

The purpose of the Teacher Story is not to provide a definitive example of effective teaching of mathematics in the sense that it is what any teacher should do when confronted by the same situation. What the Teacher Stories aim to do is show how a single teacher responded to a particular situation and how what they have done demonstrates the *Standards* in action. Faced with a student like Eric there are many approaches—the best of these will represent thoughtful action that can be mapped to the *Standards*.

TEACHER CREDENTIALING INITIATIVE: THE TEACHING STANDARDS ASSESSMENT EVALUATION PROJECT (TSAEP)

At the time of publication of the *Standards* (2002) the work for the AAMT moved from development to implementation. Of the two direct uses identified above— *recognition* and *professional development*—it was the first of these that received a positive response from the Australian Government as the most likely agency for funding the AAMT to undertake a significant research and development project[7].

As a result, the *Teaching Standards Assessment Evaluation Project* (TSAEP) was commenced in July, 2003 with funding from the Australian Government. Government officials saw the opportunity for the AAMT work on the *Standards* to be an example of how to move from the development of teaching standards to their ultimate implementation with the aim of enhancing the quality and status of teaching. A brief outline of TSAEP follows. A detailed description of the project is contained in Fraser and Morony (in preparation).

The TSAEP Steering Committee—mostly teacher members of the AAMT— developed, implemented, and piloted a model for assessing teachers against the AAMT *Standards*. The key parameters for the Assessment Model were commitments to ensure, as far as possible, that it was:

- rigorous and valid;
- adaptable to and applicable in all teaching contexts;
- fair to all candidates no matter what their teaching situation;
- equally accessible to teachers across the country;
- controlled by the candidate insofar as this is possible; and
- oriented towards contributing to professional growth of the candidate— through both the process itself and the feedback provided to all candidates.

The approach adopted was for assessment to be directly against the *Standards*. The evidence presented by the candidate was to be accumulated against each of the ten Standards. For each candidate, there were to be at least two peer assessors who were to reach a consensus decision on whether the candidate had presented sufficient evidence to demonstrate that the standard had been reached. There were no formal rubrics, checklists, scoring guides or whatever. Assessors were able, however, to use these mechanisms if they assisted their identification and weighing of evidence.

At the practical level, when it was necessary to try to resolve issues, the people developing the model often asked two 'fall-back' questions. These were: "Would this be something I would see as reasonable for myself?" and "What would we do if we were trying to assess students in this way?" These served to emphasise the teacher-oriented nature of the work, something that is a consistent feature of AAMT's work in this area.

The Assessment Model that was evaluated through TSAEP consisted of:
- Written Assessment—questions seeking candidates' personal detailed written responses. The questions simulate teaching decisions and include commenting on student work and responding to hypothetical situations. The context and content of the questions are linked to the candidate's level of teaching;
- Portfolio—five compulsory items: Professional Journey—a brief (2500 words maximum) written reflection on the candidate's professional life as a teacher of mathematics; Current Teaching and Learning Practices—an example of current/ recent classroom work; Case Study—an example of the candidate's efforts over time to address a particular issue(s) with one or a few students; Validation— some 'objective' material that attests to the candidate as a teacher (video or audio tape of a teaching episode; a report on a structured observation by a peer[8] designed to give a short snapshot of the teacher at work); Documentation— material the candidate may possess that demonstrates the range and quality of the candidate's work and achievements. The candidate is required to annotate the material by linking what they present with the *Standards*. This component of the assessment process is the most substantial and varied. It provides the greatest amount of evidence of the candidate matching the *Standards*; and
- Interview—a 30–45 minute telephone conversation to provide further confirmation of evidence, as well as an opportunity to clarify any matters that were not fully understood from the Portfolio items in particular.

The following illustrates how the assessors undertook their work. In the Portfolio the links identified by the candidate between the materials presented and the *Standards* had primacy. Assessors were also instructed to note instances of positive evidence that had not been cited by the candidate. All candidates received constructive written feedback, prepared and agreed upon by the relevant assessors.

This helped candidates—both successful and unsuccessful—to set further learning and development goals.

Six teachers were recruited as volunteer candidates. They were all from different states; four were female, two male; four primary, two secondary; four taught in government schools, two in non-government schools. This was about as good a mix as it was possible to achieve in the circumstances, although there was no-one from a non-metropolitan location. Five assessors, also volunteer classroom teachers and hailing from four states, were recruited and trained—the evidence presented by each candidate was independently assessed by at least two assessors who were currently involved in the same level of schooling.

Those successful in proving that their work met the *Standards* were to be awarded the credential Highly Accomplished Teacher of Mathematics (HAToM) by the AAMT. Four of the six candidates in the TSAEP were recommended to receive the HAToM award, with two teachers presenting insufficient evidence in relation to some *Standards*. These two teachers were subsequently advised of the areas in which there was insufficient evidence, and a process established to give them further opportunities to pursue the credential. Neither of these teachers has taken the opportunity to complete the requirements for them to be awarded the HAToM credential.

An independent external evaluator used a 'participant-observer' methodology to report on the project. Observations, document analysis, interviews with participants and feedback from participants of all kinds provided the data for an extensive evaluation report (Brinkworth, 2005). The report contains a wealth of information that can guide the thinking of the AAMT and others in relation to assessing teachers against professional teaching standards. The most significant results from the evaluation were:

- The TSAEP found that the Assessment Model works—candidates are validly and reliably identified as HAToMs.
- The assessment process is able to discriminate among teachers.
- The Model itself and the Guidelines that were provided to candidates are both transparent and flexible in allowing teachers to exercise some control over the form of their Portfolio submissions.
- Significant time and effort is required by teachers to compile a case for accreditation, and this has an impact on their personal and professional lives.
- The actual process of assessment is professionally demanding and time-intensive for the assessors.
- Conducting assessments according to the Model has a significant monetary cost.
- Being assessed using this Model is likely to appeal to a relatively small number of teachers.
- The component of the *Standards* relating to assessment of students' learning (Standard 3.4) was the most difficult to identify for all candidates. Possibly this was because the long-term achievement of students is not included in the methods of assessment the candidates undertake.

At the conclusion of the TSAEP the AAMT Council considered the evaluator's report and adopted the Assessment Model and assessment process recommended from the TSAEP.

The approach—i.e., using this Assessment Model in this way—can only be sustainable if there is a sufficient pool of candidates for whom the benefits of undertaking the assessment outweigh the costs. The Project provides some insight into likely costs for candidates. One relates to time. It is likely (Brinkworth, 2005) that the assessment process will take a minimum of 70–80 hours (50–60 hours for the Portfolio; 20 hours to prepare for and take part in the Written Assessment and Interview, and for general preparation and administration). The other cost is financial. The Candidate's fee allows for payment to assessors for their work, a contribution to the ongoing training of assessors, AAMT administration and other personal costs such as stationery, postage etc.).

On the positive side, the benefits identified by these candidates are their own personal professional learning, affirmation of their work by their peers and recognition in their school community. In the current climate there are no financial incentives in the workplace such as promotion, reclassification, a salary increment or similar to make the process more appealing. There is, however, a recent move by one educational authority to make the assessment process accessible to some of its teachers. This is discussed later in this chapter.

TEACHER PROFESSIONAL DEVELOPMENT

The *Standards* are the profession's statement of what high quality teaching of mathematics looks like, what highly accomplished teachers know and do, and what they are like. They therefore provide a framework and a common language for talking and thinking about high quality teaching in the Australian context.

Engaging with Excellence in Mathematics Teaching: Creating Excellence in the Learning Environment Project

An instructive example of the integration of the *Standards* into programs of professional learning is a program entitled *Engaging with Excellence in Mathematics Teaching: Creating Excellence in the Learning Environment*. This pilot teacher professional development program was developed and conducted by the Australian Council for Education Research (ACER) in collaboration with the AAMT in 2004.

The catalyst for the partnership was the release of some classroom videos from the *1999 Third International Mathematics and Science Study* (TIMSS) Video Study (National Center for Education Statistics, 2003). ACER was the Australian partner in this project and, as a consequence, has a commitment to the uptake of its findings and resources. The videos now available are acknowledged as an outstanding resource for teacher development, especially when the software tools and other resources that are associated with them are taken into account. Given the finalisation of the AAMT *Standards* it was agreed that these would be used as the framework for the teachers' investigations.

Given that the videos capture learning environments (physical, intellectual, emotional) in mathematics classrooms in a variety of countries, the focus area for the professional development program was Standard 3.1:

Standard 3.1: Learning environment

Excellent teachers of mathematics establish an environment that maximises students' learning opportunities. The psychological, emotional and physical needs of students are addressed and the teacher is aware of, and responds to, the diversity of students' individual needs and talents. Students are empowered to become independent learners. They are motivated to improve their understanding of mathematics and develop enthusiasm for, enjoyment of, and interest in mathematics. In an inclusive and caring atmosphere of trust and belonging, active engagement with mathematics is valued, communication skills fostered, and co-operative and collaborative efforts encouraged.

In this professional development program, participants used the AAMT *Standards* to self-identify their learning needs in mathematics—they used a form of the *Standards* that has been developed for this purpose. Another learning activity involved them in analysing, describing and discussing the learning environments represented in selected videos by using the framework and language of the *Standards*. Participants then went on to express their particular learning goals for their professional learning program, monitor their progress and note their success.

The pilot program concluded in August, 2004. Analysis of feedback from the 14 participants—all of whom had no previous detailed exposure to the *Standards*[9]— shows that they found the document useful to very useful in identifying their professional learning needs: "The *Standards* self-evaluation form in particular was identified as a most useful instrument" (Peck, Hollingsworth, & Morony, 2004, p. 375).

The participants reported that the *Standards* assisted them in working with colleagues who had not attended the face-to-face sessions. The *Standards* provided a means for focussing their learning. "Overwhelmingly, all teachers felt that they had significantly improved their awareness and appreciation of the AAMT *Standards* and were able to identify ways that their practice (or that of their colleagues) had moved closer to the *Standards*" (Peck et al., 2004, p. 376).

The attempt to focus on a single standard was not successful, however. As soon as real life school initiatives were developed these inevitably reflected a wide range of attributes of effective teaching of mathematics. The single Standard about the establishment of a positive learning environment was insufficient to cover all aspects.

The Professional Learning Using the Mathematics Standards project

The Professional Learning Using the Mathematics Standards (PLUMS) Project was a much larger scale exploration of the usefulness of the AAMT *Standards* for teacher professional learning. The AAMT *Standards* were developed to define the

273

'high end' of individual teacher performance. The HAToM process is a means for credentialing those teachers working to the high level set by the *Standards*. On the other hand, for the *Standards* to be a 'framework for professional development' they need to be applicable to the wide range of teachers of mathematics in schools. Another issue is whether the *Standards*, which were written to describe individual 'excellence,' can play a role in group approaches to professional learning.

The PLUMS Project was designed to test these issues by exploring the question: "To what extent are the AAMT *Standards for Excellence in Teaching Mathematics in Australian Schools* able to be used to support the professional learning of teachers of mathematics in the context of in-school, collaborative professional learning programs?"

PLUMS[10] set out to trial the AAMT *Standards* as a framework for supporting the professional learning of *all* teachers of mathematics on a school-by-school basis. Two groups of eight schools (primary/secondary; government and non-government) in different states were selected for the trial. One group was in a regional city and the other in a state capital.

After an initial introduction to the AAMT *Standards* and associated materials, each school designed and conducted a professional learning program in an area of mathematics teaching and learning that was important to it. It is important to note that the professional learning was *not* focussed on the teachers becoming familiar with the *Standards*. Rather, the emphasis was for them to see whether the *Standards* were useful to them, and in what ways. Schools were encouraged and supported to use the *Standards* and related materials in a range of ways including a small amount of funding to be spent at the school's discretion, some release time for project purposes (e.g., responding to an evaluator, reporting and sharing results etc.) and access to support personnel either locally or at distance.

Two independent evaluators were appointed. They gathered data from observation, documents produced by the teachers and schools, surveys and interviews with participant teachers. The evaluators prepared a detailed report (Bishop, Clarke, & Morony, 2006) on the usefulness of the *Standards* in the schools' professional learning programs.

As would be expected in a project that asked schools to design and undertake their own professional learning program, the projects in the schools varied significantly in terms of their particular foci, the way the learning took place and how the *Standards* were used. Some projects involved the whole staff in a primary school, others engaged all the teachers at a particular year level, while others involved a small group of teachers on a particular topic. Some summary observations of the programs undertaken in each of the schools include:

– The majority of projects in the regional cluster focussed on assessment, while many of the city schools focussed on pedagogy and teaching practice—this reflects current emphases in the two states and suggests that school-based decisions about professional learning are taken in these broader contexts, even when they have a 'free choice'.
– A common theme across the schools' projects is that they provided opportunities for teachers to work together on planning, development and reflection,

thus reinforcing the importance of collaborative work in teacher professional learning in these schools.
- The approach of asking schools to design their own project was a strong contributor to the high levels of teacher ownership of the work done.
- The scope of many of the projects went well beyond the funding and other support that was provided, and this was complemented by reports of high levels of enthusiasm among the teachers involved for the work and their learning.

The evaluation (Bishop et al., 2006) determined that the *Standards* were used quite extensively within these schools' professional learning programs for:
- needs analysis;
- setting directions and targets; and
- establishing 'distance travelled' by teachers in their professional learning.

These reflect the operationalisation of the *Standards* as a framework to guide teachers of mathematics in their professional learning (i.e., as a 'framework for professional learning').

Two other anticipated uses of the *Standards*—'designing actual professional learning activities' and 'guiding progress during the course of a professional learning program'—did not eventuate to any great extent. These uses may emerge as teachers become more familiar with the *Standards*, and when they work with them over a more extended timeframe.

The following major benefits from using the *Standards* have been synthesised from the evidence provided by the teachers, teacher-leaders and professional learning programs (Bishop et al., 2006):
- **structure**: help with planning enables systematic organisation of activities, affirms what is being done well, points to deficiencies, helps administrators.
- **language**: help with sharing meanings about intentions and activities enriches discussions and debates, clarifies relevance of ideas—a shared language for professional discussions.
- **priorities**: enables priorities to be determined, in specific subject area.
- **subject specificity**: important to have a focus on one subject (especially for primary teachers), not just vague generalities, recognises and names teachers' particular needs and deficiencies in mathematics
- **assessment in mathematics**: found to be a very useful section of the *Standards*, with several groups focussing on it.

The PLUMS project demonstrated that the AAMT *Standards* can be used for developmental purposes with groups of teachers. This complements their efficacy when used for individual recognition, as demonstrated in the TSAEP.

Perhaps the evidence that both justifies the efforts of the AAMT to develop and implement its *Standards* over many years as well as encourages further effort is contained in responses from teacher-leaders involved in PLUMS. These include:

"Professional development using the AAMT *Standards*... a new challenge with a specific direction/target ... and therefore a baseline to come back to and compare ..."

"The vision of a nationally recognised standards framework that was not just thrust upon us, but (the standards were) given an opportunity to be embraced as part of our planning."

"The AAMT *Standards* gave us direction and helped the program move quickly to areas that needed improvement."

"The program enabled our whole school to take a similar journey and work as a team to improve outcomes for our students." (Bishop et al., 2006, p. 48)

CURRENT ACTIVITIES

The development of the *Standards* as a consensus statement for the mathematics teaching profession represents a synthesis of the views of diverse professionals. The *Standards* are at the broad, profession-wide scale. However the diversity within that profession is profound at the level of the daily work of teachers of mathematics. Their immediate concerns are directly related to their context—students, colleagues, school, location, community, curriculum, educational authority, etc.—and all these vary markedly around the country. It is an ongoing challenge for the AAMT to try to make the *Standards* practically useful to teachers in all their diverse settings, with their diverse needs and with the diverse set of influences acting on them.

The findings from the PLUMS Project outlined above indicate that the *Standards* can have benefits for teachers in in-school professional development. Promoting those results is an important strategy. More generally, there is an ongoing need to continue to promote professional development uses of the *Standards* to teachers. Over the last several years this has been done by linking sessions at AAMT conferences, and other teacher conferences, to the *Standards*. At the time of proposing a session, presenters are required to identify the relevant *Standard(s)*. These are then published in the program and attendees can use the information to guide their choice of conference sessions. Perhaps the most important aspect of this strategy, however, is that those attending conferences are reminded of the *Standards* and, to some extent at least, engage with them.

From the middle of 2008 the AAMT will be cooperating with the Catholic Education Office of Melbourne (CEOM) on a project that will foreground the HAToM process. The CEOM is an autonomous education authority of around 300 schools centred on Australia's second largest city. Over the next five years, the CEOM will support an annual cohort of up to 12 teachers (i.e., up to 60 in all) to submit themselves for assessment by the AAMT against the AAMT *Standards*. The support will include funding the costs of assessing each teacher, provision of some release time to enable teachers to prepare for their assessment, and networking and other services provided by CEOM mathematics officers.

The project is a component of a five-year strategy of the CEOM[11] to enhance the learning and teaching outcomes in mathematics in its schools by improving overall levels of student and school performance. It is a means for enabling recognition of the CEOM's best teachers of mathematics, thereby helping to lift the quality of teaching across the board. For the AAMT this project will provide an example of the HAToM process over a sustained period. It will bring the AAMT *Standards* to the attention of teachers of mathematics in the CEOM, and hopefully, more widely.

SOME REFLECTIVE COMMENTS

The current collaboration with the CEOM represents explicit recognition by an important education authority of the AAMT's work on *Standards for Excellence in Teaching Mathematics in Australian Schools*. This is a landmark achievement for the association. In fact, recognition of the work by the CEOM predates the current project. In late 2006, officers at the CEOM developed and gathered data from a survey to identify needed improvements in the teaching of mathematics. This was part of the development of its overall five-year strategy. Those officers chose to use the AAMT *Standards* to help frame that survey.

The AAMT is pleased that its work was able to assist in this way, by providing an authoritative picture of effective teaching of mathematics. On the other hand, one might ask the rhetorical question: "Why would the CEOM *not* use the consensus view of the profession—the AAMT *Standards*—as its goal for the teaching of mathematics?"

A major factor that has in some ways limited the uptake of the AAMT *Standards* by teachers of mathematics has been the proliferation of work on teaching standards by others, as outlined earlier. At one level, there is nothing the AAMT can do about this. We are, like it or not, in 'competition' for the attention of teachers. Many of them, understandably, give their attention to the mandated standards with which they must be familiar.

These other teaching standards are generic in nature. The AAMT does not argue that they are inferior to what the association has developed and is doing, just that they are different. We have the evidence that at least some teachers find our work useful. One of the criticisms of our subject specialist approach is that primary teachers will not want to deal with separate sets of standards in different curriculum areas. It is therefore particularly noteworthy that primary teachers in the PLUMS project found the AAMT *Standards* of benefit precisely because they were subject-specific. Hence we argue that the AAMT *Standards* present a different pathway to achieving the stated goal of governments that the purpose for using professional standards for credentialing and professional development is to improve teaching. The AAMT strongly supports that goal and looks forward to a time when teachers are given choice as to which framework they use.

At the same time, a broad consensus has recently developed between governments and other education employers and teacher unions that reform of the career structure for teachers is an important strategy in efforts to improve the quality of education in this country. The most radical component of these anticipated reforms is the notion of 'performance pay' for teachers. A vision for a system for performance pay has been developed by the influential Business Council of Australia (BCA), the organisation that represents the views and interests of the one hundred largest companies in Australia. In relation to matters of education policy and practice, therefore, theirs is a voice that is independent of both government and unions.

Like many community and business groups, the BCA recognises the links between education achievement and economic and social prosperity. The BCA commissioned a report from the Australian Council for Educational Research that included a discussion of performance pay (Dinham, Ingvarson, & Kleinhenz, 2008) in which they conclude that the country needs "a new remuneration structure that rewards excellent teachers and demonstrates that, as a society, Australia values the teaching profession" (p. 2). Such a structure needs to be based on a system of certification that is developed and owned by the profession:

> The time has come, therefore, for the teaching profession to take up the challenge of developing a system for defining high-quality teaching standards, promoting development towards those standards and identifying those who reach them – a national 'certification' system. The level of ownership of and commitment to professional standards within a profession will depend on the extent to which members of the profession are entrusted with their development and application. It is in the interests of employing authorities and the public that teachers have a strong commitment to their own standards and their application. (Dinham et al., 2008, p. 31)

The AAMT's work is an example of precisely such a system, and is being promoted and increasingly recognised as such. This would not be the case if the work had been envisaged as a traditional research effort, with educational researchers leading the work. The concept of 'ownership' as envisaged by the Business Council of Australia relies on the profession (in our case, teachers of mathematics through their national professional association) pursuing and realising its goals through research and development. Educational researchers have an important role to play by working with the profession to ensure the work is rigorous and the findings defensible. However the politics of the situation in this case required the practitioners to drive the work. Given that the issue of "quality teaching" is an intensely politically charged arena, it may be that this kind of change in control is necessary for there to be practical gains for teachers. Certainly the work models collaboration between practitioners and researchers that may be an example of how currently identified distances between the two groups can be diminished.

One result of the plethora of work on professional standards is that it is common for teachers to be sceptical about the AAMT *Standards* when they hear of them for the first time. The commitment to defining 'standards' by employers makes teachers wary of the credentialing and accountability uses to which those standards are being put. Their concern can be summarised in a single question: "Who is doing what to whom, and why?" It is not possible to answer this question on behalf of employers. For the AAMT, however, the answer is quite clear. As a professional organisation it is not possible to *do* anything to members, and teachers more generally. The AAMT's capacity to influence people—in this case to take up and work with the AAMT *Standards*—relies on the quality and usefulness of what is offered. The need to inform people about the *Standards,* and to encourage them to work with them means that the uptake of the *Standards* is a necessarily long process. However, there is a resolve within the Council and management of the AAMT that what we have is useful to teachers and worth promoting and supporting. That resolve is fuelled by consistently positive feedback from projects and teachers.

Change in education is known to be a slow process. It has taken a decade to get this far. Perhaps in another decade the AAMT *Standards* will be a 'given' in the professional lives of teachers of mathematics in Australia. That is worth striving for. Or maybe it will take two decades ...

NOTES

[1] The author has been a key leader and worker in all of the AAMT's work to develop and use the *Standards.* This chapter is very much an "insider's view".

[2] See www.teachingaustralia.edu.au/ta/go/home/links/accreditation for links to websites for further information about these bodies.

[3] The *Linkage Grants* program has superseded the SPIRT program.

[4] The establishment of this group was part of achieving the third of our purposes. Useful contacts were made with a range of groups outside mathematics education and this has contributed to the acceptance of the AAMT as a legitimate and serious 'player ' in the field of teaching standards.

[5] Available from www.aamt.edu.au/Standards/Standards-document

[6] In this sense 'level' means both the age/grade of the students, and the type of mathematics being studied when students have a choice, typically in the later secondary years—the different types of subjects at Year 12 level in Australia deal with quite different 'levels' of mathematics.

[7] It is noteworthy that the then national Minister for Education was a medical practitioner who came from a background in the Australian Medical Association. Within the medical profession, the notion of standards and credentialing is well-established—he took the view that similar arrangements should be encouraged for teachers.

[8] Difficulties relating to privacy have meant that, in practice, candidates in TSAEP all chose to submit an observation report for this item.

[9] Indeed, some were not even aware of their existence.

[10] PLUMS was funded by Teaching Australia, a government funded "institute for advanced teaching and school leadership".

[11] Information about the CEOM strategy is available from www.ceo.melb.catholic.edu.au.

REFERENCES

Askew, M., Brown, M., Rhodes, V., Wiliam, D., & Johnson, D. (1997). *Effective teachers of numeracy in primary schools: Teachers' beliefs, practices and pupils' learning.* Paper presented the British Educational Research Association annual conference September, 11–14, University of York.

Australian Association of Mathematics Teachers Inc. (2002). *Standards for excellence in teaching mathematics in Australian schools.* Adelaide: Author.

Australian Association of Mathematics Teachers Inc. (2006). *Standards for excellence in teaching mathematics in Australian schools (2006 edition).* Adelaide: Author. Retrieved from www.aamt.edu.au/Standards/Standards-document

Australian Senate Employment, Education and Training References Committee. (1998). *A class act: Inquiry into the status of the teaching profession.* Canberra: Senate Printing Unit.

Bishop, A., Clarke, B., & Morony, W. (2006). *Professional standards using the mathematics standards.* Canberra: Teaching Australia: Australian Institute for Teaching and School Leadership.

Brinkworth, P. (2005). *AAMT teaching standards assessment evaluation project: Evaluation report October 2004.* Canberra: Commonwealth of Australia. Retrieved April 17, 2008, from http://www.dest.gov.au/sectors/school_education/publications_resources/profiles/aamt_tsaep_evaluation_report_oct2004.htm

Commonwealth of Australia. (2003). *Australia's teachers: Australia's future. Report of the review of teaching and teacher education* (3 Vols.). Canberra: Author.

Fraser, C., & Morony, W. (in preparation). Teacher-developed professional standards for excellence in teaching mathematics: Progressing teachers' professionalism. In G. Anthony & B. Grevholm (Eds.), *Mathematics teacher recruitment and education: An international perspective.*

Dinham, S., Ingvarson, L., & Kleinhenz, E. (2008). *Teaching talent: The best teachers for Australia's classrooms.* Report prepared for the Business Council of Australia. Retrieved from http://www.bca.com.au/DisplayFile.aspx?FileID=443

Glaser, B., & Strauss, A. (1967). *The discovery of grounded theory: Strategies for qualitative research.* Chicago: Aldine Publishing Co.

Hattie, J. (2003). *Teachers make a difference. What is the research evidence?* Paper presented at the Australian Council for Educational Research Conference, 19–21 October, Melbourne.

Ingvarson, L. (1998). Professional development as the pursuit of professional standards: The standards-based professional development system. *Teaching and Teacher Education, 14*(1), 127–140.

Ingvarson, L., & Kleinhenz, E. (2006). *Advanced teaching standards and certification: A review of national and international developments.* Canberra: Teaching Australia: Australian Institute for Teaching and School Leadership.

National Board for Professional Teaching Standards. (1989). *Towards high and rigorous standards for the teaching profession.* Detroit, MI: Author.

National Board for Professional Teaching Standards. (1996). *Adolescence and young adulthood/mathematics. Standards for national board certification.* Southfield, MI: Author.

National Center for Education Statistics. (2003). *Teaching mathematics in seven countries: Results from the TIMSS 1999 video study.* Washington, DC: Author.

National Council of Teachers of Mathematics. (1989). *Curriculum and evaluation standards for teaching mathematics.* Reston, VA: Author.

National Council of Teachers of Mathematics. (1991). *Professional standards for teaching mathematics.* Reston, VA: Author.

National Council of Teachers of Mathematics. (1995). *Assessment standards for teaching mathematics.* Reston, VA: Author.

National Council of Teachers of Mathematics. (2000). *Principles and standards for school mathematics.* Reston, VA: Author.

Peck, R., Hollingsworth, H., & Morony, W. (2004). Engaging with excellence. In B. Tadich, S. Tobias, C. Brew, B. Beatty, & P. Sullivan (Eds.), *Towards excellence in mathematics* (Proceedings of the 41st annual conference of the mathematical association of Victoria) (pp. 367–376). Melbourne: Mathematical Association of Victoria.

Rowe, K. (2003). *The importance of* teacher quality *as a key determinant of students' experiences and outcomes of schooling.* Background paper to keynote address presented at the Australian Council for Educational Research conference, 19–21 October, Melbourne.

Will Morony
The Australian Association of Mathematics Teachers Inc.

IRIS R. WEISS, P. SEAN SMITH, AND SHARON K. O'KELLEY

THE PRESIDENTIAL AWARD FOR EXCELLENCE IN MATHEMATICS TEACHING: SETTING THE STANDARD

INTRODUCTION

In 1983, the White House established The Presidential Award for Excellence in Mathematics and Science Teaching (PAEMST) program to recognize outstanding mathematics and science teachers in the United States. Administered by the National Science Foundation on behalf of the White House, the Presidential Awards are given annually to teachers who demonstrate:

— Subject-matter competence and sustained professional growth in science or mathematics and in the art of teaching;
— An understanding of how students learn science or mathematics;
— The ability to engage students in direct hands-on science inquiry or mathematics inquiry activities;
— The ability to foster curiosity and to generate excitement among students, colleagues, and parents about the uses of science and mathematics in everyday life;
— A conviction that all students can learn science and mathematics, and a sensitivity to the needs of all students' cultural, linguistic, learning, and social uniqueness;
— An understanding of the relationships of science and mathematics to each other and the interconnectedness of all subject matter;
— An experimental and innovative attitude in their approach to teaching; and
— Professional involvement and leadership.

Nominations for the award are typically sent to the state department of education, which then sends an application packet to the nominees. A selection committee reviews the applications and picks the three state finalists for each award category and then a national panel makes the final selection. Initially, Presidential Awards were restricted to secondary (grades 7–12) schoolteachers in the 50 states, District of Columbia, and Puerto Rico with two science teachers and two mathematics teachers in each jurisdiction receiving awards each year. The program was expanded in 1986 to include U.S. territories and the Department of Defense Dependent Schools and again in 1990 to include elementary (grades Kindergarten–6) teachers. Currently, the awards alternate each year between elementary and secondary-level teachers (National Science Foundation, Application Section).

J. Cai, G. Kaiser, B. Perry and N.-Y. Wong (eds.), Effective Mathematics Teaching from Teachers' Perspectives: National and Cross-National Studies, 281–301.
© 2009 Sense Publishers. All rights reserved.

Each winner is given an expense-paid trip for two to Washington, DC to attend an awards ceremony, receive a Presidential citation, meet with leaders in government and education, and attend a number of special receptions. In addition, each recipient's school receives a grant (originally $5,000, later increased to $10,000) to be used under the direction of the recipient to improve the local science or mathematics program. Activities supported by these grants have included field trips, curriculum development, purchase of laboratory and instructional materials, and professional development for teachers. In addition, Awardees and their schools often receive gifts from private sector donors in honor of their achievement and contributions.

The purpose of the Presidential Awards program is not only to honor individual achievement but also "to exemplify the highest standards of mathematics and science teaching" (National Science Foundation, About the Awards, ¶3). Recipients of the award are considered models for their peers as well as leaders in the movement to improve mathematics and science education (National Science Foundation, About the Awards). In 2000, Horizon Research, Inc. conducted a survey of Presidential Awardees as well as of a nationally representative sample of teachers. One of the purposes of surveying the Awardees was to compare their backgrounds, attitudes, and teaching practices to those of teachers in the nation as a whole. This chapter focuses specifically on the comparison of mathematics teachers in an attempt to illuminate the extent to which mathematics teaching in the United States is moving towards a greater focus on teaching for understanding.

THEORETICAL CONSIDERATIONS

Over the years much research has been conducted to analyze the type of mathematics teaching occurring in K-12 classrooms throughout the United States. What research has shown is that the mathematics teaching in American schools has followed a prevalent and predictable pattern characterized by the "demonstration-practice routine" (Hiebert, 2003, p.11) of instruction. Under this traditional style of education, teachers first provide explanations and examples of mathematical principles and then ask students to practice what they have been shown. Each class, therefore, usually follows a set routine of lecture followed by individual work time. This particular approach to teaching emphasizes the demonstration of procedures and transmission of definitions but focuses little on the development of conceptual understanding or mathematical reasoning. Without the opportunity to adequately explore and learn these higher-level skills, students in the United States have typically made poor showings on state, national, and international assessments. The results of these tests indicate that American students have lacked depth and flexibility in their mathematical knowledge. In essence, they have been unable to move past the computations and memorization they have been asked to do to apply their knowledge to new and different situations (Hiebert, 2003).

Because of weaknesses in student mathematical knowledge, educators and researchers alike have advocated for decades that mathematics education in American schools needs to be reformed (See Herrera & Owens, 2001 for a review). With the release of its *Curriculum and Evaluation Standards for School Mathematics* in 1989, the National Council of Teachers of Mathematics (NCTM) took center stage of the reform effort. In its 1991 *Professional Standards*, NCTM advocates that several fundamental shifts in mathematics teaching need to occur to bring about the implementation of its standards. These changes include transitioning (a) from seeing "classrooms as simply a collection of individuals" to promoting a sense of community among students, (b) from regarding teachers as the only arbiters of knowledge to encouraging student use of logic and reasoning to validate solutions, (c) from emphasizing rote memorization and "mechanistic answer-finding" to valuing the process of problem-solving and conjecturing, and (d) from treating mathematical topics in a disjointed manner to focusing on the connections among concepts and to applications (Introduction, ¶13). It is not enough, however, to simply say these shifts should occur. To practice the reform-based teaching the Standards advocate, teachers should have substantial academic preparation, regularly participate in professional development activities, and commit to making instructional decisions that promote long-term mathematical learning for their students.

One of the areas of debate among scholars is how much content preparation a mathematics teacher should have. The federal act of No Child Left Behind signed into law in 2001 states that each teacher in the United States must be "highly qualified" (U.S. Department of Education, Highly Qualified Teacher for Every Child, ¶2). To be highly qualified, teachers must have a degree in the subject taught, be fully certified by the state in which they practice, and be able to "demonstrate knowledge of subjects taught" (U.S. Department of Education). Corresponding to the federal law, most national committees of both the mathematics and mathematics education communities have consistently recommended that prospective teachers at the secondary level pursue a major in mathematics or its equivalent (Ferrini-Mundy & Findell, 2001). Specifically, the Conference Board of the Mathematical Sciences (CBMS) recommends that prospective secondary teachers pursue substantial coursework in mathematics including an in depth study of calculus as well as work in abstract algebra and discrete mathematics (CBMS as cited by Ferrini-Mundy & Findell, 2001). Substantial preparation is not only required at the secondary level but also at the elementary and primary levels as well. CBMS makes the recommendation that elementary and primary mathematics teachers should take courses that help them deepen their understanding of numbers and operations, Algebra and functions, Geometry and measurement, and Statistics (CBMS, 2001).

In order to bring about the reforms suggested by the NCTM and other national standards, mathematics teachers must continue their education throughout their careers. In its *Professional Standards*, the NCTM (2001) states that the standards-based movement "has a strong underlying theme in professionalism" that encourages teachers to become members "of a learning community that continually fosters growth in knowledge, stature, and responsibility" (Introduction, Standards for the Professional Development of Teachers of Mathematics. ¶3). As in any profession, the constant honing of skills and continued accrual of knowledge play a fundamental role in the ongoing development of teachers (Garet, Porter, Desimone, Birman, & Yoon, 2001). As indicated by research, a commitment to regular participation in professional development activities is crucial to this growth. For example, Smith, Desimone and Ueno used data from the 2000 National Assessment of Educational Progress to conclude that teachers who frequently participated in content-related professional development activities were more likely to stress the standards-based idea of conceptual learning in both their instructional goals as well as in their teaching strategies (2005).

As indicated in the study conducted by Smith, Desimone, and Ueno, commitment to professional development can greatly influence the pedagogical decisions a teacher makes. Under the reform-based system, NCTM advocates in its *Professional Standards* that the primary goal of mathematics instruction should be "the development of mathematical power for all students" (NCTM, 1991, ¶1). The NCTM characterizes this power as "the ability to explore, conjecture, and reason logically" as well as the ability to establish connections within mathematics and to outside applications. Moreover, this power involves the development in each student the self-confidence, inventiveness and curiosity to use "quantitative and spatial information in solving problems and making decisions" (1991, ¶1). To help develop this power in their students, teachers need to employ a wide variety of instructional strategies. They need to select tasks that engage their students, that provide connections to what students already know and to where they are going, and that demonstrate how that knowledge can be applied. In addition, teachers should guide activities that emphasize the use of technology and other tools for mathematical investigations. Teachers should also promote the use of discourse at both the group and classroom level in which students are encouraged to explore and explain various methods to solving mathematical problems (NCTM, 1991). Finally, an ongoing part of a teacher's job is to assess learning. In a standards-based system, teachers use various types of assessment on a regular basis to gain a better understanding of what students know. These types of assessments can include conducting conversations, asking open-ended questions on quizzes or tests, reading journals, and observing the presentations of portfolios (NCTM, 2000).

Despite the decades-old call for reform in mathematics teaching and the degree of specificity with which it has been described, it remains unclear the extent to which standards-based teaching has taken hold in American schools. This chapter attempts to provide some insight into the situation by comparing Presidential Awardees, the majority of whom reported using standards-based instructional methods, to a national sample of teachers. Through survey responses, both groups provide an in-depth look into their professional lives.

METHOD

In 2000, the National Science Foundation supported the fourth in a series of surveys through a grant to Horizon Research, Inc. (HRI). The first survey was conducted in 1977 as part of a major needs assessment of science, mathematics, and social studies education, consisting of a comprehensive review of the literature;

case studies of 11 districts throughout the United States; and a national survey of teachers, principals, and district and state personnel. A second survey of teachers and principals was conducted in 1985–86 to identify trends since 1977, and a third survey was conducted in 1993. The 2000 National Survey of Science and Mathematics Education was designed to provide up-to-date information and to identify trends in the areas of teacher background and experience, professional activities, curriculum and instruction, and the availability and use of instructional resources.

HRI distributed surveys to a national probability sample of approximately 9,000 teachers in grades K–12. At the same time, questionnaires were sent to all teachers who had received the Presidential Award for Excellence in Mathematics and Science Teaching.[1] The response rates were 74% for the national sample and 83% for the Presidential Awardees.

To be eligible for the Presidential Award, applicants need a minimum of five years K–12 teaching experience. At the time of the survey administration, nearly all Awardees who responded had 10 or more years teaching experience. To enable valid comparisons, only Awardees who were still employed as full or part-time teachers, and only teachers from the national sample with 10 or more years prior teaching experience, were included in the analysis. All estimates of the national teaching population were computed using weighted data, reflecting sampling probabilities.

Many of the individual survey questions were combined into a small number of composite variables through factor analysis. Differences in composite means between Awardees and national estimates were tested with two-tailed independent samples t-tests. A finite population correction was applied to the standard errors of the Awardee estimates to adjust for the large proportion of Awardees in the sample, and the Benjamini-Hochberg False Discovery Rate procedure for multiple comparisons was used to maintain an overall Type I error rate of 0.05 for the composite data. Comparisons based on individual items were done on a post-hoc basis and were significant at the .05 level, but no adjustments were made for multiple comparisons, so those data should be interpreted with that caveat in mind. Additional caution is also warranted in interpreting the results because they are based on self-report data.

RESULTS

Considering the selection criteria used in evaluating the nominees for the Presidential Awards and the resources and opportunities made available to the recipients, it was expected that they and the national sample of teachers would differ in teaching experience, subject matter background, classroom practices, and in roles in the professional community. The purpose of this analysis is to provide information about the nature and extent of these differences between the Presidential Awardees (referred to in the tables as "P.A.") and teachers of mathematics nationally ("Nat."). In keeping with the elementary (K-6) and secondary (7–12) classifications used in the Presidential Awards program, the results of the surveys are described in the same manner. In addition, the results are analyzed and classified according to the categories established earlier in the chapter – academic preparation, professional development, and teacher decision-making.

Preparation

In the category of academic preparation, it is not surprising that Presidential Awardees were more likely than others to have extensive coursework in mathematics. For example, secondary mathematics Awardees were more likely to have undergraduate majors in their field, 65% compared to 51% nationally (Table 1).

Table 1. Undergraduate Majors of Experienced Mathematics Teachers

Major	Percent of Teachers[†]			
	Grades K-6		Grades 7-12	
	P.A.	Nat.	P.A.	Nat.
Mathematics	3	1	65	51
Mathematics Education	3	1	20	19
Other Education	86	92	11	22
Other Fields	8	7	4	9

[†]Excludes the roughly 10% of respondents who indicated they had undergraduate majors in three or more fields.

In mathematics courses taken, there were large differences in the percentage of secondary Awardees and secondary teachers in the nation as a whole who had completed each of a number of types of college mathematics courses. The differences were most notable in the more advanced courses, such as abstract algebra, advanced calculus, and discrete mathematics. In addition, 59% of Awardees compared to only 40% nationally completed courses on instructional uses of computers and other technologies (see Table 2).

Table 2. Grade 7-12 Experienced Mathematics Teachers Completing Various College Courses

College Courses	Percent of Teachers	
	P.A.	Nat.
General methods of teaching	88	92
Methods of teaching mathematics	89	81
Supervised student teaching in mathematics	78	68
Mathematics for middle school teachers	36	39
Geometry for elementary/middle school teachers	26	27
College algebra/trigonometry/elementary functions	81	82
Calculus	96	85
Advanced calculus	79	56
Real analysis	53	32
Differential equations	67	56

College Courses	Percent of Teachers	
	P.A.	Nat.
Geometry	86	76
Probability and statistics	86	80
Abstract algebra	79	55
Number theory	72	55
Linear algebra	84	69
Applications of mathematics/problem solving	50	36
History of mathematics	50	35
Discrete mathematics	47	29
Other upper division mathematics	70	50
Biological sciences	51	54
Chemistry	49	46
Physics	58	46
Physical science	24	28
Earth/space science	18	22
Engineering (any)	9	9
Computer programming	67	54
Instructional uses of computers/other technologies	59	40
Any computer programming/computer science	72	59
Other computer science	33	25

Similarly, as can be seen in Table 3, elementary mathematics Presidential Awardees were more likely than their peers nationally to have taken such college courses as probability and statistics (43% versus 31%), geometry for teachers (42% versus 20%), and calculus (23% versus 10%).

Perhaps as a result of their more extensive coursework, Presidential Awardees were much more likely than teachers in the nation as a whole to indicate they felt well qualified to teach their discipline. For example, in grades K-6, 96% of Presidential Awardees compared to 57% nationally felt well qualified

Table 3. Grade K-6 Experienced Mathematics Teachers Completing Various College Courses

College Course	Percent of Teachers	
	P.A.	Nat.
Mathematics for elementary school teachers	95	97
Mathematics Education[+]	93	95
College algebra/trigonometry/elementary functions	46	38
Probability and statistics	43	31
Geometry for elementary/middle school teachers	42	20
Applications of mathematics/problem solving	30	21
Calculus	23	10

[+]Includes General methods of teaching, Methods of teaching mathematics, Instructional use of computers/other technologies, and Supervised student teaching in mathematics courses.

to teach mathematics. Similarly, as can be seen in Table 4, a larger proportion of secondary mathematics Presidential Awardees perceived themselves as well qualified to teach each of a number of mathematics concepts. Differences were most marked in the use of technology in support of mathematics (60% versus 24%) and in the more advanced mathematics topics such as calculus (43% versus 18%), functions and pre-calculus (80% versus 51%), and topics from discrete mathematics (35% versus 13%).

Table 4. Experienced Grade 7–12 Mathematics Teachers Reporting That They Are Very Well-Qualified to Teach Each of a Number of Mathematics Topics

Topic	Percent of Teachers	
	P.A.	Nat.
Numeration and number theory	74	76
Computation	89	92
Estimation	88	88
Measurement	88	87
Pre-Algebra	95	94
Algebra	95	87
Patterns and relationships	92	77
Geometry and spatial sense	86	70
Functions and pre-calculus concepts	80	51
Data collection and analysis	69	48
Probability	56	47
Statistics	44	24
Topics from discrete mathematics	35	13
Mathematical structures	19	10
Calculus	43	18
Technology in support of mathematics	60	24

In addition to feeling well prepared in the content knowledge of their discipline, Presidential Awardees tended to also feel more prepared pedagogically than their national counterparts (see Table 5). For example, 96% of elementary mathematics Presidential Awardees compared to 66% of teachers nationally considered themselves well prepared to lead a class of students using investigative strategies. Whether it was providing deeper coverage of fewer mathematics concepts, making connections between mathematics and other disciplines, using calculators to demonstrate mathematics principles, or using the Internet in their teaching, Presidential Awardees were much more likely than the general teaching population to consider themselves at least fairly well prepared.

Table 5. Experienced Mathematics Teachers Considering Themselves Well Prepared For Each of a Number of Tasks

Task	Percent of Teachers[†]			
	Grades K-6		Grades 7-12	
	P.A.	Nat.	P.A.	Nat.
Take students' prior understanding into account when planning curriculum and instruction	100	86	93	87
Encourage participation of females in mathematics	99	98	98	94
Encourage students' interest in mathematics	99	95	97	93
Listen/ask questions as students work in order to gauge their understanding	99	93	96	94
Develop students' conceptual understanding of mathematics	99	92	98	92
Use the textbook as a resource rather than the primary instructional tool	99	81	93	74
Teach groups that are heterogeneous in ability	97	88	80	75
Manage a class of students engaged in hands-on/ project-based work	97	84	91	71
Make connections between mathematics and other disciplines	97	84	86	72
Provide deeper coverage of fewer mathematics concepts	97	78	93	81
Have students work in cooperative learning groups	96	85	91	76
Lead a class of students using investigative strategies	96	66	90	67
Involve parents in the mathematics education of their children	89	68	58	42
Encourage participation of minorities in mathematics	88	89	84	88
Use calculators/computers for drill and practice	82	70	84	86
Use calculators/computers for mathematics learning games	80	70	69	58
Use calculators/computers to collect and/or analyze data	72	45	90	67
Recognize and respond to student cultural diversity	66	66	61	57
Use calculators/computers to demonstrate mathematics principles	60	45	93	74
Use calculators/computers for laboratory simulations and applications	53	41	87	57
Use the Internet in your mathematics teaching for general reference	51	22	53	29
Use the Internet in your mathematics teaching for data acquisition	46	17	47	28
Use the Internet in your mathematics teaching for collaborative projects with classes/individuals in other schools	32	12	27	16
Teach students who have limited English proficiency	27	29	19	21

[†]Includes teachers responding "very well prepared" and "fairly well prepared."

Professional Development

A series of items asked respondents to think back to "three years ago" and describe their needs for professional development at that time. Given the differences in preparedness reported earlier, it is not surprising that Presidential Awardees as a whole were less likely than teachers nationally to perceive a need for professional development in several areas (see Table 6). Substantial differences existed between national mathematics teachers and Awardees in the perceived needs to learn how to use technology in mathematics instruction and how to use inquiry/investigation-oriented teaching strategies. The differences were particularly acute at the elementary level. For example, 57% of elementary mathematics teachers nationally perceived a moderate or substantial need to learn how to use inquiry/investigation-oriented teaching strategies compared to 37% of the Presidential Awardees. In contrast, mathematics Awardees were at least as likely as their national counterparts to perceive a need for professional development in how to assess student learning.

Although Presidential Awardees generally reported less of a need for professional development, they were, in fact, more likely to spend substantial amounts of time on in-service education in their field. For example, as can be seen in Table 7, roughly 8 out of 10 secondary Presidential Awardees reported spending more than 35 hours on in-service education in their field in the past three years compared to only about 4 in 10 nationally.

Similarly, Presidential Awardees were much more likely to participate in each of a number of types of mathematics-related professional development activities (see Table 8). More than 70% of the Awardees reported teaching an in-service

Table 6. Experienced Mathematics Teachers Reporting That They Perceived a Moderate or Substantial Need for Professional Development "Three Years Ago"

Statement	Percent of Teachers*			
	Grades K-6		Grades 7-12	
	P.A.	Nat.	P.A.	Nat.
Learning how to use technology in mathematics instruction	77	79	53	71
Deepening my own mathematics content knowledge	45	41	29	26
Learning how to teach mathematics in a class that includes students with special needs	44	51	58	50
Learning how to assess student learning in mathematics	42	40	38	27
Understanding student thinking in mathematics	40	41	34	31
Learning how to use inquiry/investigation-oriented teaching strategies	37	57	39	51

Table 7. Time Spent by Experienced Mathematics Teachers on In-Service Education in Last Three Years

Number of Hours	Percent of Teachers*			
	Grades K-6		Grades 7-12	
	P.A.	Nat.	P.A.	Nat.
None	3	12	0	7
Less than 6 hours	3	22	2	6
6–15 hours	10	33	6	20
16–35 hours	15	17	11	23
More than 35 hours	69	16	81	43

Table 8. Experienced Teachers Participating in Various Professional Activities in Last Twelve Months

Professional Activity	Percent of Teachers			
	Grades K-6		Grades 7-12	
	P.A.	Nat.	P.A.	Nat.
Taught any in-service workshops in mathematics or mathematics teaching	71	6	74	17
Served on a school or district mathematics curriculum committee	68	20	73	47
Served on a school or district mathematics textbook selection committee	46	20	57	47
Mentored another teacher as part of a formal arrangement that is recognized or supported by the school or district, not including supervision of student teachers	45	20	44	22
Received any local, state, or national grants or awards for mathematics teaching	32	2	38	7

workshop in their field compared to less than 20% nationally. In addition, roughly 7 out of 10 Presidential Awardees reported serving on a school or district curriculum committee for their field compared to only 2 in 10 in grades K–6 and 5 in 10 in grades 7–12 for the national mathematics teacher population.

Given their active involvement in professional development, it is not surprising that Presidential Awardees were much more likely to be familiar with the National Council of Teachers of Mathematics (NCTM) *Standards* (see Table 9). Nationally, only 12% of elementary mathematics teachers and 23% of secondary mathematics teachers reported being "very familiar" with the NCTM *Standards* whereas 81% of elementary Awardees and 75% of secondary Awardees indicated the same level of awareness. Mathematics Presidential Awardees who were familiar with the *Standards* were much more likely than their national counterparts to report both strong agreement with the *Standards and* extensive implementation of the recommendations made by the *Standards* documents.

Table 9. Experienced Mathematics Teachers' Familiarity with the NCTM Standards

Professional Activity	Percent of Teachers			
	Grades K-6		Grades 7-12	
	P.A.	Nat.	P.A.	Nat.
Familiarity with NCTM *Standards*				
Not at all familiar	0	37	0	10
Somewhat familiar	2	30	3	28
Fairly familiar	17	21	22	39
Very familiar	81	12	75	23
Extent of agreement with NCTM *Standards*[†]				
Strongly Disagree	2	0	1	0
Disagree	0	1	1	7
No Opinion	0	17	1	14
Agree	30	69	52	68
Strongly Agree	68	13	45	10
Extent to which recommendations have been implemented[†]				
Not at all	0	0	0	2
To a minimal extent	0	18	2	20
To a moderate extent	16	56	41	57
To a great extent	84	26	56	22

[†]These analyses included only those teachers indicating they were at least somewhat familiar with the *Standards.*

Teacher Decision-making

Since the United States does not have a national curriculum, curricular and pedagogical issues are addressed at state and local levels. As can be seen in Table 10, both elementary and secondary mathematics Presidential Awardees perceive themselves as having more control over curriculum and instructional decisions than do their peers nationally. Whether the decision at hand was determining course goals and objectives; selecting the content, topics, and skills to be taught; selecting textbooks/ instructional programs; or even setting the pace for covering topics, Presidential Awardees were considerably more likely than other teachers to indicate that they had strong control over the decision.

Based on the results of a factor analysis, the items in Table 11 were combined into two composite variablesCurriculum Control and Pedagogy Control.[2] Each composite has a minimum possible score of 0 and a maximum possible score of 100. Table 11 displays the composite scores for mathematics classes by grade range and illustrates that Presidential Awardees across the board perceive much more control over decisions related to curriculum and pedagogy than do their national peers. This difference is particularly visible in the area of curriculum control at the K–6 level.

Table 10. Classes Where Experienced Mathematics Teachers Report Having Strong Control Over Various Curriculum and Instructional Decisions

Decision	Percent of Classes[†]			
	Grades K-6		Grades 7-12	
	P.A.	Nat.	P.A.	Nat.
Selecting teaching techniques	88	66	92	74
Determining the amount of homework to be assigned	74	68	92	79
Setting the pace for covering topics	73	48	75	50
Selecting the sequence in which topics are covered	72	40	75	54
Choosing tests for classroom assessment	71	42	90	77
Selecting other instructional materials (besides textbooks/instructional programs)	71	35	78	48
Choosing criteria for grading students	62	46	83	67
Determining course goals and objectives	35	12	53	28
Selecting content, topics, and skills to be taught	34	13	53	29
Selecting textbooks/instructional programs	31	9	54	28

[†] Teachers were given a five-point scale for each decision, with 1 labeled "no control" and 5 labeled "strong"

Table 11. Curriculum Control and Pedagogy Control Composite Scores for Mathematics ClassesTaught by Experienced Teachers

	Mean Score			
	Grades K–6		Grades 7–12	
	P.A.	Nat.	P.A.	Nat.
Curriculum Control	74*	52	84*	69
Pedagogy Control	89*	80	97*	92

* Presidential Awardees significantly different than teachers nationally (2-tailed independent samples t-test, $p < 0.05$).

Presidential Awardees also reported fundamentally different ideas than teachers in the nation as a whole about the objectives appropriate for mathematics instruction. Table 12 shows the percentage of mathematics Presidential Awardees and mathematics teachers nationally who reported giving heavy emphasis to each of a number of instructional objectives. Note that Awardees were more likely than their national peers to emphasize learning how mathematical ideas connect with one another, learning how to effectively explain mathematical ideas and increasing student interest in mathematics. In contrast, mathematics teachers nationally were more likely than Awardees to emphasize learning mathematical algorithms or procedures, learning to perform computations with speed and accuracy, and preparing for standardized tests.

Table 12. Mathematics Classes of Experienced Teachers with Heavy Emphasis on Various Instructional Objectives

Objective	Percent of Classes[†]			
	Grades K-6		Grades 7-12	
	P.A.	Nat.	P.A.	Nat.
Learn how to solve problems	97	84	85	77
Learn mathematical concepts	93	89	93	88
Learn to reason mathematically	95	73	89	76
Learn how mathematics ideas connect with one another	80	57	78	59
Learn to explain ideas in mathematics effectively	74	39	60	38
Increase students' interest in mathematics	71	55	50	32
Prepare for further study in mathematics	50	43	73	62
Understand the logical structure of mathematics	46	32	46	41
Develop students' computational skills	25	67	20	37
Learn mathematical algorithms/procedures	28	47	45	61
Prepare for standardized tests	16	39	14	29
Learn to perform computations with speed and accuracy	15	44	10	22
Learn how to apply mathematics in business and industry	11	11	18	17
Learn about the history and nature of mathematics	9	2	9	3

[†]Teachers were given a four-point scale for each objective, with 0 labeled "None"; 1, "Minimal Emphasis"; 2, "Moderate Emphasis"; and 3, "Heavy Emphasis."

Differences between types of objectives among grade ranges are captured in the mean scores on three composite variables Mathematics Reasoning, Basic Mathematics Skills, and Nature of Mathematics – as shown in Table 13. For both Presidential Awardees and mathematics teachers nationally, the greatest reported emphasis was on objectives related to mathematical reasoning e.g., learning mathematical concepts. Mathematics teachers in the nation as a whole, however, tended to have a greater emphasis on basic mathematics skills (e.g., developing computational skills) than did Awardees.

Table 13. Mean Composite Scores Related to Objectives in Mathematics Classes Taught by Experienced Teachers

Class Objective Composites	Mean Score			
	Grades K-6		Grades 7-12	
	P.A.	Nat.	P.A.	Nat.
Mathematics Reasoning	97*	91	95*	91
Basic Mathematics Skills	59*	77	51*	65
Nature of Mathematics	63*	55	69*	62

* Presidential Awardees significantly different than teachers nationally (2-tailed independent samples t-test, $p < 0.05$).

Differences between Awardees and the national population can also be seen in the types of activities used in the mathematics classroom. Table 14 shows that students of Presidential Awardees were more likely than others to work in groups; write reflections; engage in mathematical activities using concrete materials; record, represent, and analyze data; and design their own activity or investigation. They were, however, less likely than classes nationally to practice routine computations/ algorithms or, at the elementary level, answer textbook or worksheet questions.

Table 14. Mathematics Classes of Experienced Teachers Where Teachers Report that Students Take Part in Various Instructional Activities at Least Once a Week

Activity	Percent of Classes			
	Grades K-6		Grades 7-12	
	P.A.	Nat.	P.A.	Nat.
Engage in mathematical activities using concrete materials	96	77	49	28
Work in groups	91	70	87	56
Use mathematical concepts to interpret and solve applied problems	83	68	83	71
Follow specific instructions in an activity or investigation	72	74	74	74
Record, represent, and/or analyze data	66	47	54	37
Review homework/worksheet assignments	55	77	84	93
Practice routine computations/algorithms	51	77	47	72
Use calculators or computers for learning or practicing skills	48	36	83	79
Use calculators or computers to develop conceptual understanding	45	29	79	61
Answer textbook or worksheet questions	44	83	86	92
Write reflections	38	21	17	8
Read other (non-textbook) mathematics-related materials in class	32	23	13	9
Use calculators or computers as a tool	31	15	65	35
Design their *own* activity or investigation	25	13	15	6
Make formal presentations to the rest of the class	25	11	18	7
Listen and take notes during presentation by teacher	24	30	81	86
Work on extended mathematics investigations or projects	18	6	12	5
Read from a mathematics textbook in class	18	45	32	37

In addition, secondary mathematics Presidential Awardees as a whole were more inclined than their peers to use calculators/computers to demonstrate mathematics principles, retrieve and exchange data, and solve problems using simulations. Mathematics teachers in the nation as a whole were more likely to use those resources to do drill and practice, and at the elementary level, to play mathematical learning games (see Table 15).

Table 15. Mathematics Classes Where Teachers Report that Students Use Calculators/Computers for Various Activities at Least Once a Week

Activity	Percent of Classes			
	Grades K-6		Grades 7-12	
	P.A.	Nat.	P.A.	Nat.
Play mathematics learning games	32	45	8	7
Demonstrate mathematics principles	31	24	71	52
Do drill and practice	20	38	35	53
Solve problems using simulations	13	12	24	14
Do simulations	13	11	25	10
Retrieve or exchange data	10	6	19	9
Take a test or quiz	8	16	65	60
Collect data using sensors or probes	8	3	11	4

Table 16 displays the means for composite variables related to mathematics teaching practice. As previously noted, the data suggest that mathematics teachers nationally were more inclined to use traditional teaching practices, such as lecturing, doing worksheet/textbook problems, and practicing routine computationṣthan were Presidential Awardees. This is most apparent at the elementary level where the national mean composite score was 70 compared to the Awardee mean score of 54. In contrast, secondary Awardees were more likely to use calculators/computers for investigations than teachers in the national population (a mean score of 46 versus 32).

Data about their "most recent lesson" support the general findings that Presidential Awardees in mathematics were more likely to implement lessons that involve students in reform-oriented activities, such as doing hands-on/manipulative activities, working in small groups, and using computers and calculators. For example, as seen in Table 17, roughly 7 out of 10 lessons taught by Awardees

Table 16. Mean Scores for Teaching Practice Composite Variables in Mathematics Classes Taught by Experienced Teachers

Teaching Practice Composites	Mean Score			
	Grades K-6		Grades 7-12	
	P.A.	Nat.	P.A.	Nat.
Use of Strategies to Develop Students' Abilities to Communicate Mathematics Ideas	86*	73	80*	69
Use of Traditional Teaching Practices	54*	70	76*	81
Use of Calculators/Computers for Developing Concepts and Skills	43*	39	72*	65
Use of Calculators/Computers for Investigations	37*	27	46*	32

* Presidential Awardees significantly different than teachers nationally (2-tailed independent samples t-test, $p < 0.05$).

Table 17. Mathematics Classes of Experienced Teachers Participating in Various Activities in the Most Recent Lesson

Activity	Percent of Classes			
	Grades K-6		Grades 7-12	
	P.A.	Nat.	P.A.	Nat.
Discussion	95	89	93	92
Students doing hands-on/manipulative activities	80	67	38	23
Students working in small groups	77	51	72	52
Students completing textbook/worksheet problems	45	77	58	78
Lecture	40	66	69	85
Students using calculators	37	14	80	73
Students reading about mathematics	21	19	18	18
Students using computers	15	8	9	3
Test or quiz	10	12	16	16
Students using other technologies (besides calculators or computers)	9	3	3	2

included students working in small groups in their most recent lesson, compared to roughly 5 out of 10 nationally. Similarly, 80% of lessons taught by elementary mathematics Awardees involved students doing hands-on/manipulative activities compared to 67% of lessons taught by teachers nationally. In contrast, mathematics teachers in the nation as a whole were more likely than Presidential Awardees to implement lessons that involve students completing textbook/worksheet problems.

It is not at all surprising, therefore, that classes taught by Presidential Awardees spend a greater percentage of mathematics instructional time working with hands-on or manipulative materials (see Table 18).

Assessment practices of Presidential Awardees also differed greatly from those of their peers (see Table 19). Presidential Awardees were more likely than other

Table 18. Average Percentage of Experienced Teachers Mathematics Class Time Spent on Different Types of Activities

Activity	Percent of Class Time			
	Grades K-6		Grades 7-12	
	P.A.	Nat.	P.A.	Nat.
Working with hands-on or manipulative materials	33	25	14	7
Whole class lecture/discussion	26	29	36	41
Non-manipulative small group work	14	8	20	14
Individual students reading textbooks, completing worksheets, etc.	13	26	12	20
Daily routines, interruptions, and other non-instructional activities	8	9	10	12
Other activities	6	3	8	6

Table 19. Mathematics Classes of Experienced Teachers Where Teachers Report Assessing Students' Progress Using Various Methods at Least Monthly

	Percent of Classes			
	Grades K-6		Grades 7-12	
	P.A.	Nat.	P.A.	Nat.
Observe students and ask questions as they work in small groups	100	96	96	87
Use assessments embedded in class activities to see if students are "getting it"	100	98	99	93
Ask students questions during large group discussions	99	100	99	97
Observe students and ask questions as they work individually	98	99	95	96
Give tests requiring open-ended responses (e.g., descriptions, explanations)	82	57	90	74
Have students present their work to the class	82	53	68	55
Review student homework	79	88	96	98
Review student notebooks/journals	78	55	55	45
Conduct a pre-assessment to determine what students already know	74	68	40	45
Grade student work on open-ended and/or laboratory tasks using defined criteria (e.g., a scoring rubric)	72	39	77	46
Review student portfolios	61	41	28	20
Have students assess each other (peer evaluation)	46	34	36	25
Have students do long-term mathematics projects	45	17	37	19
Give predominantly short-answer tests (e.g., multiple choice, true/false, fill-in-the-blank)	33	59	29	48

mathematics teachers to base assessment of student progress on open-ended tasks/ tests, student presentations, and long-term mathematics projects. In contrast, mathematics teachers nationally were more likely than Awardees to use predominately short-answer tests.

These findings are summarized in the composite variables related to assessment practices. (See Table 20.) Presidential Awardees used informal assessment strategies (e.g., using assessments embedded in class activities) and journals/portfolios more frequently than mathematics teachers in the nation as a whole. Elementary Awardees used journals/portfolios quite a bit more than their national counterparts.

Table 20. Mean Scores for Assessment Practice Composite Variables in Mathematics Classes Taught by Experienced Teachers

	Mean Score			
	Grades K-6		Grades 7-12	
	P.A.	Nat.	P.A.	Nat.
Use of Informal Assessment	87*	83	83*	77
Use of Journals/Portfolios	53*	37	35*	24

* Presidential Awardees significantly different than teachers nationally (2-tailed independent samples t-test, $p < 0.05$).

SUMMARY

Given the eligibility criteria and the process of selecting Presidential Awardees, some of the differences between Awardees and the national population of mathematics teachers described in this chapter are to be expected. Presidential Awardees tended to be more highly educated than their national peers and as a consequence of the award, to have more resources to devote to their teaching. Also as expected, Awardees tended to have more opportunities to serve in leadership roles.

Still, the differences in level of involvement in professional activities are extraordinary. Presidential Awardees were much more likely to be active professionally whether serving on a school or district curriculum or textbook committee, receiving grants or awards for teaching, or providing professional development for others. Presidential Awardees were also far more likely to be familiar and in strong agreement with the NCTM *Standards* documents.

These differences in professional activities and beliefs were reflected in differences in instructional objectives. Presidential Awardees were much more likely than other teachers to emphasize objectives related to mathematics reasoning and the nature of mathematics. Teachers nationally tended to emphasize objectives related to basic mathematics skills such as learning computational skills, algorithms/procedures, and preparing for standardized tests.

The classroom pedagogical and assessment practices by which these instructional objectives were addressed result in further differences between Presidential Awardees and the national population of teachers. Presidential Awardees tended to use more investigative teaching strategies and their students were much more likely to work in small groups, use manipulative materials, and work with technology. In addition, Presidential Awardees were more likely than other mathematics teachers to use open-ended performance tasks, portfolios, or long-term projects in determining student progress. They were also much less likely to use multiple choice and other objective tests. In contrast, mathematics teachers nationally were more apt to use traditional teaching practices in which their students read a textbook in class or did drill and practice with worksheet problems.

CONCLUSION

In 1983, the White House established the Presidential Award for Excellence in Mathematics and Science Teaching to recognize teachers who have reached the "highest standards of mathematics and science teaching" (National Science Foundation, About the Awards, ¶3). With an emphasis on engaging students through experimental and innovative methods of teaching, the PAEMST program served as a precursor to the reform-based ideas of mathematics teaching that would later be advocated in the NCTM *Standards* documents. In its *Principles and Standards for School Mathematics*, the NCTM defines its idea of effective mathematics teaching. In its Teaching Principles, it states that "effective mathematics teaching requires understanding what students know and need to learn and then challenging and supporting them to learn it well" (NCTM, 2000, p. 16). To fulfill this requirement, mathematics teachers must be deeply knowledgeable about content, students, and pedagogy. They must be flexible in their understanding of all three areas in order to create or choose lessons that "capture and sustain interest, and engage students in building mathematical understanding" (NCTM, 2000, p. 18). In turn, such knowledge and flexibility are learned and sustained through an ongoing commitment to professional development and collaboration (NCTM, 2000). These are the traits at the heart of standards-based teaching that NCTM defines as effective and that the majority of the Presidential Awardees exhibit.

With the advent of the NCTM standards, the Presidential Awardees became more than examples of exemplary teaching. They became the role models of how standards-based or effective teaching might look in all mathematics classrooms. By comparing their backgrounds, professional involvement, instructional objectives and teaching methods with a national sample of teachers, this chapter examines the extent to which American teachers are transitioning from the traditional style of teaching to the standards-based methods reported by the majority of the Presidential Awardees. The data show that although some mathematics teachers who were not Presidential Awardees were using standards-based teaching, as of 2000, it was not a widespread phenomenon.

NOTES

[1] See http://2000survey.horizon-research.com/instruments/teacher.php to download a copy of the survey.
[2] See http://www.horizon-research.com/reports/2001/2000survey/pres_award.php for more information on the composite variables.

REFERENCES

Conference Board of the Mathematical Sciences. (2001). *The mathematical education of teachers.* Providence, RI and Washington, DC: American Mathematical Society and Mathematical Association of America.

Ferrini-Mundy, J., & Findell, B. (2001). The mathematical education of prospective teachers of secondary school mathematics: Old assumptions, new challenges. In *CUPM discussion papers about mathematics and the mathematical sciences in 2010: What should students know?* The

Committee on the Undergraduate Program in Mathematics, Mathematics Association of America (pp. 31–41).

Garet, M. S., Porter, A. C., Desimone, L., Birman, B. F., & Yoon, K. S. (2001). What makes professional development effective? Results from a national sample of teachers. *American Educational Research Journal, 38*(4), 915–945.

Herrera, T., & Owens, D. (2001). The "new new math"?: Two *reform* movements in *mathematics* education. *Theory into Practice, 40*(2), 84–92.

Hiebert, J. (2003). What research says about the NCTM Standards. In J. Kilpatrick, W. G. Martin, & D. Schifter (Eds.), *A research companion to principles and standards for school mathematics* (pp. 5–23). Reston, VA: National Council of Teachers of Mathematics.

National Council of Teachers of Mathematics. (2000). *Principles and standards for school mathematics*. Reston, VA: National Council of Teachers of Mathematics.

National Council of Teachers of Mathematics. (1991). *Professional standards for teaching Mathematics* [Electronic Version]. Reston, VA: National Council of Teachers of Mathematics.

National Science Foundation. (n.d.). Retrieved May 15, 2008, from http://www.paemst.org

Smith, T., Desimone, L., & Ueno K. (2001). "Highly Qualified" to do what? The relationship between NCLB teacher quality mandates and the use of reform-oriented instruction in middle school mathematics. *Educational Evaluation and Policy Analysis, 27*(4), 75–109.

U.S. Department of Education. (2006). *Highly qualified teachers for every child*. Retrieved May 15, 2008, from http://www.ed.gov/nclb/methods/teachers/stateplanfacts.html

Iris R. Weiss
Horizon Research, Inc.

P. Sean Smith
Horizon Research, Inc.

Sharon K. O'Kelley
University of Georgia

JINFA CAI, TAO WANG, NING WANG, AND TIFFANY GARBER

STUDYING EFFECTIVE TEACHING FROM TEACHERS' PERSPECTIVES

The Journey Has Just Begun

To improve students' mathematical learning through effective teaching is always at the core of mathematics education research and reform. What is effective mathematical teaching? To address this fundamental question, researchers have developed various paradigms and methods in an attempt to identify important features of effective classroom instruction (Koehler & Grouws, 1992; Porter & Brophy, 1988; Shulman, 1986). Typically researchers generate some of the features by analyzing one or more aspects of the features of classroom instruction, such as instructional tasks (Doyle, 1983, 1988; Stein, et al., 1996; Hiebert & Wearne, 1993), classroom discourse of teacher-student interaction (Cazden, 1986; Lampert, 1990; Perry, et al., 1993), and student-peer interactions (Cobb & Bauersfeld, 1995; Forman, & Cazden, 1985). Regardless of the different focuses, these researchers tend to agree that the classroom activities and behaviors are largely affected by beliefs shared by cultural members (Cooney, et al., 1998; Fennema & Franke, 1992; Thompson, 1992). Correspondingly most researchers infer the teachers' beliefs and practice of effective mathematics teaching through interpreting those observable instructional behaviours. Little has been done to reveal the teachers' beliefs from their own words by directly interviewing them, especially teachers from different cultural backgrounds, about their views on the effective teaching (Cai, 2007).

To amend this important lack of research, recently Cai and his colleagues (Cai, Perry, & Wong, 2007) used semi-structured interview questions to directly interview forty-five teachers from four regions about their views on effective teaching. The four regions—Australia, Mainland China, Hong Kong SAR, and the United States~provide a cultural spectrum across the East and West. The researchers found that although the teachers shared some common beliefs, teachers from the four regions had different views about the characteristics of effective teachers and the characteristics of effective lessons. In addition, they valued differently the contributions of memorization, understanding, and practice in students' learning (see Cai et al. in this volume). To provide a more comprehensive picture about culture and teachers' perspectives on effective teaching, this book continues the journey to study effective teaching from teachers' perspectives, by including additional studies of teachers from over 10 countries. Adding these new

J. Cai, G. Kaiser, B. Perry and N.-Y. Wong (eds.), Effective Mathematics Teaching from Teachers' Perspectives: National and Cross-National Studies, 303–317.
© *2009 Sense Publishers. All rights reserved.*

studies using various research methods not only enriches the cultural spectrum in our previous study, but also provides an opportunity to reflect on the research in this area from a methodological perspective. Table 1 shows a summary of participants' backgrounds as well as the research methods adopted by the studies in this volume.

This concluding chapter will first discuss the methodologies involved in the studies. Then we will summarize the findings about effective teaching from the teachers' perspectives across the studies. We end this chapter by providing theoretical and methodological insights for future research on studying effective teaching from the teachers' perspectives.

Table 1. Summary of the chapters in this book

Chapters	Kinds of Teachers	National or Cross-National Comparative Study	Methods Used
Cai, et al.	Experienced in-service teachers	Cross-National Comparative Study, including Australia, Mainland China, Hong Kong SAR, and the United States	Semi-structured interviews
Givvin, et al.	Teacher educators and/or researchers	Cross-National Comparative Study, including Australia, the Czech Republic, Hong Kong SAR, Japan, Netherlands, Switzerland, and United States	Evaluating video-taped lessons from TIMSS Video Study
Kuntze and Rudolph-Albertt	Experienced in-service teachers	Cross-National Comparative Study, including Germany and Switzerland	Surveys
Wilson and DuCloux	Experienced in-service teachers and pre-service teachers	National Study in the United States	Semi-structured interviews and survey
Lim	Experienced and novice in-service teachers	National Study in Malaysia	Interviews
Maass	Experienced in-service teachers	National Study in Germany	Surveys and semi-structured interviews
Huang and Li	In-service master teachers	National Study in Mainland China	Video-stimulated semi-structured interviews
Vistro-Yu and Villenda-Diaz	Experienced in-service teachers	National Study in the Philippines	Survey, semi-structured interviews, and classroom observation
Kaasila and Erkki	Student teachers	National Study in Finland	Interviews
Li, et al.	Experienced	National Study in Mainland	Surveys

Chapters	Kinds of Teachers	National or Cross-National Comparative Study	Methods Used
	in-service teachers and students in one school	China	(open-ended, free essays)
Wong, et al.	Experienced in-service teachers	National Study in Hong Kong SAR	Hypothetical situations, semi-structured interviews, and classroom observation
Weiss, et al.	Award winning and ordinary in-service teachers	National Study in the United States	Surveys

A COMPARISON ACCORDING TO METHODOLOGIES USED

In this book, teachers from 12 studies were asked to give their views on effective mathematics teaching (see Table 1). We compare the research methods employed in the studies from three perspectives: teachers involved, data collection methods, and comparative nature of the studies. In the chapter by Morony, he synthesized the work of the Australian Association of Mathematics Teachers (AAMT) about the knowledge, skills and attributes required for effective teaching of mathematics. This concluding chapter does not include the discussion of the chapter by Morony.

Teachers Involved

In addition to being from different countries with various cultural backgrounds, teachers in the studies can be classified into three groups, based on their prof-essional practice background: (1) in-service teachers, (2) teacher educators, and (3) student teachers. The in-service teacher group (the largest subject group) is divided into three subgroups based on their background in educational practice. They are outstanding teachers, ordinary or experienced teachers, and novice teachers (see Table 1). Of the three sub-groups, the group of outstanding teachers is most difficult to define because of the use of different criteria in different systems. In this concluding chapter, we define outstanding teachers based on their teaching excellence that is acknowledged by local professional organizations (e.g., awards and professional ranks). For example, in the chapter by Weiss, Smith, and O'Kelley, some teachers are Presidential Awardees for Excellence in Mathematics and Science Teaching, the highest honor in teaching profession in the United States. In the chapter by Huang and Li, in China, outstanding teachers are "master teachers" and culturally-valued "moral characters" with "expertise for others to follow." In a study included in the chapter by Vistro-Yu and Villenda-Diaz, the Philippine teachers are categorized into two groups, based on their student performance: teachers from high performing schools and teachers from low performing schools.

Teachers' belief about effective teaching is a dynamic entity that could be changed along with their teaching practice (Gusky, 1986) and could be reflected in their practice (Cooney et al., 1998). Therefore, including teachers with so many variations in their teaching experience could provide insights into how teachers hold different beliefs on effective teaching, not only across cultures, but also within cultures.

Data Collection Methods

Across the studies in this volume, most researchers used interviews and surveys to collect data about teachers' view on effective teaching. Other methods included evaluating video-taped lessons, observation, and hypothetical situations. Although interviewing was one of the most popular forms of data collection in the studies, the types of interviews varied. In general, there are two types of interviews: semi-structured interviews and more open-ended interviews. The difference lies in the types of questions asked by researchers. The semi-structured interview includes pre-designated questions aimed toward research questions about effective teaching. In addition, there are often some follow-up questions to get clarifications and examples from the interviewees. For example Cai, et al. used this method to ask the teachers to respond questions about their views on the nature of mathematics and features of effective teaching and learning. Wilson and DuCloux reported two studies in their chapter. They used semi-structured interview in their first study and a survey in their second study. The second type of interview asks questions about teachers' concrete life experiences in classrooms; therefore, the responses are more narrative than those in the semi-structured interviews. For example, in Lim's study, ten Malaysia teachers were first asked to recall one of their own teachers as an example of an "effective" mathematics teacher and then to list the characteristics and teaching practices of those teachers. Using this list, the ten teachers were asked to do a self-assessment on their own teaching to see if they themselves were effective mathematics teachers. The teachers were then asked for the characteristics of ideal effective teaching and finally asked about any challenges and constraints they faced in their efforts to be effective mathematics teachers. Kaasila and Erkki's chapter involving student teachers from Finland also used interviews to collect data when their portfolios and questionnaires were examined.

One special semi-structured interview is in the chapter by Huang and Li where they used video-taped lessons to stimulate teachers' responses as well as semi-structured questions. In their study of master teachers in China, the researchers used two video-taped lessons of geometry in grade eight. One lesson was recognized by local educational experts as a successful reform-oriented teaching style and the other as a traditional style of teaching. The master teachers watched the videos and were interviewed to understand their views of effective teaching for each of the two lessons.

Like the interviews, there were different forms of surveys. In Kuntze and Rudolph-Albert's study, surveys were given to the 53 participants from Germany and Switzerland. The data were collected in two paper and pencil questionnaires.

Multiple and differing criteria were used by the teachers to judge effective teaching. The first questionnaire contained a unit on individual criteria of instructional quality, in which participants were asked to name characteristics for effective mathematics instruction from an external observational view. On the second questionnaire about individual views of instructional success, participants were asked to imagine situations in which they were satisfied or not satisfied with lessons they had taught. They were also asked to give reasons for the unsatisfying lessons. Li, et al.'s study used open-ended, free essays. Sixth-grade students and their teachers were assigned a free essay in which they were asked to discuss a good mathematics lesson. The question asked in the essay was, "What is a good mathematics lesson?"

In the chapter by Weiss, et al., they constructed and used a well-structured survey instrument. The teachers receiving Presidential Award for Excellence in Mathematics and Science Teaching and a national sample of teachers in grades K-12 were asked to complete the survey about their background, preparation, classroom practices, and professional activities. Not only are the findings from the study significant, but also is the survey instrument significant.

Unlike the studies that were performed by interviews and surveys, the study by Givvin, et al. evaluated video-taped lessons by teacher educators. In this study, a common set of video-taped eighth-grade mathematics lessons was evaluated by the mathematics educators in the different countries. Two lessons from each of the six countries were selected, and then the educators were asked to focus on the methods used to teach mathematics—the kinds of learning opportunities provided and the nature of the reasoning evidenced by the teacher or students. Each group spent two hours per country, evaluating lessons from the country. This report was designed to indicate and note the dimensions that the group members used to compare the lessons and the comments about each country's lessons. The groups were then asked to summarize their conclusions regarding major similarities and differences among the lessons.

The study by Wong, et al. used multiple methods, specifically hypothetical situations/case studies, semi-structured interviews, and classroom observation. The researchers first administered a questionnaire to gather the views and self-reported teaching practices from a large sample of teachers; then they interviewed each teacher (consisting of 4 interviews per participant), observed the teacher (which was videotaped), and produced hypothetical situations to ask participants whether "doing mathematics" was involved in each case.

Comparative Analysis

Most of the studies are comparative in nature. Some compared teachers across nations some within a nation. Studies by Cai, et al., Givvin, et al., and Kuntze and Rudolph-Albert are cross-national comparisons. The chapter by Weiss, et al. was a within-nation study comparing two groups of U.S. teachers, the Presidential Awardees and a national sample of ordinary teachers. Maass identified and compared two groups (*Gymnasium* and *Hauptschule*) of German teachers' perspectives about effective teaching. Li, et al. compared teachers' views with students' views about what makes teaching effective. Vistro-Yu and Villenda-Diez summarized studies in the Philippines comparing teachers from high performing schools and low performing schools. Wilson and DuCloux compared teachers' views and researchers' viewers about effective teaching.

FINDINGS ABOUT EFFECTIVE TEACHING FROM TEACHERS' PERSPECTIVES

Given the diverse backgrounds of the participant teachers and various methods of data collection, it was quite challenging to summarize the findings—across the studies—about effective teaching from teachers' perspectives. However, we found that these studies clearly showed that both the participants' cultural background and professional experience affect their views on effective teaching. For example, the cultural influence on teachers' views about effective teaching is quite evident in the study by Cai and his colleagues, who found that the teachers from Eastern regions emphasize a "teacher-led" method of instruction in the classroom, and the Western regions emphasize a "student-centered" method of effective teaching. The study by Weiss, et al., is a typical example of showing why experience matters in terms of views on effective teaching between award winning teachers and ordinary teachers.

In general, all researchers in this volume viewed effective teaching as a cognitive and cultural activity, which is organized by effective teachers. Therefore, it is reasonable to summarize the results from two aspects: characteristics of effective teaching and characteristics of effective teachers.

Characteristics of Effective Teaching

In discussing the characteristics of effective teaching, there are different focuses among teachers studied in this volume. For example, Malaysian teachers in Lim's study claimed that effective teaching includes anything added to the lesson that can make it more effective for teachers to teach and for students to learn. The attributes that are added to lessons include creative and innovative use of teaching aids, clear explanations, and student-centered activities. The teachers characterize these attributes as effective mathematics teaching.

Classroom discourse, norms, and building relationships were crucial in establishing the quality of classroom practice according to the master teachers in East Asia. To them, a quality lesson is one that depends on teachers facilitating meaningful discourses that can lead to socially negotiated understanding. Thus, effective teaching should include clarity of the lesson's instructional goals and objectives, extent of students' participation, and extent of fulfilling the lesson's instructional goals and objectives.

The attributes of effective teaching highlighted in Kuntze and Rudolph-Albert's study included four basic dimensions: instructional efficiency, student orientation, cognitive activation, and clarity/structure. In the study by Givvin, et al., the teachers from six different countries greed upon the demand of content (that it requires deep understanding), expectations for students (that they be actively engaged in reasoning and in presenting their thinking), and ways in which they define important features of effective teaching.

In general, all studies in this volume showed that each country has its own culture that may have an impact on teachers' views about effective teaching, but we can still identify a number of common themes concerning teachers' views of effective teaching across the studies.

Active engagement of students. Actively engaging students was seen as important to effective teaching in every country studied. However the teachers in different countries emphasized different approaches to create the active engagement. In the United States, the teachers view effective teaching as engaging students in hands-on activities, such as manipulatives for mathematical exploration. Australian teachers stated that students' verbal involvement, more than physical involvement, arises by tapping into the curiosity of the students. Teachers from Hong Kong said that participation and involvement are keys for understanding and achieving learning objectives. For the teachers from Australia and Hong Kong, student engagement refers more to verbal interactions than to physical activity in the classroom. For the Chinese teachers, a lively and comfortable learning environment is necessary for students to engage in important mathematics. In China, instructional content is much more important than the forms of classroom activities (e.g., whether a class includes hands-on manipulatives). The teachers in China believe posing cognitively challenging problems effectively engages students' verbal and mental participation. In Malaysia, students viewed effective teaching as the process that ensures active participation of students. In other words, active participation of students in classroom can make positive change in their behaviors and attitudes toward learning mathematics. In Germany and Switzerland, the motivation, presentation, and activation of students were seen as most important.

Group activities/in-class student collaboration. The teachers from almost all the countries and regions studied in this volume recognized the importance of student-peer collaboration and interaction in the effectiveness of teaching. Among them, the teachers from the United States believed it to be especially significant and believe that peer interaction provides a comfortable social and cognitive environment in which students become active learners. According to the master teachers in China, students need opportunities to share mathematics thinking and discuss alternative solutions to solving problems, and class time should be self-exploratory as well as spent in discussions as groups. German teachers believed that group work was effective and should be used in the classroom. In Hong Kong, the teachers believed students should learn from one another in order to understand better and learn more effectively.

Classroom climate. The climate of the classroom is important to the overall lesson provided to students. The effective lessons were described as relaxed but well-disciplined by the Australian teachers, whereas as formal and "very intense, focused, and disciplined" were the descriptions of the teachers from Hong Kong and the Czech Republic. The climate of effective lessons described by teachers from Netherlands seemed quite informal and laid-back in contrast to the classroom climate described by the teachers from China and Hong Kong. The teachers from Switzerland and the United States tended to describe the climate for effective lessons as respectful and friendly and the teaching was a good combination of the relaxed and disciplinary styles. It thus becomes evident that most teachers in the studies see a balance between a controlling and relaxing environment as a positive classroom climate conducive to student learning.

Coherence and flexibility. Teachers from Mainland China and Hong Kong hold a firm belief that effective teaching should be a coherent and well-structured for students. While coherence is critical for effective teaching, the delivery process of an effective lesson should be flexible according to students' understanding. For the teachers from Mainland China and Hong Kong, effective teaching builds a path for students to go from rigid to flexible, from imitating the "right way" of solving mathematics problems to solving problems on their own. Such flexibility is an important feature of a coherent lesson. In a similar vein, the teachers from Finland also viewed the flexibility, changing a lesson plan and adopting according to what is happening in class, as an important feature of effective teaching. For the teachers from the United States, teaching flexibly to fit students' needs is a prominent characteristic of an effective lesson. Australian teachers agreed, and commented that an effective lesson should be planned yet flexible. It should be indicated that the word "coherence" may have different meanings in different countries. The approaches to achieve coherence in different countries may be different as well. The studies in this volume do not include enough information for us to accurately point out how the meanings of coherence and approaches to achieve coherence differ across countries.

Cultivating students' interests. The fact that teaching is effective when students' interests are cultivated has been highlighted by the teachers from Australia, Mainland China, Finland, Germany, Hong Kong, and the United States. For example, Australian teachers commented that if a lesson begins with an interest-capturing activity, students' interests are more likely to be maintained for the rest of the lesson. Teachers from the United States found that active involvement increases interest and thus makes lessons effective. When talking about how to cultivate students' interests, teachers from different countries commented on different approaches. In particular, teachers from Finland and Hong Kong suggested that students' interests can be cultivated by making connections among different mathematical ideas. Chinese teachers pointed out that a good question-and-answer technique would stimulate students' interests toward mathematics. German teachers used the development of logical problems to increase students' interests by enhancing their spatial thinking and the application of mathematics.

Types of teaching. For the teachers from Malaysia, student-centered activities promote understanding. Vistro-Yu and Villena-Diaz in their chapter found that the

Philippine teachers from high performing schools tend to accept the inquiry-based teaching as an effective style. For the Chinese teachers, effective teaching should always focus on student learning, which includes student motivation. Student-centered instruction provides space for student exploration, discovery, and learning with understanding. These teachers were less focused on the teacher and teaching, which includes having innovative instruction, low pressure, reaching instructional objectives, and using different techniques. Included in the student-centered learning is the students' engagement and overall development in the students. For the Finnish teachers, problem-centered teaching, which includes open problems and complex situations, is an important teaching approach. The German teachers commented that two types of teaching styles are effective: transmission teaching, which includes explanation of rules and exercises, and process-based teaching, which includes independent problem solving processes with open-ended asks. The teachers from Hong Kong stressed that they would be more rigid in early grades and more relaxed as the students grew up and became more experienced. Unfortunately, the terms such as student-centered teaching, problem-centered teaching, transmission teaching, and process teaching are not clearly defined in these studies. Thus, it is not completely clear if these terms were used in the same way in different countries.

In general, all the teachers involved in the studies believed that teaching should foster understanding; that is, students should not simply imitate what teachers do but internalize and personalize what is learned. Understanding, thinking, and problem solving were highly regarded by the teachers in all the studies.

It should be indicated, however, that in most of the studies there were discrepancies in what each country states as effective teaching and what is actually practiced.

Characteristics of Effective Teachers

There is a difference between the Eastern and Western regions' concepts of what constitutes an effective teacher. Eastern concepts include more content-oriented features, such as a well-prepared and effective presenter, a stimulator of thinking, and understanding the texts in order to teach them. In contrast, Western concepts focus more on the person-oriented features, including being a good listener, enthusiastic, and able to manage the classroom effectively. According to Li et al., when comparing teachers and students in China, teachers focused on students and learning, and the way they were motivated to participate and learn; students focused on self-discipline and participation. Hong Kong teachers focused most on understanding mathematics and problem solving. Teachers that were seen as effective were those who challenged students' thinking and abilities. Teachers from the United States focused more on group activities and the ability of their students to thoroughly understand the material and apply it.

Almost every country stated that the teacher must have goals set forth and must strive to meet these goals in order to be effective. Thus, it is important that to be an effective teacher, one must set goals and overcome constraints to reach them.

It is also important to study the ideas of what constitutes effective teaching in order to improve teaching by learning from others about what works and what fails.

There are also many similarities when teachers across the studies discussed the characteristics of an effective teacher. The following common themes were identified as characteristics of effective teachers across the studies.

Strong mathematics knowledge. Regardless of the nations they are from, all the teachers involved in the studies believed that an effective teacher should have a strong background in mathematics. For example, teachers in Australia, Mainland China, and Hong Kong named a strong background in mathematics as extremely critical. In the United States, the award-winning teachers took many more mathematics courses and participated in more extensively in professional development than did ordinary teachers. In particular, teachers in China commented that an understanding of the textbooks and curriculum—exploring and studying texts intensively to try to help students overcome difficulties—is a very important characteristic of an effective teacher. Competent knowledge is important to effective teachers in Finland and Malaysia.

Teacher personality. The teachers from Australia, China, Malaysia, and the United States view personality as important for an effective teacher. In particular, Australia and the United States view teachers' enthusiasm about teaching and rapport with students as important characteristics. The Malaysian teachers expect an effective teacher to be patient, helpful, rewarding (i.e. using verbal praise), and caring. The Chinese teachers emphasized their personal impact on students. The teachers from Australia, China, and the United States see that having a desire to understand the needs of students as an important feature of the effective teachers. The Chinese teachers further stated to create nurturing classroom environments for understanding, the effective teachers must first understand their students' background in mathematics and psychological readiness and then set appropriate instructional goals.

Good preparation. The teachers studied from the Eastern regions regarded being well-prepared as a characteristic of an effective teacher. The teachers from Hong Kong and Mainland China commented that effective teachers must be well-prepared so that they can present the information well and have the ability to provide clear explanations of the points to be covered in each lesson. The Malaysian teachers viewed good planning and presentation as effective characteristics. According to the Malaysian teachers, proper training of effective teaching behaviors provides teachers with the opportunity to help students do well in examinations. For the teachers from Finland, effective teachers must be oriented by goals that include developing pupils' understanding and calculation skills.

Stimulating thinking. In addition to good preparation, those teachers from the Eastern regions also emphasized the effective teacher's ability to stimulate student thinking. The teachers from China and Hong Kong saw the teacher's ability to provide insightful explanation and stimulate thinking as important characteristics. Further, the Hong Kong teachers stated that the role of teachers was to demonstrate enhanced understanding. Understanding and thinking were repeated features stressed by the teachers from other nations. For example, the teachers from the Czech Republic claimed that the teaching content provided by the effective teacher should be "demanding," "difficult," and "rich." The emphasis in these teachers' response was placed on rules and procedures as well as on concepts and processes.

Interactive teaching. Many teachers emphasize positive interactions with students as a major characteristic of an effective teacher. The teachers from Australia and the United States believed that effective teachers should be good listeners so that they can interact with their students effectively. The Malaysian teachers claimed that to interact with their students productively, the effective teachers should give extra time and individual attention to students and encourage students' participation by cultivating their learning interests. For the teachers from Finland, listening to students and understanding their thinking was an aspect of interactive teaching. To do this, effective teachers should learn their students' problem-solving strategies, and even their errors in practice.

Classroom management. Among all the participants, only the teachers from United States and Malaysia noted that the ability to manage the classroom was an important feature for the effective teacher. Although the teachers from other nations didn't explicitly mention this management ability, it might be assumed by these teachers as default ability for effective teachers.

ISSUES OF STUDYING EFFECTIVE TEACHING FROM TEACHERS' PERSPECTIVES

The summary above provides a general picture of a just-begun research journey to explore effective teaching from the teachers' perspectives. Regardless of various research methods and diverse background of participating teachers, the studies in this volume yield significant insights into our reflections on two interrelated research components, the existing theoretical frameworks of the research on effective teaching and the research methods.

Theoretical Perspective

The research findings from the studies in this volume clearly show that the teachers' beliefs about effective mathematics teaching constitute a complex and culture-related system.

This belief system is complex because it consists of multiple interrelated belief facets. As Thompson (1980, quoted in Philipp, p. 259) once suggested, the complex nature of this belief system can be discussed from at least two perspectives: its hierarchical structure and the inter-connectedness of different beliefs in the system. It is hierarchical, according to Thompson, because beliefs within a belief system may be primary or derivative, and central or peripheral. It is clear in this volume that for most teachers some features are more primary and central than others. For example, for almost all the teachers some features (e.g., student-cantered teaching and teaching for understanding) are always central features, while other features (e.g., good classroom management) are derivative and peripheral. In addition, the reports in this volume also reveal that the features of effective teaching are interconnected, or exist "in clusters," to use Thompson's words. For example, the main features of an effective teacher, as reported by the participants, largely reflect personal traits and professional skills required for fulfilling the effective teaching.

The findings of the studies in this volume also show that the teachers' belief system about effective mathematics teaching is culture-related. Although sharing some features of effective teaching and effective teachers, teachers from different cultures clearly demonstrate different preferences on the two questions. While the views from most Asian teachers are more mathematics content-oriented, those from most American and European teachers tend to be more person-oriented. For example, most Asian teachers emphasized that an effective teacher should understand the content thoroughly and the teaching should follow well-structured lesson plans. In contrast, what most American and European teachers highlighted about an effective teacher was the teacher's passion about mathematics, good listening skills, and providing enough space and time for students to learning for understanding.

By situating the teachers' beliefs in very different cultures, this volume generally reconfirms the existing theories about the complex and culture-related nature of the teachers' belief systems. However it also generates some new questions urging us to reconsider some aspects of current theories and plan for further research in the journey ahead.

The first issue enerated from this volume is about the problem of the dichotomization of effective teaching models in existing theories. For example, the student-centred model and transmissive model are two popular terms in literature on effective teaching. There are two general theoretical assumptions in literature about the two models. First, the two models are mutually exclusive. Second, the student-centered model predominant in Western culture is superior to the transmissive model predominant in the Eastern culture. Recently the two assumptions of the theoretical dichotomy have been questioned by findings in some cross-national studies, which showed that Chinese students from transmissive classrooms scored over their Western peers who were exposed to the student-centred teaching. This so-called "Chinese learner's paradox" has been addressed from both pedagogical and learning perspectives (Fan, Wong, Cai, & Li, 2004). Studies in this volume address this paradox from a perspective of culture and teachers' beliefs. For example, Vistro-Yu and Villen-Diaz argued that a seemingly transmissive teaching style in Western culture could be actually very child-centered in Eastern culture.

Memorization is part of the process of understanding. To the Chinese, discouraging memorization is tantamount to discouraging understanding, truly a disservice to the child. Thus, to the East Asians, the above belief statement is not "anti-child." It is clear from this argument that such a theoretical dichotomization could be problematic especially when it is considered from a cultural perspective. This aspect has recently been echoed by some researchers. For example, Clarke

(2006) claimed that different belief models should be viewed as complementary rather than necessarily oppositional alternatives. Thus, we need to develop more inclusive theories by considering the complementarities and interrelatedness of different pedagogical and belief models.

The second issue rising from this volume is that we found an inconsistency in some reports between the teachers' beliefs and their practices. Although this inconsistency had been identified in other research (e.g., Skott, 2001), this phenomenon is especially conspicuous in the cross-cultural studies in this volume. For example, in the chapter by Cai, et al., the Chinese teachers believe that teacher should care about individual student's need and teaching should be flexible. However when responding about their own teaching practice, effective teaching was often described as nicely fulfilling their well-structured lesson plans. One approach taken by researchers to explain inconsistencies is to examine whether particular beliefs within a belief system are more central or primary, and hence play a greater role in influencing practice, than do other beliefs (Philipp, 2007). While this approach may provide a phenomenological description of relationships among different beliefs, it fails to explain why some specific beliefs are more central for teachers in one culture but not for those in another culture. By considering local contingencies, constraints and available supportive resources in the cultural environments,

Ernest (1989) created a model to explain the inconsistency between what the teachers believe about effective teaching and what they practiced in classroom. In this model, Ernest argued that the teachers' beliefs about effective mathematics teaching has two interrelated parts, espoused beliefs and enacted beliefs. According to Ernest, the teacher's mental or espoused models of teaching and learning mathematics, subject to the constraints and contingencies of the school context, are transformed into classroom practices. These are the enacted (as opposed to espoused) model of teaching mathematics, the use of mathematics texts or materials, and the enacted (as opposed to espoused) model of teaching mathematics. With a full consideration of the powerful influence of the social and cultural context that the teacher is exposed to, this model explains well some findings in this volume. For example, Vistro-Yu and Villen-Diaz in this volume also noted that in the Philippines regardless of teachers' belief in a more child-centred or transmissive class, they always teach in the way that their supervisors tell them to do.

The inconsistency between what the teachers believe about effective teaching and what they practiced in classroom may also reflect the fundamental inconsistency between the views of teachers and researchers. Wilson and DuCloux found that teachers are viewing effective teaching in the paradigm of a teacher-centered classroom whereas scholars of decades past and the NCTM documents are viewing good teaching in the paradigm of a student-centered classroom.

In either case, this belief inconsistency definitely needs more future studies especially in different cultural contexts because such studies could provide insights into the relationship between culture and teachers' beliefs.

Methodological Perspective

The studies in this volume also yield an insight into research methods for future cross-national studies about teachers' beliefs. As we stated at the beginning of this chapter, the diverse research methods adopted by the authors in this volume have made the comparison of research findings extremely difficult. Therefore it would be quite helpful if we could develop some standardized tools to measure teachers' beliefs in different cultures. Given the hierarchical structure of mathematics teachers' belief system, one promising approach is to develop an appropriate Likert-scale survey to determine and compare the belief systems of teachers in different cultures. Although some Likert-scale surveys already exist (see a review in Philipp, 2007), most of them were developed from the Western cultural model and hence lack a full spectrum of features of effective mathematics teaching. This volume and other future studies will provide an important source for developing such an important measurement tool.

Given the complex nature of teachers' belief system, while developing standardized measurement tools is emerging for generating a general cross-cultural picture of teachers' beliefs about effective teaching, other research methods (e.g., case studies) are indispensable in our future journey.

REFERENCES

Cai, J. (2007). What is effective mathematics teaching? A study of teachers from Australia, Mainland China, Hong Kong SAR, and the United States. *ZDM - The International Journal on Mathematics Education, 39*(4), 265–270.

Cai, J., Perry, R., & Wong, N.-Y. (2007). What is effective mathematics teaching? A dialogue between East and West. *ZDM - The International Journal on Mathematics Education, 39*(4).

Cazden, C. B. (1986). Classroom discourse. In. M. C. Wittrock (Ed.), *Handbook of research on teaching* (3rd ed., pp. 432–463). New York: Macmillan.

Clarke, D. (2006). Using international research to contest prevalent oppositional dichotomies. *ZDM The International Journal on Mathematics Education, 38*(5), 376–387.

Cobb, P., & Bauersfeld, H. (Eds.). (1995). *The emergence of mathematical meaning: Interaction in classroom cultures* (pp. 131–162). Hillsdale, NJ: Erlbaum.

Cooney, T. J., Shealy, B. E., & Arvold, B. (1998). Conceptualizing belief structures of preservice secondary mathematics teachers. *Journal for Research in Mathematics Education, 29*(3), 306–333.

Doyle, W. (1983). Academic work. *Review of Educational Research, 53,* 159–199.

Doyle, W. (1988). Work in mathematics classes: The context of students' thinking during instruction. *Educational Psychologist, 23,* 167–180.

Ernest, P. (1989). The impact of beliefs on the teaching of mathematics. In P. Ernest (Ed.), *Mathematics teaching: The state of the art* (pp. 249–254). New York: The Flamer Press.

Fan, F., Wong, N. Y., Cai, J., & Li, S. (Eds.). (2004). *How Chinese learn mathematics: Perspectives from insiders.* Singapore: World Scientific.

Fennema, E., & Franke, M. L. (1992). Teachers' knowledge and its impact. In D. A. Grouws (Ed.), *Handbook of research on mathematics teaching and learning* (pp. 147–164). New York: Macmillan.

Forman, E. A., & Cazden, C. B. (1985). Exploring Vygotskian perspectives in education: The cognitive value of peer interaction. In J. W. Wertsch (Ed.), *Culture, communication, and cognition* (pp. 323–347). Cambridge: Cambridge University Press.

Guskey, T. (1986). Staff development and the process of teacher change. *Educational Researcher, 15*(5), 5–12.

Hiebert, J., & Wearne, D. (1993). Instructional tasks, classroom discourse, and students' learning in second-grade arithmetic. *American Educational Research Journal, 30*(2), 393–425.

Koehler, M. S., & Grouws, D. A. (1992). Mathematics teaching practices and their effects. In D. A. Grouws (Ed.), *Handbook of research on mathematics teaching and learning* (pp. 115–126). New York: Macmillan.

Lampert, M. (1990). When the problem is not the question and the solution is not the answer: Mathematical knowing and teaching. *American Educational Research Journal, 27*, 29–63.

Perry, M., VanderStoep, S. W., & Yu, S. L. (1993). Asking questions in first-grade mathematics classes: Potential influences on mathematical thought. *Journal of Educational Psychology, 85*(1), 31–40.

Philipp, R. A. (2007). Mathematics teachers' beliefs and affect. In F. K. Lester, Jr. (Ed.), *Second handbook on research on mathematics teaching and learning: A project of the National Council of Teachers of Mathematics* (pp. 257–315). Charlotte, NC: Information Age Publishing.

Porter, A. C., & Brophy, J. (1988). Synthesis of research on good teaching: Insights from the work of the institute for research on teaching. *Educational Leadership, 45*, 74–85.

Shulman, L. S. (1986). Paradigms and research programs in the study of teaching: A contemporary perspective. In M. C. Wittrock (Ed.), *Handbook of research on teaching* (3rd ed., pp. 3–36). New York: Macmillan.

Skott, J. (2001). The emerging practices of a novice teacher: The roles of his school mathematics images. *Journal of Mathematics Teacher Education, 4*, 3–28.

Stein, M. K., Grover, B. W., & Henningsen, M. (1996). Building student capacity for mathematical thinking and reasoning: An analysis of mathematical tasks used in reform classrooms. *American Educational Research Journal, 33*(2), 455–488.

Thompson, A. G. (1992). Teachers' beliefs and conceptions: A synthesis of the research. In D. A. Grouws (Ed.), *Handbook of research on mathematics teaching and learning* (pp. 127–146). New York: Macmillan.

Jinfa Cai
University of Delaware

Tao Wang
The University of Tulsa

Ning Wang
Widener University

Tiffany Garber
University of Delaware

EDITORS AND CONTRIBUTORS

Jinfa Cai is a Professor of Mathematics and Education at the University of Delaware. He is interested in how students learn mathematics and solve problems, and how teachers can provide and create learning environments so that students can make sense of mathematics. He has explored these questions in various educational contexts, both within and across nations. His research projects were funded by various foundations, such as the U.S. National Science Foundation and Spencer Foundation. He received a number of awards, including a National Academy of Education Spencer Fellowship, an American Council on Education Fellowship, an International Research Award, and a Teaching Excellence Award. He has been serving on the Editorial Boards for several international mathematics education research journals, such as the Journal for Research in Mathematics Education. He was a visiting professor in various institutions, including Harvard University in 2000–2001.

Meixia Ding is an Assistant Professor of Mathematics Education at the University of Nebraska-Lincoln (2007–). She is interested in how to foster students' mathematical thinking and how to equip teachers with Mathematical Knowledge for Teaching (MKT). She has explored these questions in various educational contexts, both cooperative and directive classrooms, within and across nations. Her current research projects, funded by internal grants, are investigating (a) the development of preservice elementary teachers' algebraic thinking, and (b) preservice elementary teachers' misconceptions about number and operations as appeared in their mathematics content course work. These pilot studies are expected to contribute to her future work when seeking external funding support for her research.

Kanita K. DuCloux is completing her PhD in Mathematics Education at the University of Georgia where she is an active researcher in the Center for Proficiency in Teaching Mathematics funded by the National Science Foundation. She earned an Educational Specialist degree (1999) in Mathematics Education from State University of West Georgia, a MA degree (1990) in Mathematics from Clemson University and a BA (1987) in Mathematics from Wittenberg University. She taught mathematics at Miles College, a historically black college in Alabama, for a year before beginning an 11-year career teaching secondary mathematics in Georgia. At the University of Georgia, she teaches courses for students preparing to teach mathematics in grades 6-12. She works with practicing teachers and supervises student teachers. Her research interests include teacher preparation, assessment of student learning in mathematics, and issues of equity in mathematics education.

Tiffany Garber graduated from the University of Delaware with a BA in English. She was a research assistant at the LieCal Project, under the direction of Dr. Jinfa Cai. She currently lives in Newark, Delaware.

Karen Bogard Givvin is a Research Scientist at the LessonLab Research Institute in Santa Monica, CA. She joined LessonLab in 1998 to work on the TIMSS 1999 Video Study, serving as the Dutch Country Associate on the mathematics portion of the study. Since then, her work has been on studies of mathematics and science teacher professional development and training programs, as well as on studies of the relationship between teacher knowledge, classroom practice, and student achievement. Karen is interested in research, professional development, and teacher training in mathematics and science and the use of video in support of those activities.

James Hiebert is the Robert J. Barkley Professor of Education at the University of Delaware, where he teaches in programs of teacher preparation, professional development, and doctoral studies. His professional interests focus on mathematics teaching and learning in classrooms. He has edited books on students' mathematics learning and co-authored the books Making Sense: Teaching and Learning Mathematics with Understanding and The Teaching Gap: Best Ideas from the World's Teachers for Improving Education in the Classroom. He served on the National Research Council committee that produced Adding It Up and Helping Children Learn Mathematics, was director of the mathematics portion of the TIMSS 1999 Video Study, and is a Principal Investigator on the NSF-funded Mid-Atlantic Center for Teaching and Learning Mathematics.

Hilary Hollingsworth is a freelance education consultant who works with schools, universities, and education organizations in Australia and the United States. Her current interests, which focus on the use of video cases for teacher professional learning, were generated through her work at LessonLab in Santa Monica, California. While there, she was the Australian Country Associate on the mathematics portion of the TIMSS 1999 Video Study, and a Director for the Teacher Learning Division of the company. She has previously worked as a lecturer at the University of Melbourne, a mathematics consultant in Victorian schools, and a primary teacher in Victoria. Hilary has a strong interest in the relationship between teacher professional learning and student learning.

Rongjin Huang is a mathematics educator who had been working as a secondary mathematics teacher and then a university faculty member in China for many years. He is currently continuing his further study at Texas A&M University. He is a member of Learner's Perspective Study which is a well-known international classroom research project with more than 14 participating countries. His interests include mathematics classroom research with a focus on Chinese pedagogy of mathematics, and mathematics teacher education. He completed several research projects funded by the University of Hong Kong and University of Macau and published more than thirty journal papers and book chapters both nationally and internationally. He organized and chaired several topic study sessions at various regional and international professional conferences such as EARCOME 3, 4, and ICME-11.

Jennifer Jacobs is a Faculty Research Associate at the University of Colorado-Boulder in the Institute of Cognitive Science. She was the U.S. Country Associate on the mathematics portion of the TIMSS 1999 Video Study. Jennifer currently works on several research projects in the area of middle school mathematics professional development, all with a focus on using video to support teachers' professional learning. Her primary interests are in educational and comparative research, including instructional practice, mathematics education, and methodological issues.

Raimo Kaasila is a senior lecturer in the field of mathematics education at the University Lapland. He is interested in elementary teacher education, especially in student teachers' beliefs of mathematics, its learning and teaching and students' collaborative planning. He is also interested in the use of narrative inquiry as a research method.

Gabriele Kaiser holds a master's degree as a teacher for mathematics and humanities, which she completed at the University of Kassel in 1978. She has taught in school from 1979–2000. She completed her doctorate in mathematics education in 1986 on applications and modelling and her post-doctoral study (so-called 'Habilitation') in pedagogy on international comparative studies in 1997, both at the University of Kassel. Her post-doctoral study was supported by a grant of the German Research Society (DFG). From 1996 to1998 Gabriele Kaiser worked as a guest professor at the University of Potsdam. Since 1998, she is professor for mathematics education at the Faculty of Education of the University of Hamburg. Her areas of research include modelling and applications in school, international comparative studies, gender and cultural aspects in mathematics education and empirical research on teacher education. She has received grants from the German Research Society (DFG) in order to support this research.

At present she is Editor-in-Chief of the journal "ZDM – The International Journal on Mathematics Education (formerly Zentralblatt fuer Didaktik der Mathematik), published by Springer Publishing House and Editor of a monograph series "Advances in Mathematics Education" published by Springer Publishing House too.

Since July 2007 she serves as president of the International Study Group for Mathematical Modelling and Applications (ICTMA), an ICMI affiliated Study Group.

Gerald Kulm is Curtis D. Robert Endowed Professor of Mathematics Education in the College of Education and Human Development, Texas A&M University. His areas of research are mathematics assessment, curriculum evaluation, and teacher development. Kulm is the author or editor of more than a hundred publications on teaching, problem solving, attitudes, and assessment in mathematics and science education. His work includes editing the AAAS volumes Blueprints for Reform in

Science, Mathematics, and Technology Education and Middle Grades Mathematics Textbooks: A Benchmarks-Based Evaluation. He is the author of Mathematics Assessment: What Works in the Classroom. Kulm currently serves as Editor of the journal School Science and Mathematics.

Sebastian Kuntze is full professor for mathematics and mathematics education at Ludwigsburg University of Education (Germany) since 2008. After his academic studies in Munich and Paris, he worked as a secondary mathematics teacher (1997–2002) and as an assistant professor at the universities of Augsburg (2002–2005) and Munich (2005–2008). His research interests in mathematics education concentrate on professional knowledge and instruction-related beliefs of in-service and pre-service mathematics teachers, on the scientific evaluation of in-service teacher trainings including video-based training programmes, on argumentation and proof in the mathematics classroom, as well as on competencies of learners in the domain of statistical literacy.

Chi-Chung Lam is the Dean of students and professor at the Department of Curriculum and Instruction, the Hong Kong Institute of Education. His research interest includes curriculum change and implementation, teacher and student beliefs. He is particularly interested of the curriculum development in Hong Kong and the Chinese mainland. He has served three secondary schools and the University of Hong Kong, and he was a professor at the Chinese University of Hong Kong before he moves to the Hong Kong Institute of Education in 2008. He was a visiting scholar in a number of institutions, the latest one was the University of Hong Kong.

Yeping Li is currently Associate Professor of Mathematics Education at Texas A&M University. He is interested in examining issues related to mathematics curriculum and teacher education in various education systems, and understanding how factors related to mathematics curriculum and teachers may come together in shaping effective classroom instruction that is valued in different cultures. His research projects were supported by various funding agencies, such as the Spencer Foundation. His work has been published extensively in many journals internationally. He has been serving as an Associate Editor for the journal of School Science and Mathematics, and a guest editor for other journals including the International Journal of Educational Research and ZDM-The International Journal on Mathematics Education. He organized and chaired many group sessions at various prominent national and international professional conferences, such as ICME-10 in 2004 and the ICME-11 in 2008.

Chap Sam Lim gained a PhD from Exeter University (UK) in 1999 with a thesis on the public images of mathematics. She is currently an Associate Professor in mathematics education at Universiti Sains Malaysia. She is active members of several international and national research projects especially on cross cultural comparative study of mathematics teaching and learning in schools. She was awarded a fellowship by the Asia Scholarship Foundation (ASF) in the year

2004–5 where she spent six months in Shanghai to carry out a cross-cultural comparison study on mathematics teaching between China and Malaysia. She is the co-editor of a book entitled "*Improving the Teaching and Learning of Mathematics: from research to practice*". She has published numerous research articles, focusing on cross-cultural study, public images of mathematics, teaching mathematics in second language, and lately Lesson Study as a professional development for mathematics teachers in both international and national journals.

Katja Maass has been working as a researcher and teacher trainer at the University of Education in Freiburg since 2004. Before taking up her position at university, she worked as a mathematics and biology teacher for 10 years. Her main research interests are in modelling and applications and the beliefs and professional development of teachers. She also works in the area of materials design. Her PhD thesis is a qualitative study of the impact of modelling and applications on students' beliefs and competencies. Since completing her thesis, she has continued to deepen her insight into the impact of modelling on day-to-day teaching as part of an international project of professional development and a national quantitative study about low achieving students.

Will Morony is currently Executive Officer of the Australian Association of Mathematics Teachers. He came to the role in 1997 after a career as a teacher of secondary mathematics and physics in South Australian schools, and 10 years as a senior mathematics officer in the curriculum section of the South Australian education department. During this time he was involved in a range of national initiatives in mathematics, as well as a range of state-wide research and development projects. In his work with the AAMT, Will has taken a leadership role in the Association's work in a range of areas including policy development, professional learning, progressing the national numeracy agenda and teacher professional teaching standards.

Sharon K. O'Kelley is currently a doctoral student in Mathematics Education at the University of Georgia. She holds a BA in English from Erskine College, a JD from Seattle University School of Law, and a Master's Degree in Mathematics Education from Montana State University. Prior to coming to the University of Georgia, she taught high school mathematics for 11 years in Tacoma, Washington. Her professional interests are in preservice teacher education and the role communication plays in the mathematics classroom.

Dr. Erkki Pehkonen is a full professor in the field of mathematics and informatics education at the University of Helsinki in Finland. He is interested in problem solving, a focus on motivating middle grade pupils with open-ended problems, as well as in understanding pupils' and teachers' concepttions about mathematics teaching and learning.

Bob Perry is currently Professor of Mathematics Education in the Faculty of Education at Charles Sturt University in Albury, Australia. He teaches mathematics education and research methods subjects in the Murray School of Education. Bob has worked in tertiary institutions in Australia and overseas since 1972. His research agenda includes transition to school, early childhood mathematics education, researching with children, teacher beliefs about mathematics learning and teaching, education of Indigenous children and community capacity building. Bob has published widely in all of these areas and has been invited to speak at gatherings ranging from individual prior-to-school settings and schools through to keynote addresses at international research meetings.

Patrick Sean Smith, Senior Research Associate at Horizon Research, Inc. (HRI), received a Bachelor's Degree in Chemistry, a Master's Degree in Science Teaching, and a PhD in Curriculum and Instruction from the University of North Carolina at Chapel Hill. Prior to joining HRI in 1991, Dr. Smith taught high school chemistry and physics. In addition, he was a member of the Education Studies Department at Berea College, where he taught courses in elementary science methods and the philosophical foundations of education. He was the project manager for the 2000 National Survey of Science and Mathematics Education. He is currently the principal investigator of ATLAST (Assessing Teacher Learning About Science Teaching), a project that is creating instruments to measure teacher and student science content knowledge, as well as teacher and student opportunity to learn.

Rosemarievic Villena-Diaz is an educator at heart with 19 years of teaching experience both in the undergraduate and graduate teaching programs of the Philippine Normal University, a teacher-training state university. Over the period, she has been a lecturer/resource person in pre-service and in-service training programs. Her training and experience include designing, reviewing and revising curricula, and preparing instructional materials across levels. She has also served the graduate school in various capacities: as adviser of graduate students in thesis writing and as examiner in graduate theses oral examinations. Rosemarievic obtained her BS Math degree (Magna Cum Laude) from the Philippine Normal College; MS Math and PhD in Science Education major in Mathematics both from De La Salle University, Manila. She also attended Professional Studies in Education at Queensland University of Technology, Brisbane, Australia under the RP-Australian Project in Basic Education (PROBE) in 1997. She is currently president of the Philippine Council of Mathematics Teacher Educators (MATHTED), Inc.

Catherine P. Vistro-Yu is a professor at the Mathematics Department of the Ateneo de Manila University in Quezon City, Philippines, where she has been teaching since 1991 after finishing her EdD and MEd in mathematics education from the University of Georgia, USA. She teaches general courses in mathematics to undergraduate students, mathematics content and courses on curriculum, assessment, and special topics in mathematics education to teachers enrolled in their graduate programs. Her most important research works have centered on children's concepts on mathematics, mathematical literacy, teachers' beliefs and on how teachers' implement curriculum. She has co-authored papers on teachers' beliefs, the social aspects of mathematics education, and professional development of mathematics teachers. She also conducts special in-service seminars for mathematics teachers. Catherine was president of the Philippine Council of Mathematics Teacher Educators (MATHTED), Inc. for 4 years. During this time, she spearheaded a 3-year writing project that produced the Mathematics Framework for Basic Education and Framework for Mathematics Teacher Education for the Philippines.

Ning Wang received her PhD in Educational Measurement and Statistics from the University of Pittsburgh. She also received a master's degree in Research Methodology and another master's degree in mathematics education. Currently, she is am Associate Professor at the Center for Education, Widener University, teaching research methodology courses at the Master's and Doctoral level. Dr. Wang has extensive experience in the validation of assessment instruments in various settings, scaling using Item Research Theory (IRT), and conducting statistical data analysis using Hierarchical Linear Modeling and Structural Equation Modeling. In particular, she is interested in the applications of educational measurement, statistics, and research design techniques into the exploration of the issues in the teaching and learning of mathematics.

Tao Wang received his Docter in Education (2005) and Master in Education (2001) from Harvard University. He is an assistant professor and the graduate advisor of the School of Education at The University of Tulsa, Oklahoma USA. Currently he is teaching courses of Child Development, Testing and Measurement, and Classroom Discourse Analysis. He has taught in primary school and university level in Shanghai for eight years after he obtained his master degree in Psychology from East China Normal University in 1989. He studies how teachers in different cultures teach mathematics. Related topics include culture and teacher beliefs, classroom discourse analysis, and mathematics learning and teaching. He is also interested in the study of early child development in different cultures.

Iris R. Weiss is President of Horizon Research, Inc. (HRI), a contract research firm in Chapel Hill, NC specializing in science and mathematics education research and evaluation. Dr. Weiss received a Bachelor's Degree in Biology from Cornell University, a Master's Degree in Science Education from Harvard University, and a PhD in Curriculum and Instruction from the University of North Carolina at Chapel Hill. Before establishing HRI in 1987, Dr. Weiss was Senior Educational Research Scientist at the Research Triangle Institute (RTI). While at RTI, she directed numerous education research, development, and evaluation projects, including the 1977 and 1985-86 National Surveys of Science and Mathematics Education. She was the principal investigator on the 1993 and 2000 National Surveys as well. Dr. Weiss has provided consultation to the National Science Foundation, the US Department of Education, the American Association for the Advancement of Science, the National Science Teachers Association, the National Council of Teachers of Mathematics, the Congressional Office of Technology Assessment, the Council of Chief State School Officers, and the National Assessment of Educational Progress. She has also been involved in the evaluation of a wide variety of mathematics/science professional development and systemic reform projects, including the Local Systemic Change Initiative. Dr. Weiss is currently Principal Investigator of a knowledge management and dissemination project for NSF's Math-Science Partnership program.

Patricia S. Wilson is a Professor at the University of Georgia where she is Project Director of the Center for Proficiency in Teacher Education funded by the National Science Foundation. After receiving a BS degree in Mathematics, she taught mathematics in Columbus OH. She earned her PhD degree at The Ohio State University and continued her career in Georgia. She has taught courses in mathematics and mathematics education at both the graduate and undergraduate levels. Her research interests include the preparation of mathematics teachers as well as the development of mathematics teacher educators. She is currently collaborating with researchers at Georgia and Penn State University to develop a framework of Mathematical Knowledge for Teaching at the secondary level.

Ngai-Ying Wong is Professor, Department of Curriculum and Instruction, The Chinese University of Hong Kong, founding president of the Hong Kong Association for Mathematics Education. His research areas include conception of mathematics, mathematics teachers' professional knowledge and the CHC learners' phenomenon. His research project "Enhancement of students' mathematics problem solving abilities by the systematic introduction of variations" won the competitive earmarked grant of the Hong Kong Research Council. He received a number of awards, including the Faculty's Exemplary Teaching Award in 2005, the University's Research Excellence Award in 2008 and Class III Award for excellent research output in educational science, Ministry of Education, Peoples' Republic of China in 2006.

Qian-Ting Wong received M.Phil. in the Department of Curriculum and Instruction, The Chinese University of Hong Kong. She worked on teachers' beliefs about mathematics, mathematics learning and mathematics teaching. She has been council member of the Hong Kong Association for Mathematics Education and research assistant in the Hong Kong Institute of Education. She is co-author of a popular primary mathematics textbook in Hong Kong and is now freelance worker on mathematics teaching and learning.

Qiao-Ping Zhang is a doctoral candidate, Department of Curriculum and Instruction, The Chinese University of Hong Kong. His research interests include conception of mathematics and pedagogical expertise. He is a member of the Hong Kong Association for Mathematics Education and an editor of the Journal of Zhong Xue Shu Xue [Secondary School Mathematics]. He also served as teacher assistant at the Faculty of Mathematics and Computer Science, Hubei University.

CPSIA information can be obtained
at www.ICGtesting.com
Printed in the USA
LVOW13s0113261017
553808LV00012B/392/P